SOCIOLOGICAL INVESTIGATIONS

J. Dan Cover

DPG

The Dushkin Publishing Group, Inc.

Printed in the United States of America

Library of Congress Catalog Card Number: 92-74475

International Standard Book Number (ISBN) 0-87967-896-8

First Printing

The Dushkin Publishing Group, Inc., Sluice Dock, Guilford, Connecticut 06437

PREFACE

In one sense, this book is primarily a reader. The articles that are reprinted here focus upon themes that are central to the study of sociology: values, social roles, primary groups, deviance, social stratification, class ideology, minorities, religion, politics, marriage, and alienation. In a different sense, this book is an innovative and practical workbook. The eleven investigations in this book involve students in the process of conducting research using real-life data. The research they conduct emulates that of the original research articles; the data they use is their own. Before beginning their sociological investigations, students are asked to complete a Student Survey, which is found in the back of the book. The results are collected by the instructor and entered onto the preprogrammed computer disk provided. The student responses are tallied, analyzed, and returned to the students as raw data to be used in testing hypotheses.

To help keep sight of the larger theoretical issues that may well get lost in research details, an introduction to each investigation presents a historical perspective of the topic, using the conflict and functional theories. (The symbolic interaction theory, a third widely used orientation, is not included because it focuses on the individual or small-group level.) This book begins, therefore, with an article by Randall Stokes that introduces the functional and conflict perspectives.

The investigations themselves are organized into five sections:

1. **Introduction:** Discusses the background of the research and provides key definitions and information.
2. **Background:** Introduces the specific research to be undertaken and describes the findings of the original research article.
3. **Replication:** Takes students step-by-step through the process of interpreting their Student Survey results and comparing them to the original article's findings.
4. **Topics for Further Investigation:** Expands on the student's findings and explores new hypotheses and ideas not necessarily addressed in the reading.
5. **References and Recommended Readings:** Suggests a wealth of additional reading material that students will find interesting and relevant to the topic.

No investigation requires more statistical knowledge than that covered in the Investigation Tools section near the end of the book. This section covers the basics of reading and understanding percent tables, and the correlation and comparison of variables. Also provided in this section are four exercises that may be assigned by the instructor to test the students' understanding of these concepts.

I do not expect that these investigations will make students qualified sociologists, any more than a one-semester course can make them fluent in a foreign language. But I hope that they will find the investigations meaningful and enlightening, and that they will increase their powers of social discovery and insight.

Sociological Investigations has two parts: the book itself and the instructor's materials. In addition to the instructor's manual, a computer disk is provided to instructors. The disk includes the following programs:

Utilities: Allows instructors to customize the program.
Student Survey: Collects the answers to the Student Survey.
Analysis: Analyzes Student Survey responses statistically and provides a printout.
Graphs: Presents graphic interpretations of survey results.

The use and features of the disk are discussed in more detail in the Instructor's Guide.

TO THE STUDENT

The purpose of *Sociological Investigations* is to help you develop your ability to use sociological insights by reading and interpreting research results. The evidence from this research is the foundation of all sociological analysis. Science is based on observation (what we call empirical data)—not faith. Yet, most students taking introductory sociology do not have the chance to do any actual data-gathering themselves. Paradoxically, you seem to be asked to accept our conclusions on faith. You may wonder if the data *really* does support the sociological generalizations. You may become skeptical of all statements made in your textbook.

Some kinds of skepticism are healthy. In fact, Robert K. Merton suggests that "organized skepticism" is a "norm of science." The key word here is "organized." If being skeptical leads to checking the facts for yourself in a systematic way, then it is fruitful. This book is designed to allow you to do just that—check the facts for yourself. Of course, it would not be possible to repeat all of the studies mentioned in your textbook. But, with the aid of this book, you *can* replicate some of them.

The purpose of this reader/workbook, then, is to allow you to get the feel of sociological research with real data about areas of interest to sociologists. The results will not be known until you and your fellow students do the research. *Nothing is made-up or pre-cooked.* It is altogether possible that the results will not support your hypotheses. However, you may also find that human social behavior is much more predictable than you ever thought. Whatever the results, they will not be based on faith or the authority of your instructor or the author of your textbook. They will be based on your own interpretation of the data gathered by you and your fellow students.

The text will guide you, but your results will be unique to your class. Throughout, you will want to ask three things: First, do you understand how we gather data and draw conclusions in sociology? Second, do the data support our hypotheses? And, finally, what have you learned about human behavior?

Science can be as exciting as a detective story, with you playing the role of Sherlock Holmes, the great fictional detective. But science is not fictional, and what we discover affects each of us because social science is about us. When you come to the end of the course, I hope you will have gained a new appreciation of the scientific approach and a deeper understanding of the social forces shaping our lives.

J. Dan Cover

CONTENTS ─────────────────────────────────────

(Continued on the next page.)

INVESTIGATION TOOLS

SOCIOLOGICAL THEORY AND PERSPECTIVES

Randall Stokes

Philosophers who specialize in the study of the methods and procedures of science impose rigorous standards on definitions of a theory. **Theories** typically are described as sets of interrelated propositions, or "laws," from which may be derived testable hypotheses. This definition implies a very high degree of precision in underlying generalizations and concepts, and also a degree of "closure" (completeness), which sociology has yet to achieve. While certain specialized areas of study within sociology have theories that approach the standards of the philosophy of science, the major theories in sociology do not.

The major sociological theories might best be regarded as **perspectives,** or as conceptual guides. Each of these major perspectives has a limited number of central concepts and an even more limited number of broad generalizations about the way society works. A perspective, in other words, consists of a set of concepts. The concepts highlight important social processes, while the perspective is the overall viewpoint to which the concepts are related. In the words of Herbert Blumer (1931), the major sociological perspectives should be characterized as **sensitizing devices:** They sensitize us to important elements and processes in social behavior and organization. Their greatest value is not that they can provide testable hypotheses but that they provide researchers with a "map" of the social world, which guides investigation. They provide a way of thinking about what is important and of seeing what is important amid the seeming turmoil of human behavior.

Both of the two major sociological perspectives—structural-functionalism and conflict theory—attempt to provide a more or less complete image of society, and each differs from the other in several important ways.

Structural-functionalism

Like all the major perspectives, **structural-functionalism** (more commonly referred to as functionalism) has its roots in the nineteenth century, particularly in the work of Herbert Spencer (1820–1903). Spencer's great insight (1898) was that human society could be likened to a physical organism (that is, the body of a living creature). Like a physical organism, society is composed of parts, each of which is related to other parts by its **function** (what it does). Just as the brain, heart, and stomach are dependent on each other if the organism is to survive, so are the various segments of society dependent on each other.

Reprinted with permission from *Introduction to Sociology* by Randall Stokes. Dubuque, IA: Wm. C. Brown, 1984, pp. 23–33.

Spencer's writings about the nature of society were also influenced by *social Darwinism.* According to the social Darwinist view, societies, like physical organisms, are continually under survival pressures. Those organisms and societies that manage to develop attributes capable of coping with the environment survive and prosper, while those that do not perish. Thus, according to Spencer, all aspects of any living society could be explained by looking for the function they performed for the larger society. Specific forms of government, the family, and religion were seen by Spencer as existing because they had stood the test of survival; they existed because evolutionary pressures had created them.

As might be expected, Spencer's ideas gained great popularity among nineteenth-century businesspeople, particularly in the United States. Robber barons could (and did), for example, defend their great wealth as the natural evolutionary result of "survival of the fittest." Spencer provided the ideal counter to the radical notions of Karl Marx, who saw the great success of modern business as resting on worker exploitation.

Among the major influences on the development of modern functionalism have been Émile Durkheim (1858–1917), and the contemporary sociologists, Talcott Parsons and Robert K. Merton. In its modern form, functionalism is considerably more sophisticated than the simple organic theory proposed by Spencer. Modern functionalists see society as a system made up of related parts, and the nature and organization of the system receive the greatest attention. This perception is evident in the major functionalist concepts of consensus, system integration, and equilibrium.

Consensus

A fundamental assumption of functionalism is that societies are based on widely shared agreement, or **consensus,** about basic values. Values are beliefs about what is right or wrong, legitimate or illegitimate, justified or unjustified, desirable or undesirable, and similar moral and esthetic issues.

According to functionalists, shared values are the central organizing principles of all societies. Parsons (1961, 1966) argues that values serve much the same purpose in human societies as the genetic pool serves in animal species. The genes of an animal, drawn from the genetic pool of the species, determine the physical characteristics of particular animals. In an analogous fashion, the basic values of a society shape the organization of particular segments of society and the behavior of persons in those segments. Thus, according to Parsons, the same fundamental values determine the character of such diverse segments of society as business enterprises, universities, the military, and government. While the activities and organization of each of these segments differ, all have roots in the same values.

System integration

The second major assumption of functionalism is that, just as Spencer argued, societies experience **system integration;** that is, societies are systems that are bound together by the interdependent functions of their parts. From this point of view, any given aspect of society is connected to other aspects of society by exchanges among them. Schools, to take a simple example, exchange trained workers for resources and financial support from the economy.

An important offshoot of this assumption is that particular segments of society are determined by the *needs* of other segments. Over long periods of time, every aspect of society is shaped by the needs of other aspects so that the entire system exists in a state of harmonious integration.

Equilibrium

The third and final major functionalist assumption is that societies have mechanisms for maintaining their state of integration. System **equilibrium,** or balance, conveys the image of society as a tightrope walker, leaning this way and that to maintain balance on the rope. Functionalists believe that society corrects for events and trends that might upset the harmonious balance between its various parts. Thus, for example, the entire law enforcement and legal system are society's way of preserving itself from the threat of persons who do not abide by the rules. Deviance, as such rule breaking is known in sociology, is dealt with by legal punishment in serious cases and by informal means (for example, ridicule, rejection) in less serious cases.

A different kind of threat to the system may result from the failure of one segment of society to carry out its proper function. Some readjustment of the system must then take place if integration is to be restored.

In any case, the functionalist view is of a society that is essentially in balance, or moving toward a balance.

To summarize, functionalists view society as a system made up of many diverse parts, ranging from organizations and groups to particular ways of acting and believing. The overall system is bound together by consensus, with all of the system's diverse parts stemming from the same widely shared values, and by functional integration. The system is also equipped with mechanisms to maintain itself in the face of deviance and disorganization.

Strengths, limits, and illustrative analyses of structural-functionalism

A strong point of the functionalist perspective is that it provides a relatively clear guide for analysis. As noted previously, one of the major assumptions of functionalist theory is that all parts of society perform some function for other parts and for the survival of the system. If this assumption is valid, then it would seem possible to explain any particular aspect of society by looking for its function for the larger society. Two brief illustrations should clarify this point.

Functionalists argue that the nature of the modern nuclear family can be explained by its functional relationship to other sectors of society. In a modern industrial society, workers must be free to move about to find jobs as first one and then another sector of the economy undergoes growth. The nuclear family is mobile and is thus functional in an industrial society. The extended family, however, with its larger number of persons working, is **dysfunctional** (that is, detrimental or not beneficial) in an industrial economy because it impedes mobility. The functionalist explanation of the nuclear family would thus cite the functional compatibility of the nuclear family with an industrial economy as the reason for the nuclear family's existence.

A second example concerns the nature of romantic love in Western industrial societies. The expectation in such societies is that people marry for love and that husband and wife remain in love with each other. Many observers have noted that for many of the world's societies, it is entirely irrelevant whether or not husbands and wives love each other, and, indeed, the idea seems faintly improper and silly in some. Functionalists would, following the logic of their perspective, assume that romantic love serves some function in Western industrial societies and that this function explains its existence. One functionalist analysis concludes that romantic love is needed because so few other forces bind the nuclear family together (Davis, 1932). In contrast to the extended agricultural family, the nuclear family is not an economically productive unit, marriage does not represent an alliance between extended families, and other family members are not present on the scene to support the marriage. Under these circumstances, functionalists argue that romantic love solves the problem of how to induce people to marry and to stay married.

The same logic of analysis can be applied to virtually any aspect of society, including those that may appear to have no function or even a dysfunction for the larger society. Thus, for example, Kingsley Davis (1947) notes that the persistence of prostitution can be explained by the fact that it serves *latent* (hidden) functions for the preservation of the system. Among other things, prostitution provides an outlet for certain sexual desires that might threaten marital stability and also moderates the

Émile Durkheim (1858–1917) One of the leading contributors to sociology and the founder of the French school of sociological thought. Born in Epinal in eastern France and educated in France and Germany, Durkheim quickly established a reputation as a brilliant scholar of social science, philosophy, and law. He was appointed as the first professor of sociology at the University of Bordeaux, where he taught until 1902 before moving to the Sorbonne. Durkheim's reputation is based largely on four books: *The Division of Labor in Society* (1893), *The Rules of the Sociological Method* (1894), *Suicide* (1897), and *The Elementary Forms of Religious Life* (1917).

Durkheim combined rigorous empirical research with penetrating theoretical insights. He saw social order as arising from a commonly held system of values and norms. Durkheim believed that in modern societies this system plays a smaller role in regulating individual behavior than in more primitive societies, and the resulting state of normlessness may lead to social disorder and other sociological phenomena.

frustration of men otherwise unable to find sexual partners. Unfortunately, Davis fails to consider possible functions of prostitution for women in the society.

There are two main criticisms of functionalism. The first has to do with the difficulty the functionalist perspective has in accounting for social change. Functionalism's emphasis on accounting for the existence and maintenance of particular features of society has hindered adequate investigation of how societies change.

The second criticism of functionalism is that it produces a conservative view of societies. The functionalist rule that particular features of society should be explained by looking at their function for the larger society tends to result in unthinking approval of the larger society. The system is treated as a given, and there is thus no clear way for functionalists to be critical of the existing order. Social problems, such as crime, breakdown of the family, or loss of commitment to important values, for example, tend to be seen by functionalists as situations that threaten integration. From a different point of view, however, these may not be problems at all. Some crimes could be seen as a justified reaction to inequalities created by the social system. A breakdown of families (that is, increasing number of couples not marrying and high rates of divorce and desertion) could be interpreted as a needed move away from the outmoded institution of marriage. A decline in mass commitment to certain values could be positive. In other words, functionalists tend to see social problems as threatening to the system, rather than as problems with the system itself.

Another often-noted reflection of the conservatism of functionalism is its tendency to overlook conflict. Critics charge that functionalism presents an unrealistically optimistic view of the relations between different groups within the society. The oppression and coercion of some groups by other more powerful groups tend either to be ignored or to be seen as minor flaws in the social system. The overwhelming emphasis of functionalism on integration and consensus, it is argued, conceals the equally wide prevalence of coercion, inequality, fraud, and conflict. This criticism is made with particular vigor by sociologists who identify with conflict theory.

Conflict Theory

The dominant voice in the development of **conflict theory** was Karl Marx (1818-1883). Marx's central insight was that all societies could best be understood as arenas of conflict between groups whose interests were fundamentally opposed. These groups, which Marx called *classes,* are determined by economic factors. Marx believed that all societies are divided into the classes that own the currently most important means of production and the classes that do not. **Means of production** refers to the commodity or material that is most important to the kind of economic activity in which a particular society is engaged. In preindustrial (feudal) times, Marx believed that the central means of production was land and that society was split by the distinction between landowners and nonlandowners. In industrial societies, the essential means of production is *capital*—assets that can be used to finance industrial production. Marx thus saw industrial societies as divided into a dominant group of capitalists—the *bourgeoisie*— and workers without capital— the *proletariat.*

From Marx's point of view, all other aspects are secondary to and determined by the opposition between economic classes. Politics is simply another way in which the bourgeoisie enforces its will on society. Religion is a means by which the bourgeoisie distracts the proletariat from realising its dismal state. Marx called government "a committee to manage the affairs of the bourgeoisie" and referred to religion as "the opiate of the people."

Marx believed it was inevitable that the steadily increasing exploitation of the workers would eventually result in violent revolution that would destroy the capitalist system. Workers would be reduced to little more than appendages of the machines they operated, and human skill would be replaced by automation. As workers became less uniquely useful and more interchangeable, wages would fall until they lived in the direst poverty. Furthermore, the successful growth of capitalism would gradually increase the size of the proletariat, as unsuccessful capitalists fell to the level of workers and as all sectors of the society were brought into the capitalist system. Ultimately, Marx believed that the proletariat would become conscious of itself as a group with a common interest in destroying the system that enslaved them. Once such **class consciousness** was achieved, it would only be a matter of time before the capitalist system would be replaced by socialism and the private ownership of the means of production would be abolished. The socialist state, as envisioned by Marx, would be a classless state, and the ceaseless conflict between classes that had shaped the course of all history would thus be at an end.

Among the more widely known modern conflict theorists is Ralf Dahrendorf (1959). Dahrendorf's major contribution has been to generalize the sources of conflict in society. As noted previously, Marx saw economic factors as the single source of conflict. Once the private ownership of property was abolished, therefore, he believed conflict would cease. Dahrendorf feels that this view is too narrow and argues that conflict stemming from economic sources is really only one variety of the more pervasive conflict that results from differences in authority. Dahrendorf feels that all social organization inevitably produces inequality of power and authority. If organizations are to function, certain people must make decisions and others must be bound by those decisions. Thus, regardless of whether the society is socialist or capitalist, Dahrendorf believes that there is always conflict between those with power and those without power. Dahrendorf sees conflict as an inescapable element in human affairs, and not something that can be eliminated simply by socializing the means of production.

Dahrendorf also proposes that conflict need not be total to be important. Marx's real interest was the radical confrontation between capitalists and workers, out of which the entire nature of society would change. Dahrendorf argues that such radical conflict is the exception and that all societies are routinely shaped and molded by countless numbers of more limited conflicts. Unions and management, producers and consumers, racial groups, and special interests of all sorts constantly engage in conflict. Most such conflict, however, is controlled in a way that prevents widespread violence.

According to Dahrendorf, these numerous minor conflicts exert constant pressure on society for change. For example, the gradual improvement in the wages and working conditions of unionized workers could be interpreted as the result of controlled conflict between workers and management. Similarly, the legal and economic status of American blacks has been significantly improved by the controlled conflict of the civil rights movement. From this point of view, conflict can be seen as functional for the larger society, a view most clearly put forward by Lewis Coser (1956).

Overall, conflict theory directs our attention to the ever-present facts of coercion, inequality, and oppression. In sharp contrast to the functionalist view of society as a stable, integrated system in which conflict is abnormal and exceptional, advocates of the conflict perspective see stability as fleeting, soon to be replaced by conflict.

The contrasts between functionalism and conflict theory have been vividly summarized by Dahrendorf (1959). According to Dahrendorf, the key assumptions of the functionalist perspective are:

1. Every society is a relatively persistent, stable structure of elements.
2. Every society is a well-integrated structure of elements.
3. Every element in a society has a function, that is, renders a contribution to its maintenance as a system.
4. Every functioning social structure is based on a consensus of values among its members.

Karl Marx (1818–1883) Founder of the economic, political, and social school of thought known as Marxism, whose ideas provided the inspiration for modern communism. Born in Prussia, Marx studied at the universities of Bonn and Berlin before receiving his doctorate from the University of Jena in 1841. His main areas of study were philosophy, law, and history, and he was greatly influenced by the works of the German philosophers Georg Hegel and Ludwig Feuerbach. In 1847 and 1848 he collaborated with Friedrich Engels on *The Communist Manifesto*, and in 1867 published the first volume of *Capital (Das Kapital)*. He also wrote numerous pamphlets, articles, editorials, and essays. He edited or wrote for several newspapers and weeklies (including acting as European correspondent for the *New York Tribune* from 1851 to 1862), and helped organize and write the constitutions for the International Working Men's Association and workers' parties in England, Germany, and France.

Marx's writings have had a profound influence on historical interpretation and theory as well as on history itself. He saw all history as the story of class conflict: According to him, the mode of production in any society determines not only the character of the economy, but the character of the society as well.

According to Dahrendorf, the basic tenets of the conflict view are:

1. Every society is at every point subject to processes of change; social change is ubiquitous.
2. Every society displays at every point dissensus and conflict; social conflict is ubiquitous.
3. Every element in a society renders a contribution to its disintegration and change.
4. Every society is based on the coercion of some of its members by others.

Another view of the basic principles of conflict analysis is presented by Randall Collins, in the box opposite.

Strengths, limits, and illustrative analyses of conflict theory

One of the major values of the conflict perspective is that it has provided a corrective, at least within American sociology, to the long dominance of the functionalist viewpoint. Perhaps because American society has itself experienced long periods of what appears to be freedom from internal strife, American sociology has tended to emphasize stability and integration. The emergence of modern conflict theory over the past several decades has opened the way to reevaluation of both American society and American sociology. Studies of stratification (inequality), racial relations, politics, and the law have received a valuable new source of stimulation.

Conflict theory also has provided new leads for the study of social change. As noted previously, functionalism has had particular difficulty in accounting for social change within the confines of a system. The conflict conception of society as a tense arena of conflict between groups and classes with opposed interests has provided a clear approach to the study of social change. Social change, from the conflict view, is a by-product of the struggle for power between groups. Thus, for example, the major changes in the government's stance toward social welfare, which took place during the Great Depression of the 1930s, can be seen as a result of conflict between aroused and angry workers and the entrenched interests of the business community. It seems unlikely that Social Security, unemployment insurance, and the other reforms enacted during the Depression would have come to pass without conflict and the threat of even greater conflict.

A third major contribution of the conflict perspective is that it produces a critical stance toward society. As noted previously, the functionalist viewpoint tends to lead to an unquestioning acceptance of the existing order. Problems tend to be seen as those situations that threaten the system, and the possibility that the system itself may be a problem is overlooked. Proponents of the conflict perspective, however, look for inequality and inequalities that are built into the normal working of the society. Conflict theorists see what are normally regarded as social problems (for example, crime, pollution, poverty) as symptoms of more basic problems of the society itself, rather than as flaws in an otherwise integrated system.

Some illustrations of the way in which conflict-oriented sociologists have approached the study of particular issues may make the advantages of this view clearer. The first illustration concerns the giving of relief money.

Frances Fox Piven and Richard A. Cloward (1971) discovered certain inconsistencies in the historical timing of expansions and contractions of relief giving in the United States. Contrary to the notion that relief money is stimulated by humanitarianism, Piven and Cloward found that the flow of relief money increased and decreased in a way that did not correspond to the degree of societal need. The expansion of relief programs during the later years of the Depression and also during the mid-1960s, for example, did not coincide with an increase in the numbers of people in need. Neither did the subsequent phasing out of these programs follow sharp declines in the level of need.

By investigating *whose* interests were being served by social policies and institutions (the central element of conflict analysis), Piven and Cloward came to

Some Principles of Conflict Analysis

1. Think through abstract formulations to a sample of the typical real-life situations involved. Think of people as animals maneuvering for advantage, susceptible to emotional appeals, but steering a self-interested course toward satisfaction and away from dissatisfaction.

2. Look for the material arrangements that affect interaction: the physical places, the modes of communication, the supply of weapons, devices for staging one's public impression, tools, and goods. Assess the relative resources available to each individual: their potential for physical coercion, their access to other persons with whom to negotiate, their sexual attractiveness, their store of cultural devices for invoking emotional solidarity, as well as the physical arrangements just mentioned.

3. Apply the general hypothesis that inequalities in resources result in efforts by the dominant party to take advantage of the situation; this need not involve conscious calculation but a basic propensity of feeling one's way towards areas of greatest immediate reward, like flowers turning to the light. Social structures are to be explained in terms of the behavior following from various lineups of resources, social change from shifts in resources resulting from previous conflicts.

4. Ideals and beliefs likewise are to be explained in terms of the interests that have the resources to make their viewpoint prevail.

5. Compare empirical cases; test hypotheses by looking for the conditions under which certain things occur versus the conditions under which other things occur. Think causally; look for generalizations. Be awake to multiple causes—the resources for conflict are complex.

Note: From *Conflict Sociology: Toward an Explanatory Science* by Randall Collins, 1975, New York: Academic Press. Copyright 1975 by Academic Press. Adapted by permission.

some very interesting conclusions. They noted that the expansion of relief programs could be explained by the degree of threat that exists to civil order and to the continued control of the dominant groups. If deprivation produces widespread and dangerous discontent, as in the radical movements of the 1930s and the urban riots of the 1960s, relief programs are initiated or expanded. Deprivation alone, however, does not stimulate a flow of relief. Similarly, Piven and Cloward explain the phasing out of relief programs by the passing of the threat to dominant groups and not by any decline in the numbers of people experiencing deprivation. During periods when there is no political threat, relief giving once again becomes grudging and is limited by the dominant group's desire to keep people's work motivation high.

A second illustration of conflict analysis is found in the work of Richard Quinney (1974) and concerns the nature of the legal system. Laws and law enforcement have usually been seen by sociologists, particularly those with a functionalist orientation, as based on the values of the entire society. As mentioned earlier, functionalism sees agreement over basic values as an essential foundation of any society. Laws are regarded as the formal statement of these values and law enforcement as a means to preserve them. Quinney, on the contrary, argues that law reflects the interests of dominant classes and works to their advantage. People from the upper classes write the laws and determine how and against whom they will be enforced. Rather than being an expression of the beliefs of the entire society, Quinney regards the legal system as one of many ways the upper classes have of retaining control over the society. Like Piven and Cloward, Quinney seeks to explain the nature and existence of particular elements of society by asking who benefits. From the conflict perspective, the legal system benefits the upper classes, as did the giving of relief money in Piven and Cloward's study.

One major limitation of the conflict perspective is that it does not adequately account for the fact of long periods of apparent stability in many societies. Just as functionalism is not able to explain social change, conflict theory does not provide an adequate understanding of stability. It does not seem feasible that all periods of stability in a society can be simply a result of the successful oppression of some groups by others. It is particularly difficult for conflict theory to account for the stability of customs and values. Even when major change occurs, as in the Russian and Chinese revolutions, there is much about the society that does not change. The daily life of the average Russian or Chinese undoubtedly has many features that were not changed by the revolutions the two countries experienced. Manners, preferences in food, relations between men and women, patterns of recreation, and a host of other details that make up daily life are likely to be persistent over time.

REFERENCES

Blumer, H. 1931. Science without concepts. *American Journal of Sociology, 36* (January), 11–17.

Coser, L. 1956. *The functions of social conflict.* New York: The Free Press.

Dahrendorf, R. 1959. *Class and class conflict in industrial society.* Stanford, Calif.: Stanford University Press.

Davis, K. 1932. The sociology of prostitution. *American Sociological Review, 2,* 744–755.

Davis, K. 1947. Final note on a case of extreme isolation. *American Journal of Sociology, 52* (March), 432–437.

Parson, T. 1961. Some considerations of the theory of social change. *Rural Sociology, 26,* 219–239.

Parson, T. 1966. *Societies: Evolutionary and comparative perspectives.* Englewood Cliffs, N.J.: Prentice Hall.

Piven, F. F., & Cloward, R. A. 1971. *Regulating the poor: The functions of public welfare.* New York: Random House.

Quinney, R. 1974. *Critique of legal order.* Boston: Little, Brown.

Spencer, H. 1898. *First principles.* New York: Appleton.

VALUES

> During the time men live without a common power to keep them in awe, they are in that condition which is called Warre; and such a warre, as is of every man against every man . . . and worst of all [there will be] continual fear and danger of violent death; and the life of man, solitary, poore, nasty, brutish and short.
>
> Thomas Hobbes
> *Leviathan*

It is one o'clock in the morning and you are tired after a long day at work. You decide to take a shortcut to get home sooner. It takes you through a little-traveled part of the city that was burned out in riots some years ago. Rushing through the dark, deserted streets, you feel a sensuous pleasure in the air conditioning that gives escape from the steamy heat of the night. You are suddenly jolted awake as a spiked board flashes in front of the headlights and is immediately swept under the car. A loud crash is followed by tearing and the explosive decompression of the front tires. The car swerves uncontrollably. A shower of sparks erupts as steel rims slide across the concrete. The car grinds to a halt amid the smoke of smoldering rubber shards.

When you regain your composure, you turn off the headlights and are plunged into blackness. As your eyes adjust to the dark you see broken streetlights, piles of brick rubble, and boarded-up buildings. The place looks like a war zone. It is rarely patrolled by the police, so you have no choice but to leave your car and go for help. You trudge off into the darkness, hoping to find an all-night store. Almost immediately you feel you are being watched. You stop and peer anxiously into the darkness. In the dim outline of an abandoned building you catch the furtive movements of figures and a metallic reflection. Was that a knife or a gun? Who are they? What are they doing here? What do they want with you? Did they put the board in the street? Your mouth is dry and you shiver despite the heat. You sense movement behind you. You're trapped! Gripped by fear, your heart beats faster and faster until it pounds hard against your chest. You wish you were anywhere but here.

This story reminds us that danger and violence can be found at the frontiers of even the most civilized societies. The story also warms up our imagination for a difficult challenge—imagining what life would be like without the protective cloak of societal order. Let me give you your wish and let you escape

from society to a time and place without society. Without police, family, friends, or neighbors, you are now alone in the most primitive, primordial place imaginable. It might look like a post-holocaust movie or like William Golding's novel *Lord of the Flies* (1962). His description of what such a "state of nature" might be like takes place on an uninhabited tropical island. The characters are all well-bred school-age children who have survived the crash of their airplane. There are no adult survivors. The children are on the island only a few days before their aristocratic English manners dissolve. Underneath the veneer of civility we find that even the most civilized humans are unreconstructed savages after all. The children's descent into barbarism leads to paganism, blood sacrifice, and terror, and culminates with a child's death. If this is the natural condition of humanity, how is it possible to end the savagery? How is civilized society possible?

The conditions described by Golding introduce us to the Hobbesian problem of order, or the "Hobbesian question." It is called this because the question was raised in its modern form by the English philosopher Thomas Hobbes (1588–1679). He believed that all humans find happiness by avoiding pain and maximizing pleasure. Because many of the things that bring pleasure are in short supply, the struggle for happiness is virtually identical to the struggle for power. It is not morality or love, but power and self-interest that are the basic elements of human nature. Under natural conditions, like those described by Golding, unregulated individual interests create struggle and continuous human warfare. Life in the state of nature is "solitary, poore, nasty, brutish and short." How, then, is it possible to bring an end to the fearful anarchy that prevails on the frontier or in the state of nature?

To end the chaos, people must build a civil society. This requires that the individual surrender "the Right of doing anything he liketh" (in Hobbes's words) and accept law and order. Law and order must then be safeguarded. This is done by having the people that want the security of civil society enter

---

This investigation is based on "Generational Value Differences" by James A. Christenson, 1977, reprinted on pages 16–21.

into a contract with a sovereign. The contract grants the sovereign, whom Hobbes termed "the Leviathan," the authority to protect order and maintain peace. Hobbes believed that people will recognize the benefits of civil society and will readily surrender those liberties they had in the state of nature to gain the peace and security of the commonwealth.

In a closely related solution to the problem of order, the anarchy in Golding's novel ends when a British warship rescues the children. The warship could well have been named *Leviathan*, because, upon boarding it, the children are forced to accept the authority of a powerful sovereign. Golding and Hobbes express a widely held conflict view of order: that civil order is a necessary evil imposed upon us by our desire for power. The origins of society lie in struggle, opposition, and conflict. Social order is possible only when coercive restraints are placed on the unregulated struggle for power.

Functional Perspective

Functionalists reject the solution that Hobbes and Golding offer for the question of order. Why, Émile Durkheim asks, will an individual abide by the rules of the contract with the sovereign when circumstances make it not in his or her interest to do so? Durkheim answers that there must be some preexisting basis of trust or moral order. This is what he means when he says the basis of the contract is the noncontractual. Functionalists assume that to be human means to live in human groups. By sharing common dangers and experiences with others, one develops a foundation of trust. Three of the most important elements of this trust are (1) *norms,* or rules of behavior; (2) *symbols,* or beliefs that permit members to have a shared understanding of reality; and (3) *values,* which are the emotionally charged principles members use to judge whether what they experience is good, bad, or indifferent. You cannot acquire the morality of a group without being socially transformed. The problem of order is managed, but not eliminated, as your self-interest converges and is fused with the collective interest. Conflict between individuals is reduced as what one thinks becomes what others think. Opposition between you and the group diminishes in direct proportion to the values held in common. By providing standards by which the experiences of life are judged to be worthwhile, values justify social arrangements. They provide an organizational core around which diverse people and cultural elements are woven into a coherent, meaningful whole. This is the "order" model of society shown in Table 1–1.

Conflict Perspective

Hobbes told us that fear of the Leviathan's force imposes order on the opposed interests of individuals and groups within society. We become aware of the divisions and hatreds that are contained by the Leviathan when the latter loses authority. We get a glimpse of the "state of nature" in the collapse of the Soviet leviathan. With the Soviet Union no longer able to assure order, ethnic and religious wars have spread throughout the region, taking a frightful toll.

Table 1–1

DUALITY OF SOCIAL LIFE
Assumptions of Order and Conflict Models of Society

Question:	What is the fundamental relationship among the parts of society?	
	ORDER	**CONFLICT**
Answer:	Harmony and cooperation	Competition, conflict, domination, and subordination
Why:	The parts have complementary interests; basic consensus on societal norms and values	The things people want are always in short supply; basic disagreement on societal norms and values
Degree of Integration:	Highly integrated	Loosely integrated; whatever integration is achieved is the result of force and fraud
Type of Social Change:	Gradual, adjustive, and reforming	Abrupt and revolutionary
Degree of Stability:	Stable	Unstable

Note: From *In Conflict and Order: Understanding Society,* 5th ed., by D. Stanley Eitzen and Maxine Baca Zinn, 1991. Boston: Allyn & Bacon, p. 41. Copyright 1991 by Allyn & Bacon. Reprinted by permission.

Conflict theorists point out that social order is based on more than consensus. From this view, the basic reality of social life is social inequality. The basic social process is the struggle of groups to use culture to create and maintain an advantage. Groups with greater wealth and power can impose their values on the less powerful. Culture is not neutral: it favors those who have shaped it. Those with the power can then use it as a weapon to achieve narrowly defined class interests. In the United States, for example, the values of patriotism, achievement, practicality, and work all support the interests of profit-making corporations. According to conflict theorists, these values hide several facts from workers: that they are powerless to do anything but sell their labor to make owners more wealthy; that they are forced to compete as individuals with other workers, thereby prohibiting the development of meaningful social relationships; and that they work at monotonous jobs over which they have little, if any, control. Thus, the cultural values reflect the interests of the dominant class rather than those of society as a whole.

Background

Although there is disagreement among sociologists about the proper theoretical interpretation of values, few sociologists question the importance of values. Both functionalists and conflict theorists, for example, agree that some level of willingness to accept a common set of values is essential to the functioning of a civil society.

As a result, values have been the focus of a significant body of sociological research. This research, conducted by many sociologists using different theories over many decades, has produced many useful and interesting findings. Often these findings have challenged or refuted popular conceptions. The research by Glenn (1974) mentioned in Reading 1, for example, calls into question the popular belief that people tend to become more conservative as they age. (See pages 16–17.)

One objective of sociological research on values has been to identify and compare the *dominant values* of different societies in an attempt to better understand the significance of different value patterns. One influential researcher in this area is the sociologist Robin Williams. In his 1960 research, Williams suggested we can use four criteria to determine the dominant values of a society: (1) the *extensiveness* of the value throughout the society. Are there many people and activities that express the value? (2) The *duration* of the value. For how long a period of time has the value been considered important? (3) The *intensity* by which people hold the value. Are people outraged by behavior that violates the value? (4) The *prestige of the value carriers*. Who are the cultural heroes and what values do they represent? Williams used these criteria to identify the distinctive value patterns of American society.

Williams's research (1960) identified a set of 14 values that dominate American culture. These can be divided into two types: *social values* and *personal values*. Social values are those that focus on social issues and relate the individual to society. Personal values are more individual and psychological in nature. Williams's list of values is as follows:

Social Values

1. *Moral integrity.* Seeing and judging the world in ethical terms, right or wrong, good or bad.
2. *National patriotism.* Loyalty and allegiance to national symbols and slogans, and pride in one's country. Based upon the belief that America symbolizes values that deserve allegiance and/or unquestioned nationalism ("my country, right or wrong").
3. *Democracy.* Belief in majority rule and limited authority through uncoerced consensus. Supports the "cult of the common man." Rejects elitist and aristocratic principles.
4. *Helping others.* An emphasis on any type of disinterested concern and helpfulness, such as personal kindness and comfort, spontaneous aid in mass disasters, and philanthropy.
5. *Progress.* The belief that things are improving. Optimistic view of the future. A belief that forward is better than backward, that new is better than old. Belief in the perfectibility of human beings.
6. *Equality.* Commitment to social, political, and economic equality that leads to equality of opportunity rather than equality of conditions. Rejects rigid class distinctions.
7. *Science and rationality.* An emphasis on controlling nature. The belief that the universe is ordered and that rational human beings can improve their situation by approaching problems rationally and scientifically.

Personal Values

8. *Freedom.* Belief in the ability of individuals to run their own lives. Americans have traditionally understood this to be freedom *from* (the restraints of a centralized state) rather than freedom *to* (have such things as economic security).
9. *Activity and work.* An emphasis on work as an end in itself, strenuous competition, ceaseless activity, and business.
10. *Practicality and efficiency.* An emphasis on getting things done, adaptability, standardization, mass production, technological innovation, and expediency.
11. *Achievement and success.* An emphasis on personal achievement, especially secular occupational achievement.
12. *Material comfort.* An emphasis upon obtaining maximum pleasure and a high standard of living with minimal effort. Emphasis upon comfort and spectator gratification.
13. *Individualism.* "Rugged individualism" places high value on independence, responsibility, and self-respect.
14. *External conformity.* Whereas individualism rejects dependence, especially upon the state, conformity recognizes dependency upon group membership through conformity to patterns of speech, standards of dress, recreation, manners, and standardized public opinions.

James Christenson and Choon Yang (1976) set out to measure the relative importance people attached to these 14 values. They asked a sample of 5,082 North Carolina residents to rate each value on a scale from low (1) to high (4), in the same way that you were asked to do in question 12 of the Student Survey (reprinted on the following page). This made it possible to rank the 14 values by their relative order of importance.

Christenson and Yang found that social values were generally more important (rated higher) than personal values. They also found greater agreement on the order in which people ranked social values than was true for personal values. The largest differences were found between whites and nonwhites. Nonwhites placed greater importance than whites on racial equality and humanitarianism and less importance than whites on patriotism and political democracy. While such differences could be indicators of potential racial conflict, the magnitude of these differences was relatively small. Furthermore, any differences in the overall ranking of values among the various groups included in Christenson and Yang's sample were relatively minor. In short, Christenson and Yang's 1976 research suggested that there was broad agreement among Americans on the relative importance of the 14 values identified by Williams, and thus little potential for value-based social conflict.

Our investigation of social values will be based on Christenson's subsequent 1977 research on generational value differ-

STUDENT SURVEY QUESTION 12

Below are listed some commonly expressed American values. How important are each of these to you?

IMPORTANCE OF THIS TO YOU
(circle your response)

VALUE	Slight	Moderate	Great	Very Great
A. Achievement (getting ahead)	1	2	3	4
B. Moral integrity (honesty)	1	2	3	4
C. Being practical and efficient	1	2	3	4
D. National progress	1	2	3	4
E. Individualism (nonconformity)	1	2	3	4
F. Personal freedom	1	2	3	4
G. Material comfort	1	2	3	4
H. Equality (racial)	1	2	3	4
I. Equality (sexual)	1	2	3	4
J. Patriotism (to country)	1	2	3	4
K. Political democracy	1	2	3	4
L. Work	1	2	3	4
M. Leisure	1	2	3	4
N. Helping others	1	2	3	4

ences.* In this study, which appears as Reading 1 on pages 16–21, Christenson explored another potential source of value-based social conflict: differences in value preferences among different generations. As his article indicates, he found some such differences. He concluded, for example, that young adults attach slightly more importance to work, leisure, and achievement than do older adults. Overall, however, he found little evidence of significant generational value differences. These results tend to reinforce Christenson and Yang's earlier findings. If Christenson's research is valid, there is little evidence that differences in value preferences among major American social groups are a likely source of potential social conflict.

Replication

In this investigation, we will attempt to test the validity of some of Christenson's 1977 findings. We will begin by using the findings from our Student Survey to test three hypotheses that are based on findings from Christenson's study. Using data from both studies, we will then go on to investigate the relationship between one dependent variable and two independent variables. The *dependent variable* (what we are trying to explain) is the relative importance Americans attach to various social and personal values. The two *independent variables* (the variables whose influence on the dependent variable we are investigating) are sex and generational membership. In conducting our investigation, we will make use of the following data sources:

- Table 1 from Christenson's 1977 article
- The class's responses to questions 1 and 12 on the Student Survey

You will find the first of these sources, Table 1 from Christenson's article, on page 18. The class's responses to questions 1 and 12 on the Student Survey will be provided by your instructor. You will receive three pages of results from the Student Survey for this investigation:

- The first page contains mean rankings for all 14 values by sex from both Christenson's 1977 study and the Student Survey. (Note that although Christenson's article was published in 1977, his data were actually gathered in 1973.)
- The second page displays the results of tests of the three hypotheses described below. Hypotheses that are not supported will be noted with an asterisk (*).
- The third page contains a brief interpretation of the Student Survey results for this investigation. Although provided by your instructor, it should not be viewed as the final word on this topic. Rather, it is intended to provide a basis from which you can begin a more thorough analysis and interpretation of the results.

The hypotheses we will investigate are:

Hypothesis 1:

Moral integrity will be the highest rated social value on the Student Survey.

Hypothesis 2:

Personal freedom will be the highest rated personal value on the Student Survey.

Hypothesis 3:

There will be greater agreement on the rankings for social values between the 1973 study and the Student Survey than there will be for personal values.

To test these hypotheses, we will proceed as follows:

Step 1:

Locate question 12 on your own Student Survey questionnaire. Compare your ranking of the 14 values to the overall results for the class as reported on page one of the Student Survey, and to the results of Christenson's survey.

Step 2:

Use the data provided on page one of the Student Survey results to fill in the Investigation Results table, opposite.

*Christenson and Yang altered Williams's list of values slightly: where Williams listed the values of "equality" and "science and rationality," Christenson and Yang substituted "equality (racial)" and "equality (sexual)"; likewise, whereas Williams listed "external conformity," Christenson and Yang substituted "leisure."

Table 1–2

INVESTIGATION RESULTS 1

Dominant American Values

Social Values

Value Hierarchy	Males				Females			
	Christenson		Student Survey		Christenson		Student Survey	
	Mean	Rank	Mean	Rank	Mean	Rank	Mean	Rank
Moral integrity[a]	3.61*	(1)	__.__	(__.__)	3.60	(1)	__.__	(__.__)
Patriotism	3.20	(2)	__.__	(__.__)	3.06	(2.5)	__.__	(__.__)
Political democracy	3.07	(3)	__.__	(__.__)	2.92	(4)	__.__	(__.__)
Helping others	2.97	(4)	__.__	(__.__)	3.06	(2.5)	__.__	(__.__)
National progress	2.76	(5)	__.__	(__.__)	2.55	(6)	__.__	(__.__)
Equality (racial)	2.65	(6)	__.__	(__.__)	2.77	(5)	__.__	(__.__)
Equality (sexual)	2.34	(7)	__.__	(__.__)	2.51	(7)	__.__	(__.__)

Correlation[c] between social values for 1973 and this survey for: Males = _____   Females = _____

Personal Values

			Mean	Rank			Mean Rank	
Personal freedom[b]	3.58	(1)	__.__	(__.__)	3.55	(1)	__.__	(__.__)
Work	3.36	(2)	__.__	(__.__)	3.17	(2)	__.__	(__.__)
Practicality	3.13	(3)	__.__	(__.__)	3.06	(3)	__.__	(__.__)
Achievement	3.08	(4)	__.__	(__.__)	2.90	(4)	__.__	(__.__)
Leisure	2.89	(5)	__.__	(__.__)	2.85	(5)	__.__	(__.__)
Material comfort	2.67	(6)	__.__	(__.__)	2.51	(7)	__.__	(__.__)
Individualism	2.60	(7)	__.__	(__.__)	2.75	(6)	__.__	(__.__)

Correlation[c] between personal values for 1973 and this survey for: Males = _____   Females = _____

Number of males = _____   Number of females = _____   Total = _____

[a]These Student Survey results are used in Hypothesis 1.
[b]These Student Survey results are used in Hypothesis 2.
[c]These correlations are used in Hypothesis 3.
*Means for values obtained from Christenson's 1973 survey are taken from Table 3 (in the Christenson article, p. 20) for males and females less than 40 years old.

Step 3:

Use the data provided on page two of the Student Survey results to fill in the blank spaces beneath each of the three hypotheses listed below.

Hypothesis 1:

Moral integrity will be the highest rated social value on the Student Survey.

	Moral integrity		Highest other social value	
Men	_____	>	_____	Men
Women	_____	>	_____	Women

Hypothesis 2:

Personal freedom will be the highest rated personal value on the Student Survey.

	Personal freedom		Highest other personal value	
Men	_____	>	_____	Men
Women	_____	>	_____	Women

Hypothesis 3:

There will be greater agreement on the rankings for social values between the 1973 study and the Student Survey than there will be for personal values.

	Correlation Social values		Correlation Personal values	
Men	_____	>	_____	Men
Women	_____	>	_____	Women

Checking Your Findings

Hypothesis 1: Christenson found that among North Carolinians in 1973 the most important social value was moral integrity. Was this also true for your class?

Hypothesis 2: North Carolinians ranked personal freedom as the most important personal value in Christenson's survey. Do the results of the Student Survey indicate that this is still true for you and your classmates?

Hypothesis 3: Christenson found greater agreement among the groups he studied concerning the ranking of social values than he did for personal values. Is this also true of the Student Survey results?

After analyzing the findings, summarize your conclusions in Table 1–3 on page 15 labeled Support for Hypotheses. Indicate whether or not moral integrity and personal freedom are still the most important social and personal values. Are the correlations between the original survey and your survey statistically significant? You may want to consult pages 160–161 in the Investigation Tools section at the back of this book, where statistical significance is discussed.

Topics for Further Investigation

1. Christenson's most important finding was that there were no major differences in the order of the value rankings among the various groups included in his study. In particular, he noted no significant differences between the value preferences of men and women. This suggests that our first independent variable, sex, has little effect on our dependent variable, value preferences. Do the results of the Student Survey tend to confirm or disconfirm the above hypothesis?

2. Christenson (1977) concluded "no age strata even with adjustment for socioeconomic situations seemed to be radically or even moderately disaffiliated with other age groups toward Williams' 'dominant' values of American society"(p. 20).

    a. How do the results of the Student Survey compare to Christenson's? Are the hierarchies of values in the two studies comparable?

    b. If not, which values rose or fell in importance?

    c. If the Student Survey value hierarchy differs from Christenson's, does it also have a distinctive theme (spiritual, materialistic, hedonistic, success-oriented)?

3. If the value rankings in your Student Survey are very different from those reported by Christenson, do you believe this is because your college is unusual or because of generational differences?

    a. If the former, do students in your college represent a subculture because of their distinctive socioeconomic background, religious denomination, ethnic composition, or geographic region?

    b. If you think that the differences between the two value hierarchies are caused by generational differences, what basic cultural changes (such as the feminist movement, affirmative action, and civil rights legislation) have occurred since 1973—when Christenson collected his data—that might explain these differences?

    c. One of the most difficult challenges a researcher faces is translating a vague idea like "new morality" into a more specific research idea. Inverse or negative correlations might be used to indicate a different morality in this survey compared to the Christenson survey. Can you think of other ways we might research new or different value profiles?

    d. If, in your judgment, the Student Survey value hierarchy does represent a "new morality," do you believe it is sufficiently distinctive to warrant the label "generation gap"?

4. In your judgment, are the findings of the Student Survey more consistent with a functionalist or a conflict theory interpretation? Why?

5. Can you suggest a way in which the disagreement between functionalists and conflict theorists over the origin and role of values might be scientifically resolved? Please explain.

Table 1–3

SUPPORT FOR HYPOTHESES

	Significantly Supported	Partially Supported	Not Supported	Indeterminate
Hypothesis 1: Integrity top social value				
(Men)	_____	_____	_____	_____
(Women)	_____	_____	_____	_____
Hypothesis 2: Freedom top personal value				
(Men)	_____	_____	_____	_____
(Women)	_____	_____	_____	_____
Hypothesis 3: Social values > personal values				
(Men)	_____	_____	_____	_____
(Women)	_____	_____	_____	_____

Indicate the amount of support you found for each hypothesis.

We began our investigation by raising the Hobbesian problem of order. Durkheim's solution was the development of social solidarity through consensus. We can see in the prolonged internal struggles of societies such as Lebanon, and more recently the former Yugoslavia, evidence of the potentially tragic impact of an absence of consensus on values. But even in Northern Ireland, where the groups in conflict share a largely common set of values, we see the war between the Protestants and the Roman Catholics. From a sociological point of view such developments raise a number of important questions for further investigation. Perhaps chief among these is the question of whether there is a minimal level of consensus on values needed to establish and maintain social order. Can you think of others?

References and Recommended Readings

Bellah, R., Madsen, R., Sullivan, W., Swidler, A., & Tipton, S. (1985). *Habits of the heart: Individualism and commitment in American life.* New York: Harper & Row.

Christenson, J. (1977). Generational value differences. *The Gerontologist, 17,* 367–374.

Christenson, J. (1979). Value orientations of potential migrants. *Rural Sociology, 44,* 331–344.

Christenson, J., & Yang, C. (1976). Dominant values in American society: An exploratory analysis. *Sociology & Social Research, 60,* 461–473.

Golding, W. (1962). *Lord of the flies.* New York: Coward, McCann & Geoghegan.

Hobbes, T. (1947). *Leviathan.* New York: Macmillan.

Hoge, D. (1976). Changes in college students' value patterns in the 1950s, 1960s and 1970s. *Sociology of Education, 49,* 155–163.

Hyman, H. H. (1966). The value systems of different classes. In R. Bendix & S. Lipset (Eds.), *Class, status and power.* New York: The Free Press.

Kohn, M. (1957). Social class and parental values. *American Journal of Sociology, 64,* 337–351.

Starr, J. (1974). The peace and love generation: Changing attitudes toward sex and violence among college youth. *Journal of Social Issues, 30,* 73–106.

Williams, R. M., Jr. (1970). *American society* (3rd ed.). New York: Alfred A. Knopf.

Williams, R. M., Jr. (1971). Change and stability in value systems. In B. Barber & A. Inkeles (Eds.), *Stability and social change.* Boston: Little, Brown.

Yankelovich, D. (1974). *The new morality: A profile of American youth in the seventies.* New York: McGraw-Hill.

Yankelovich, D. (1981). *New rules: Searching for fulfillment in a world turned upside down.* New York: Random House.

Yinger, M. (1982). *Contracultures.* New York: The Free Press.

Generational Value Differences

This research assesses the relative importance which adults in various age strata attach to Robin Williams' "dominant" American values. The influence of other social and economic factors are also considered. Data were obtained from a statewide survey in North Carolina. The findings indicate that older adults differ most from younger adults in the importance which they attach to personal values, particularly work, leisure, and achievement regardless of their social and economic situation. Only slight differences are found in the relative importance attached to social values.

James A. Christenson
University of Arizona

Maturation, exposure to different historical situations, and life cycle experiences are assumed to influence people's perception of themselves and society. Bengtson and Kuypers (1971) point out that aging, in terms of developmental time, creates maturation and life cycle differences in perceiving and evaluating reality. For example each emerging generation experiences anew the existing configuration of the social structure. Thus, each generation questions from a slightly different perspective the institutional and ideological foundation of society.

Do such differences in perception and experiences lead to fundamental differences in the importance attached to "dominant" or core values within a society? Williams (1970) states that the stability of culture is premised upon the dynamic process whereby a delicately balanced system of values is maintained. The core or dominant values of a society serve an essentially integrative function incorporating each new generation into the dominant cultural fabric. Although integration through values will not likely lead to cultural homogeneity because of maturation, historical experiences, and life cycle experiences, large dissimilarity in value patterns between various age segments of society could indicate tension within the social system. Such tension or differences between age strata in adherence to core societal values are important mechanisms in social change (Bengtson, 1975; Riley, Johnson, & Foner, 1972). Thus, an investigation of differences in value adherence between various age strata can provide insights of present and perhaps future social changes and problems.

The purpose of this paper is (1) to explore the relative importance which adults of various age strata attach to dominant American values, (2) to look particularly at the value system of the expanding older population, (3) to assess the effect which other social and economic factors in relation to age have on value adherence, and (4) to discuss the social implication of similar or dissimilar value adherence for various age groupings.

THE PROBLEM

Generational analysis, in the broad sense, examines the contribution of emerging age groups to the changing configuration of social order (Bengtson, Furlong, & Laufer, 1974). Generational value differences are often viewed from the perspective of youth versus parent. The emergence of a rapidly increasing number and proportion of older people in USA society poses new social order implications. This phenomenon labeled "societal aging" also may have considerable political and social consequences (Cowgill, 1974). Value differences between age strata, if they exist, may not be dichotomous but periodic or sporadic. For example, in a cross-sectional national study of adult Americans by Rokeach (1973), the presence of several generation gaps were discovered. The most divergent age groups appeared to be adults in their 20s and those over 60.

The value patterns of the rapidly increasing older segment of society is of particular interest. Considerable evidence exists which points to the physical, social, and economic problems resulting from the expanding older segment of American society. The socio-physical implications (particularly health) of an expanding older population have been extensively discussed (Cottrell, 1974; Kent & Matson, 1972; Streib, 1972). Likewise the economic difficulties encountered by older, particularly retired persons, with fixed incomes and growing inflation has been dramatized in both the popular and professional media (Clemente & Summers, 1973; Kent & Matson, 1972; Montgomery, 1972, Riley et al., 1972; Robbins, 1971). Studies also show how retirement frequently results in self-reorientation and self-redefinition because of loss in social status and positive role support from others (Blau, 1956; Cavan, 1962; Miller, 1965).

The temptation exists to take such socio-physical differences compounded with social and economic factors as the foundation for assertions about socio-psychological differences in values and attitudes. For example, Glenn (1974) has noted the

Reprinted by permission of *The Gerontologist, 17*, No. 4, 1977, pp. 367–374. Copyright © by The Gerontological Society of America.

popular notion of the relation between aging and conservatism. However, upon empirical investigation, he shows that the relationship is quite weak and that middle-aged and older people only tend to become more conservative in the sense that their liberalization has not kept pace with changes in the total adult population. The same popular assertions are apparent in studies of the relation between age and popular issues. The term "generation gap" has been sensationalized in terms of such salient issues as political activity and drugs (Braungart, 1971; Feuer, 1969; Flacks, 1967; Suchman, 1968).

Although several studies have looked at the effect of age on adherence to specific values (Bengtson, 1970, 1975; Friedenberg, 1969; Mead, 1970; Riley et al., 1972; Rokeach, 1973) little empirical attention has been given to Williams' (1970) conceptualization of values. Williams' description of "dominant" American values seems to be most appropriate for the broad investigation of generational value differences because of his careful documentation of value configurations from the historical fabric of American society.

Williams (1970) synthesized and abstracted basic value orientations which characterized American culture. For example, he noted in the USA Constitution and the writings of the founding fathers a strong emphasis on the values freedom, equality, and justice. From investigation of the Puritan ethic and popular literature like the Horatio Alger stories, he identified such values as work, achievement, and practicality. Williams also documented the concern of Americans for the "good life," progress, democracy, individualism, and patriotism. Such a historical synthesis of values, though somewhat abstract, can be helpful in providing an analytical framework for studying the relative importance which various groups attach to these values.

Building on the recent efforts of Christenson and Yang (1976) to operationalize Williams' value scheme for empirical investigation, this paper studies the relative importance which adults of different age strata attach to Williams' values. Values are defined as conceptions of the desirable focusing on generalized end-states arranged in a hierarchy of order (Kluckhohn, 1951; Nye, 1967; Rokeach, 1973). Values are studied in the context of a value system which Rokeach (1973) defines as a "hierarchical arrangement of values, a rank-ordering of values along a continuum of importance." It is assumed that individuals, while manifesting overall similarity toward dominant cultural values, would show some variation in the relative importance attached to certain values within a value system because of divergent maturational, historical, and life cycle experiences. However, differences may be due to factors other than age. Thus, variables (namely income, race, and sex), which past research has found to be predictive of differences in the importance attached to values, will be included in the analysis (Christenson & Yang, 1976; Han, 1969; Hyman, 1966; Rokeach & Parker, 1970).

SAMPLE AND DATA COLLECTION

Data were gathered during 1973 as part of a statewide survey of people's goals and needs in North Carolina. Mail questionnaires were sent to 5,082 heads of households. Respondents' names were systematically pulled from telephone listings of every locality throughout the State. In 1973, approximately 85% of the households had telephone service.

* * * *

MEASUREMENT OF VARIABLES

In operationalizing Williams' value scheme, his descriptive presentation of value configurations were capsulized in 14 specific concepts as suggested by Christenson and Yang (1976). These 14 value concepts were further differentiated along social and personal dimensions (Table 1). Social values focused on the relation of the individual to the larger society and personal values focused on the individual's orientation toward self (Christenson & Yang, 1976).

Respondents were requested to indicate the relative importance of these values on a scale ranging from 1 (low) to 4 (high). . . . Respondents reacted to the question: "There are many things in life which we value. Below are listed some American values and beliefs. How important are these to you?" Responses were: Slight, moderate, great, and very great.

* * * *

In order to accommodate these perspectives of crucial periods in aging, the analysis will first present age strata groupings for 10-year intervals: those heads of households under 30 years of age constitute the youngest age group and those heads of households 70 years of age or older the oldest age group. This procedure will afford an assessment of any marked changes in value patterns across six age groups. In order to investigate the influence of other social and economic factors of generational value systems, subsequent analysis will collapse respondents into three age categories: those less than 40 years of age, 40 to 59 years of age, and 60 or more years of age.

HIERARCHY OF VALUES

Moral integrity received the highest mean scores among the social values from all age groups (Table 1). Personal freedom received the highest mean scores among the personal values from all six age groupings. The social values patriotism and equality (both racial and sexual) showed the greatest statistical variation among the six age groupings. However, the dissimilarities in mean scores did not alter greatly the relative ordering of the values. Younger adults attached more importance to both equality concepts than did older adults. However, these values ranked very low for all age groupings.

The most noticeable differences between the six age groupings appeared among the personal values. A clear drop was apparent in the importance attached to the value work for those over 60 years of age. The same held true for the values achievement, leisure, and to a lesser extent freedom and individualism (although in these last two values the relative importance attached to the values decreased more gradually). In summary, work, leisure, achievement, and equality were of greater importance to younger adults than to older adults. These findings

Table 1

MEANS OF DOMINANT VALUES FOR DIFFERENT AGE GROUPINGS

Values	Age						
	Less than 30 Years (N = 511)	30–39 (N = 576)	40–49 (N = 566)	50–59 (N = 488)	60–69 (N = 294)	70 + (N = 117)	F
Social values							
Moral integrity (honesty)	3.53(1)**	3.66(1)	3.65(1)	3.65(1)	3.66(1)	3.53(1)	4.41*
Patriotism (to country)	3.00(2)	3.31(2)	3.39(2)	3.38(2)	3.28(2)	3.30(2)	16.52*
Political democracy	2.99(3)	3.09(3)	3.08(3)	3.11(3)	3.04(3)	2.97(3)	1.41
Helping others (humanitarianism)	2.98(4)	3.00(4)	2.97(4)	3.05(4)	3.01(4)	2.90(4)	1.09
National progress	2.66(6)	2.77(5)	2.81(5)	2.87(5)	2.87(5)	2.68(5)	4.80*
Equality (racial)	2.70(5)	2.64(6)	2.52(6)	2.57(6)	2.41(6)	2.29(6)	6.52*
Equality (sexual)	2.48(7)	2.28(7)	2.25(7)	2.23(7)	2.11(7)	1.92(7)	9.53*
Personal values							
Personal freedom	3.57(1)	3.57(1)	3.47(1)	3.44(1)	3.43(1)	3.34(1)	5.38*
Work (your job)	3.32(2)	3.34(2)	3.35(2)	3.30(2)	3.04(3)	2.79(3)	17.98*
Being practical and efficient	3.05(4)	3.18(3)	3.14(3)	3.20(3)	3.16(2)	3.09(2)	2.98
Achievement (getting ahead)	3.12(3)	2.98(4)	2.91(4)	2.80(4)	2.66(4)	2.62(5)	16.96*
Leisure (recreation– taking it easy)	2.98(5)	2.76(5)	2.62(6)	2.44(7)	2.44(6)	2.57(6)	26.44*
Material comfort	2.62(7)	2.66(6)	2.68(5)	2.67(5)	2.65(5)	2.70(4)	0.50
Individualism (nonconformity)	2.69(6)	2.57(7)	2.51(7)	2.51(6)	2.42(7)	2.33(7)	5.13*

* Significant at .001 level or less.
** Rank based on ordering of mean scores.

concerning work and leisure supported the earlier findings of Noe (1969) that work and leisure were interrelated. However, in Goudy's (1973) comparison of students' and parents' orientation toward leisure and the work ethic, he found a more positive orientation among students than parents toward leisure while parents scored higher on work ethic items.

When the three collapsed age groupings were adjusted for level of income ($10,000 being the cutting point) leisure, work, and achievement were still clearly of greater importance to younger adults (Table 2 [p. 19]). The value for work varied most noticeably for those of lower income and only slightly for those of higher income levels. The same was true but to a lesser extent for leisure, achievement, individualism, and freedom. Overall, most personal values appeared to be of greater importance to younger than to older adults.

Except for the values focusing on equality, all the social values tended to be of greater importance to older adults, although some differences were quite small. Patriotism and national progress manifested the strongest relationship across the age categories. In general, income had greater influence than age on social values. Those of lower income levels attached less importance than those of higher levels of income to political democracy, patriotism, national progress and slightly more

importance to sexual equality and work. Older persons with higher income differed most from younger persons with lower income on the social values. However, the interaction effect of age and income was not statistically significant for any social or personal value.*

An analysis of the influence of both race and age on adherence to social and personal values clarified previously noted variations in age groupings. Race was a major influence on the importance attached to social values with nonwhites attaching greater importance to equality (both sexual and racial) and humanitarianism, while whites placed a greater value on patriotism. The opposite situation was true for the personal values. Again leisure, work, and achievement were of greater importance to younger adults than to older adults with adjustment for race. However, personal freedom and individualism were not statistically affected by age variations (with adjustment for race). For older nonwhites, leisure dropped to the personal value of least importance. It was interesting to note that differences in the relative importance attached to patriotism

---

*Analysis was also conducted on age with adjustment for educational attainment. Results were essentially the same as that for age with adjustment for income.

Table 2

MEANS OF DOMINANT VALUES FOR DIFFERENT AGE GROUPS VARYING BY INCOME LEVELS

Values	Low Income			High Income			F Age	F Income	F Age × Income
	< 40 (461)	40–59 (414)	60 + (298)	< 40 (626)	40–59 (640)	60 + (113)			
Social values									
Moral Integrity	3.57	3.59	3.58	3.62	3.68	3.74	2.3	12.1*	1.4
Patriotism	3.10	3.29	3.23	3.20	3.45	3.42	19.7*	14.6*	0.5
Political democracy	2.96	2.94	2.95	3.10	3.20	3.23	0.7	29.6*	1.4
Helping others	3.13	3.07	2.96	2.88	2.97	3.01	0.2	7.6	5.0
National progress	2.66	2.78	2.75	2.75	2.87	2.97	7.5*	11.5*	0.9
Equality (race)	2.71	2.69	2.39	2.64	2.45	2.36	13.2*	6.7	2.7
Equality (sex)	2.50	2.41	2.10	2.28	2.13	1.93	19.2*	24.1*	0.5
Personal values									
Personal freedom	3.57	3.44	3.35	3.57	3.47	3.45	9.1*	5.2	2.5
Work	3.32	3.27	2.88	3.33	3.36	3.21	18.6*	16.2*	5.6
Practicality	3.11	3.13	3.09	3.12	3.20	3.27	1.5	7.0	1.6
Achievement	3.02	2.88	2.61	3.07	2.84	2.73	27.7*	1.1	1.4
Leisure	2.87	2.50	2.45	2.86	2.56	2.53	46.9*	0.9	0.7
Material comfort	2.64	2.70	2.64	2.64	2.66	2.73	0.9	0.2	1.0
Individualism	2.66	2.55	2.37	2.61	2.48	2.46	7.9*	0.0	0.9

*Significant at .001 level or less.

(previously shown to be higher for older adults) disappeared with adjustment for race. This implied that older adults were not necessarily more patriotic.

One might expect that values for work, leisure, and achievement would be influenced by the sex of the respondent. Men are believed to be socialized to fulfill a more work-achievement role than women. However, the findings did not support this popular notion (Table 3 [p. 20]). Variations in age groupings still had a strong effect on the relative importance given to personal values after adjustment for the influence of sex. Younger adults still placed a higher priority on work, leisure, achievement. It was interesting to note that women in their middle years had a priority similar to that of men's toward work. This could be explained in that heads of households were studied. Thus, women in the sample would more likely have a stronger commitment to work and achievement than would a more representative sample of the female population.

Older adults appeared to attach greater emphasis to all social values except equality (even with adjustment for sex). Both age and sex affected the priority afforded to racial equality. Young adults, particularly females, attached greater importance to this value. Unexpectedly, sex seemed to have minimal influence on sexual equality, while age had a stronger influence.

Overall, personal values of work, leisure, and achievement appeared related to differences in age categories regardless of sex, race, or income. Adjustment for the studied socioeconomic variables in many cases intensified the magnitude of the relationship between age and the personal values. Most social values (except equality) were only slightly influenced by age and more influenced by the socioeconomic variables considered.

SUMMARY AND IMPLICATIONS

Did adults in different age strata show major variations in their value adherence? In terms of social values the answer seemed to be "no." While older people did attach a slightly greater importance to such values as patriotism and national progress and less importance to such values as racial and sexual equality, these differences did not entail any reordering of the relative priority attached to the seven social values studied. Even though younger adults attached greater importance to the two measures of equality, these values still stood last. Differences in the seven social values seemed to be influenced more by income, race, or sex, than by age.

In terms of personal values, the answer seemed to be "yes." The greatest amount of reordering of values appeared as a result of age differences, while income, race, and sex had little or no influence. The personal values most divergent for the various age groups were work, leisure, and achievement. Younger adults attached greater importance to these values than did older adults.

Table 3

MEANS OF DOMINANT VALUES FOR AGE GROUPS VARYING BY SEX

Values	Males			Females			F Age	F Sex	F Age × Sex
	< 40 (904)	40–59 (873)	60 + (314)	< 40 (172)	40–59 (187)	60 + (106)			
Social values									
Moral integrity	3.61	3.65	3.61	3.60	3.70	3.67	2.0	1.1	0.6
Patriotism	3.20	3.42	3.26	3.06	3.32	3.36	13.7*	1.2	2.3
Political democracy	3.07	3.14	3.02	2.92	3.01	3.11	1.3	1.6	2.1
Helping others	2.97	2.96	2.94	3.06	3.27	3.17	2.2	25.4*	2.9
National progress	2.76	2.83	2.77	2.55	2.88	2.90	10.3*	0.1	5.4
Equality (race)	2.65	2.51	2.32	2.77	2.75	2.58	7.8*	16.7*	0.8
Equality (sex)	2.34	2.23	2.04	2.51	2.34	2.12	12.8*	5.4	0.3
Personal values									
Personal freedom	3.58	3.47	3.41	3.55	3.45	3.38	7.2*	0.7	0.0
Work	3.36	3.33	3.00	3.17	3.31	2.90	26.2*	7.0	1.6
Practicality	3.13	3.17	3.13	3.06	3.26	3.14	4.2	0.1	2.0
Achievement	3.08	2.88	2.59	2.90	2.79	2.82	12.4*	0.1	6.5
Leisure	2.89	2.56	2.47	2.85	2.45	2.54	31.7*	0.4	1.2
Material comfort	2.67	2.69	2.68	2.51	2.65	2.67	2.1	2.9	1.5
Individualism	2.60	2.51	2.42	2.75	2.56	2.40	8.6*	1.4	0.9

*Significant at .001 level or less.

It appeared that older adults (particularly those over 60 years of age), while having more leisure time than younger adults, value it the least. The relative low importance attached to leisure by older people could be interpreted as either a result of historical events (such as the Depression or World War II) or a cultural norm experienced by older adults while young and carried through life. It also could be indicative of a certain frustration with a forced secondary role because they no longer had ready access to the culturally prescribed role of work. Since the findings presented were based upon static cross-sectional data, such interpretations could only be taken as speculations. However, the popular notion "that at least when we get old we will have more time to relax and take it easy" did not appear to be of great value to older people.

The high value for work by young adults particularly those under 30 was somewhat surprising in light of the "turn on, drop out" subcultural norms to which many of these young people were exposed in the 60s. The same assertion could be made about the greater importance attached by young people to achievement. For older adults the work-achievement ethic appeared to be of considerably less importance.

No support was found for a dichotomy or trichotomy of value patterns. Individual value differences which existed showed a gradual increase or decrease in importance across the various age strata. While these results must be generalized with caution, since they represented the results of one statewide survey of adults at one point in time, no age strata even with adjustment for socioeconomic situations seemed to be radically or even moderately disaffiliated with other age groups toward Williams' "dominant" values of American society. While age groups may differ on such salient issues as political activity or drugs, at the more abstract level of values all studied age strata seemed to be more similar than dissimilar. The behavioral implications of the overall similarities and the noted dissimilarities toward certain personal values have yet to be explored. Particular emphasis should be placed on increasing understanding of the relatively low priority which older adults place on leisure. With an expanding older population, greater insight is needed concerning the interrelation between work and leisure and whether the importance attached to these values indicates a decrease in importance among older adults or an increase in importance among young adults.

REFERENCES

Bengtson, V. L. (1970). The generation gap: A review and typology of social-psychological perspectives. *Youth & Society, 2,* 7–32.

Bengtson, V. L. (1975). Generation and family effects in value socialization. *American Sociological Review, 40,* 358–371.

Bengtson, V. L., & Kuypers, J. A. (1971). Generational differences and the developmental stake. *Aging & Human Development, 2,* 249–260.

Bengtson, V. L., Furlong, M. J., & Laufer, R. S. (1974). Time, aging, and the continuity of social structure: Themes and issues in generational analysis. *Journal of Social Issues, 30,* 1–30.

Blau, Z. S. (1956). Changes in status and age identification. *American Sociological Review, 21,* 198–208.

Braungart, R. G. (1971). Status politics and student politics: An analysis of left- and right-wing student activists. *Youth & Society, 3,* 195–209.

Cavan, R. S. (1962). Self and role in adjustment during old age. In A. M. Rose (Ed.), *Human behavior and social processes.* Boston: Houghton Mifflin.

Christenson, J. A. (1976). Religious involvement, values, and social compassion. *Sociological Analysis, 37,* 218–227.

Christenson, J. A., & Yang, C. (1976). Dominant values in American society: An exploratory analysis. *Sociology & Social Research, 60,* 461–473.

Clemente, F., & Summers, G. F. (1973). Industrial development and the elderly: A longitudinal analysis. *Journal of Gerontology, 28,* 479–483.

Cottrell, F. (1974). *Aging and the aged.* New York: Wm. C. Brown.

Cowgill, D. O. (1974). The aging of populations and societies. *Annals of American Academy of Political & Social Science, 415,* 1–18.

Dillman, D. A., Christenson, J. A., Carpenter, E. H., & Brooks, R. (1974). Increasing mail questionnaire response: A four state comparison. *American Sociological Review, 39,* 744–756.

Feuer, L. S. (1969). *The conflict of generations.* New York: Basic Books.

Flacks, R. (1967). The liberated generation: An exploration of the roots of student protest. *Journal of Social Issues, 23,* 52–72.

Friedenberg, E. (1969). Current patterns of generational conflict. *Journal of Social Issues, 25,* 21–38.

Glenn, N. D. (1974). Aging and conservatism. *Annals of American Academy of Political & Social Science, 415,* 176–186.

Goudy, W. J. (1973). The magical mystery tour: An encounter with the generation gap. *Youth & Society, 5,* 212–226.

Han, W. S. (1969). Two conflicting themes: Common values versus class differential values. *American Sociological Review, 34,* 679–690.

Hyman, H. H. (1966). The value system of different classes. In R.

Bendix & S. M. Lipset (Eds.), *Class, status, and power.* New York: The Free Press.

Kent, D. P., & Matson, M. B. (1972). The impact of health on the aged family. *Family Coordinator, 21,* 29–39.

Kluckhohn, C. (1951). Value and value orientations. In T. Parsons & E. A. Shils (Eds.), *Toward a general theory of action.* New York: Harper Torchbooks.

Mead, M. (1970). *Culture and commitment: A study of the generation gap.* New York: Langman.

Miller, S. J. (1965). *The dilemma of a social role for the aging.* Papers in Social Welfare, No. 8. Waltham, MA: Heller Graduate School, Brandeis University.

Montgomery, J. (1972). The housing patterns of older families. *Family Coordinator, 21,* 37–46.

Noe, F. P. (1969). An instrumental conception of leisure for the adolescent. *Adolescence, 4,* 385–400.

Nye, F. I. (1967). Values, family and a changing society. *Journal of Marriage & Family, 27,* 241–248.

Riley, M. (1973). Aging and cohort succession: Interpretations and misinterpretations. *Public Opinion Quarterly, 37,* 35–49.

Riley, M., Johnson, A., & Foner, A. (1972). *Aging and society.* Col. 2. *A sociology of age stratification.* New York: Russell Sage Foundation.

Robbins, I. (1971). *Housing the elderly: Background and issues.* White House Conference on Aging, Washington.

Rokeach, M. (1973). *The nature of human values.* New York: The Free Press.

Rokeach, M. (1974). Change and stability in American value systems, 1968–1971. *Public Opinion Quarterly, 38,* 222–238.

Rokeach, M., & Parker, S. (1970). Values as social indication of poverty and race relations. *Annals of American Academy of Political & Social Science, 388,* 97–111.

Streib, G. F. (1972). Older families and their troubles: Familial and social responses. *Family Coordinator, 21,* 5–19.

Suchman, E. A. (1968). The hang-loose ethic and the spirit of drug use. *Journal of Health & Social Behavior, 9,* 140–155.

Williams, R. M., Jr. (1970). *American society* (3rd ed.). New York: Alfred A. Knopf.

SOCIAL ROLES

The first class antagonism which appears in history coincides with the development of monogamian marriage and the first class oppression with that of the female sex by the male.

Friedrich Engels
The Origin of the Family, Private Property, and the State

Conflict is so fundamental to human relationships that many believe it is the logical point to begin studying society. Lewis Coser (1956) starts his analysis of social conflict by defining it as "a struggle over values and claims to scarce status, power and resources in which the aims of the opponents are to neutralize, injure or eliminate rivals" (p. 8). Since conflict is a normal part of human relationships, the presence or absence of conflict is not a simple and direct indicator of the health and vitality of a group. What is important is whether or not the conflict has long-term consequences that are destructive or constructive. Conflict is most constructive when the opponents (1) are struggling over a realistic issue and (2) share a communal interest.

Realistic conflict is based on scarce resources like money, land, and power. This conflict is not irrational, and is not a problem that will go away with better communication between the opponents. One of the forms of realistic conflict is the zero-sum struggle, a form of conflict in which winnings are matched by losses. When losses are subtracted from winnings the sum is zero. In a no-growth economy, the demands of minorities—for example, women and blacks—for increased pay and better jobs may only be possible with equal losses to the majority (white males). By contrast, nonrealistic conflict does not deal with mutually exclusive goals. It is concerned with the emotional need to reduce tension. An individual form of this is scapegoating. After being treated unfairly by the boss, for example, one might become abusive to one's spouse upon returning home.

Communal conflict exists when the combatants share common basic aims. If blacks and whites share the belief that all people are created equal, then civil rights conflict can lead to constructive ends. If they have mutually exclusive goals, like white supremacy and black supremacy, then conflict is divisive

and not integrative. Realistic communal conflict provides a means of defining a new balance of power or of dividing up scarce resources between men and women, young and old, rich and poor. To the extent that conflict resolves tensions between the opponents, it has stabilizing consequences and becomes an integrating element of the relationship.

Conflict Perspective

Conflict can be found in all human relationships—even in the most intimate between men and women. Gibbs states (1991) that 1 in 4 women will be raped in their lifetimes. Citing a 1990 House committee report, she estimates that 1 in 7 married women will be raped by their spouses. Even among college couples, violence is widespread. Ellen Sweet (1985) discovered in a nationally representative sample of 35 colleges that the majority of female respondents had experienced some sort of victimization. Nadine Joseph (1981) reported that in a survey of 371 Arizona State University students, 60 percent said they had experienced some form of violence during dating and courtship. To feminists, like Susan Faludi, the author of *Backlash: The Undeclared War Against American Women* (1991), female victimization has become an epidemic in American society.

Neil Gilbert (Collison, 1992) discounts claims of female victimization. He claims that feminists have exaggerated the statistics to impose new norms on sexual relationships. What previously was considered seduction has been redefined as date rape. Norman Podhoretz (1991, p. 29) agrees and concludes that feminists have politicized nonviolent sexual coercion into acquaintance rape. Americans are divided by sex and generation over these conflicting claims. Men, for example, tend to see sexual overtones in the actions of the opposite sex more often than women do. Research by Abby and Melby (1986) indicates that after viewing couples in photographs and videotapes, men report more sexual intent in the behavior of females depicted than women do. These different perceptions are reflected in national polls (*The American Enterprise*, 1992) that indicate that

---

This investigation is based on "The Intergenerational Socialization of Sex-Role Attitudes: A Gender or Generation Gap?" by Mary Zey-Ferrell, William L. Tolone, and Robert H. Walsh, 1978, reprinted on pages 29–34.

males and those over 50 are less likely than females to define sexually aggressive behavior of men as rape. As a consequence, whether or not one sees women as victims may depend on whether one is male or female.

Individual victimization can become the basis for group conflict when women recognize shared interests and join interest groups to gain power in numbers and resources. The 1992 Senate confirmation hearings of the Supreme Court justice nominee Judge Clarence Thomas provided an occasion for large numbers of women to discover that they shared with Anita Hill the experience of sexual harassment in the workplace. Outraged by what they felt was an insensitive hearing by an all-male Senate committee, women organized politically to deal with problems of sexual harassment and discrimination. Conflict theorists maintain that if significant problems remain unresolved and persist over time, interest groups may become classes and form a permanent basis for class struggle. This was the view of Friedrich Engels (1820–1895), who claimed that the exploitation of women was the first class conflict in history. He believed that men's work was more highly valued. This allowed men to control wealth and power—an economic advantage that permitted men (bourgeoisie) to employ women as a servant class (proletariat). Thus, women were forced to sell their domestic and child-rearing labor for little or no wages. Engels (1844/1978) claimed, "The modern individual family is based on the open or disguised domestic enslavement of the woman" (p. 774). He concluded that in a capitalistic society the wife is little more than a "legalized prostitute." The difference that does exist is that the prostitute sells her services by the hour, while the wife is enslaved for life.

Other conflict theorists trace the origins of sexual exploitation to the greater physical strength of men (Collins, 1971), the reproductive function of women (Firestone, 1970), and patriarchy (Cronan, 1978). Whatever the origins of the battle of the sexes, Helen Hacker (1951) concludes that women are as oppressed as other racial, religious, or ethnic groups who have been exploited and persecuted. She illustrates her point by noting many similarities between the role attributes of blacks and women: both are disadvantaged by ascribed physical characteristics, both are highly visible socially because of their physical characteristics (race and sex), both are seen as inferior and weak, both are seen as happiest in a subordinate role, both are prohibited from certain occupations, and both are paid at a lower rate than their white male counterparts.

Functional Perspective

Functionalists believe that conflict theorists have overdrawn the differences in the self-interests of men and women. Talcott Parsons and Robert Bales (1955) argue that family sex roles have developed to reduce competition and conflict. According to Parsons and Bales, the family faces two basic sets of problems around which the division of labor is based. The first is to provide for the necessities of the "external" world. The second deals with managing personal and emotional problems, or the "internal" world of the family. These problems constitute

a dilemma that is extremely difficult for one person to handle. The family division of labor manages this dilemma with complementary "instrumental" and "expressive" roles. The "instrumental" role, traditionally that of the father, deals with external tasks. The "expressive" role, traditionally that of the mother, is adapted to internal tasks. Socialization of men and women to instrumental and expressive roles serves family needs and reduces the potential bases of conflict between spouses.

The functional perspective gives special significance to society and how the roles in the system fit together. For example, nineteenth-century improvements in sanitation, nutrition, and medicine produced a spectacular decline in the death rate. This reduced the number of births needed to replace those who died. Reduced fertility requirements provided a favorable climate for the legalization of abortion, acceptance of contraceptive devices, and family planning. The result has been a dramatic decline in the average number of children women bear. The number of children per woman fell from 7.0 in 1800 to 2.0 in 1990. In the case of a woman who has two children by age 20, spaced 2 years apart, both her children can be expected to be in school all day by the time she is 28. The woman can also expect to live approximately 50 more years. Liberated from many childbearing responsibilities, women have increasingly found new roles in the work force. These demographic changes, Kingsley Davis (1986) argues, allowed twentieth-century feminists and the sex-role revolution to succeed where nineteenth-century feminists had failed.

Both functional and conflict theorists recognize that the sex-role revolution requires changes in traditional sex-role attitudes of men and women. The functional perspective stresses the adjustive and complementary nature of these role changes to the new and emerging needs of society. Having developed child-rearing skills, women leave the home and seek employment that takes advantage of these skills: nurse, doctor, teacher, social worker, interior designer, and so on. The conflict perspective stresses the opposed interests of men and women. Women are seen competing with men for a limited amount of power, wealth, and jobs. If the economy is not expanding, the successes of one sex must result in losses to the other. This leads to a struggle between men and women for these scarce resources.

Background

As we have seen, functional and conflict theorists disagree over the causes and interpretation of differences in Western society, but they agree that these differences do exist and that sex roles evolve over time. Some sociologists have also questioned to what extent differences in sex-role *attitudes* (that is, beliefs about what roles are proper or improper for each sex) exist, and if these attitudes also change over time. Functional theorists would be more likely to predict that differences in sex-role attitudes from generation to generation are greater than differences in attitudes between the sexes, whereas conflict theorists (with their emphasis on the opposed interests of men and women in their struggle for power) would anticipate substantial differences between the sexes in sex-role attitudes.

In 1978 Mary Zey-Ferrell, William L. Tolone, and Robert H. Walsh set out to examine whether or not there were significant differences in sex-role attitudes between groups within our society, and, if there were, the causes of these differences. They administered a questionnaire known as the Feminine Social Equality Scale (FSE), designed to evaluate people's sex-role attitudes, to four groups of subjects: freshman* females, freshman males, and the mothers and fathers of these students. The items on the questionnaire were similar to questions 27 to 31 on your Student Survey: a list of statements was presented concerning women's participation in occupational, political, and family roles. Respondents were asked to indicate whether they agreed or disagreed with these statements, and to what extent they did so. Depending on their agreement or disagreement with the various statements on the FSE, respondents were rated as either "egalitarian" (in this case, being supportive of equal opportunities for women) or "nonegalitarian." The four groups of subjects were then compared to see which groups had the most egalitarian sex-role attitudes. As you will find in the reading (pp. 29–34), Zey-Ferrell et al. concluded (among other things) that the differences in ratings between groups were more often related to gender than to generation. Our investigation will test whether or not this still holds true.

Replication

Zey-Ferrell et al. began by advancing six hypotheses and then testing them. We will examine the first five of these hypotheses, and test two hypotheses of our own.

Gender Gap Hypotheses

In the first two hypotheses we will test the effect that a "gender gap" between respondents has on sex-role attitudes. Zey-Ferrell et al. argued that it is in the interest of females to be more supportive than males of sex-role egalitarianism. From this we can expect freshman females to be more egalitarian than males, and mothers more egalitarian than fathers.

Hypothesis 1:

Freshman females will be more egalitarian than freshman males.

Hypothesis 2:

Mothers will be more egalitarian than fathers.

---
*The term "freshman" is used here to maintain consistency with the terminology used in Zey-Ferrell et al.'s original research. This does not mean that your class must be made up only of first-year students, or that only their responses need be tabulated.

Generation Gap Hypotheses

Research literature reviewed by Zey-Ferrell et al. suggests that egalitarianism is increasing over time. We will evaluate this trend with our next two hypotheses, which compare generational differences. These hypotheses state that sons will be more egalitarian than fathers, and daughters more egalitarian than mothers.

Hypothesis 3:

Freshman males will be more egalitarian than their fathers.

Hypothesis 4:

Freshman females will be more egalitarian than their mothers.

Gender-Generation Gap Hypotheses

Our third set of questions deals with the combined effects of gender and generation. The greatest differences in levels of egalitarianism should be found in these comparisons. Hypothesis 5 is expected to show the greatest differences of the six comparisons. Hypothesis 6 is modified from the original hypothesis presented by Zey-Ferrell et al., to emphasize the expectation that the combined effects of gender and generation would produce the highest levels of egalitarianism among freshman females.

Hypothesis 5:

Freshman females will be more egalitarian than their fathers.

Hypothesis 6:

The gender gap is more pervasive than the generation gap, especially with regard to freshman females. Freshman females will have the highest egalitarian scores of all groups.

We will examine a final hypothesis after the results of these six are known.

In conducting our investigation, we will use as our data source your class's responses to questions 27 through 31 on the Student Survey. The class's response to these questions will be tabluated by your instructor and handed out to you.

The independent variables for this investigation (gender and generation) are measured by question 1 (gender) on the Student Survey and the "Mother" and "Father" categories in questions 27 through 31. The dependent variable (egalitarian sex-role attitudes) was measured by Zey-Ferrell et al. by using the Feminine Social Equality (FSE) scale listed in Appendix A of their article (pp. 33–34). We have taken 5 items (numbered 9, 10, 11, 14, and 15 on the original scale) and asked you to evaluate these sex-role attitudes on a four-point scale. The results were then divided into Egalitarian (E) and Nonegalitarian (N) responses. Note that agreement with Student

---

STUDENT SURVEY QUESTIONS 27–31

Answer questions 27–31 by circling the number in the "Me" column that best represents your attitude toward the statements. In the columns labeled "Father" and "Mother," make your best guess as to your parents' attitudes toward these statements.

27. If there are two candidates for a job, one a man and the other a woman, and the woman is slightly better qualified, the job should nevertheless go to the man because he is likely to have a family.

Me	Father	Mother	
1	1	1	Strongly Agree
2	2	2	Agree
3	3	3	*Disagree
4	4	4	*Strongly Disagree

28. The talk we hear nowadays about women being an oppressed group in American society is really ridiculous.

Me	Father	Mother	
1	1	1	Strongly Agree
2	2	2	Agree
3	3	3	*Disagree
4	4	4	*Strongly Disagree

29. I would support the candidacy of a woman for president of the United States.

Me	Father	Mother	
1	1	1	*Strongly Agree
2	2	2	*Agree
3	3	3	Disagree
4	4	4	Strongly Disagree

30. If a male and female student are equally qualified for a scholarship, it should be awarded to the male student on the grounds that he has greater career potential.

Me	Father	Mother	
1	1	1	Strongly Agree
2	2	2	Agree
3	3	3	*Disagree
4	4	4	*Strongly Disagree

31. Women who insist on competing in the male world of work and politics tend to lose their femininity.

Me	Father	Mother	
1	1	1	Strongly Agree
2	2	2	Agree
3	3	3	*Disagree
4	4	4	*Strongly Disagree

*Egalitarian Response

Survey question 29 is considered an egalitarian response, whereas *disagreement* with each of the other questions (27, 28, 30, 31) is considered an egalitarian response.

When you have received the class's data from your instructor, proceed as follows:

Step 1:

Find your answers to items numbered 27–31 in the Student Survey and record your ratings in the box above, where the questions are reprinted. This will help you compare your answers to the investigation findings. Because it would take too

much time to survey your parents, we have asked you to answer for your parents. The risk this presents is that you will see your parents as more like yourself or perhaps more traditional than they really are. This will work against our hypotheses by reducing differences between generation and gender.

Step 2:

Use the numbers provided on page one of the Student Survey results to fill in the Investigation Results table on the following page.

Step 3:

Use the averages for the four groups ($\bar{X}ff$, $\bar{X}fm$, $\bar{X}M$, and $\bar{X}F$) to test the six hypotheses we have advanced:

Hypothesis 1:

Freshman females ($\bar{X}ff$) will be more egalitarian than freshman males ($\bar{X}fm$).

$\bar{X}ff$ _____ > $\bar{X}fm$ _____

Hypothesis 2:

Mothers will be more egalitarian than fathers.

$\bar{X}M$ _____ > $\bar{X}F$ _____

Hypothesis 3:

Freshman males will be more egalitarian than their fathers.

$\bar{X}fm$ _____ > $\bar{X}F$ _____

Hypothesis 4:

Freshman females will be more egalitarian than their mothers.

$\bar{X}ff$ _____ > $\bar{X}M$ _____

Hypothesis 5:

Freshman females will be more egalitarian than their fathers.

$\bar{X}ff$ _____ > $\bar{X}F$ _____

Hypothesis 6:

The gender gap is more pervasive than the generation gap, especially with regard to freshman females. Freshman females will have the highest egalitarian scores of all groups.

$\bar{X}ff$ _____ > $\bar{X}fm$ _____

> $\bar{X}M$ _____

> $\bar{X}F$ _____

The subtitle of the Zey-Ferrell et al. article asks whether there is a gender or a generation gap. We are now in a position to answer that question. To determine the gender gap, add the scores for women ($\bar{X}ff$ + $\bar{X}M$) and men ($\bar{X}fm$ + $\bar{X}F$) and compare the differences. To determine the generation gap, add

(continued on p. 27)

Table 2-1

INVESTIGATION RESULTS 2
Sex-Role Attitudes

Student Survey Findings

Feminine Social Equality (FSE) Scale Item	Percent Endorsing Egalitarian Response			
	Freshman Males	Freshman Females	Fathers	Mothers
27. Woman better qualified; job to man	_____% N = ____	_____% N = ____	_____% N = ____	_____% N = ____
28. Woman oppressed; ridiculous.	_____% N = ____	_____% N = ____	_____% N = ____	_____% N = ____
29. Woman for president of the United States	_____% N = ____	_____% N = ____	_____% N = ____	_____% N = ____
30. Equally qualified; scholarship to male	_____% N = ____	_____% N = ____	_____% N = ____	_____% N = ____
31. Women compete; lose femininity	_____% N = ____	_____% N = ____	_____% N = ____	_____% N = ____
Investigation averages	$\bar{X}fm$ = ____	$\bar{X}ff$ = ____	$\bar{X}F$ = ____	$\bar{X}M$ = ____
Use these four group averages to test Hypotheses 1–6	↑	↑	↑	↑

Zey-Ferrell et al. Findings

	Freshman Males	Freshman Females	Fathers	Mothers
27. Woman better qualified; job to man	71.9% N = 75	93.8% N = 114	71.8% N = 188	76.4% N = 186
28. Woman oppressed; ridiculous	39.7% N = 73	73.3% N = 112	37.7% N = 183	40.3% N = 186
29. Woman for president of the United States	50.8% N = 75	75.4% N = 114	56.7% N = 187	58.5% N = 188
30. Equally qualified; scholarship to male	63.9% N = 73	92.1% N = 114	72.2% N = 184	84.1% N = 188
31. Women compete; lose femininity	53.5% N = 74	90.3% N = 114	47.9% N = 186	73.9% N = 188
Zey-Ferrell 1978 Averages	$\bar{X}fm$ = 56.0%	$\bar{X}ff$ = 85.0%	$\bar{X}F$ = 57.3%	$\bar{X}M$ = 66.6%

Note: Zey-Ferrell et al.'s data are from Table 1, p. 32.

the scores for male and female students ($\bar{X}$fm + $\bar{X}$ff) and those for mothers and fathers ($\bar{X}$M + $\bar{X}$F) and compare the differences between students and parents. Using Zey-Ferrell et al.'s results (see the bottom half of Investigation Results 2), we would get the following:

Add the scores for women and men:

$\bar{X}$ff	=	85.0	$\bar{X}$fm	=	56.0
$\bar{X}$M	= +	66.6	$\bar{X}$F	= +	57.3
Women	=	151.6	Men	=	113.3

Then subtract "men" from "women":

Women	=	151.6
−Men	=	− 113.3
Gender Gap	=	38.3

Add the scores for students and parents:

$\bar{X}$ff	=	85.0	$\bar{X}$M	=	66.6
$\bar{X}$fm	= +	56.0	$\bar{X}$F	= +	57.3
Students	=	141.0	Parents	=	123.9

Then subtract "parents" from "students":

Students	=	141.0
− Parents	=	− 123.9
Generation Gap	=	17.1

From this we find the gender gap is larger (38.3) than the generation gap (17.1). After analyzing their findings, Zey-Ferrell et al. concluded that "where gender and generational differences are involved, gender differences are more closely related to egalitarian sex-role attitudes: being female is a better predictor of sex-role egalitarianism than being of the younger generation" (p. 32). If this remains the case, we can hypothesize: Gender gap > Generation gap. The results can be compared as follows:

Add the scores for women and men:

$\bar{X}$ff	=	_____	$\bar{X}$fm	=	_____
$\bar{X}$M	= +	_____	$\bar{X}$F	= +	_____
Women	=	_____	Men	=	_____

Then subtract "men" from "women":

Women	=	_____
−Men	=	− _____
Gender Gap	=	_____

Add the scores for students and parents:

$\bar{X}$ff	=	_____	$\bar{X}$M	=	_____
$\bar{X}$fm	= +	_____	$\bar{X}$F	= +	_____
Students	=	_____	Parents	=	_____

Then subtract "parents" from "students":

Students	=	_____
− Parents	=	− _____
Generation Gap	=	_____

Hypothesis 7:

Gender gap _____ > _____ Generation gap

Checking Your Findings

Hypotheses 1 and 2 concern the gender gap. Do your findings indicate that a gender gap exists? If it does, is it greater for students or for parents? Hypotheses 3 and 4 deal with the existence of a generation gap. Does it exist? If so, is it greater for father and son or for mother and daughter? Hypotheses 5 and 6 combine the effects of gender and generation. Are these two hypotheses supported? How many of the six hypotheses were supported? Which were not? Why do you feel they were not supported?

Summarize the findings by checking the amount of support found for each hypothesis in Table 2–2 on the next page.

Topics for Further Investigation

1. Zey-Ferrell et al. concluded (p. 33) that "sex-role attitudes which were in their [males' or females'] best interest were adopted. Theoretically, a vested interest thesis is a stronger theoretical approach to explaining differential sex-role attitudes . . . than is socialization." Are the results of your survey best explained by a vested interest thesis (a conflict perspective)?

2. If your results are best explained by the vested interest view, do you feel that conflict between men and women has a realistic (zero-sum) or non-realistic basis (reflecting an irrational commitment to outdated traditions)?

3. The conflict theorist Vilfredo Pareto (quoted in Lopreato 1965, p. 73) claimed that equality "is not related to any abstraction, as a few naive 'intellectuals' still believe; [rather] it is related to the direct interests of individuals who are bent on escaping certain inqualities not in their favor, and setting up new inequalities that will be in their favor, this latter being their chief concern." Thus, minority groups may lay claim to equality as an ideological weapon to further their vested interests, rather than as a means to advance a commonly shared value. If the former is the case, struggle and conflict will revolve around the narrow vested interests of the contending parties. On the other

Table 2–2

SUPPORT FOR HYPOTHESES

	Significantly Supported	Partially Supported	Not Supported	Indeterminate
Gender Gap:				
Hypothesis 1	_____	_____	_____	_____
Hypothesis 2	_____	_____	_____	_____
Generation Gap:				
Hypothesis 3	_____	_____	_____	_____
Hypothesis 4	_____	_____	_____	_____
Gender + Generation Gap:				
Hypothesis 5	_____	_____	_____	_____
Hypothesis 6	_____	_____	_____	_____
Gender Gap > Generation Gap:				
Hypothesis 7	_____	_____	_____	_____

Indicate the amount of support you found for each hypothesis.

hand, if men and women share important beliefs and values about equality, then conflict may promote community integration. Comment upon which aspects of the conflict are communal (shared values) and which aspects are non-communal (vested interests) in nature.

4.   What sort of differences in personal values (such as freedom) and social values (such as equality) do you expect are associated with those who have high levels of egalitarianism? (See Investigation 1)

5.   Are freshman females who indicate substantial differences in egalitarianism between themselves and their parents less attached to their families than females with similar egalitarianism levels as their parents? (See Investigation 3)

References and Recommended Readings

Abby, A., & Melby, C. (1986). The effects of nonverbal cues on gender differences in perceptions of sexual intent. *Sex Roles, 15,* 283–298.

Collins, R. (1971). A conflict theory of sexual stratification. *Social Problems, 19,* 3–12.

Collison, M. (1992). Berkeley scholar clashes with feminists. *The Chronicle of Higher Education, 38,* A35.

Cook, S. F. (1973). The significance of disease in the extinction of the New England Indians. *Human Biology, 45,* 485–508.

Coser, L. (1956). *The functions of social conflict.* New York: The Free Press.

Cronan, S. (1978). Marriage. In A. Jagger & P. Struhl (Eds.), *Feminist frameworks.* New York: McGraw-Hill.

Davis, K. (1986). Demographic foundations of the sex role revolution. *Social Science, 71,* 1–5.

Engels, F. (1884). The origin of the family, private property, and the state. In R. Tucker (Ed.), *The Marx-Engels reader,* pp. 734–759. New York: W. W. Norton, 1978.

Faludi, S. (1991) *Backlash: The undeclared war against American women.* New York: Random House.

Firestone, S. (1970). *The dialectic of sex.* New York: William Morrow.

Gibbs, N. (1991). When is it rape? *Time,* June 3, 1991, 48.

Hacker, H. (1951). Women as a minority group. *Social Forces, 30,* 60–69.

Helmerich, R., Spence, J., & Gibson, R. (1982). Sex role attitudes: 1972–1980. *Personality and Social Psychology Bulletin, 8,* 656–663.

Joseph, N. (1981, June 23). Campus couples and violence. *New York Times,* p. A20.

Lopreato, J. (1965). *Vilfredo Pareto.* New York: Thomas Y. Crowell.

Mason, K., & Bumpass, L. (1975). U.S. women's sex role ideology. *American Journal of Sociology, 80,* 1212–1226.

Mezydlo, L. (1980). Perceptions of ideal sex roles as a function of sex and feminist orientation. *Journal of Counseling Psychology, 42,* 282–285.

Parelius, A. P. (1975). Emerging sex-role attitudes, expectations and strains among college women. *Journal of Marriage and the Family, 37,* 146–153.

Parsons, T., & Bales, R. F. (1955). *Family: Socialization and interaction process.* New York: The Free Press.

Podhoretz, N. (1991). Rape in feminist eyes. *Commentary, 92,* 29.

Roper, B. S., & Labeff, E. (1977). Sex roles and feminism revisited: An inter-generational attitude comparison. *Journal of Marriage and the Family, 39,* 113–119.

Smith, M. D., & Self, G. (1980). The congruence between mothers' and daughters' sex role attitudes. *Journal of Marriage and the Family, 27,* 105–109.

Sweet, E. (1985, October). Date rape: The story of an epidemic and those who deny it. *Ms., XIV,* pp. 56, 58–59, 84–85.

Thornton, A., Alwin, D., & Camburn, D. (1983). Causes and consequences of sex-role attitudes and attitude change. *American Sociological Review, 48,* 211–227.

What's OK on a date. (1992). *The American Enterprise, 3,* 102.

Young, R. F. (1977). Current sex-role attitudes of male and female students. *Sociological Focus, 10,* 309–323.

Zey-Ferrell, M., Tolone, W., & Walsh, R. (1978). The inter-generational socialization of sex-role attitudes: A gender or generation gap? *Adolescence, 13* (49), 95–107.

Zinsser, H. (1960). *Rats, lice and history.* New York: Bantam Books.

READING 2

The Intergenerational Socialization of Sex-Role Attitudes: A Gender or Generation Gap?

Mary Zey-Ferrell
Texas A & M University

William L. Tolone
Illinois State University

Robert H. Walsh
Illinois State University

BACKGROUND

Sex-roles in our society are centered around the division of labor in the home and socio-political-economic structures outside the home. Traditional sex-roles for women have prescribed behavior, regardless of marital status and age, which is related to homemaking as opposed to occupationally oriented behavior. Consequently, this sex-based division of labor is a form of social inequality by which males have traditionally been assigned activities and positions of greater prestige and power (e.g., careers), while females have been relegated to those of less prestige and power (i.e., family and home). Although American society espouses the virtues of parenthood, in fact, it places greater value on occupational achievement. The validity of this statement is found in social status indicators employed by the Census Bureau, the Duncan Scale, etc. (e.g., the achieved statuses of education, occupation, and income).

Until recently, few social scientists applied the concept of "stratification" to the sexes. However, in 1964, William Goode analyzed the division of labor in numerous societies and observed that whatever the strictly male activities are, "they are defined as being more honorific." This, Goode suggested, is similar to "racial and caste restrictions."

> The low ranking race, caste, or sex is defined as not being able to do certain types of prestigious work. Obviously, if women really cannot do various kinds of male tasks, no moral or ethical prohibition would be necessary to keep them from it (Goode, 1964: 70).

In defining forms of sex-role inequality, Rossi (1972) identified inequality existing in both the *public sector* (citizens, employees, consumers) and the *private sector* (family, friend-ship groups, etc.). According to Rossi, inequalities in the private sector will be more difficult to eliminate because of the

rights of privacy of "home, family and person." For example, in the private sector, parents may repress a daughter's aspirations to become an engineer or physician, while at the same time encouraging a son to fulfill or exceed his aspirations and capacities. Thus, parental influences are of major importance in assessing sex-role attitudes. To test the theory that the private sector factors (parental attitudes) influence sex-role attitudes of adolescents, we analyzed the difference between sex-role attitudes of female freshmen and mothers, female freshmen and fathers, male freshmen and mothers, and male freshmen and fathers.

Meier's Feminine Social Equality (FSE) Scale items, which were employed as our dependent variables, focus specifically on female roles. Female occupational, political and family roles form the content of these items. Obviously, male roles must also change in order to form a more egalitarian social structure, but Meier's scale items deal only with female roles.

Although much research has been conducted on sex-role attitudes in the past decade, most has dealt exclusively with the sex-role attitudes of women. And, the samples have consisted predominantly of students. Thus, the change toward more egalitarian role definitions among women has been well documented (Mason, Arber, and Czajka, 1976); but little research, if any, has dealt with differential sex-role attitudes between genders and generations.

Because it is generally assumed that parents are a major socializing agent of American youths, our purpose was to determine if sex-role attitudes (FSE) were transmitted from parents to children. For example, if mother-father differences in FSE attitudes were found, were those sons' and daughters' attitudes more likely to be related to those of mothers or fathers? Gender and generational similarities and differences can occur in a variety of configurations (i.e., son-daughter, mother-father, father-daughter, mother-son, etc.). Our object was to define these relationships as sex, gender, or sex and gender related effects.

College freshmen were sampled because they had just spent close to eighteen or nineteen years continuously exposed to the attitudes and influences of their parents. At the same time, these freshmen had not experienced the "liberalizing" effects of college life and education. And, these freshmen along with their parents provided us with the T1 basis for a panel to be completed during the students' senior year.

Reprinted with permission from *Adolescence, 13* (49), 1978, pp. 95–107.

RATIONALE AND HYPOTHESES

Generational Differences

According to recent research analyzing women's sex-role attitudes, past generations were less egalitarian than the present generation. A division of labor has often been justified by beliefs about innate sex differences and children's needs to have a parent (the mother) in the home. These beliefs were used to justify differential opportunities and rights for males and females outside the home (Blake, 1972). Mason, Arber and Czajka (1976: 574) suggested that support for this division of labor has been high in the past perhaps due to perceived benefits for both women and men. They posited and found that to some extent social conditions are now either reducing such benefits for women or are undermining the beliefs rationalizing traditional female sex-roles. Thus, we expected that when persons of the same sex but different generations (mothers and daughters or fathers and sons) were compared, a larger proportion of the younger generation would exhibit more egalitarian sex-role attitudes than their same-sex parent.

Gender Differences

Research has also shown that males are more likely to endorse traditional sex-roles for women (Zey-Ferrell, Tolone, and Walsh, 1976; Komarovsky, 1973, and Meier, 1972). In order to reduce competition from females in the labor market and to increase labor and emotional support from the wife in the home, even males with high educational and occupational expectations have a vested interest in keeping the female out of the labor market and in the home. Because of their vested interest in maintaining the traditional sex-roles of women, we then expected that among persons of the same generation, males would exhibit less egalitarian sex-role attitudes. Likewise, females perceive benefits accruing from greater participation in economic, political, and occupational roles and would therefore be more likely to endorse egalitarian sex-roles for women.

Combined Gender and Generational Differences

Comparing freshman females with their fathers was expected to result in an overwhelming proportion of the former endorsing an egalitarian sex-role position. This would be produced by the combined egalitarian effects of female gender and younger generation. On the other hand, comparing freshman males with their mothers was expected to produce few intergenerational differences in sex-role attitudes. Where attitudes differed, we felt that a larger portion of mothers due to the gender effects would endorse the egalitarian position. Thus, gender differences were anticipated to be stronger than generation differences.

The following hypotheses were constructed and tested. The first two deal with gender differences, while generation is

controlled. Hypotheses 3 and 4 deal with generational differences, while gender is controlled. The last two deal with the combined effects of gender and generation.

Gender Effects:
1. Larger proportions of freshman females than males will support the egalitarian sex-role position.
2. Larger proportions of mothers than fathers will support the egalitarian sex-role position.

Generational Effects:
3. Larger proportions of freshman males than fathers will support the egalitarian sex-role position.
4. Larger proportions of freshman females than mothers will support the egalitarian sex-role position.

Combined Effects:
5. Larger proportions of freshman females than fathers will support the egalitarian sex-role position.
6. There will be little differences in the proportions of mothers and sons endorsing the egalitarian sex-role position. If differences do occur, larger proportions of mothers than freshman males will support the egalitarian sex-role position.

OPERATIONALIZATIONS

Dependent Variable

The Feminine Social Equality (FSE) Scale items, developed by Meier (1972: 116), measured the dependent variable, sex-role attitudes. All items consisted of statements supporting a traditional or egalitarian norm or belief. Respondents were asked to strongly agree, agree, disagree, or strongly disagree to these items (see Appendix A). Our analysis dichtomized these responses into egalitarian and traditional categories. Thus, the percentage of respondents endorsing the egalitarian position on a given item was the dependent variable. Freshman females, freshman males and both parents (mothers and fathers) responded to the items.

Independent and Control Variables

Gender and generation were used [as] both independent and control variables. When differences in gender were analyzed, generation was controlled; when differences in generation were analyzed, gender was controlled. Both gender and generation varied in analyzing differences between freshman females and fathers and freshman males and mothers.

DATA COLLECTION AND SAMPLE

Our original sample consisted of over 800 freshman students (61 percent female and 39 percent male) enrolled in a large midwestern state university in early 1975. The sample was obtained in the same manner as the university employs when conducting institutional research. Based on the assumption that a representative cross-section of students will be in attendance at 10:00

a.m. classes on Wednesday, we selected a number of these classes which predominantly contained freshmen. We supplemented these classes to bring the sample size to about 20 percent of the freshman class. The sex ratio closely approximated that of the total freshman class. Although sophomores, juniors and seniors were unavoidably sampled along with the freshmen (as they were members of the same classes as those sampled for freshmen), we chose to focus on freshmen for longitudinal reasons.

A self-administered questionnaire was completed by the respondents and on a separate piece of paper they were requested to provide their questionnaire code number and their parent(s)' current mailing address. Questionnaires which contained many of the same or similar questions as those in the student instrument were then mailed to both parents of the freshmen.

For the present research, we obtained 189 sets of mother, father and freshman student (114 female students, 75 male students, and their respective parents). In order to more adequately control the parameters of this study, we analyzed only single (never-married), white freshmen and their parents. The extremely small number of nonwhites within the parent-student sample and the confounding influence of mixing married and non-married student responses dictated that we operate in this manner.

FINDINGS AND CONCLUSIONS

Proportions of All Types of Respondents Endorsing the Egalitarian Position

The data in Table 1 [p. 32] indicate that on all items, with the exception of 11 and 17, more respondents agreed than disagreed with the egalitarian position. Generally, each type of respondent (freshman males, freshman females, mothers and fathers) was more egalitarian than non-egalitarian in their endorsement of sex-role attitudes. On each attitude item, without exception, a larger portion of freshman females than any other respondent type endorsed the egalitarian position. With the exception of item 16, either freshman males or fathers were the lowest proportion of any respondent types endorsing the egalitarian position (see Table 1).

Gender Differences

Hypothesis 1 stated that a larger proportion of freshman females than freshman males would endorse the egalitarian sex-role position. With the exception of items 7, 8, and 16, freshman females were significantly more egalitarian in their sex-role attitudes. . . . Hypothesis 1 was generally supported by these data and we concluded that a gender-gap in sex-role attitudes between freshman males and freshman females existed.

Hypothesis 2 stated that a larger proportion of mothers than fathers would endorse the egalitarian sex-role position. Contrary to our expectations, there were no significant differ-

ences between mothers and fathers on fourteen of the seventeen items. Only on items 14, 15, and 17 did a significantly larger proportion of mothers endorse the egalitarian position. . . . Thus, there was generally little support for hypothesis 2, and we concluded that mothers were not more egalitarian in their sex-role attitudes than fathers. There was little sex-role attitude gender-gap between mothers and fathers.

Generational Differences

Hypothesis 3 stated that a larger proportion of freshman females than their mothers would endorse the egalitarian sex-role position. As expected, significant differences between freshman females and their mothers were found on fourteen of the seventeen items. The only exceptions were for items 3, 8, and 17 where no significant differences appeared. . . . Thus, hypothesis 3 was supported and we concluded that freshman females were significantly more egalitarian in their sex-role attitudes than are their mothers. Our data demonstrated a generation-gap in sex-role attitudes of freshman females and their mothers.

Similarly, hypothesis 4 stated that a larger proportion of freshman males than their fathers would support the egalitarian sex-role position. Contrary to our expectation, this occurred on only four of the seventeen items (3, 6, 7, and 13). . . . There is little or no generation-gap between freshman males and their fathers. Further, on two of the items (7 and 13), a significantly larger proportion of freshman males endorsed the egalitarian position. But, on two other items ("Women in Congress" and "Woman general manager of General Motors," respectively), a significantly larger proportion of fathers than freshman males endorsed the egalitarian position.

Combined Gender and Generation Differences

Hypothesis 5 stated that a larger proportion of freshman females than fathers would endorse the egalitarian position. Because freshman females are more egalitarian as a result of combined gender (being female) and generational (younger) effects, it was expected that these differences would be greater and thus more significant than in any other comparison. On all 17 items, the proportion of freshman females endorsing the egalitarian position was significantly greater than that of fathers, providing overwhelming support for this hypothesis. There is a combination gender- and generation-gap between freshman females and their fathers.

Finally, hypothesis 6 stated that there would be no difference in the proportion of freshman males and mothers endorsing the egalitarian sex-role position. Freshman males, as members of a younger generation, socialized during a period of change toward more egalitarian sex-role attitudes, should be more egalitarian than mothers due to generation. On the other hand, mothers, due to gender, should be more egalitarian than their sons. Thus, it was hypothesized that these effects would cancel each other and there would be little difference in

Table 1

PERCENTAGE OF RESPONDENT TYPES AGREEING
WITH EQUALITARIAN POSITION

	FSE Item[a]	Freshman Males	Freshman Females	Fathers	Mothers
1.	Women not hold offices in government.	78.7 N = 75	88.5 N = 114	71.9 N = 187	75.6 N = 188
2.	Women not compete for male occupations.	76.0 N = 75	91.2 N = 114	79.2 N = 187	79.7 N = 187
3.	Women in Congress.	69.4 N = 72	86.7 N = 113	79.2 N = 183	82.4 N = 187
4.	Woman's place in the home.	70.8 N = 74	89.3 N = 113	62.6 N = 187	70.0 N = 187
5.	Top leadership positions held by males.	70.8 N = 75	84.1 N = 113	74.5 N = 184	72.4 N = 189
6.	Woman general manager of G.M.	51.4 N =73	79.0 N = 114	65.0 N = 186	67.9 N = 187
7.	Qualified woman refused admission to Plumbers Union.	98.7 N = 74	99.1 N = 114	90.3 N = 187	94.7 N = 188
8.	Woman continues to work after children	53.5 N = 74	61.9 N = 113	47.0 N = 185	52.7 N = 188
9.	Woman President of the United States	50.8 N =75	75.4 N = 114	56.7 N = 187	58.5 N = 188
10.	Woman better qualified; job to man.	71.9 N = 75	93.8 N = 114	71.8 N = 188	76.4 N = 186
11.	Woman oppressed; ridiculous.	39.7 N = 73	73.3 N = 112	37.7 N = 183	40.3 N = 186
12.	Woman not need education equal to man.	79.2 N = 74	95.5 N = 114	82.8 N = 187	84.5 N = 188
13.	Woman organizes to gain equal pay.	88.7 N = 75	96.5 N = 113	79.8 N = 188	79.2 N = 187
14.	Equally qualified; scholarship to male.	63.9 N = 73	92.1 N = 114	72.2 N = 184	84.1 N = 188
15.	Women compete; lose femininity.	53.5 N = 74	90.3 N = 114	47.9 N = 186	73.9 N = 188
16.	Women clergy.	73.3 N = 75	82.5 N = 114	71.5 N = 186	65.0 N = 189
17.	Married woman with children not work.	45.8 N = 70	58.5 N = 114	39.1 N = 187	50.8 N = 187

[a]This table exhibits abbreviated forms of each item. For the full items, see Appendix A.

freshman males' and mothers' endorsement of egalitarian sex-role attitudes. This hypothesis was generally supported. There were significant differences between freshman males and mothers on five items (3, 6, 13, 14, and 15). There were no significant differences on twelve of the seventeen items.

With regard to the items in which there were significant differences in freshman males and mothers, we expected a larger proportion of mothers to endorse the egalitarian position. This expectation was also supported. Shown in Table 1, in four of the five items where there was a significant difference (3, 4, 14, and 15), a larger proportion of mothers than freshman males endorsed the egalitarian position. . . . This demonstrates that

where gender and generational differences are involved, gender differences are more closely related to egalitarian sex-role attitudes: being female is a better predictor of sex-role egalitarianism than being of the younger generation.

SUMMARY AND IMPLICATIONS

Our analysis produced a number of interesting empirical results. When generation was controlled, gender differences in attitudinal sex-role egalitarianism appeared between freshman females and males, but not between mothers and fathers. When gender was controlled, generational differences appeared between freshman females and mothers, but not between freshman males and fathers. Finally, combined gender and generational effects demonstrated differences in the proportion of freshman females and fathers endorsing the egalitarian position, but generally not between freshman males and mothers.

The proportion of freshman females endorsing the egalitarian sex-role positions differed from that of (1) freshman males, supporting the gender-gap thesis; (2) mothers, supporting the generation-gap thesis; and (3) fathers, supporting both the gender- and generation-gap theses. The portion of freshman males endorsing the egalitarian sex-role position differed only from that of the freshman females, supporting the gender-gap thesis. A generation-gap between freshman males and fathers did not exist. Further, the combined effects of gender and generation generally did not produce a gap in the attitudes of freshman males and mothers.

From these findings, it can be seen that the gender-gap is more pervasive than the generation-gap; especially with regard to freshman females. Such gender differences will be more difficult to eliminate than generational differences in sex-role attitudes. Although the older generation will pass away and the new generation has promise of being more egalitarian, gender-related differences show little indication of decreasing. In their sex-role attitudes, the present generation of freshman males was more similar to the older generation of males (their fathers) than to the present generation of freshman females. Assuming that freshman males' attitudes are based on maintaining a more advantageous social position for their sex, one implication is that a change in social structure is needed to eliminate these attitudinal differences. If this happens, the next generation of males and females would experience interaction in which females hold positions which are politically, economically, and socially equal to that of males. Consequently, vested interest could become a more individualized phenomenon as opposed to one which is structurally based and sex-related.

Also from the findings discussed above, it is obvious that freshman females are more likely than freshman males to experience the effects of the generation-gap in egalitarian sex-role attitudes. The proportions of both parents endorsing the egalitarian sex-role position were more similar to that of freshman males than females. Thus, regardless of whether the male was egalitarian or non-egalitarian, he was more likely to find parental support for his sex-role attitudes than were freshman females.

The sex-role socialization thesis explored in this research was substantiated for freshman males, but not for freshman females. A significantly larger proportion of freshman females than mothers and fathers endorsed the egalitarian sex-role position. The females probably acquired their sex-role attitudes from significant role models other than parents, such as female peers. More plausibly, they may have rejected the sex-role attitudes of one or both of their parents because these parental attitudes were no longer beneficial to them or in their best interest. Subsequently, sex-role attitudes which were in their best interest were adopted. Theoretically, a vested interest thesis is a stronger theoretical approach to explaining differential sex-

role attitudes of freshman females, and probably other females, than is socialization.

It is easy to determine that the consequences of the gender- and generation-gaps for females are pervasive and of grave magnitude. Because more freshman females than males experience a gender- and generation-gap in sex-role attitudes, they are more likely to experience both psychological and behavioral role-conflict. This results from differences between their attitudes and those of parents and the opposite sex. If parental sex-role attitudes are generalized to other adults of the same generation, freshman females are also likely to experience role-conflict in relationships with these adults. Thus, sex-role attitudes of these adolescent females, though undoubtedly in their vested interest, clearly differ from those of many with whom they interact. As these differences are perpetuated, the insensitive stereotypes expeditiously used in the process of daily interaction will be perpetuated. Progress in removing these structurally-based, sex-role stereotypes will be impeded, resulting in maintenance of the status quo.

APPENDIX A

FEMININE SOCIAL EQUALITY ITEMS AND ABBREVIATED FORMS

1. It is all right for the woman to participate in local politics such as precinct work, but they should not hold the most important offices in government. (Women not hold offices in government.)
2. Women should try not to compete with men in occupations that have always belonged to men. (Women not compete for male occupations.)
3. There ought to be more women in the Congress of the United States. (Women in Congress.)
4. The old saying that "a woman's place is in the home" is still basically true and should remain true. (Woman's place in the home.)
5. In groups that have both male and female members, it is appropriate that top leadership positions be held by a male. (Top leadership positions held by males.)
6. A woman takes over as general manager of General Motors Corporation. (Woman general manager of G.M.)
7. A woman is refused admission into the Plumbers Union, even though she has passed all tests and is qualified. (Qualified woman refused admission to Plumbers Union.)
8. A woman continues to work after she has children even though her husband is making an adequate income to support the family. (Woman continues to work after children.)
9. A woman is elected President of the United States. (Woman President of the U.S.)
10. If there are two candidates for a job, one a man and the other a woman, the woman is slightly better qualified, the job should nevertheless go to the man because he is likely to have a family to support. (Woman better qualified, job to man.)

11. The talk we hear nowadays about women being an oppressed group in American Society is really ridiculous. (Women oppressed; ridiculous.)

12. A woman does not need as much education as a man. (Woman not need equal education to man.)

13. A working woman attempts to organize her co-workers to demand that the employer pay women on the same pay scale as male employees. (Woman organizes to gain equal pay.)

14. A male student and a female student are equally qualified for a certain scholarship; it is awarded to the male student on the grounds that he has greater "career potential." (Equally qualified; scholarship goes to male.)

15. Women who insist on competing in the male world of work and politics tend to lose their femininity. (Women compete; lose femininity.)

16. A woman becomes a clergyman in the church. (Woman clergy.)

17. Unless it is economically absolutely necessary, married women should not work when they have children. (Married women with children not work.)

REFERENCES

Bayer, A. E. (1975). Sexist students in American colleges: A descriptive note. *Journal of Marriage and the Family, 37,* 391–397.

Blake, J. (1972). Coercive pronatalism and American population policy. In R. Parke, Jr., & C. F. Westoff (Eds.), *Aspects of population growth and the American future research reports* (pp. 81–108). Washington, DC: U.S. Government Printing Office.

Epstein, G., & Bronzaft, A. L. (1972). Female freshmen view their roles as women. *Journal of Marriage and the Family, 34,* 621–672.

Ferree, M. M. (1974). A woman for president? Changing responses: 1958–1972. *Public Opinion Quarterly, 38,* 390–399.

Goode, W. J. (1964). *The family.* Englewood Cliffs, NJ: Prentice-Hall.

Kohn, M. L. (1963). Social class and parent-child relationships: An interpretation. *American Journal of Sociology, 68,* 471–480.

Komarovsky, M. (1973). Cultural contradictions and sex roles: The masculine case. In J. Huber (Ed.), *Changing women in a changing society.* Chicago: University of Chicago Press.

Mason, K. O. (1973). Studying change in sex-role definitions via attitude data. In *Proceedings of the American Statistical Association, Social Statistics Section,* pp. 138–141.

Mason, K. O., Arber, S., & Czajka, J. L. (1976). Change in U.S. women's sex-role attitudes, 1964–1974. *American Sociological Review, 41,* 573–596.

Mason, K. O., & Bumpass, L. L. (1975). U.S. women's sex-role ideology, 1970. *American Journal of Sociology, 80,* 1212–1219.

Meier, H. C. (1972). Mother-centeredness and college youths' attitudes toward social equality for women: Some empirical findings. *Journal of Marriage and the Family, 34,* 115–121.

Osmond, M. W., & Martin, P. Z. (1975). Sex and sexism: A comparison of male and female sex-role attitudes. *Journal of Marriage and the Family, 34,* 774–758.

PRIMARY GROUPS

> If civilization imposes such great sacrifices not only on man's sexuality but on his aggressivity, we can understand better why it is hard for him to be happy in civilization. In fact, primitive man was better off in knowing no restrictions of instinct. . . . Civilized man has exchanged a portion of his possibilities of happiness for a portion of security.
>
> Sigmund Freud
> *Civilization and Its Discontents*

In her last recording, Janis Joplin sang "freedom's just another word for nothing left to lose." The song was a tragic omen, as she was to die a month later from what may have been a suicidal overdose of heroin. Her warning to us suggests that our social needs, like love, security, and support, can only be fulfilled through membership in and attachment to groups. To be free or detached from the groups that satisfy these needs is to leave us alone and empty, with nothing else to lose. We are, however, ambivalent about the advice contained in the message. We resist the restraints and responsibilities that come with our attachment to groups and civilization. Because of this, Sigmund Freud (1856–1939) would have disagreed with Janis Joplin's view. He saw the needs of the individual and society as being in opposition. This chapter investigates the nature of the attachment that exists between the individual and the group.

Conflict Perspective

Freud was convinced that there was an irremediable antagonism between the demands of human instincts and the restrictions of society. Each new generation threatens civilization with an invasion of barbarians whose aggressive and pleasure-seeking instincts must be contained. The repression of these instincts begins in the family. In one of the great dramas of human life, according to Freud, the young man struggles to be free of the social taboos imposed on him by his father. Because he is smaller and weaker, he fails in this struggle. The youngster then internalizes the father's standards as a conscience. Civilization develops other means for repressing human instincts, and

correspondingly is responsible for increasing the misery of civilized people. Because of this, modern people sometimes feel that they would be happier if they gave up civilization and returned to primitive conditions. To conflict theorists like Freud, human happiness is elusive and rarely enduring. Freud was especially attracted to Greek plays like *Oedipus Rex* because of their insight into the human condition. The tragedy concludes: "Count no mortal happy till he has passed the final limit of his life secure from pain." Civilization demands a high price.

Functional Perspective

Functionalists reject the individualistic views of Freud. As humans, our distinctive qualities are those that have been learned socially. We speak a language we did not make, use tools we did not invent, and use knowledge passed on to us by others. If somehow it were possible to remove these social characteristics of an individual, the person would fall to the rank of an animal. The individual and the social order are fused, not opposed. To oppose the two is to destroy both.

Émile Durkheim believed the demands of the individual and social order must be balanced. When the demands of the group overwhelm those of the individual, the result can be the sacrifice of the individual to the needs of the group. Examples of this may be found in the Japanese ritual of hara-kiri and the kamikaze pilots of World War II who suicidally crashed their planes into American ships. Americans usually commit suicide not out of social duty or oppression, but because they are free of commitments that would keep them from choosing suicide. Durkheim observed that through group attachment there is a "constant interchange of ideas and feelings of each to all, something like a mutual moral support, which instead of throwing the individual on his own resources, leads him to share

This investigation is based on "Relative Attachment of Students to Groups and Organizations" by Charles B. Spaulding, 1966, reprinted on pages 41–44.

35

in the collective energy and supports his own when exhausted"
(1897/1951, p. 210).

Group attachment is essential to the mental health of
individuals. Detached individuals have higher rates of mental
disorder (Faris & Dunham, 1939), schizophrenia (Jaco, 1954;
Kohn & Clausen, 1955), feelings of powerlessness (Seeman,
1964), and deviance (Rabb & Selznick, 1959). The strength of
group attachment is related to the size of the group. Erwin
Smigel (1956) found that social control became a greater
problem the larger the scale of the social organization: "If
obliged to choose, most individuals would prefer to steal from,
and be more approving of others stealing from, large scale,
impersonal rather than small scale, personal organizations" (p.
320). Thus, attachment to small groups serves a dual function.
For the individual, attachment brings security and social support. For the social order, attachment increases the means by
which the individual may be subjected to social control.

The small groups to which we have the greatest attachment
Charles Horton Cooley called *primary groups.* They are primary because it is in them that we have our first social
experiences and develop our most complete sense of social
unity. "Psychologically [there] is a certain fusion of individu-
alities in a common whole, so that one's self, for many purposes
at least, is the common life and purpose of the group. Perhaps
the simplest way of describing this wholeness is by saying that it
is a 'we'; it involves the sort of sympathy and mutual identification for which 'we' is the natural expression" (Cooley, 1909, pp.
26–27). Primary groups are highly personal and evoke the
strongest feelings of mutual identification among their members. The primary group attaches and integrates the individual
into the social order. These features led Cooley to conclude that
the primary group is universal and essential to society.

Secondary groups are more often found in industrial urban
society than in rural agricultural villages. Secondary groups are
made up of people who are brought together to accomplish
specific goals. In working toward these goals, the individuals
specialize in tasks that make their relations to one another more
calculated and impersonal. In the most extreme cases the sole
basis of the relationship may be money. In secondary groups,
face-to-face communication is replaced by written messages
and organizational policy. As organizational size increases,
personal knowledge of others decreases. This provides less
emotional attachment and support than the individual enjoyed in
primary groups. But secondary groupings also pose organizational problems, since they exert less control over the behavior
of individuals, as Smigel's survey showed. In large-scale urban
society, the bond becomes an increasingly urgent issue for both
individual and society. The differences between primary and
secondary groups are summarized in Table 3–1.

Durkheim observed that in rural areas there was more
community attachment. He was concerned that as the scale and
size of society increased, the character of social relationships
would change and the sense of community would be eroded. He
feared that weakening social bonds would result in individuals'
feeling disconnected from society. In such a "mass society,"
people would become strangers to one another. Isolated and

Table 3–1

PRIMARY AND SECONDARY GROUP CHARACTERISTICS

	Type of Group	
	Primary	Secondary
Scale	Small	Large
Society	Rural	Urban
Division of Labor	Unspecialized	Specialized
Intimacy	Personal	Impersonal
Identity	"We"	"Me"
Community	Moral	"Mass"
Bonds	Strong	Weak
Beliefs	Sacred	Secular
Involvements	Enduring	Temporary
Investments	Many	Few
Attachment	Emotional	Calculative

alienated from society, religious faiths would be abandoned,
kinship ties would dissolve, and individuals would drift in
search of purpose and community.

The social bond of which Durkheim spoke has been found
by Rodney Stark (1992, pp. 187–190) to consist of at least four
elements:

1. *Beliefs.* Socially acquired ideas penetrate our conscience
   and consciousness, mentally linking us with others.
2. *Involvements.* The more time we spend in a group, the
   more absorbed we become in the ways of that social
   order.
3. *Investments.* The costs of group membership means that
   the individual risks losing these investments if he or she
   rejects group standards. The group can exert restraints
   on individuals who are unwilling to sacrifice their
   careers, social contacts, earned licenses, and seniority.
4. *Attachments.* This refers to more or less stable relationships that carry an emotional commitment. It was this
   degree of attachment that Cooley found to be so different in primary and secondary groups.

Background

The research of Charles Spaulding, which you will read about in
Reading 3 on pages 41–44, investigated the nature of the
individual's attachment to the group. Spaulding hypothesized
that groups with a preponderance of primary characteristics will
have greater member attachment and be more cohesive than
groups of a secondary character. He found this hypothesis to be
supported. He also found that there were certain clear exceptions to this general rule: the United States, for instance, which
is a secondary group, received a higher rank than many of the
primary groups. In replicating Spaulding's research through our
Student Survey, we will see whether or not his findings are still
true.

Replication

Our first hypothesis will investigate whether, overall, our Student Survey results match those reported by Spaulding.

Hypothesis 1:

There is a significant correlation between group attachments in Spaulding's 1966 study and our study.

Next, we will test two of the specific hypotheses that Spaulding examined.

Hypothesis 2:

The members of groups that are relatively small, face-to-face, intimate, permanent, informal, or spontaneous will, on the whole, be more emotionally attached to those groups than to groups that are opposite in character.

Hypothesis 3:

The United States* will be the object of a greater degree of emotional attachment than will other formal organizations and many quasi-primary groups.

To test these hypotheses, we will need two data sources:

- Table 1 from Spaulding's 1966 article
- The class's responses to question 10 on the Student Survey

You will find the first of these sources, Table 1 from Spaulding's article, on page 43. The class's responses to question 10 on the Student Survey will be provided by your instructor.

In this investigation, the dependent variable is group attachment. Spaulding measured this with a six-point scale (with scores 0–5), rating "feeling of attachment."

The independent variable is the degree to which the group possesses primary qualities. We have sampled 12 of Spaulding's original 38 groups and included them in question 10 on the Student Survey, reprinted below. They are then divided into primary and secondary groups. *Primary groups* include "steady" or fiancé(e), immediate family, same-sex best friend, and close friends. *Quasi-primary* or *secondary groups* include extended family, nation, work organization, local community, city of residence, state or province of residence, United Nations, and military organization.

STUDENT SURVEY QUESTION 10

Study the list that follows. Think carefully of ALL the organizations and informal groups to which you belong. Then rate these organizations by circling the number that most nearly expresses your feeling toward the group or organization. If you belong to two or more groups or organizations of a single type (such as if your parents were separated and remarried), evaluate the one for which you have the greatest positive feeling.

Feeling of Attachment

Very Great (5) / Great (4) / Moderate (3) / Slight (2) / Neutral (1) / Antagonism (0)

		0	1	2	3	4	5
A.	Your immediate family	0	1	2	3	4	5
B.	Your extended family (aunts, uncles, cousins, grandparents)	0	1	2	3	4	5
C.	Your "steady" or fiancé(e) (if you have one) [On the computer survey, enter "X" if no steady or fiancé(e)]	0	1	2	3	4	5
D.	The United States of America*	0	1	2	3	4	5
E.	Your state/province	0	1	2	3	4	5
F.	Your city	0	1	2	3	4	5
G.	Your local community or neighborhood	0	1	2	3	4	5
H.	The United Nations	0	1	2	3	4	5
I.	The organization for which you work	0	1	2	3	4	5
J.	A military organization (e.g., Army, Navy)	0	1	2	3	4	5
K.	Your best friend of your own sex	0	1	2	3	4	5
L.	A small informal group of friends (your clique, gang, or crowd)	0	1	2	3	4	5

If you belong to several such groups, answer in terms of the one that means the most to you.

---

*If survey is taken in Canada, substitute "Canada."

Table 3–2

INVESTIGATION RESULTS 3

Attachment to Groups

Groups and Organizations	Group Type†	Spaulding's Attachment	Student Survey Attachment	My Rating
Steady or fiancé(e)	(P)	4.31	_____	_____
Immediate family	(P)	3.97	_____	_____
Same-sex best friend	(P)	3.94	_____	_____
United States*	(Q-S)	3.67	_____	_____
Close friends	(P)	3.52	_____	_____
State/province of residence	(Q-S)	3.04	_____	_____
Extended family	(Q-S)	2.80	_____	_____
Your work organization	(Q-S)	2.65	_____	_____
City of residence	(Q-S)	2.62	_____	_____
Your local community	(Q-S)	2.46	_____	_____
The United Nations	(Q-S)	2.36	_____	_____
Military organization	(Q-S)	2.09	_____	_____

Spaulding's Average Attachment = 3.12

*If survey is taken in Canada, substitute "Canada."
†P = primary group
Q-S = quasi-primary or secondary group
Note: Spaulding's data are from Table 1, p. 43.

Overall Student Survey attachment (P + Q-S) =	_____
Average attachment to primary groups (P) =	_____ ←
Average attachment to secondary groups (Q-S) =	_____ ←
Correlation between your class's study and Spaulding's (1966) study: Rho =	_____ ←
My average group attachment (add your attachment ratings and divide by 12) =	_____
Hypothesis 1	_____
Hypothesis 2	_____

To test our hypotheses, we will proceed as follows:

Step 1:

Use the information provided by your instructor to fill in Table 3–2 (Investigation Results, 3 above).

Step 2:

At the bottom of the Investigation Results table you will find, marked by arrows, the results needed to fill in the blanks in hypotheses 1 and 2 below.

Hypothesis 1:

There is a significant correlation between group attachments in Spaulding's 1966 study and our study.

Evaluation: With 12 groups, significance at the .05 level requires a correlation larger than + .504. (See Table A, "Critical Values of Rho," on page 201.)

Correlation 1966 to present _____ ≥ Rho + .504

Hypothesis 2:

The members of groups that are relatively small, face-tro-face, intimate, permanent, informal, or spontaneous will, on the whole, be more emotionally attached to those groups than to groups that are opposite in character.

Evaluation: There will be greater attachment to primary groups (P) than to secondary groups (Q-S).

Average attachment

Primary groups		Secondary groups
_____	>	_____

Step 3:

To complete hypothesis 3, find the Student Survey score to the right of Spaulding's United States rating (3.67) and record the Student Survey score in the left blank of hypothesis 3, below.

Table 3–3

SUPPORT FOR HYPOTHESES

	Significantly Supported	Partially Supported	Not Supported	Indeterminate
Hypothesis 1: Rho Spaulding and Student Survey	_____	_____	_____	_____
Hypothesis 2: Primary group attachment	_____	_____	_____	_____
Hypothesis 3: United States* attachment	_____	_____	_____	_____

Indicate the amount of support you found for each hypothesis.

Then identify the highest-ranked secondary group (Q–S) other than the United States.* Record that attachment score in the right blank below.

Hypothesis 3:

The United States* will be the object of a greater degree of emotional attachment than will other formal organizations and many quasi-primary groups.

Evaluation: The United States* will be ranked above all other quasi-primary and secondary groups (Q–S) as well as above some primary groups.

United States*
rank _____ > _____ Highest ranked secondary group (excluding U.S.*)

Checking Your Findings

Hypothesis 1 deals with the types of groups that we consider to be important. We hypothesized that the order of group attachment found in 1966 will continue to the present. Support for this hypothesis requires a Rho greater than or equal to +.504. Do your results support the hypothesis? Note any groups that rose or fell more than three ranks. If any changed more than three ranks, how do you explain these changes?

Hypothesis 2 concerns the nature of the attachment of individuals to primary and secondary groups. You can now compare primary and secondary group attachment scores and evaluate whether individuals are more attached to primary groups than to secondary groups.

Hypothesis 3 states that the only large, formally organized group to compare to the emotional attachment of primary groups will be the nation. To test this we have hypothesized that the United States* will be the highest-ranked secondary group. Did you find this to be true?

Summarize your findings by checking off the amount of support for each hypothesis in Table 3–3 above.

*If survey is taken in Canada, substitute "Canada."

Topics for Further Investigation

1. In addition to the questions raised by Spaulding, you may wish to consider changes in the level of social cohesion. The average attachment reported for these 12 groups by the students in Spaulding's study was 3.12, or between "Moderate" and "Great Attachment." How does this compare to your average attachment and the class's average attachment?

2. Do you think the level of attachment is affected by the student's religion (low vs. high attendance), residence (rural vs. urban), family (broken vs. unbroken) or social class (lower vs. upper)? Do you feel these are characteristic of society as a whole? If the level of attachment has fallen, what are the implications of this for individuals and society?

3. One would expect that attachment levels for steady or fiancé(e) would be closely connected to romantic love (Student Survey question 34, items A–M) and liking (items N–Z). Does this seem to be the case? (Loving and liking are explored further in chapter 10).

4. Durkheim believed that the fewer attachments an individual has to social groupings the higher will be the level of anomie (discussed further in chapter 11). Do the attachment scores appear to be related to responses to our indicators of anomie (Student Survey questions 13–17)?

5. Many believe anomie and extremist political views and prejudice are connected. Do you find that group attachment is also connected to support for civil liberties (Student Survey questions 18–23, discussed in chapter 9) or social distance (question 11–A, discussed in chapter 11)?

References and Recommended Readings

Bellah, R., Madsen, R., Sullivan, W., Swidler, A., & Tipton, S. (1985). *Habits of the heart: Individualism and commitment in American life.* New York: Harper & Row.

Cooley, C. H. (1909). *Social organization.* New York: Charles Scribner's Sons.

Crutchfield, R., Geerkin, M., and Grove, W. R. (1983) "Crime rates and social integraiton." *Criminology* 20:467–478.

Durkheim, E. (1897). *Suicide.* Reprint. New York: The Free Press, 1951.

Erikson, K. (1976). *Everything in its path.* New York: Simon & Schuster.

Faris, R. E. L., & Dunham, H. W. (1939). *Mental disorders in urban areas.* Chicago: University of Chicago Press.

Jaco, E. G. (1954). The social isolation hypothesis and schizophrenia. *American Sociological Review, 19,* 567–577.

Kohn, M., & Clausen, J. (1955). Social isolation and schizophrenia. *American Sociological Review, 20,* 265–273.

Olmsted, M., & Hare, P. (1978). *The small group* (2nd ed.). New York: Random House.

Rabb, E., & Selznick, G. (1959). *Major social problems,* New York: Harper & Row.

Seeman, M. (1964). Organizations and powerlessness: A test of the mediation hypothesis. *American Sociological Review, 29,* 216–226.

Smigel, E. (1956). Public attitudes toward stealing as related to the size of the victim organization. *American Sociological Review, 21,* 320–327.

Spaulding, C. B. (1966). The relative attachment of students to groups and organizations. *Sociology and Social Research, 50,* 421–435.

Stark, R. (1992). *Sociology.* 4th ed. Belmont, CA: Wadsworth.

Stark, R., Doyle, D. P., & Kent, L. (1980). Rediscovering moral communities: Church membership and crime. In T. Hirschi & M. Gottfredson (Eds.), *Understanding crime: Current theory and research.* Beverly Hils, CA: Sage.

Stark, R., Doyle, D. P., & Rushing, J. L. (1983). Beyond Durkheim: Religion and suicide. *Journal for the Scientific Study of Religion, 22,* 120–131.

Swanson, G. E. (1968). To live in concord with society: Two empirical studies of primary relations. In A. J. Reiss (Ed.), *Cooley and sociological analysis.* Ann Arbor, MI: University of Michigan Press.

Relative Attachment of Students to Groups and Organizations

Students in a Western university indicate generally closer attachment to primary and quasi-primary groups than to other types. Important partial exceptions exist for the nation-state and the university, and among the most loyal members of some other organizations. Strong attachment to primary and quasi-primary groups tends to increase attachment to larger organizations with which the former are associated.

Charles B. Spaulding
University of California, Santa Barbara

It has often been assumed that people feel closer attachment to primary and quasi-primary groups than to secondary groups and organizations.[1]* While the research here reported generally supports this assumption, it suggests that certain important exceptions exist in the cases of entities such as the nation-state and the university as well as among the most loyal members of certain other organizations. The findings also indicate that strong attachment to primary and quasi-primary groups tends to increase attachment to larger and more formal organizations when the former are perceived as being associated with the latter.

A great deal of effort has gone into the study of primary, small, or informal groups. While much of this work has been directed toward relatively artificial laboratory groups, some of it has also been concerned with groups established for other purposes, many of which may properly be described as primary or quasi-primary.[2] The implications of much of the research are that persons tend to value primary-group relationships relatively highly, but no one has stopped to ask specifically whether people do in truth feel greater attachment to primary and quasi-primary groups than to other groups and organizations. And while a considerable amount of attention has been given to the relationships between group membership and organizational behavior, the analysis is far from clear and complete.

In his original discussion of the primary group Cooley's emphasis was on its effect upon the behavior of people,[3] and this emphasis has been retained in the literature along with efforts to determine how structure develops within groups. Considerable attention has also been given to cohesiveness of groups. Although some writers have emphasized the importance of personal

satisfaction as one necessary aspect of "primary relations,"[4] the approach has usually been to determine those factors which are associated with relative cohesiveness in small groups rather than to consider specifically the relative cohesiveness of different types of groups and organizations.[5] Cohesiveness has often been defined as "attraction to the group,"[6] and several different methods of measuring it have been employed. In this research emotional attachment has been assumed to be one possible measure of cohesiveness.[7]

One conceptual difficulty involves the question of whether or not the primary group is by very definition cohesive, satisfying, or emotionally attractive. As with so many sociological concepts the definitions of the primary group vary somewhat among writers,[8] and the question of whether emotional attachment is an essential part of the definition is debatable. In his original writings Cooley seems to have assumed that such was the case, for he emphasized the "we" feeling of such groups, the sympathetic attitudes of the members toward each other, and the cooperative behavior among them.[9]

No matter whether cohesiveness be regarded as an attribute which is necessary to the definition or whether it be regarded as a separate variable, the empirical question concerning the actual association of cohesiveness with the other attributes normally used in defining a primary group may still properly be raised. A formulation of the principal attributes of the primary group worked out by two of Cooley's students will serve the purposes of the present research. They defined the primary groups as being face-to-face, unspecialized, permanent, small, and intimate.[10] Although these writers recognized that Cooley considered unity or wholeness to be a normal development within groups so characterized,[11] their definition leaves open the question of whether cohesiveness is a necessary attribute.

In any case, much evidence suggests that people do find primary and quasi-primary groups to be attractive. In addition to what appear to have been Cooley's original assumptions, much of the writing on the diversified or mass society seems to grieve for the more primary world. From *Gemeinschaft und Gesellschaft*[12] to *The Lonely Crowd*[13] and beyond[14] this under-

---

*Footnotes for this article will be found on page 44.

Reprinted with permission from *Sociology and Social Research*, 50, 1966, pp. 421–435.

lying feeling persists. There are also famous instances of more direct evidence. Long John suffered nightmares when the Norton Street gang disintegrated;[15] the girls in the Relay Assembly Room at Hawthorne liked to come to work;[16] and absenteeism in an aircraft factory varied with group membership.[17] Conversely, at the New York State Training School for Girls the isolate tended to run away,[18] and the German soldier without a group attachment more frequently deserted or surrendered.[19] Also people who find themselves in cohesive groups tend to be less anxious according to Seashore's data,[20] and Asch's study of the acceptance of obvious error under group pressure indicates anxiety on the part of the aberrant members.[21] In addition to fulfilling the sheer need for association, the primary or quasi-primary group may be a real help in solving certain practical problems and in integrating a member's perceptions and conceptions.[22]

The well-established power of the primary and quasi-primary group to influence behavior also suggests its appeal to its members, for exclusion is often its most drastic form of punishment. And this power has been often demonstrated. For instance, the family has a powerful impact on the child,[23] the clique[24] or gang[25] on its members, the cohesive work group upon workers,[26] the squad or company upon the soldier.[27]

In the light of these data, the *first* formal *hypothesis* for investigation was: The members of groups which are relatively small, face-to-face, intimate, permanent, and informal or spontaneous (i.e. primary and quasi-primary groups) will, on the whole, be more emotionally attached to those groups than to groups and organizations of opposite character.

Only one large formally organized body seemed likely to challenge primary and quasi-primary groups in terms of the emotional attachment of its members and that was the United States of America, the nation-state. This judgment was based on an analysis of world history drawn from the writings of many persons in many disciplines. What these writings show is that in Western Europe around 1500 A.D. localism, tribalism, feudalism, and imperialism began to give way to nationalism. Loyalties began to pass from city, tribe, or local region to larger units, and men began to think of themselves as Spaniards, Frenchmen, Englishmen, etc.[28] Gradually, this movement has been sweeping much of the world, and we are now witnessing the attempts of the African peoples (among others) to throw off imperialism and tribalism and achieve nationalism.

While nationalistic emotions have thus been spreading across the face of the earth, internationalism has been making much slower progress. The United Nations boasts some 117* members, but citizens of the world are few, and the mighty nations have released little of their pride and power to the United Nations.

The *second hypothesis,* therefore, was: The United States of America will be the object of a greater degree of emotional attachment than other formal organizations and than many quasi-primary groups.

If it is true that people feel relatively strong attachment to quasi-primary groups, the basic concept of conditioning would suggest that many of them should also become relatively more closely attached to the organizations with which those friendship groups are associated. Of course, informal groups may oppose the larger organization, as in the famous case of the Bank Wiring Room at Hawthorne,[29] but the general trend might well be that primary relationships would bind members to the organization. Seashore's data on work units in a plant manufacturing heavy equipment suggest this very thing, for of the low-cohesive groups 31 per cent viewed the company as supportive, while among the highly cohesive groups 72 per cent so perceived it.[30]

* * * *

PROCEDURE AND SAMPLE

In order to explore the various suggested relationships, a questionnaire, which either listed or provided a place for listing all of the groups and organizations to which persons might belong, was developed and pretested. Respondents were asked to complete a listing of their current memberships and then to indicate their relative attachment to each group or organization by an appropriate check on a crude scale with subdivisions and code values as follows: antagonism 0, neutral feeling 1, slight attachment 2, moderate attachment 3, great attachment 4, and very great attachment 5.[31] A student who belonged to two or more groups or organizations of a single type (as where parents were separated and remarried) was directed to evaluate the one for which he had the greatest positive feeling.

A summary of selected data resulting from the analysis of the 343 completed questionnaires is presented in Table 1 [opposite]. While the referents of many of the categories in this table are obvious, some of them appear to require explication. Among these are items 5, 12, and 20 which refer to subgroups of fraternities or sororities, churches, and political organizations. These subgroups include those which were listed by students in response to the directions to name subgroups attached to organizations listed.

Where students listed comparable subgroups without listing the obvious parent organization (as they sometimes did), the subgroups so listed were included in the counts on which Table 1 is based. . . .

Brief explanations of other categories used in Table 1 may be presented in outline form identified by number as follows:

Item 9. Was identified in the questionnaire as "a small informal group of friends (your clique, gang, or crowd)."

Item 10. Coded as referring primarily to church groups maintained for college students by the various denominations under the auspices of the University Religious Conference or nearby local churches.

Item 11. Certain students listed special committees within the residence halls. They did not, in most cases, seem to regard these as subgroups of the Residence Halls Association but as aspects of the residence hall group.

Item 13. Activities such as folk dance and drama groups, cycling club, band, and forensic squad were coded here.

Editor's note: As of 1992, this number was closer to 175.

Item 17. Coded as an identifiable group with which respondent currently lived—not a named fraternity or sorority.

Item 22. Described in questionnaire as "your large family group, including such relatives as aunts, uncles, cousins, grandparents, grandchildren, etc."

Item 30. The questionnaire asked for rating of "your community or neighborhood (if different from the city in which you live)." No directions were given concerning whether reference was to present college address or "regular" home, beyond general instructions to rate grouping of greatest attachment.

Item 31. Coded to refer to a cooperative association of the residence halls and the interfraternity council.

Items 34 and 36. R.O.T.C. was usually listed as an independent military unit and was always so coded.

FINDINGS AND DISCUSSION

Table 1 demonstrates that the respondents' evaluations of attachment generally followed the pattern predicted by hypothesis 1. When the items were arranged in order of relative attachment, eight of the first nine were of a generally primary or quasi-primary type, and the one exception was the United States. Even the items listed as numbers 10 through 13 appear to display more primary-group characteristics (and in greater degree) than most of the succeeding items with higher numbers.

In view of the recent trend among writers to emphasize the continuing importance to urban dwellers of their kindred,[32] the relatively low (No. 22) position of the large family group is of some theoretical interest. Why does it not rate higher?

A reexamination of some of the relevant literature suggests a part of the answer. Since our descent system stresses both lines of parentage, each set of siblings has a different kindred, and this circumstance militates against overt devices for identification and ready perception of the kindred as an objective reality—as tends to be the case where one line or the other is stressed.[33] But this condition does not negate the importance of relatives. What the studies of Sussman, Zimmerman, and others[34] suggest is that, from the pool of possible friends created by kinship, certain relatives are selected on the basis of geographic proximity, mutual interests, and needs, and harmonious personalities to be the intimates of any particular family. The resultant intimate relationships are apparently thought of in specific terms rather than in terms of loyalty to some larger social entity.

While the studies in the literature have largely analyzed relationships of married couples with relatives, these patterns probably carry over to the children of those couples. The very small use made by college students of the kin name only for aunts and uncles also suggests the validity of this interpretation.[35] The child, then, may be very fond of Uncle Joe, Cousin Sue, and Grandmother Jones, but quite neutral or even antagonistic toward other members of his kindred, and not particularly conscious of the kindred as an entity.

The one item among the top nine which was not a primary or quasi-primary group was the United States of America, a fact well in line with hypothesis 2.

Table 1

STUDENTS' RELATIVE ATTACHMENT TO GROUPS AND ORGANIZATIONS

Groups and Organizations	Attachment Score	Number of Responses
1. Conjugal Family	4.66	41
2. Steady or Fiancé(e)	4.31	160
3. Parental Family	3.97	340
4. Best Friend	3.94	332
5. Fraternity or Sorority Subgroup	3.72	18
6. Athletic Team	3.68	38
7. The United States	3.67	343
8. College Fraternity or Sorority	3.61	87
9. Clique	3.52	319
10. Church Group (at university)	3.45	11
11. Residence Hall Committees, etc.	3.44	16
12. Church Subgroup (off campus)	3.32	38
13. Special Interest Groups (campus)	3.21	66
14. U.C.S.B.	3.17	293
15. A Church	3.16	141
16. Academic Department	3.09	107
17. Residence Hall or Living Group	3.04	70
18. State of Residence	3.04	343
19. Campus Honorary or Service Club	2.83	23
20. Political Organization Subgroup	2.82	11
21. Political Organization	2.81	37
22. Large Family Group	2.80	335
23. Special Interest or Recr. Grp. (off campus)	2.78	49
24. Work Associates	2.68	168
25. Work Organization	2.65	171
26. Departmental Club or Honorary Fraternity	2.62	58
27. City of Residence	2.62	341
28. A Lodge	2.59	17
29. Student Body Committee	2.58	19
30. Community or Neighborhood	2.46	220
31. Cooperative Associations	2.38	66
32. United Nations	2.36	331
33. Class (i.e. Jr., Sr.) Council	2.36	11
34. Any Military Organization	2.09	57
35. Associated Men and Women Students	1.91	11
36. R.O.T.C.	1.88	26
37. Union	1.67	12
38. Associated Student Body Organization	1.10	241
Number of Respondents		(343)

CONCLUSIONS

The original propositions tested in this research have on the whole been well supported. Entities for which relatively great emotional attachment was expressed by students may generally be characterized as primary or quasi-primary groups, except that the United States was also well toward the top of the list. Most formal organizations and secondary groups tended to be rated lower. . . .

That there are limits to the generally greater relative attractiveness of quasi-primary groups is further suggested by the relatively high attachment to the United States and to the university campus. Some larger entity which comes to symbolize a constellation of values and relationships may well come to outrank certain primary and quasi-primary relationships for certain persons at certain times.

FOOTNOTES

1. This idea seems to underlie Homan's emphasis on the importance of the small group for the happy life. See: George C. Homans, *The Human Group* (New York: Harcourt, Brace and Company, 1950), 112, *et passim*; E. L. Trist and K. W. Bamforth, "Some Social Psychological Consequences of the Longwall Method of Coal Getting," *Human Relations*, 4, 1 (1951), 3–38; and also references in subsequent footnotes in this paper, especially numbers 9, 12, 13, 14, and 15–21.

2. Two summaries of considerable bodies of this research are: Dorwin Cartwright and Alvin Zander, *Group Dynamics: Research and Theory,* (Evanston, Illinois: Row Peterson and Company, 1960, Second Edition); and A. Paul Hare, *Handbook of Small Group Research* (New York: The Free Press, a Division of the Macmillan Co., 1962).

3. Charles H. Cooley, *Social Organization* (New York: Charles Scribner's Sons, 1927), especially chapters III and IV.

4. Cf. Leonard Broom and Philip Selznick, *Sociology,* (New York: Harper and Row, 1963, Third Edition), 139.

5. See the collections cited in footnote 2.

6. Cf. Dorwin Cartwright and Alvin Zander, *op. cit.*, 74, and Hare, *op. cit.*, 146–147.

7. For some suggested indices see Warren O. Nagstrom and Hanan C. Selvin, *Two Dimensions of Cohesiveness in Small Groups, Sociometry*, 28:30–43 (March, 1965), especially 31 and 32; also Dorwin Cartwright and Alvin Zander, *op. cit.*, 69–72.

8. Compare: Leonard Broom and Philip Selznick, *op. cit.*, 135–40; George A. Lundberg, Clarence C. Schrag, and Otto N. Larsen, *Sociology* (New York: Harper and Row, 1963, Third Edition), 67 and 68; William F. Ogburn and Meyer F. Nimkoff, *Sociology* (Boston: Houghton Mifflin Co., 1964, Fourth Edition), 133.

9. Charles Horton Cooley, *op. cit.*, especially 23 and 24.

10. Charles Horton Cooley, Robert Cooley Angell, and Lowell Juilliard Carr, *Introductory Sociology* (New York: Charles Scribner's Sons, 1933), 55.

11. *Ibid.*, 56.

12. As is so often the case, there is argument about this point. See the Foreword, Preface, and Introduction to Ferdinand Tönnies, trans. and ed. Charles P. Loomis, *Community and Society* (East Lansing, Michigan: Michigan State University Press, 1957).

13. David Riesman, Nathan Glazer, Reuel Denny, *The Lonely Crowd* (Garden City, New York: Doubleday Anchor Books, 1963).

14. See, for instance, Walter M. Gerson, "Alienation in Mass Society: Some Causes and Responses," *Sociology and Social Research,* 49 (January, 1965), 143–152.

15. William Foote Whyte, *Street Corner Society,* (Chicago: University of Chicago Press, 1964, Second Edition), 48.

16. Stuart Chase, *Men at Work* (New York: Harcourt, Brace and Co., 1945), 20.

17. Elton Mayo and George Lombard, *Teamwork and Labor Turnover in the Aircraft Industry of Southern California* (Boston: Graduate School of Business Administration, Harvard University, 1944).

18. J. L. Moreno, *Who Shall Survive?* (Washington: Nervous and Mental Disease Publishing Co., 1943), 217.

19. Edward A. Shils and Morris Janowitz, "Cohesion and Disintegration in the Wehrmacht in World War II," *The Public Opinion Quarterly,* 12 (Summer, 1948), 280–315, especially 285.

20. Stanley E. Seashore, *Group Cohesiveness in the Industrial Work Group* (Ann Arbor: Survey Research Center, Institute for Social Research, University of Michigan, 1954), especially 14, 61–62, and 98. Some relevant literature is cited on 15.

21. Solomon E. Asch, "Opinions and Social Pressure," *Scientific American,* 193 (November, 1955), 31–35, especially 33.

22. Charles B. Spaulding, "Cliques, Gangs, and Networks," *Sociology and Social Research,* 32 (July–August, 1948), 928–937, especially 933 and 934.

23. This point scarcely needs specific support, but one of the most compelling bodies of data is found in Sheldon and Eleanor Glueck, *Unraveling Juvenile Delinquency* (Cambridge, Massachusetts: Harvard University Press, 1950), especially chapters VIII–XI.

24. For instance, Leon Festinger, Stanley Schachter, and Kurt Bach, *Social Pressures in Informal Groups* (Stanford University Press, 1963, c. 1950), especially Chapter 5.

25. Frederick M. Thrasker, *The Gang* (Chicago: University of Chicago Press, 1927), especially Chapter XV.

26. F. J. Roethlisberger and William J. Dickson, *Management and the Worker* (Cambridge, Massachusetts: Harvard University Press, 1961, c. 1939), especially Chapter XXII.

27. Shils and Janowitz, *loc. cit.*

28. For a classic statement see, John Herman Randall, Jr., *The Making of the Modern Mind* (Cambridge: The Riverside Press, 1926), especially Book II, Chapter VIII, and 173–178.

29. Roethlisberger and Dickson, *op. cit.*, Part IV.

30. Stanley E. Seashore, *op. cit.*, 76. Percentages calculated by the present writer.

31. Students were requested to "rate all groups and organizations to which you belong by placing an 'x' on the line opposite each one, under the phrase which most nearly expresses your feeling toward the group or organization."

The anonymous questionnaire was administered by the author to 344 students in upper division (junior and senior) courses on the Santa Barbara campus of the University of California. With the exception of one department which was being terminated, a course generally taken primarily by junior students majoring in the particular department was chosen from each academic department on the campus, and permission was secured to present the questionnaires at a regularly scheduled meeting of each class. Only one student refused to complete the questionnaire, and one questionnaire was discarded during processing because the general tone of the answers appeared to involve jocular good humor rather than veracity. The analysis is based on the remaining 343 completed questionnaires.

32. Much of the literature is cited in, Marvin B. Sussman, "Isolated Nuclear Family: Fact or Fiction" *Social Problems,* 6 (Spring, 1959), 333–340. See also, Carle C. Zimmerman and Lucius F. Cervantes, *Successful American Families* (New York: Pageant Press Inc., 1960) 39–40.

33. George P. Murdock, *Social Structure* (New York: The Macmillan Co., 1949), 60–61.

34. Sussman, *op. cit.*; and Zimmerman and Cervantes, *op. cit.*

35. Warren O. Hagstrom and Jeffrey K. Hadden, "Sentiment and Kinship Terminology in American Society," *Journal of Marriage and the Family,* 27 (August, 1965), 324–332, 329.

DEVIANCE

> If criminal behavior, by and large, is the normal behavior of normally
> responding individuals in situations defined as undesirable, illegal, and
> therefore criminal, then the basic problem is one of social and political
> organizations. . . . Crime, in this sense, is political behavior and the
> criminal becomes in fact a member of a "minority group" without sufficient
> public support to dominate and control the police power of the state.
>
> George Vold
> *Theoretical Criminology*

As long as humans have lived together, security and collective order have been threatened by deviants. In spite of the importance and antiquity of the problem of order, the first truly scientific studies of deviants were not undertaken until the latter part of the nineteenth century. These ground-breaking investigations studied the supposed qualities of deviants: low intelligence, physical defects, and psychological and moral maladjustment. While these studies promised to enlighten us about the nature of individual deviants, they were unable to explain why deviance varies by group (social class, race, religion, neighborhood). Individual approaches overlooked the fact that the origins of crime lie not in the individual or even in the behavior itself. Crime is, rather, a *social judgment* made about individual behavior. This is amply illustrated by historical and anthropological evidence that shows that what is considered a crime at one time and place has undoubtedly been considered normal or even praiseworthy at another time and place. To overcome the limitations of individualistic theories, sociologists have focused their research efforts on the social nature of deviance.

Functional Perspective

Functional and conflict theories are two of the most important perspectives guiding sociologists in the study of the social organization of deviance. The functional view begins with the assumption that society is composed of many groups that are organized in such a way as to form a coherent whole. Social values (see chapter 1) explain and coordinate the arrangement of

individuals in society. From values, rules develop and are justified. For example, in capitalistic society, private property is valued and laws are enacted to ensure rights and privileges of individual owners. In communistic society, collective property is valued and laws ensure rights and privileges of collective ownership.

Functionalists believe that law emerges from shared values and agreement about the way society should operate. The legal system develops from customs that have passed into law and are now enforced by the state. The state represents the collective will and legislates, adjudicates, and enforces laws in the broadly defined interests of society. To protect collective agreements, government must not represent the narrow interests of any particular group or stratum of society.

Deviance is inherent not in the individual but in the collective creation and enforcement of rules. When capitalists define property rights they simultaneously define crimes against the individual owner. When communists define state-owned property, they also define crimes against the state. Whether the values are capitalistic or communistic, functionalists reason that unless the majority accept the rules, societal organization is not possible. Since an inevitable result of rules will be rule-breakers (according to the functionalists), deviance is a "normal" and inescapable part of social organization. As times change, the moral boundaries of society also change, but the boundaries are always clarified through the prosecution of deviants. Public punishment of a criminal signifies that the justifications given in defense of the deviant act are less important than the values they violate. Seen in this light, deviants may serve to increase conformity and solidarity by dramatizing the limits of acceptable behavior.

According to Raymond Michalowski (1977), there are three key assumptions implicit in the functionalist view of deviance and society:

This investigation is based on *"The Seriousness of Crimes: Normative Structure and Individual Differences"* by Peter H. Rossi, Emily Waite, Christine E. Bose, and Richard E. Berk, 1974, reprinted on pages 52–59.

1. *Law reflects the collective will of the people.* All members of a society agree upon the basic definitions of right and wrong, and the law is merely the written statement of this collective agreement.
2. *The law serves all people equally.* Because it reflects the collective will of all the people, the law neither serves nor represses the interests of any particular group of individuals.
3. *Those who violate the law represent a unique subgroup.* Because the majority agree upon the definitions of right and wrong, the small group who violate the law must share some common element that distinguishes them from the law-abiding majority.

Conflict Perspective

Conflict theorists agree with functionalists that society is composed of many subgroups that are organized into a society on the basis of values. The two viewpoints differ, however, about how well the subgroups (rich and poor, black and white, men and women) are integrated. They also disagree about whose values the laws are based upon. And if there is considerable disagreement, then society can only be held together by coercion instead of consensus.

Karl Marx believed that throughout history the most important features of society had been determined by the struggle between social classes. He believed that the group that owned and controlled the most important industries would become the most powerful group. They would then use their advantages to secure what they felt was in their self-interest. In capitalistic society, for example, business exists to make a profit. To maximize profit, businesses seek to minimize corporate liability, corporate taxes, pollution controls, worker safety standards, unions, high wages, and free competition. The profits of the capitalists are achieved at the expense of less-powerful groups like workers, consumers, and small businesses.

Businessmen further advance their interests by financing advertising campaigns to sway public opinion, by contributing to political candidates, and by congressional lobbying. They may also use economic rewards, blacklists, intimidation, coercion, and violence to achieve their goals. As the influence of businessmen grows, their interests pass into law. Law, then, does not evolve from agreement but from the need to control those who *disagree*. It expresses the ratio of strength between the dominant class and subordinate classes.

The dominant class has the power not only to pass laws, but also to judge what is criminal. In capitalist countries, since laws are administered by the state as a means through which capitalists maintain their economic advantage, it is only when crimes threaten the capitalist class itself that the state is likely to intervene. Although white-collar crime and corporate crimes involve far greater economic losses to society, lower-class crimes of violence are considered more serious. Thus, in the capitalists' view, the rich who steal from the poor are not to be judged as harshly as the poor who steal from the rich.

According to the conflict theorists, innumerable evils of the capitalistic order stem from the defense of private property.

Among these are the evils of selfishness, egoism, injustice, and crime. According to Steven Spitzer (1975), capitalism creates two common classes of deviants who often then become criminals. The first, and the less threatening to capitalists, is the alienated minority group Spitzer calls "social junk": "hippies," welfare recipients, drug addicts, and alcoholics. Capitalists control this group through welfare agencies. The second group is rebellious and potentially dangerous. Spitzer calls them "social dynamite" because they question the authority of the dominant group. Social dynamite includes such groups as students, labor unions, and religious and political organizations. Capitalists control social dynamite through the legal system (courts, prisons, police, and the military).

Spitzer says that these two groups will be labeled as more or less deviant according to the extent to which they challenge any of the following: (1) the capitalistic modes of appropriating the products of human labor, (2) the social conditions under which capitalistic production takes place, (3) the patterns of distribution and consumption in capitalistic society, (4) the socialization of productive and nonproductive roles, or (5) an ideology that supports capitalistic society.

In summarizing the view of conflict theory, Raymond Michalowski (1977, pp. 24–25) states that there are five key assumptions to this perspective:

1. *Society is composed of diverse social groups.*
2. *There exist differing definitions of right and wrong.* Social groups have diverse values, goals, and interests, and at times these conflict with one another.
3. *The conflict between social groups is one of political power.* At all times there is an imbalance of political power, with those who have it struggling to maintain it, and those who do not have it struggling to obtain it.
4. *Law is designed to advance the interests of those with power to make it.* The law is not a value-neutral forum for dispute settlement. It is a mechanism by which those with the power to make the law can advance their own interests, without particular concern for the overall good of society.
5. *A key interest of those with the power to make and enforce law is maintaining their power.* Much of law is concerned with keeping those with interests different from those in power from gaining political power.

Background

The conflict model asserts that the seriousness of a crime is determined by the degree to which the behavior threatens the interests of the dominant class. This view holds that the seriousness of crimes will be seen quite differently by dominant and minority groups. By contrast, functionalists believe there is substantial agreement between groups regarding the seriousness of crimes.

Research conducted in 1974 by Peter H. Rossi, Emily Waite, Christine E. Bose, and Richard E. Berk, which you will read about in Reading 4 (pp. 52–59), indicated that there is general agreement in our society on the relative ordering of crimes. Although females and blacks tend to judge crimes as less serious than males or whites do, there is nevertheless considerable agreement on the ratings from one subgroup of respondents to another. Rossi et al. also found that an individual's judgment of crime seriousness depends heavily on the amount of his or her formal education.

Replication

In this investigation we will look at the characteristics that determine the seriousness of crime and then see if there is general agreement about the ratings of the seriousness of crimes. Rossi et al.'s research provides information that will help us examine these questions in some detail. The article claims that a small number of characteristics of criminal acts account for much of the perceived seriousness of the crime. For example, (1) crimes against police officers are regarded as more serious than acts against others, (2) crimes involving strangers are considered more serious than crimes involving persons known to the offender, (3) crimes against persons are rated as more serious than crimes against property, and (4) crimes against persons are considered more serious than white-collar crimes, victimless crimes, and crimes against order.

To see if Rossi et al.'s findings remain valid, we will investigate six questions. The first question is whether crimes against police officers are rated as more serious than equivalent crimes against strangers. The seriousness of acts against the police will be measured by the averages of the seriousness ratings for offenses that ranked, on the Rossi et al. survey (see Table 1, pp. 54–55), 5 (impulsive killing of a police officer), 11 (assault with a gun on a police officer) and 48 (beating up a police officer). The combined average for these offenses will be compared to the combined average for crimes against others, which ranked 20 (impulsive killing of a stranger), 24 (assault with a gun on a stranger), and 64 (beating up a stranger).

Hypothesis 1:

Crimes against police officers will be rated as more serious than equivalent crimes against strangers.

The second question concerns whether or not greater seriousness is attached to crimes against strangers than to crimes against persons known by the offender. The seriousness of crimes against strangers will be measured by the responses to items 24 (assault with a gun on a stranger) and 64 (beating up a stranger). The seriousness of crimes against known persons is measured by items 38 (assault with a gun on a spouse) and 91 (beating up a spouse).

Hypothesis 2:

Crimes against strangers will be rated as more serious than equivalent crimes against a spouse.

The third question is whether it is considered more serious to commit crimes against others or against property. The seriousness of crimes against others will be measured by responses to items 35 (armed street holdup stealing $200 in cash) and 43 (armed street holdup stealing $25 in cash). Crimes against property include items 72 (passing worthless checks for more than $500), 78 (theft of a car for the purpose of resale), and 104 (passing worthless checks involving less than $100).

Hypothesis 3:

Crimes against others will be rated as more serious than crimes against property.

The fourth question concerns the greater seriousness of crimes against others as compared to white-collar crimes, victimless crimes, and crimes against order. The seriousness of crimes against others will be measured by the average of items 20 (killing a stranger), 24 (assault with a gun on a stranger), 35 ($200 holdup), 43 ($25 holdup), and 64 (beating up a stranger). White-collar crimes include items 74 (employee embezzling company funds) and 107 (willfully neglecting to file income tax returns). Victimless crimes are items 108 (soliciting for prostitution), 123 (male homosexual acts with consenting adults), and 128 (selling pornographic magazines). Crimes against order are items 135 (disturbing the peace) and 140 (being drunk in public places).

Hypothesis 4:

Crimes against others will be rated as more serious than white-collar crimes, victimless crimes, and crimes against order.

The most important theoretical question raised by this research is whether or not there is a consensus regarding the seriousness of the rated offenses. Rossi et al. found agreement in ratings across subgroups. If this remains true, the correlation between the rankings of men and women should not be explainable by chance in more than 5 cases out of 100. To be confident that the similarities between men and women in the ratings of the 20 offenses did not happen by chance, Table A in the back of this book (p. 201) indicates that our Rho must equal or exceed a value of $+.377$. Another way of saying this is that the probability (P) of such a correlation occurring is less than or equal to .05. You may want to review the section on correlation (pp. 158–162) for more details on determining the significance of a correlation.

Hypothesis 5:

There will be a significant correlation between the crime seriousness ratings of men and women.

Durkheim believed deviance was a "social fact," the characteristics of which would show consistency over time. This suggests there should be an association between the 1974 study and our ratings. To test this we will use the procedure employed in the previous hypothesis.

Table 4–1

INVESTIGATION RESULTS 4
The Seriousness of Crimes

Rossi et al. Rank	Offense	Rossi et al. Average	Class Average	Class Rank
5	Impulsive killing of a police officer	8.214	__.__	___
11	Assault with a gun on a police officer	7.938	__.__	___
20	Impulsive killing of a stranger	7.821	__.__	___
24	Assault with a gun on a stranger	7.662	__.__	___
35	Armed street holdup stealing $200 cash	7.414	__.__	___
38	Assault with a gun on a spouse	7.323	__.__	___
43	Armed street holdup stealing $25 cash	7.165	__.__	___
48	Beating up a police officer	7.020	__.__	___
64	Beating up a stranger	6.604	__.__	___
72	Passing worthless checks for more than $500	6.309	__.__	___
74	Employee embezzling company funds	6.207	__.__	___
78	Theft of a car for the purpose of resale	6.093	__.__	___
91	Beating up a spouse	5.796	__.__	___
104	Passing worthless checks less than $100	5.339	__.__	___
107	Willfully neglecting to file income tax returns	5.157	__.__	___
108	Soliciting for prostitution	5.144	__.__	___
123	Male homosexual acts with consenting adults	4.736	__.__	___
128	Selling pornographic magazines	4.526	__.__	___
135	Disturbing the peace	3.779	__.__	___
140	Being drunk in public places	2.849	__.__	___
	Overall average =	6.155	= __.__	___

Note: Rossi et al.'s data are from Table 1, pp. 54–55.

Hypothesis 6:
There will be a significant correlation between the Rossi et al. crime seriousness ratings and the Student Survey ratings.

To investigate these six hypotheses, we will use the following data sources:

- Table 1 from the Rossi et al. article
- The class's responses to question 36 on the Student Survey

You will find the first of these sources, Table 1 from the Rossi et al. article, on pages 54–55. The class's responses to question 36 on the Student Survey will be provided by your instructor. (Question 1, sex of the rater, is used in hypothesis 5.) Question 36 on the Student Survey consists of a selection of 20 crimes taken from the list of 140 crimes presented in Table 1 of the Rossi et al. study. Crimes were selected to allow comparison of eight crime classifications (crimes against police, others, strangers, spouse, property, order, and white-collar and victimless crimes). Each crime was rated on the Student Survey on a scale from (1) "Not Serious at All" to (9) "Extremely Serious."

When you have received the class results from your instructor, proceed as follows:

Step 1:

Using the data provided by your instructor, fill in the class average for each type of crime in the Investigation Results table above.

Step 2:

In our hypotheses we are not comparing the average ratings of individual crimes, but of crime classifications. The classification "crimes against police," for example, is made up of offenses that ranked, on the Rossi et al. survey, 5 (impulsive killing of a police officer), 11 (assault with a gun on a police officer), and 48 (beating up a police officer). To obtain an average rating for this crime classification, we would average the crime seriousness ratings for those three offenses. In Table 4–2, the 10 crime classifications that we are interested in are

Table 4–2

AVERAGE RATED SERIOUSNESS BY CRIME CLASSIFICATION

Crimes against police (5, 11, 48): Hypothesis 1   =   _____

Crimes against strangers (20, 24, 64): Hypothesis 1   =   _____

Crimes against strangers (24, 64): Hypothesis 2   =   _____

Crimes against spouse (38, 91): Hypothesis 2   =   _____

Crimes against others (35, 43): Hypothesis 3   =   _____

Crimes against property (72, 78, 104): Hypothesis 3   =   _____

Crimes against others (20, 24, 35, 43, 64): Hypothesis 4   =   _____

White-collar crimes (74, 107): Hypothesis 4   =   _____

Victimless crimes (108, 123, 128): Hypothesis 4   =   _____

Crimes against order (135, 140): Hypothesis 4   =   _____

listed, along with the Rossi et al. ranks (in parentheses) of the individual crimes that constitute the classifications. In the blanks provided in Table 4–2, fill in the average seriousness ratings for the 10 crime classifications. These will be used to test hypotheses 1 though 4.

Step 3:

Use the averages for the crime classifications listed in Table 4–2 to fill in the blank spaces in hypotheses 1 through 4 below.

Hypothesis 1:

Crimes against police officers will be rated as more serious than equivalent crimes against strangers.

Ratings of crimes ——— > ——— Ratings of crimes
against police   against strangers
(5, 11, 48)   (20, 24, 64)

Hypothesis 2:

Crimes against strangers will be rated as more serious than equivalent crimes against a spouse.

Ratings of crimes ——— > ——— Ratings of crimes
against strangers   against a spouse
(24, 64)   (38, 91)

Hypothesis 3:

Crimes against others will be rated as more serious than crimes against property.

Ratings of crimes ——— > ——— Ratings of crimes
against others   against property
(35, 43)   (72, 78, 104)

Hypothesis 4:

Crimes against others will be rated as more serious than white-collar crimes, victimless crimes, and crimes against order.

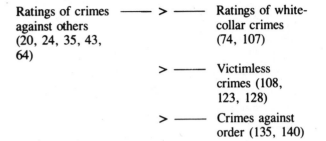

Ratings of crimes ——— > ——— Ratings of white-
against others   collar crimes
(20, 24, 35, 43,   (74, 107)
64)
                          > ——— Victimless
                                 crimes (108,
                                 123, 128)

                          > ——— Crimes against
                                 order (135, 140)

Step 4:

For hypothesis 5 we need to find out the degree of correlation between the crime seriousness ratings of men and women in your class. The average ratings given by men and women will be provided to you by your instructor. Your instructor may also provide you with the correlation between these ratings, or may ask you to determine the correlation yourself, using the method described on pages 158 to 162 in the Investigation Tools section of this book. Alternatively, your instructor may provide you with the probability (P) of such a correlation occurring purely by chance.

When you have obtained the correlation or probability, enter it in the appropriate blank space in hypothesis 5 below. Table A, "Critical Values of Rho," on page 201 tells us that for 20 pairs of items, the correlation must be greater than or equal to .377 if we want to be sure that the probability (P) of such a correlation occurring by chance is less than or equal to 5 times in 100 (P $\leq$ .05).

Hypothesis 5:

There will be a significant correlation between the crime seriousness ratings of men and women.

Correlation   +.377
Men and Women   _____ $\geq$ for .05 level of
Rho   significance
P   _____ $\leq$ .05

Step 5:

To test the validity of hypothesis 6 we will need to know the degree of correlation between Rossi et al.'s findings and our Student Survey findings. Again, your instructor may provide you with this correlation or probability, or you may be asked to calculate the correlation yourself. When you have obtained either a correlation or probability, enter it in the appropriate blank space in hypothesis 6 below.

Hypothesis 6:

There will be a significant correlation between the Rossi et al. crime seriousness ratings and the Student Survey ratings.

Table 4–3

SUPPORT FOR HYPOTHESES

	Significantly Supported	Partially Supported	Not Supported	Indeterminate
Hypothesis 1: Police vs. strangers	_____	_____	_____	_____
Hypothesis 2 Strangers vs. spouse	_____	_____	_____	_____
Hypothesis 3: Others vs. property	_____	_____	_____	_____
Hypothesis 4 Others vs. order	_____	_____	_____	_____
Hypothesis 5: Rho men and women	_____	_____	_____	_____
Hypothesis 6: Rho 1974 and student survey	_____	_____	_____	_____

Indicate the amount of support you found for each hypothesis.

Correlation   _____ $\geq$ $+.377$
1974 and present   for .05 level of
Rho   significance
P   _____ $\leq$ .05

Checking Your Findings

Hypothesis 1 proposed that attacks on representatives of law and order would be considered more serious than attacks on others. Are equivalent crimes against the police rated as more serious than those against strangers?

For hypothesis 2, Rossi et al. found that attacks against strangers were considered more serious than the same type of attacks against people known to the attacker. Presumably the latter crime was impulsive, while the former implies a deliberate or intentional injury without just cause or reason. Did you find crimes against strangers to be rated higher than those against a spouse?

Hypothesis 3 was derived from Rossi et al.'s finding that violent crimes are more serious than crimes against property. Do your findings support the previous study?

Hypothesis 4 postulates that white-collar crimes, victimless crimes, or crimes against order will not be considered as serious as crimes against others. What do your findings indicate?

Hypothesis 5 concerns agreement about the seriousness of crimes across various groups. Conflict theorists expect agreement within social classes: distinct groups will have distinct values and self-interests. Functional theorists expect there will be agreement about the seriousness of crimes throughout society. Did you find agreement and a high correlation between the ratings of men and women?

Hypothesis 6 concerns the consistency of crime seriousness over time (your current survey and Rossi et al.'s 1974 survey) and across groups (your class and the Baltimore survey group). Functionalists like Durkheim believe the normative structure of crime is a social fact that has persistence across generations. If so, changes over time will be evolutionary rather than revolutionary. Functionalists also believe there is more agreement between subgroups of society than do the conflict theorists. If the correlation between your class and the Baltimore survey group is larger than $+.377$ (or if the probability of such a correlation is less than .05), you may conclude that the agreement between the two studies did not happen by chance. Such a finding would be more consistent with a functional than a conflict perspective.

After analyzing your findings, summarize your conclusions in Table 4–3, above.

Topics for Further Investigation

1. In the United States, research indicates the rated seriousness of crimes is consistent over time. Clyde Coombs (1967) and David Krus, Jay Sherman, and Patricia Krus (1977) compared ratings of crimes in 1926, 1966, and 1976, based on a rating scale devised by Louis Thurstone. The results suggest increased homogeneity and agreement over time. Some differences were noted. A lowering in seriousness of sex offenses was found, while crimes against persons tended to be judged more serious. The overall results reflected more continuity than discontinuity.

   a. On the average, did your class rate crimes higher or lower than did the Rossi et al. (1974) study?

b. Compare your class's ratings and the 1974 ratings. Which crimes rose more than five ranks? Which crimes fell more than five ranks? Is there a pattern to the types of crimes that have changed their order of importance (such as crimes against order, victimless crimes, crimes against others)?

c. Do you feel that differences between your class ratings and the Rossi et al. ratings are the result of changes over time, or of some unusual characteristics of students in your class? If you feel that they are the result of changes over time, you should relate this to hypothesis 6.

2. Hypotheses 5 and 6 highlight the differences between conflict and functional theories. The former expects disagreement and the latter expects agreement between classes regarding the seriousness of crime.

a. Do you see evidence of great differences between classes of people (rich and poor, men and women, black and white)?

b. Do the findings in hypotheses 5 and 6 indicate significant consensus or disagreement regarding the seriousness of crime?

c. On balance, do the results seem to support the functional or conflict view?

References and Recommended Readings

Chamblis, W. J. (1976). Functional and conflict theories of crime: The heritage of Émile Durkheim and Karl Marx. In W. Chamblis & M. Mankoff (Eds.), *Whose law, whose order?* New York: John Wiley & Sons.

Cooms, C. H. (1967). Thurstone's measurement of social values revisited forty years later. *Journal of Personality and Social Psychology, 6*, 85–91.

Cullen, F., Link, B., & Polanzi, C. (1982). The seriousness of crime revisited. *Criminology, 20*, 83–102.

Cullen, F., Link, B., & Polanzi, C. (1985). Consensus in crime seriousness: Empirical reality or methodological artifact? *Criminology, 23*, 99–118.

Durkheim, E. (1933). *The division of labor in society.* New York: The Free Press.

Durkheim, E. (1938). *The rules of sociological method.* New York: The Free Press.

Evans, S., & Scott, J. (1984). The seriousness of crime cross-culturally. *Criminology, 22*, 39–59.

Krohn, M. (1978). A Durkheim analysis of international crime rates. *Social Forces, 57*, 654–670.

Krus, D., Sherman, J., & Krus, P. (1977). Changing values over the last half-century: The story of Thurstone's crime scales. *Psychological Reports, 40*, 207–211.

Lukes, S., & Scull, A. (Eds.). (1983). *Durkheim and the law.* New York: St. Martin's Press.

Michalowski, R. J. (1977). Crime, perspective and paradigm. In R. F. Meyer (Ed.), *Theory in criminology*, pp. 17–39. Newbury Park, California: Sage Publications.

Miethe, T. (1982). Public consensus on crime seriousness. *Criminology, 20*, 515–526.

Newman, G. (1976). *Comparative deviance.* New York: Elsevier.

Rossi, P., Waite, E., Bose, C., & Berk, R. (1974). The seriousness of crimes: Normative structure and individual differences. *American Sociological Review, 39*, 224–237.

Sinden, P. G. (1980). Perceptions of crime in capitalist America: The question of consciousness manipulation. *Social Focus, 13*, 75–85.

Spitzer, S. (1975). Toward a Marxian theory of deviance. *Social Problems, 22*, 638–651.

Vold, G. B., & Bernard, T. (1985). *Theoretical criminology* (3rd ed.). New York: Oxford University Press.

The Seriousness of Crimes: Normative Structure and Individual Differences

Using ratings of the seriousness of a set of 140 crimes obtained from a household sample taken in Baltimore in 1972, the study explores certain collective characteristics of these ratings. Respondents largely agree on the relative ordering of crimes. Very few descriptive characteristics of the crimes account for much of the variation from crime to crime in the average ratings received. The more highly educated and the younger the respondents, the more likely were their ratings to agree with average ratings computed over the entire sample. These findings indicate that norms concerning crime seriousness are widely diffused throughout subgroups of our society.

Peter H. Rossi
Emily Waite
The Johns Hopkins University

Christine E. Bose
State University of New York at Albany

Richard E. Berk
UCLA

The seriousness of criminal acts represents a conceptual dimension of criminality indispensable in everyday discourse, in legal theory and practice, and in sociological work. The seriousness of a criminal act may be viewed as a normative evaluation, an overall judgment which allows comparison among criminal acts, cultural values in different societies and cultures, and individual value differences. To be of theoretical or practical use, a measure of crime "seriousness" requires that a society show consensus about the order of seriousness of specific criminal acts. This consensus should be reflected in the criminal code, the behavior of judges and juries, and the actions of law enforcement agencies. It is a moot question whether seriousness is defined by the actions of criminal justice systems or vice versa; but societal consensus and the operations of criminal justice systems should correspond to some degree.

In many ways, "seriousness" as applied to criminal acts, resembles "prestige" as applied to occupations or other social statuses: both terms resist precise abstract definition; both can be easily translated into operational forms through the use of sample surveys; both are important in empirical research; and both remain obstinately necessary in technical and vernacular vocabularies.

Of course, whether consensus exists over seriousness or consistency in the legal code or actions of a criminal justice system is a matter for empirical investigation. This issue is relevant to the current controversy over conflict versus consensus models of deviant behavior. The conflict model implies disagreement over what is to be considered serious, with dissensus generated by the varying interests of subgroups in a society. To the extent that empirical investigation shows great consensus, the conflict model loses support.

Building on an important research tradition, our research further specifies crime "seriousness" and investigates its properties. This paper develops measures of the seriousness of criminal acts by examining the nature and degree of popular consensus concerning a reasonable sample of acts deemed criminal offenses in most of this country's legal jurisdictions, applying these measures to more representative populations, and trying to get at what it is about criminal acts which leads them to be regarded as more or less serious in the popular eye.

The most extensive previous treatment measuring crime seriousness is the pioneering work of Sellin and Wolfgang (1964). Using samples of judges, police and college students in Philadelphia, they obtained ratings of the seriousness of 141 offenses, using an eleven point rating scale for some respondents, and a magnitude (ratio) scale for others. A small subgroup (fifteen) of criminal acts was selected from these 141, the offenses being supplemented by descriptions of the consequences to victims of the criminal acts (e.g. amounts of property stolen or personal injury). The end result of the Sellin-Wolfgang researches is a set of fifteen descriptions of criminal acts along with scale scores for each act.

Sellin and Wolfgang observed several important properties of these seriousness measures. First, respondents were able to handle both the rating and magnitude estimation tasks easily, suggesting that respondents make such assessments in their daily lives. Secondly, Sellin and Wolfgang note considerable

Reprinted with permission from *American Sociological Review*, 39, 1974, pp. 224–237.

agreement among subgroups about both the relative ordering of criminal acts and the scale scores given.

The Sellin-Wolfgang results have not gone unchallenged. Rose (1966) questions the representativeness on the samples of raters and the evidence presented of subgroup consensus, asserting that it is unclear whether the seriousness scores are generalizable and whether in fact raters agreed as much as Sellin and Wolfgang allege. Nevertheless, several replications support the Sellin-Wolfgang work. Normandeau (1966) finds much agreement among French Canadian students, and (modified by a scaling factor) between his student group and those studied by Sellin and Wolfgang. Another Canadian replication, by Akman, Normandeau and Turner (1967), reports similar agreement among Canadian university students, judges, police and white collar workers (N = 2745) with Sellin and Wolfgang's respondents. Velez-Diaz and Megargee's (1970) study of 175 young lower class offenders and non-offenders in Puerto Rico is similarly supportive.

All these (see also McConnell and Martin, 1969) are vulnerable on grounds of internal and external validity. The samples used appear to be "haphazard." The methods of ascertaining agreement among subgroups and between samples range from visual inspection of data arrays to regression coefficients.

THE DESIGN OF THE BALTIMORE CRIME SERIOUSNESS STUDY

Our research was conducted to develop measures of crime seriousness for a much larger study of the potential support for penal reforms among state elites. We needed some rational basis for selecting a sample of crimes that varied according to seriousness and with which quantitative measurers of the "amount of seriousness" were associated.

The vehicle used was a sample survey of the adult population of Baltimore city conducted in the fall of 1972. We chose Baltimore mainly for convenience, bolstered by the expectation that consensus among our sample would be so strong that one could safely generalize results to other parts of the United States having quite different population mixtures.

* * * *

The core of the interview administered was a rating task in which respondents were asked to judge the seriousness of a list of offenses. Two lists of eighty offenses were used, sharing twenty offenses in common, sixty offenses being different on each list. Thus, 140 offenses were rated by the Baltimore sample. The rated offenses were picked by expanding the *Uniform Crime Reports* listing, transforming general crime categories into specific acts (e.g. "burglary" became "breaking and entering a house, stealing a transistor radio") and by adding offenses not normally reported, especially white collar crimes and crimes in the process (at least in some states) of decriminalization. In addition to rating the eighty crimes, each respondent was questioned concerning perceptions of the crime problem in Baltimore and such "background" identifying variables as age,

occupation of household head, and educational attainment. Each interview lasted about half an hour.

The main body of the interview consisted of a card sorting task in which the respondent placed each of eighty IBM cards (each containing a short description of an offense) into a box containing nine slots, each slot corresponding to a level of crime seriousness. The instructions called for crimes considered most serious to be placed in the slot labelled "9" and crimes least serious in the slot labelled "1" with crimes of intermediate seriousness being placed closer or further away from those two poles depending on the respondent's perception. There was no attempt in the interview to define for the respondent what was meant by "seriousness."

Interviewers reported that most respondents performed the rating task easily. The survey design called for 16,000 ratings (two hundred respondents each rating eighty crimes); 15,521— or 97%—were finally obtained. The distribution of ratings tended to be more dense on the high serious end of the nine point scale: the most popular rating was "9," with the lower ratings decreasing in popularity. The average rating given all crimes was 6.27, indicating that the typical crime was placed above the median more often than below it.

THE CRIME SERIOUSNESS RATINGS

Table 1 [pp. 54–55] shows the average ratings received by the 140 offenses, with the offenses arranged in rank order. A word of caution should be sounded with respect to this rank order: Adjacent crimes ordinarily are not statistically significantly different. A typical standard error for a score is between .1 and .3: Most crimes in adjacent ranks differ in the third decimal place.

There are few surprises in the ratings shown in Table 1. Crimes against persons, especially murder, receive very high seriousness ratings. Crimes against property in which no action is taken against people are rated significantly lower; and at the end of the list are offenses often classified as misdemeanors, e.g. "disturbing the peace," or "being drunk in public places."

Although the general ordering of the crimes accords with common sense expectations, it is still interesting to note where some offenses fall in the ordering of crimes. For example, crimes involving action taken against police officers are almost always regarded as more serious than similar actions taken against others. Another tendency is for crimes involving persons known to the offender to be regarded as less serious than crimes committed against strangers: apparently respondents feel that when a victim is known to the offender, the offense is, in some sense, understandable and possibly justified. Finally, it may be noted that "white collar" crimes (e.g. embezzlement, and price gouging) and "crimes without victims" (e.g. homosexuality) are not regarded as particularly serious offenses.

THE QUESTION OF CONSENSUS

The usefulness of the ratings in Table 1 rests heavily on the extent to which significant subgroups in the general population agree with each other. If the disagreement is great, then the seriousness ratings reflect individual preference, conditioned

(continued on p. 56)

Table 1

AVERAGE SERIOUSNESS RATINGS GIVEN TO 140 OFFENSES IN BALTIMORE SURVEY
(N is at least 100)

Rank	Crime	Mean	Variance
1	Planned killing of a policeman	8.474	2.002
2	Planned killing of a person for a fee	8.406	2.749
3	Selling heroin	8.293	2.658
4	Forcible rape after breaking into a home	8.241*	2.266
5	Impulsive killing of a policeman	8.214	3.077
6	Planned killing of a spouse	8.113*	3.276
7	Planned killing of an acquaintance	8.093	3.273
8	Hijacking an airplane	8.072	2.776
9	Armed robbery of a bank	8.021	8.020
10	Selling LSD	7.949	3.048
11	Assault with a gun on a policeman	7.938	3.225
12	Kidnapping for ransom	7.930	3.844
13	Forcible rape of a stranger in a park	7.909	3.737
14	Killing someone after an argument over a business transaction	7.898	3.536
15	Assassination of a public official	7.888	5.400
16	Killing someone during a serious argument	7.867	3.663
17	Making sexual advances to young children	7.861	3.741
18	Assault with a gun on a stranger	7.847*	2.172
19	Impulsive killing of a spouse	7.835	3.952
20	Impulsive killing of a stranger	7.821*	3.429
21	Forcible rape of a neighbor	7.778	3.726
22	Impulsive killing of an acquaintance	7.717	4.205
23	Deliberately starting a fire which results in a death	7.707	4.189
24	Assault with a gun on a stranger	7.662**	2.976*
25	Manufacturing and selling drugs known to be harmful to users	7.653	3.280
26	Knowingly selling contaminated food which results in a death	7.596	5.202
27	Armed robbery of a company payroll	7.577	3.080
28	Using heroin	7.520	4.871
29	Assault with a gun on an acquaintance	7.505	3.482
30	Armed holdup of a taxi driver	7.505	3.336
31	Beating up a child	7.490	3.840
32	Armed robbery of a neighborhood druggist	7.487*	3.221
33	Causing auto accident death while driving when drunk	7.455	3.904
34	Selling secret documents to a foreign government	7.423*	5.722
35	Armed street holdup stealing $200 cash	7.414	3.633
36	Killing someone in a barroom free-for-all	7.392	4.637
37	Deliberately starting a fire in an occupied building	7.347	5.177
38	Assault with a gun on a spouse	7.323	4.650
39	Armed robbery of a supermarket	7.313	3.911
40	Assault with a gun in the course of a riot	7.245	3.218
41	Armed hijacking of a truck	7.198	3.866
42	Deserting to the enemy in time of war	7.194	4.673
43	Armed street holdup stealing $25 in cash	7.165	4.431
44	Armed robbery of an armored truck	7.163	5.210
45	Spying for a foreign government	7.135	7.024
46	Killing a pedestrian while exceeding the speed limit	7.122	3.964
47	Seduction of a minor	7.021	5.729
48	Beating up a policeman	7.020	5.734
49	Selling marijuana	6.969*	7.216
50	Father-daughter incest	6.959	7.112
51	Causing the death of an employee by neglecting to repair machinery	6.918	4.556
52	Breaking and entering a bank	6.908	4.641
53	Mugging and stealing $25 in cash	6.873*	5.305
54	Selling pep pills	6.867	5.683
55	Cashing stolen payroll checks	6.827	4.784
56	Mugging and stealing $200 cash	6.796	5.051
57	Causing the death of a tenant by neglecting to repair heating plant	6.704	6.314
58	Killing spouse's lover after catching them together	6.691	7.695
59	Blackmail	6.667	5.122
60	Advocating overthrow of the government	6.663	7.715
61	Neglecting to care for own children	6.660	6.977
62	Forcible rape of a former spouse	6.653	6.394
63	Manufacturing and selling autos known to be dangerously defective	6.604	5.968
64	Beating up a stranger	6.604	5.379
65	Using LSD	6.557	7.479
66	Driving while drunk	6.545	6.006
67	Practicing medicine without a license	6.500*	6.908
68	Burglary of a home stealing a color TV set	6.440*	5.048
69	Knowingly passing counterfeit money	6.392	5.220
70	Beating up someone in a riot	6.368	5.788
71	Performing illegal abortions	6.330	5.723
72	Passing worthless checks for more than $500	6.309	5.119
73	A public official accepting bribes in return for favors	6.240	6.467

Rank	Crime	Mean	Variance
74	Employee embezzling company funds	6.207˙	5.030
75	Knowingly selling stolen stocks and bonds	6.138˙	4.960
76	Refusing to obey lawful order of a policeman	6.118˙	5.806
77	Burglary of a home stealing a portable transister radio	6.115˙	5.871
78	Theft of a car for the purpose of resale	6.093˙	5.085
79	Knowingly selling defective used cars as completely safe	6.093	5.023
80	Burglary of an appliance store stealing several TV sets	6.062	5.371
81	Looting goods in a riot	6.043	5.052
82	Knowingly selling stolen goods	6.021	4.463
83	Leaving the scene of an accident	5.949	6.620
84	Printing counterfeit $10 bills	5.948	6.820
85	Shoplifting a diamond ring from a jewelry store	5.939	5.466
86	Mother-son incest	5.907	9.189
87	Theft of a car for joy-riding	5.876	6.047
88	Intimidating a witness in a court case	5.853	4.850
89	Brother-sister incest	5.825	8.709
90	Knowingly selling worthless stocks as valuable investments	5.821	5.021
91	Beating up a spouse	5.796	7.051
92	Selling liquor to minors	5.789	7.572
93	Burglary of a factory stealing machine tools	5.789	5.317
94	Using stolen credit cards	5.750	5.832
95	Using pep pills	5.656	9.512
96	Joining a riot	5.656	6.750
97	Lending money at illegal interest rates	5.653	5.775
98	Knowingly buying stolen goods	5.596	5.794
99	Refusal to serve when drafted in peace time	5.535	8.863
100	Resisting arrest	5.449	6.271
101	Impersonating a policeman	5.449	7.405
102	Using false identification to obtain goods from a store	5.438	6.628
103	Bribing a public official to obtain favors	5.394	6.198
104	Passing worthless checks involving less than $100	5.339˙	5.921
105	Desertion from military service in peace time	5.323	7.526
106	Under-reporting income on income tax return	5.305	6.321
107	Willfully neglecting to file income tax returns	5.157˙	6.470
108	Soliciting for prostitution	5.144	7.687
109	Proposing homosexual practices to an adult	5.140	9.361
110	Overcharging on repairs to automobiles	5.135	6.455
111	Shoplifting a dress from a department store	5.070	6.308
112	Beating up an acquaintance	5.032	5.644
113	Driving while license is suspended	5.031	7.988
114	Pouring paint over someone's car	4.938	7.449
115	Shoplifting a pair of shoes from a shoe store	4.990	6.781
116	Overcharging for credit in selling goods	4.970	6.213
117	Shoplifting a carton of cigarettes from a supermarket	4.969	6.793
118	Smuggling goods to avoid paying import duties	4.918	5.618
119	Killing a suspected burglar in home	4.868˙	8.930
120	False claims of dependents on income tax return	4.832	6.801
121	Knowingly using inaccurate scales in weighing meat for sale	4.786	5.902
122	Refusal to make essential repairs to rental property	4.781	6.678
123	Engaging in male homosexual acts with consenting adults	4.736	9.396
124	Engaging in female homosexual acts with consenting adults	4.729	9.042
125	Breaking a plate glass window in a shop	4.653	6.697
126	Fixing prices of a consumer product like gasoline	4.629	6.069
127	Fixing prices of machines sold to businesses	4.619	6.218
128	Selling pornographic magazines	4.526	7.826
129	Shoplifting a book in a bookstore	4.424˙	6.551
130	Repeated refusal to obey parents	4.411	9.074
131	Joining a prohibited demonstration	4.323	6.486
132	False advertising of headache remedy	4.083	7.972
133	Refusal to pay alimony	4.063	6.670
134	Refusal to pay parking fines	3.583˙	6.475
135	Disturbing the peace	3.779	7.174
136	Repeated truancy	3.573	7.658
137	Repeated running away from home	3.571˙	6.342
138	Loitering in public places	3.375	8.111
139	Refusal to answer census taker	3.105	7.329
140	Being drunk in public places	2.849	6.021

Note: Scores have a range of 9 (most serious) to 1 (least serious).
˙Crimes rated by all members (200) of the Baltimore sample.
˙˙This offense was inadvertently repeated (see crime rank No. 18), indicating that differences in scores as much as .185 can be obtained through response unreliability.

perhaps by subcultural norms, but certainly not generalized social norms.

It is easier to assert that there should be consensus than it is to devise a suitable standard against which a given degree of consensus should be measured. In other words, how much agreement should consensus require? The answer to this question depends in part on what device is used to measure consensus: In this section we will use correlations, and we will use an arbitrary standard to define consensus, i.e. that the correlations among subgroups should meet the requirements of a "reliable test." That is, if a test is to be regarded as reliable, we ordinarily expect correlations between alternative forms of the test or test-retest correlations to be .70 or more.

The correlations between certain major divisions of the Baltimore sample are shown in Table 2 [on p. 57]. All the correlations in that table meet the "reliability" requirement, the correlation between blacks and whites being .89, between males and females .94 and between the better educated and the less well educated, .89. These coefficients indicate that knowing the scores given by one group, the scores given by the other group can be fairly well predicted. A correlation of .89 indicates that such predictions can be made with a high degree of accuracy.

* * * *

A large variety of subgroups is of potential interest, but with so small a total sample, one can only compare a few of the more complex subgroup combinations. In Table 3 [p. 58] correlations are shown among subgroups defined by the cross classification of sex, race and educational attainment. Eight subgroups in all are created.

Note that in Table 3 the numbers of persons in each subgroup who contribute individual ratings to the averages that go into the comparisons are small. For example, the average ratings for relatively well educated black males are based on samples of seven and eight. Given the small number of ratings over which these averages were computed, the subgroup correlations must be considered quite high. The lowest correlation is .61 and the highest .93, the average of all the correlations among subgroups being .75. Note also that it is poorly educated black males who disagree most with the other subgroups in the sample, only one correlation involving this subgroup being as high as .70.

In the last column of Table 3, the correlations are given for each subgroup's ratings with the overall sample ratings. These correlations are high, above .86, except for poorly educated black males. In short, the eight subgroups defined by race, educational attainment, and sex do not vary much from the ratings given by the total sample.

The correlations in Table 3 were computed over all 140 crimes. For a small subset of twenty crimes (marked by an asterisk in Table 1) all two hundred respondents contributed to the ratings; and hence by considering this set of crimes alone, we can double the number of individual ratings used in computing subgroup average seriousness ratings. Doing so significantly raises the correlations. None are below .70, and only three are below .80. The range is from .75 to .96, averaging

.86. Furthermore, the correlations of the subgroup ratings with the ratings of the total sample are all above .88.

The subgroup in least agreement with the total sample consists of black males with less than high school education. Inspection of the residuals of the regression of total sample means on the average seriousness scores of this group suggests that the main points of disagreement center around certain crimes against the person, particularly those in which the offender and the victim are known to each other. For example, compared to the total sample, "beating up an acquaintance" is regarded much less seriously by poorly educated black males. The line between manly sport and crime can be thin indeed.

These findings are the only hint of subcultural differences, along the lines of a "subculture of violence" (cf. Wolfgang and Ferracuti, 1967) or a lower class subculture that defines certain acts quite differently (cf. Miller, 1968). Of course, one would want to see whether these findings would be replicated in a larger sample of poorly educated black males before accepting them as definitive evidence of subcultural differences.

All told, the amount of consensus among subgroup averages is impressive. Obviously, the correlations presented mask some differences among the groups. The measurement of these differences will be taken up later in this paper.

WHAT IS SERIOUSNESS?

In asking the respondent to rate crimes, we did not specify what was "seriousness." Nor did we ask respondents what they meant by their ratings. Obviously, respondents imparted some meaning to the term, a meaning shared sufficiently by others to produce the degree of consensus reported above.

We may never know what our respondents had in mind when they placed each card bearing a description of an offense in a slot corresponding to their judgments. However, we can construct some of the principles that guided them by examining the way in which characteristics of the crimes influenced their ratings. We shall see that a very crude crime classification system can account for a great deal of variation from crime to crime in the average ratings given.

The crime classification system used was developed ad hoc by the senior author of this paper and applied by two researchers to each crime. The system consists of the following binary judgments applied to each offense:

1. Crimes Against the Person I: Murder, manslaughter.
2. Crimes Against the Person II: Assault, rape and incest.
3. Crimes Against the Person III: All other crimes involving actual or threatened personal injury exclusive of those shown above.
4. Crimes Involving Property I: Cases in which the value of goods involved was more than $25.
5. Crimes Involving Property II: All other crimes involving property.
6. Selling Illegal Drugs: Heroin, LSD, Marijuana, Pep Pills.
7. "White Collar Crimes": Embezzlement, income tax cheating, fraudulent business practices, etc.

Table 2

**CORRELATIONS AMONG AVERAGE CRIME RATINGS
FOR MAJOR SUBGROUPS: RACE, SEX, AND
EDUCATIONAL ATTAINMENT (N = 140)**

Subgroups	Correlation	n* =
Blacks and whites	.89**	(100)
Males and females	.94**	(100)
Less than high school graduation and high school graduation or better	.89**	(96–104)

*In this context, n denotes the number of respondents who rated each of the crimes. Note that for 20 of the crimes shown in Table 1, all respondents (200) contributed to the ratings. Hence, n refers to the number who rated all but the common 20 crimes. Since the correlations were computed across all 140 pairs of average scores generated by each pair of subgroups, the essential N for each correlation is 140.
**p < .01.

8. "Victimless" Crimes: Prostitution, homosexuality, etc.
9. Subversion (Crimes Against the State): Desertion, spying for enemy, etc.
10. Crimes Involving Action Against Policemen.
11. Crimes Involving Offenses Against Order: Loitering, disturbing the peace, etc.

* * * *

Note that certain types of crimes are regarded as not particularly distinguishable from the base crimes, in particular "white collar crimes" and "victimless crimes." Our respondents do not see these offenses as particularly serious.

The findings of this section can be summarized in two statements: First, it is clear that collectively respondents were reacting to the simple characteristics of the crimes they rated, as indicated by the fact that these eleven binary variables account for so much variation in the mean ratings given. Second, crimes against persons and illegal drug selling are seen as especially serious offenses, compared to crimes against property.

SUBGROUP VARIATION IN MEAN SERIOUSNESS RATINGS

Earlier in this paper, we found considerable agreement on the ordering of crime seriousness among subgroups of the sample defined by cross classifying race, sex and educational attainment. However, subgroups can still differ in the extent to which they consider the entire set of crimes to be more or less serious. We now turn to this question.

Subgroups of a sample may have different thresholds concerning what is or is not to be regarded as a highly serious crime. Some subgroups may regard crime less seriously than other subgroups. We have already seen in Table 2 that females and blacks have a lower threshold of seriousness respectively, than males or whites.

To pursue this line of analysis, mean seriousness ratings were computed for each of the crimes for each of the subgroups we wanted to distinguish. For example, in studying the effects of age, sex and race simultaneously, we divided the sample into eight subgroups based on the cross classification of these three characteristics. Average ratings were computed for each of the 140 crimes, leading to a total of 1,120 average seriousness ratings (eight subgroups times 140 crimes).

* * * *

In short being black, female, or younger leads to a generally higher seriousness rating over all the crimes. The amount of the increment varies, being least (and statistically insignificant) for young white males and greatest (1.00) for older black males.

* * * *

The findings of this section indicate that subgroup characteristics contribute only moderately to the overall ratings of crime seriousness. . . . In other words, if all the raters were composed of the average subgroup, the ratings shown in Table 1 would vary at most by less than half a unit on the rating scale.

The implications of these findings are quite important: because subgroups vary so little from each other, the fact that our sample is not representative does not seem to be a fatal flaw. For example, our Baltimore sample is 37% black, more than twice the national percentage for the United States as a whole. However, since blacks add as a group .8 to the average seriousness score, this over-representation adds to the scores of seriousness only .05 scale units compared to scores computed if we weight blacks according to national racial proportions. Furthermore, since blacks tend to agree quite closely with whites (r = .89) on the relative ordering of scores, the scores may be inflated slightly (.05) by the over-representation of blacks; but the resulting scores may still be used with little error to order crimes according to their seriousness.

INDIVIDUAL DIFFERENCES IN CRIME SERIOUSNESS RATINGS

The overall large amounts of agreement among subgroups tends to obscure the fact of individual differences in crime seriousness ratings. Around each of the means used above is some degree of individual variation. Indeed, it is possible to have a great deal individual variation and still have considerable between subgroup consensus.

It is to these individual differences that we now turn. In part, differences among individuals may arise from individual value disagreements with the general ordering of crimes given by the total sample. For example, some individuals may place all crimes against property higher than crimes against persons. In part, these differences represent "error," possibly created by misunderstanding the rating task, not being familiar with the vocabulary used in the crime descriptions, by respondents making mistakes in placing cards in the spaces intended, or by interviewers making mistakes in gathering the cards from the slots in which they were placed. As long as such "errors" are

Table 3

CORRELATIONS AMONG SUBGROUP MEANS COMPUTED FOR ALL 140 CRIMES: RACE, EDUCATIONAL ATTAINMENT, AND SEX SUBGROUPS (N = 140)

	Subgroup								
	Less than High School Graduation				High School Graduation or Better				
	Black Females (1)	White Females (2)	Black Males (3)	White Males (4)	Black Females (5)	White Females (6)	Black Males (7)	White Males (8)	Overall Sample (9)
Less Than High School Graduate									
Black Female (1)		.76	.70	.77	.74	.75	.78	.74	.86
White Female (2)			.61	.83	.76	.78	.77	.77	.88
Black Male (3)				.66	.65	.67	.63	.65	.77
White Male (4)					.73	.79	.79	.79	.90
High School Graduate or Better									
Black Female (5)						.78	.80	.74	.86
White Female (6)							.83	.93	.94
Black Male (7)								.84	.90
White Male (8)									.93
n* =	[9]	[14]	[16–17]	[18–19]	[9–10]	[17]	[7–8]	[18]	[100]

*"n" indicates the number of respondents whose ratings contribute to the computer averages. "n" can vary within a subgroup because of slight variations in the numbers of persons who were administered each of the two versions of the basic questionnaire, each containing a different set of 60 crimes to be rated.

not systematically related to some characteristics of individuals or of the criminal acts being rated, they will tend to be ironed out in computing averages for subgroups. To the extent that individual differences are based on value differences, the analysis in Table 3 would tend to pick up such differences provided they were correlated with the subgroup characteristics used.

The mode of analysis of individual differences used below is particularly sensitive to individual differences that lead to an individual's ratings differing from those of the total sample. Such differences may be either generated by "error" in the sense used above or generated by more systematic biases. The analysis attempted here is not sensitive to differences between the two sources of individual differences.

To obtain a measure of the degree to which individual respondents agreed with each other, a correlation was computed between each respondent's ratings and the average ratings given by the entire sample. Thus for each respondent, the scores given to the eighty criminal act descriptions he or she rated were paired off with the average ratings given to those acts by the entire Baltimore sample.

Of the two hundred correlations so computed, 195 (98%) were positive, covering a range from −.78 to .86. The average correlation was .54, with a standard deviation of .23. In short, even on the individual level where we can expect to find idiosyncratic factors at work, there is a great deal of agreement between individuals and the total sample. Indeed, given the

amount of inter-subgroup consensus, it would be surprising to find otherwise.

This finding is not an artifact of arithmetic. Although each individual contributes to the averages computed, his contribution is not enough to more than negligibly influence these averages. For 120 of the crimes, each respondent is only one of one hundred individuals whose ratings are used; and for the remaining twenty criminal acts he is but one of two hundred individuals involved.

* * * *

These findings suggest strongly that educational attainment is the major determinant of agreement. A reasonable interpretation is that educational attainment fosters a more accurate cognition of the normative structure of society. The process can be viewed as twofold. First, exposure to the normative structure of the society is a concomitant of formal instruction. Second, educational attainment reflects skills in handling verbal and written communication, the use of which in the years after school completion reinforces knowledge of the normative structure. Reading newspapers, magazines, and listening or viewing provides continual clues to societal evaluations of criminal acts. This interpretation is bolstered by the finding that age is also a determinant of agreement with societal consensus: The younger the respondent, and therefore the closer in time to formal educational experience, the more the individual respondent is likely to agree with the sample consensus.

CONCLUSIONS

Building on the pioneering work of Sellin and Wolfgang (1964) this study is an extension to a more representative population and attempts a more detailed analysis of certain salient characteristics of crime seriousness ratings.

Using a sample survey undertaken in Baltimore in 1972, in which two hundred adults rated 140 descriptions of criminals according to how "serious" the respondents believed the acts to be, average ratings were constructed for each crime and for subgroups of the sample. In addition, an analysis was undertaken of the determinants of individual levels of agreement with the total sample.

Three sets of findings may be viewed as strongly supported in the resulting data: First, there is considerable agreement from subgroup to subgroup on the relative ordering of the criminal acts rated and on the relative "distance" between such acts on the scale used.

Second, a small number of characteristics of the crimes account for a large proportion of the variation from crime to crime in the average rating given to the acts in question.

Third, the more highly educated and the younger respondents were, the more likely were their individual ratings of criminal acts to agree with the average computed for the entire sample.

These findings greatly support the following generalizations: First, the norms defining how serious various criminal acts are considered to be, are quite widely distributed among blacks and whites, males and females, high and low socioeconomic levels, and among levels of educational attainment. Second, there is strong evidence that whether an individual's ratings of crimes agree with the general normative trends depends heavily on formal educational attainment, suggesting that exposure to the normative structure and language handling ability lead to better knowledge of the normative structure.

REFERENCES

Akman, D. D., Normandeau, A., & Turner, S. (1967). The measurement of delinquency in Canada. *The Journal of Criminal Law, Criminology and Police Science, 58,* 330–337.

McConnell, J. P., & Martin, J. D. (1969). Judicial attitudes and public morals. *American Bar Association Journal, 55,* 1129–1133.

Miller, W. (1958). Lower class culture as a generating milieu of gang delinquency. *Journal of Social Issues, 14,* 5–19.

Normandeau, A. (1966). The measurement of delinquency in Montreal. *The Journal of Criminal Law, Criminology and Police Science, 57,* 172–177.

Rose, G. N. G. (1966). Concerning the measurement of delinquency. *The British Journal of Criminology, 6,* 414–418.

Sellin, T., & Wolfgang, M. E. (1964). The measurement of delinquency. New York: John Wiley & Sons.

Sudman, S. (1967). Reducing the cost of surveys. Chicago: Aldine.

Velez-Diaz, A., & Megargee, E. I. An investigation of differences in value judgments between youthful offenders and non-offenders in Puerto Rico. *Journal of Criminal Law, Criminology and Police Science, 61,* 549–553.

Wolfgang, M. E., & Ferracuti, F. (1967). *The subculture of violence.* London: Social Science Paperbacks.

SOCIAL STRATIFICATION

L'homme c'est rien—l'oeuvre c'est tout.*

Sherlock Holmes
in Sir Arthur Conan Doyle's
The Redheaded League

No social indicator tells us more about an individual's standing in the social hierarchy than does his or her occupation. The occupation, in turn, tells us a great deal about the individual's life chances; that is, the opportunities that affect one's chances for survival and growth. For example, the lower the social rank, the greater the risk of death at birth, malnutrition, physical and mental illness, occupational injury, substandard housing, limited education, arrest, and innumerable other handicaps and disadvantages. Occupations are more than types of work that provide a means of livelihood; they also define your general status in the community. This in turn creates opportunities for meeting people who are rich or poor, educated or uneducated, law-abiding or criminal, and to a large extent influences the neighborhood in which you will live and even the kinds of friends you will have. More than anything else, work shapes the course and content of your life. Whether or not something so profoundly basic to you and society as stratification is inevitable is a question over which conflict and functional theorists disagree.

Conflict Perspective

Karl Marx assumed that the first social act is the production of the goods and services necessary for material life. How people produce their material necessities causes them to enter into definite relationships with each other. Furthermore, these relationships develop a force greater than the will of any particular system. Marx observes that "insofar as millions of families live under economic conditions of existence that separate their modes of life, their interests, and their culture from those of other classes and put them in a hostile opposition, they form a

class" (quoted in Giddens, 1971, pp. 37–38). In the *Communist Manifesto* (1848/1954, pp. 9–10), he went on to conclude:

> The history of all hitherto existing society is the history of class struggles.
> Freeman and slave, patrician and plebian, lord and serf, guildmaster and journeyman, in a word; oppressor and oppressed, stood in constant opposition to one another, carried on an uninterrupted, now hidden, now open fight, a fight that each time ended, either in a revolutionary reconstitution of society at large, or in common ruin of the contending classes.

The effective production of material needs requires a division of labor. The most distinctive features of this division of labor are then determined by the class of people who own the productive process and who set the terms for those who work for them. This divides capitalistic society into social classes— the bourgeoisie, who are the owners of production; the middle class, who are small businessmen, intellectuals and entrepreneurs; the proletariat, who are the workers; and the lumpenproletariat, who are the social refuse created by capitalists: criminals, addicts, and outcasts.

Motivated by profit, capitalists extend their monopoly over the means of production. The result is a society polarized between an increasingly smaller wealthy class of bourgeoisie and an impoverished class of the proletariat. The poverty this produces is not the result of economic necessity but of capitalistic domination. Inequality is functional for the dominant class, not for society. Marx concluded that when the unfair advantages of the capitalists are ended, equality will be achieved and all workers will be paid wages "from each according to his ability to each according to his needs." When that happens, inequality and the class system will wither and disappear from industrial society.

Functional Perspective

Kingsley Davis and Wilbert Moore (1945, 1953) do not share the view of Marx that inequality is produced primarily as a result of a dominant class exploiting other classes. Instead,

*"The man is nothing, the work everything."

This investigation is based on "Occupational Prestige in Comparative Perspective" by Donald J. Treiman, 1977, reprinted on pages 66–71.

Davis and Moore argue that social inequality is organizationally necessary for the survival and effective operation of society. Davis (1949, pp. 367–368) sums up the argument as follows:

> The rights and prerequisites of different positions in a society must be unequal. . . . Social inequality is . . . an unconsciously evolved device by which societies insure that the most important positions are conscientiously filled by the most qualified persons. Hence, every society, no matter how simple or complex, must differentiate persons in terms of both prestige and esteem and must therefore possess a certain amount of institutionalized inequality.

All societies develop a division of labor to deal with the basic issues of survival. There must, for example, be adequate production and distribution of food, housing, and clothing; individual needs must be managed; and some level of domestic harmony must be assured. Occupations develop to serve these and other socially important needs. Since everyone does not have equal skill and talent, there must be incentives to attract people who have the skills necessary to do the job. The incentives may be unequal rewards of prestige, power, and wealth. These incentives are the price tags attached to occupations to ensure that the jobs are done satisfactorily. If, for example, demand is constant and the supply of teachers declines, the price (as in wages, prestige, and power) will rise. If demand is constant and there is a surplus of farmers, the price of that occupation will fall. Functionalists believe inequality is not simply the result of capitalists dominating workers, but a motivational necessity faced by every society.

If the functional theory of inequality is correct, Robert Hodge, Paul Siegel, and Peter Rossi (1964) reasoned, there should be a high degree of agreement in ratings of occupational prestige. This should even hold true over time. To see if the ratings are consistent, they compared their 1963 National Opinion Research Center (NORC) survey with surveys taken in 1925 and 1947. The occupational prestige rankings proved to be remarkably similar. Small differences were noted in a rise in the prestige of scientific occupations and a drop in prestige in artistic occupations. While there was a decline in governmental prestige scores, police officers experienced an upward swing in prestige.

Hodge, Siegel, and Rossi believe that there are three reasons for the stability of occupational prestige: (1) educational requirements, monetary rewards, and even functional importance are not subject to rapid change in industrial society; (2) any abrupt or dramatic changes in the prestige attached to an occupation would upset the connection that exists between the social rewards of an occupation and its importance to society; and (3) the meaning of achievement, career, seniority, and occupational mobility would be fundamentally altered if occupational prestige were subject to large-scale changes.

Donald Treiman carries the functional argument even further. He asserts that prestige rankings are not only consistent over time within societies but are also universal across societies. Treiman (1977, p. 2) claims that "the division of labor creates inherent differences in the power associated with various occu-

Table 5–1

COMPARISON OF TWO THEORIES OF STRATIFICATION

Functionalist Theory	Conflict Theory
1. Stratification is universal and necessary	1. Stratification is universal but is NOT necessary
2. Stratification is an expression of commonly shared social values	2. Stratification is an expression of the values of powerful people
3. Tasks and rewards are fairly allocated	3. Tasks and rewards are unfairly allocated
4. Stratification facilitates the optimal functioning of society and the individual	4. Stratification impedes the optional functioning of society and the individual
5. Stratification can change gradually as an evolutionary process	5. Stratification can change drastically as a revolutionary process

Note: From "Some Empirical Correlates of the Davis-Moore Theory of Stratification" by A. Stinchombe. In *Social Stratification in the United States* (p. 55) edited by J. Roach, 1969, Englewood Cliffs, NJ: Prentice Hall. Copyright 1963 by Arthur Stinchombe. Adapted by permission.

pational roles, wherever they are found, [that] these differences, in turn, create differences in privilege, and that power and privilege beget prestige." From this he concludes (p. 2) that

> the relative prestige of the social roles known as occupations is essentially invariant in all complex societies, past and present, and that this must be so as a consequence of inherent features of the division of labor as it exists in all societies. Competing hypotheses—that the prestige hierarchy of each society reflects idiosyncratic cultural values, that worldwide similarity exists but only because a Western system of occupation has diffused throughout the world as an adjunct to Western hegemony, or that worldwide similarity is a consequence of the constraints imposed by an industrial structure and industrial technology—are considered and rejected.

Background

At the end of Reading 5, on page 70, Treiman states that his

> data favor the pure structural theory. . . . In all complex societies, industrialized or not, a characteristic division of labor arises that creates intrinsic differences among occupational roles with respect to power; these in turn promote differences in privilege; and power and privilege create prestige. Since the same process operates in all complex societies, the resulting prestige hierarchy is relatively invariant in all such societies, past or present.

Marx's and Treiman's hypotheses concerning occupational prestige therefore differ in three ways: (1) The Marxian view suggests changes in occupational prestige over time, while Treiman does not. (2) The Marxian view expects a different consciousness of occupational prestige by class, while Treiman does not. (3) The Marxian view suggests different prestige hierarchies across cultures, while Treiman does not.

Our investigation is based on these three points of difference. By comparing data from our Student Survey and other sources, we will be able to decide which view is better supported.

Replication

The primary question raised by Treiman's research concerns consistency of occupational prestige ratings over time. Therefore, the first question that we will try to answer in our investigation is whether or not such a consistency exists.

Hypothesis 1:

Occupational prestige ratings will remain consistent over time.

We will test this hypothesis by comparing our Student Survey ratings to the occupational prestige ratings given by respondents to NORC surveys in 1947 and 1963, reported by Robert Hodge, Paul Siegel, and Peter Rossi (1964). If occupational prestige ratings remain consistent over time, we should see significant correlations between these earlier studies and our Student Survey.

How will we know if our correlations are statistically significant? By consulting Table A, "Critical Values of Rho," on page 201 of the Investigation Tools section. In this investigation we are rating 19 occupations. Since Table A does not have that number (n = 19), we will use the more conservative significance value for n = 18. The table indicates that we will need a correlation value greater than or equal to .399 if we are to be sure that the probability (P) of such a correlation occurring purely by chance is 5 in 100 or less (P ≤ .05). Thus, in order to test hypothesis 1, we will see if the following expectations hold true in our investigation:

Correlation 1947 to present   ≥   Rho +.399
                           P   ≤   .05

Correlation 1963 to present   ≥   Rho +.399
                           P   ≤   .05

The second hypothesis we will examine is concerned with the agreement of raters within a society regarding the ranking of occupational prestige.

Hypothesis 2:

Occupational prestige ratings will remain consistent throughout our society.

Current study and U.S. Census   ≥   Rho +.399
                             P   ≤   .05

Current study and another school   ≥   Rho +.399
                                 P   ≤   .05

We will test this consensus hypothesis by comparing our ratings to the occupational prestige ratings of the United States Department of the Census and with the ratings of other schools, which will be provided by your instructor.

The final hypothesis deals with Treiman's claim that inherent features of the division of labor make the occupational prestige hierarchy similar worldwide.

Hypothesis 3:

Occupational prestige ratings will remain consistent between societies.

Current study and New Zealand   ≥   Rho +.399
                            P   ≤   .05

Current study and Inter. Standard   ≥   Rho +.399
                                 P   ≤   .05

This hypothesis will be evaluated by comparing our prestige ratings to the ratings of another country and to Treiman's Standard International Occupational Prestige Scale (SIOPS).

To test our hypotheses, we first need to obtain occupational prestige ratings from the following sources:

- The National Opinion Research Center, 1947
- The National Opinion Research Center, 1963
- The United States Bureau of the Census
- A school other than your own
- Treiman's New Zealand study
- Treiman's Standard International Occupational Prestige Scale
- Your class's responses to question 35 on the Student Survey

The first two sources (the NORC data) will be found in Table 5–2, Investigation Results 5, on the opposite page. All of the other data will be provided to you by your instructor.

Strictly speaking, this is a correlational study. One could, however, consider earlier prestige ratings in 1925 and 1963 as independent variables and the current (Student Survey) occupational prestige ratings a dependent variable. The Student Survey prestige ratings are measured by the scale in question 35, reprinted on page 64.

When you have received the necessary data from your instructor, proceed as follows:

Step 1:

Begin by turning to the Occupational Prestige Exercise you completed in the Student Survey (question 35). Record your ratings in the Investigation Results table (Table 5–2 on the next page), in the right-hand column labeled My Rating.

Step 2:

Use the Student Survey data provided by your instructor to fill in the rest of the Investigation Results table.

Table 5–2

INVESTIGATION RESULTS 5

Changes in Occupational Prestige Ratings—1925–1963

Counts, 1925[a]		NORC, 1947[b]		NORC, 1963[b]		Student Survey		
Occupation	Rank	Occupation	Score	Occupation	Score	Occupation	Class Rating	My Rating
Banker	1	Physician	93	Physician	93	_____	_____	_____
Professor	2	College professor	89	College professor	90	_____	_____	_____
Physician	3	Banker	88	Lawyer	89	_____	_____	_____
Minister	4	Minister	87	Minister	87	_____	_____	_____
Lawyer	5	Lawyer	86	Banker	85	_____	_____	_____
Teacher	6	Teacher	78	Teacher	81	_____	_____	_____
Manager	7	Farmer	76	Electrician	76	_____	_____	_____
Farmer	8	Electrician	73	Farmer	74	_____	_____	_____
Bookkeeper	9	Manager	69	Police officer	72	_____	_____	_____
Electrician	10	Bookkeeper	68	Bookkeeper	70	_____	_____	_____
Police officer	11	Police officer	67	Carpenter	68	_____	_____	_____
Conductor	12	Conductor	67	Manager	67	_____	_____	_____
Carpenter	13	Carpenter	65	Conductor	66	_____	_____	_____
Clerk	14	Operator	60	Operator	63	_____	_____	_____
Barber	15	Barber	59	Barber	63	_____	_____	_____
Operator	16	Clerk	58	Clerk	56	_____	_____	_____
Miner	17	Miner	49	Miner	50	_____	_____	_____
Janitor	18	Waiter	48	Waiter	49	_____	_____	_____
Waiter	19	Janitor	44	Janitor	48	_____	_____	_____
		Arithmetic *Mean* of sampled prestige scores =	69	Arithmetic *Mean* of sampled prestige scores =	70	Arithmetic *Mean* of sampled prestige scores =	_____	
		Range of sampled prestige scores =	49	*Range* of sampled prestige scores =	45	*Range* of sample prestige scores =	_____	

[a]Counts data are from "The Social Status of Occupations: A Problem in Vocational Guidance" by G. Counts, 1925. *School Review, 33,* pp. 16–27.
[b]NORC data are from "Occupational Prestige in the United States: 1925–1963" by R. Hodge, P. Siegel, & P. Rossi, 1964. *American Journal of Sociology, 74,* pp. 703–716. Copyright 1964 by the University of Chicago Press. Reprinted by permission.

Step 3:

Test the validity of the three hypotheses by filling in the appropriate blanks on the next page. Your instructor may provide you with the correlation coefficients (rho) or the probability values (P), or both. Alternatively, your instructor may ask you to calculate rho for yourself (see page 162 of the Investigation Tools section for how to do this). In any case, your findings will enable you to test each hypothesis: if the correlation rho is greater than or equal to .399, the correlation is significant because it would not occur by chance more than 5 times in 100. This is just another way of saying that its probability (P) is .05 or less.

Hypothesis 1:

Occupational prestige ratings will remain consistent over time.

STUDENT SURVEY QUESTION 35
Occupational Prestige Exercise

For each occupation mentioned, please circle the rating that gives your own personal opinion of the general standing or prestige that such an occupation has.

Occupational Category	Excellent	Good	Average	Below Average	Poor	Don't Know
Banker	100	80	60	40	20	DK
Barber	100	80	60	40	20	DK
Bookkeeper	100	80	60	40	20	DK
Carpenter	100	80	60	40	20	DK
Clerk in store	100	80	60	40	20	DK
Coal miner	100	80	60	40	20	DK
College professor	100	80	60	40	20	DK
Electrician	100	80	60	40	20	DK
Farmer	100	80	60	40	20	DK
Janitor	100	80	60	40	20	DK
Lawyer	100	80	60	40	20	DK
Machine operator	100	80	60	40	20	DK
Manager of small store	100	80	60	40	20	DK
Minister	100	80	60	40	20	DK
Physician	100	80	60	40	20	DK
Police officer	100	80	60	40	20	DK
Public school teacher	100	80	60	40	20	DK
Railroad conductor	100	80	60	40	20	DK
Restaurant waiter	100	80	60	40	20	DK

Correlation 1947 to present _____ $\geq$ Rho +.399
                          P _____ $\leq$ .05

Correlation 1963 to present _____ $\geq$ Rho +.399
                          P _____ $\leq$ .05

Hypothesis 2:

Occupational prestige ratings will remain consistent throughout our society.

Current study and U.S. Census _____ $\geq$ Rho +.399
                            P _____ $\leq$ .05

Current study and another school _____ $\geq$ Rho +.399
                            P _____ $\leq$ .05

Hypothesis 3:

Occupational prestige ratings will remain consistent between societies.

Current study and New Zealand _____ $\geq$ Rho +.399
                            P _____ $\leq$ .05

Current study and Inter. Standard _____ $\geq$ Rho +.399
                            P _____ $\leq$ .05

Checking Your Findings

Summarize your overall findings in Table 5–3 on page 65. Analyze these findings in terms of the theories—and the predictions—of Marx and Treiman.

As we draw our investigation to a close, we need to return to the original question that prompted our research. We began by comparing conflict and structural-functional views of occupational inequality. One interpretation of Marx suggests that there are differing perceptions of occupational prestige depending on the respondent's class position (bourgeoisie, middle class, proletariat, or lumpenproletariat). These different class ratings of occupational prestige would be reflected in low correlations between classes and generations. On the other hand, Treiman argued that unequal rewards inhere in occupations and are a function of the unequal importance of occupations to the operation of society. This condition would produce common perceptions of prestige rankings and significant correlations. Do your results show occupational prestige ranks are consistent over time? Do the correlations show significant intercultural consistency? Does the overall weight of evidence support Marx or Treiman?

Topics for Further Investigation

If you think the results of your investigation support Treiman, is the evidence sufficient that you are willing to agree with his quote on page 61 that "the relative prestige of the social roles known as occupations is essentially invariant in all complex societies, past and present"? Treiman does not stop here. He goes on to add that "this must be so as a consequence of inherent features of the division of labor as it exists in all

Table 5–3

SUPPORT FOR HYPOTHESES

	Significantly Supported	Partially Supported	Not Supported	Indeterminate
Hypothesis 1: Temporal consistency	_____	_____	_____	_____
Hypothesis 2: Intracultural consistency	_____	_____	_____	_____
Hypothesis 3: Intercultural consistency	_____	_____	_____	_____

Indicate the amount of support you found for each hypothesis.

societies." This is not only true of past and present societies, but he sees no reason why any future society will be different. Do you now accept this? If not, what kinds of additional evidence would you need to accept Treiman's conclusion of the inevitability and universality of inequality?

Caveats

If you are uncomfortable with the results of the investigation, you might consider problems that may be internal and/or external to the survey. *Internal factors* are those that are peculiar to your study and, therefore, make your findings unique and nongeneralizable. Bernard Berelson and Gary Steiner (1964) note three internal factors that relate to the characteristics of the raters: (1) Occupations closer to the rater's own rank tend to be given higher ratings. (2) Well-known occupations are rated more consistently by raters. (3) Raters evaluate occupations at the extremes of the distribution more consistently than occupations in the middle. Your class may also have a number of distinctive characteristics that make its results unique and nongeneralizable. Such may be the case if your class has selectively attracted a particular academic major, such as nurses, or has an unusual socioeconomic, religious, or regional composition.

External factors are those that are independent of the study. These include real shifts in occupational prestige. Political scandals, for example, are associated with a substantial drop in the prestige ratings of politicians. During periods of economic recession or depression, businessmen typically have a corresponding decline in occupational prestige. Determine which occupations have had the greatest shifts in prestige and then determine the influence that internal and external factors have had in these changes.

References and Recommended Readings

Abrahamson, M. (1973). Functionalism and the functional theory of stratification. *American Journal of Sociology, 78,* 1239–1246.

Berelson, B., & Steiner, G. (1964). *Human behavior: An inventory of scientific findings.* New York: Harcourt, Brace & World.

Blau, P., & Duncan, O. (1967). *The occupational structure.* New York: John Wiley.

Collins, R. (1971). Functional and conflict theories of educational stratification. *American Sociological Review, 36,* 1002–1018.

Counts, G. (1925). The social status of occupations: A problem in vocational guidance. *School Review, 33,* 16–27.

Davis, K. (1949). *Human society.* New York: Macmillan.

Davis, K., & Moore, W. (1945). Some principles of stratification. *American Sociological Review, 10,* 242–249.

Davis, K., & Moore, W. (1953). Replies to Tumin. *American Sociological Review, 18,* 394–396.

Gans, H. (1972). The positive functions of poverty. *American Journal of Sociology, 78,* 275–289.

Giddens, A. (1971). *Capitalism and modern social theory.* New York: Cambridge University Press.

Grandjean, B. (1975). An economic analysis of the Davis-Moore theory of stratification. *Social Forces, 53,* 543–552.

Guppy, N. G. (1984). Consensus on occupational prestige: A reassessment of the evidence. *Social Forces, 62,* 709–725.

Hatt, P. (1950). Occupational and social stratification. *American Journal of Sociology, 55,* 538–543.

Hodge, R., Siegel, P., & Rossi, P. (1964). Occupational prestige in the United States: 1925–1963. *American Journal of Sociology, 74,* 703–716.

Inkeles, A., & Rossi, P. (1956). National comparisons of occupational prestige. *American Journal of Sociology, 66,* 329–339.

Lipset, S., & Bendix, R. (1959). *Social mobility in industrial society.* Berkeley, CA: University of California Press.

Marx, K. (1848). *The communist manifesto.* Reprint. New York: Gateway Editions, 1954.

Rossides, D. (1976). *The American class system.* Boston: Houghton Mifflin.

Treiman, D. (1977). *Occupational prestige in comparative perspective.* New York: Academic Press.

Tumin, M. (1953). Some principles of stratification: A critical review. *American Sociological Review, 18,* 387–393.

Occupational Prestige in Comparative Perspective

Donald Treiman
UCLA

THE DIVISION OF LABOR AND OCCUPATIONAL STRATIFICATION

Men are known by their work. It is no accident that when strangers meet, a standard opening gambit is the question, "What sort of work do you do?," for this information provides the best single clue to the sort of person one is. It marks a person as "someone to be reckoned with" or as one who can be safely ignored, one to whom deference is due or from whom deference can be expected. Moreover, it permits at least crude inferences regarding attitudes, experiences, and style of life. In short, occupational roles locate individuals in social space, thereby setting the stage for their interaction with one another.

This is possible because people in all walks of life share understandings about occupations—how much skill they require, how physically demanding they are, whether they are considered men's work or women's work, and so on—but particularly about their prestige. Every adult member of society ordinarily is able to locate occupations on a hierarchy of prestige. These perceptions form part of the *conscience collective*. This permits one to rank oneself and others with respect to the social honor derived from occupational status. Of course, occupational prestige is not the only basis of rank, but it is an important one in all societies with any substantial degree of occupational role differentiation.

It is therefore important to understand the nature of occupational prestige systems: What determines the relative prestige ordering of occupations? Do the same factors operate in all societies? If not, what accounts for the differences that do exist?. . . . I propose a theory that argues that prestige ultimately is rooted in power relations. . . .

A Theory of Occupational Prestige

. . . The structural theory of prestige determination . . . predicts that the prestige ordering of occupations will be fundamentally invariant in all complex societies, past or present. The theory consists of four propositions, which are outlined here and elaborated below.

First, the similarity in the "functional imperatives" faced by all societies results in a basic similarity in the specific

functions that have to be accomplished. This, together with inherent limitations in possible organizational forms, results in a basically similar configuration of occupational roles in all societies beyond those of the most rudimentary size and organizational complexity. That is, a division of labor will necessarily develop and, moreover, will develop in a similar way in all societies.

Second, differentation inherently implies stratification. Specialization of functions carries with it inherent differences in the control over scarce resources, which is the primary basis of stratification. These resources include skill, authority, and property, each of which functions in a somewhat different way. Together they create differential power, in the most general sense of that term. Thus, the division of labor creates a characteristic hierarchy of occupations with respect to power exercised.

Third, the power resulting from control over scarce resources creates the opportunity for, and almost invariably results in, the acquisition of special privilege; thus the basic similarity among all complex societies in the relative power exercised by various occupations creates a corresponding similarity with respect to occupational differences in privilege.

Fourth, power and privilege are everywhere highly valued, and hence powerful and privileged occupations are highly regarded in all societies.

Thus, since the division of labor gives rise to characteristic differences in power, and power begets privilege, and power and privilege beget prestige, there should be a single, worldwide occupational prestige hierarchy. . . .

The Division of Labor and Occupational Specialization

. . . The basic factor promoting the division of labor is its efficiency. Relative to unspecialized labor, specialized labor is far more efficient. There are several reasons for this.

First, some tasks can be more efficiently performed by individuals with particular personal traits—great strength, height, agility, speed, stamina, sharpness of eyesight, intelligence, tenacity, aggressiveness, and so forth. Sporting events provide a good illustration. No crew that expected to win would allow the coxswain and the oarsman to trade roles; the one is chosen for his small size and light weight and the other for his strength. Differences in the physical traits demanded by various kinds of work are recognized by all societies in a division of labor based on age and sex; some tasks are performed exclusively by women and others exclusively by men in virtually every known society (Murdock, 1937); similarly, some activities are rigidly age stratified virtually everywhere. But physical differences are not the only ones that come into play in determining occupational capabilities. Personality differences, differences in talent, and differences in general capacity, all of which are probably as much a matter of socialization as of genetic endowment, are also important in occupational performance.

Second, most tasks require learned skills, many of which take considerable time to master. Hence, individuals ordinarily can only learn one or a few skills. This is recognized in the adage, "jack of all trades and master of none." Beyond the apprenticeship required for learning a skill, the experience gained in continuously performing it will serve to reinforce the skill. Weekend craftsmen can hardly expect to be as expert as those who perform a craft on a full-time basis; but weekend craftsmen will be more skilled than those with only intermittent and sporadic practice.

* * * *

INTRASOCIETAL CONSENSUS IN OCCUPATIONAL PRESTIGE EVALUATIONS

One of the most striking features of occupational prestige systems in almost all societies is the lack of subgroup variation in prestige ratings. On the average, people in all walks of life, rich and poor, educated and ignorant, urban and rural, male and female, view the prestige hierarchy in the same way. With minor exceptions, there is extraordinary consensus throughout each society regarding the relative prestige of occupations. The prestige hierarchy appears to be a genuine Durkheimian social fact that exists independently of the particular values and attitudes of raters. Regardless of their views about what the prestige hierarchy ought to be, people are generally capable of reporting what it actually is. Those in low-prestige occupations correctly perceive their own low status and those in high-prestige occupations correctly perceive their own high status. Blacks perceive the same hierarchy as whites despite their severely disadvantaged position, and women perceive the same hierarchy as men.

This, of course, need not be so. Other sorts of prestige evaluations do not display such consensus. For example, ratings of the prestige of 20 religious denominations in the United States conform to a "social distance" rather than a "prestige" model. Raters tend to accord the highest prestige to their own religion and the least prestige to religions that are theologically and organizationally farthest removed from their own.[1] The contrast between the consensus that characterizes occupational prestige evaluations and the lack of consensus that characterizes the evaluation of other social categories is striking and serves to bolster a conception of occupational prestige ratings as peculiarly collective perceptions of social reality rather than expres-

sions of personal values. In this conception, occupations *have* prestige and people learn the prestige hierarchy along with the other lore and knowledge they acquire as part of their socialization to adult roles. . . . The prestige of occupations is rooted in the structure of relationships of power and privilege that arises from the division of labor. These relationships produce a society-wide system of evaluations of occupations, which are known more or less well by every fully socialized member of society.

Of course, all individuals need not and do not share identical perceptions of the prestige hierarchy. There is, indeed, a relatively large idiosyncratic component in the prestige ratings made by each individual, so that the typical correlation in the ratings made by any pair of individuals is about .6. The point is that differences in perceptions of the prestige hierarchy are not socially structured; it is very hard to find systematic differences among subgroups of the population with respect to the way they hierarchically order occupations. While it is possible to locate isolated instances of differences in the evaluation of particular occupations, these exceptional cases are too few to seriously discredit the claim of near-perfect consensus across population subgroups in the prestige evaluation of occupations.

. . . The evidence supports the claim of intrasocietal consensus in occupational prestige evaluations. Prestige judgments are not importantly affected by the occupational status, ethnic status, or sex of raters, either in the United States or in other societies. Furthermore . . . prestige ratings by students in nonindustrialized countries are not particularly deviant and are no more Western than ratings by nonstudents, which means that it is valid to use data from student samples to estimate the prestige hierarchies of countries for which no better data are available. Finally, . . . the prestige hierarchy tends to be extremely stable over time, even in countries undergoing rapid industrialization or other social change. Thus we need not be concerned about the fact that the available data span nearly a quarter of a century; they can be taken as representing the range of societies in the contemporary world.

* * * *

The sex of raters has virtually no effect on ratings in any society for which pertinent data are available. First, in the United States at least, women are as willing to rate occupations as are men (Reiss, 1961: 13–14, 196) and give as wide a range of ratings as men (Bose, 1973: 50). Second, the correlations between the mean ratings by men and women are near unity in both industrialized and nonindustrialized societies. In the United States, the correlation is .98 (Reiss, 1961: 189); in Denmark it is .99; both in the Philippines and in Zambia (Hicks, 1969) the rank correlation is .98; and in South-West Africa the correlation is .94. The relatively lower correlation in South-West Africa may be due to the slightly greater tendency for men than for women to downgrade male incumbents of traditionally female service occupations. . . . But the overall pattern is one of striking agreement between men and women in their perceptions of the relative prestige of occupations. Indeed, in Denmark the correlation between the standard deviations of male and female ratings is .82.

---

1. Unpublished analysis of data from a 1964 National Opinion Research Center survey conducted in conjunction with the project "Occupations and Social Stratification."

In sum, occupational prestige evaluations are not importantly structured by occupational position, ethnic group membership, or sex, despite the relationship of these factors to differential life chances. There is, however, one group that requires special consideration because of its unique position in the social structure of all societies, but especially in that of developing societies. This is the student group.

How Representative Are Students in Their Occupational Evaluations?

In societies such as the United States, where most of the population gets at least a secondary education, we would expect students to perceive the occupational prestige structure in the same way as the general population does. And indeed they do. By early adolescence, children in the United States have acquired adult prestige perceptions (Simmons, 1962: Table 5; Gunn, 1964) and high school students are indistinguishable from adults in their occupational evaluations (Siegel *et al.*, 1974: Table 5.2). This also appears to be true for Brazil (São Paulo), Chile, Germany, Great Britain, Japan, the Netherlands, Norway, the Philippines, and Poland, since for all of these places it was possible to combine prestige data from student and nonstudent samples (recall that the criterion for combining data sets is a correlation of at least .95).

However, in nonindustrialized countries one cannot assume that students are similar to nonstudents in their prestige perceptions. First, educational opportunities are generally very limited in such places so that only a small fraction of the population obtains secondary schooling. Hence, secondary students must be regarded as constituting the incipient elites of their countries. Second, in many nonindustrialized countries higher education (including secondary schooling) follows a Western model. Often the teachers are Europeans or are locals who have gone abroad for their own advanced schooling. Hence, the norms and values imparted along with instruction may promote a pattern of occupational evaluation that is more similar to that of the industrialized nations of the West than is that of the remainder of the population. Insofar as this is true, the use of prestige ratings by students to represent the prestige hierarchies of nonindustrialized societies may result in an overstatement of the degree of worldwide similarity in prestige evaluations.

Fortunately, the available evidence suggests that the "Western bias" of student prestige evaluations, insofar as it exists at all, is rather small. If we regard the United States as epitomizing advanced industrial societies, we can use the degree of agreement with United States' prestige ratings as a measure of bias toward prestige perceptions of industrialized Western societies. If such bias exists, the prestige ratings of students should be more similar to American prestige ratings than are the ratings of nonstudents from the same societies. . . . [Data were collected] for four societies: [Nigeria (Kano)], the Congo, . . . Spain, and Zambia. . . .

. . . All [of the latter] three show a similar pattern: Students are similar to most, but not all, of the occupational

groups in the extent of their agreement with American prestige evaluations. In each case the lowest-status occupational group exhibits substantially less similarity to the United States' evaluations than the students or the other groups. But even here caution is in order. The Congolese correlations are based on 11 occupations, so minor fluctuations in rankings can have large effects on the size of the correlations. And in the Zambian case, . . . the mine recruits were largely new arrivals in the Copperbelt who may not yet have learned the prestige structure of the mining area.

But even accepting the validity of these occupational differences, the data provide striking evidence of consensus in the prestige perceptions of students and nonstudents within each society. First, the correlations between the prestige ratings of students and nonstudents are, with three exceptions, all above .96. The exceptions are the correlation between those with no education and those with primary or secondary education in Kano (.92); the correlation between students and unskilled laborers in the Congo (.86); and the correlation between students and mine recruits in Zambia (.92). Second, there is almost no overlap between countries in the degree of prestige similarity to the United States displayed by various subgroups. The conclusion that the Congo, Nigeria (Kano), Spain, and Zambia display increasingly great similarity to the United States would, with a single minor exception, hold regardless of which subgroup was used to represent the prestige hierarchy of each country. The differences between countries in the degree of prestige similarity to the United States are much larger than the differences among subgroups within each country.

Taken together, these results give us considerable confidence that the use of student samples, or for that matter other samples of unrepresentative population groups, will not seriously distort conclusions regarding the extent of cross-cultural similarity in occupational prestige evaluations.

* * * *

To sum up, the results . . . clearly favor a structural model of occupational prestige determination. Wherever we have data we find basic intersocietal similarity in the relative education required to perform various occupations and in the relative income returned to them. Second, for the most part the connections between educational requirements, income gained, and prestige are similar throughout the world. Thus, it cannot be the case that occupational prestige hierarchies are similar merely as a consequence of the imposition of a Western value system on the non-Western world. Rather, it is evident that to a large degree occupational prestige hierarchies are similar throughout the world because occupational skill and hence income hierarchies are similar throughout the world and these features of occupations determine their prestige.

Occupational Structures in Past Societies

Having shown that occupational structures are essentially similar throughout the contemporary world, we now ask whether this is the consequence of the homogenizing effect of industrialization or whether occupational structures are similar in all complex societies, industrialized or not. To decide between these alternatives we examine data from past societies. Since industrialization is, at best, about 150 years old (the rapid expansion of industry known as the "industrial revolution" first occurred in Great Britain during the period 1750–1825, in the United States and Western Europe during the nineteenth century, and elsewhere still later, if at all: Hughes, 1968), demonstration of substantial similarity in occupational structures between pre–nineteenth-century societies and the present will constitute strong evidence for a pure structural theory of occupational prestige.

As usual, appropriate data are extremely sparse. Not only are there no data on authority or economic power, but there are no data for past societies on skill levels of occupations. I have, however, located systematic data on the wealth or income of occupational incumbents for six past societies and "prestige" data for two past societies. Let us consider the prestige data first.

In 1395 a rank ordering of castes was promulgated by Raja Jayastihi Malla of Nepal (Wright, 1958: 111–112). Since this was the official ordering of castes and since fourteenth-century Nepali occupations were almost exclusively organized on the basis of caste membership (in fact, at the time castes were named by the occupations of their members), it seems reasonable to interpret such a caste ranking as an occupational prestige ranking. Similar data are available for fifteenth-century Florence, in the form of a ranking of guilds. An official rank order of guilds was maintained by the Florentine Commune, and a history of the guilds of Florence interpolates various subguilds and individual occupations into the official list (Staley, 1906: 61–62). The rank order of guilds as of 1427 was used here to correspond to wealth data described below.

The wealth data consist of estimates, of varying quality, of either the average wealth held by incumbents of various occupations or the average income returned to particular occupations. Data are available for fifteenth-century Florence, late–seventeenth-century England, late–eighteenth-century America, mid–nineteenth-century Philadelphia, mid–nineteenth-century Hamilton, Ontario, and late–nineteenth-century London.

In order to assess the stability over time in the ordering of occupations with respect to income or wealth and prestige, it was necessary to match occupational titles from each of the historical data sets to . . . standard categories. . . . Since these categories were developed inductively from mid–twentieth-century data the ease with which the matches could be made itself constitutes a partial test of the claim . . . that despite the proliferation of new jobs as a result of changes in technology, and despite the massive and ubiquitous shift in the distribution of labor forces associated with industrialization (out of agricultural and laboring jobs and into nonmanual jobs), the organization of functions into specific occupations has remained strikingly stable. Most of the differences between occupational structures, I claim, represent greater or lesser subdivision of functions into separately named occupational titles; they do not represent differences in the actual distribution of functions among occupational categories.

Furthermore, differences in the degree of differentiation of occupations tend to reflect the relative importance of specific functions in particular economies. Thus, in fifteenth-century Florence, fine distinctions were made between various kinds of wool workers; and in medieval Nepal several varieties of priests were distinguished. But since highly specialized subcategories of occupations tend to be relatively homogeneous with respect to their economic or prestige status, little precision is lost by aggregating such categories for comparative purposes.

The best evidence for the stability of occupational categories over time is the very fact that it was possible to carry out the task described here. In very few instances did it prove difficult or impossible to find a match between the historical data and contemporary titles. (And, for the most part, those difficulties that did arise resulted from vaguely defined titles, e.g., "agent," which are as common to contemporary data as to the historical material analyzed here.) Nearly all the lists of occupations include high government officials, clergy, lawyers, physicians, teachers, large merchants, shopkeepers, artisans of various sorts—smiths, masons, carpenters, and so on—and unskilled laborers. Although specific occupational titles are present in some of the data sets and not in others, the extent to which the basic categories remain the same is striking. Even in medieval Nepal, by far the most nearly unique society under consideration here, the occupational categories are generally quite recognizable and are surprisingly comparable to occupations in the modern world. . . .

Let us now consider how stable occupational status hierarchies have been over time. . . . The size of these correlations is striking. For each historical period, going back to fifteenth-century Florence, the relative levels of occupational wealth or income are strongly related to the contemporary worldwide average occupational prestige hierarchy. In fact, the historical correlations are approximately as strong as the contemporary ones. For past societies the average correlation of occupational wealth (or income) levels with the Standard Scale is .75, whereas the corresponding average correlation for contemporary societies is only .70.[2] Similarly, the average intercorrelation of occupational wealth levels over the four and one-half centuries between 1427 and 1890 is .75, suggesting that the intertemporal stability of occupational structures within Europe is possibly greater than the intersocietal similarity within the contemporary world. Lending support to this view is the striking demonstration by Brown and Hopkins (1955) of stability in the relative wages of building craftsmen and laborers in England for more than 5 centuries:

after [about 1410] there was no sustained change until the First World War. In the fifteenth century the craftsman

---

2. It may seem anomalous that the average correlation for the historical data is actually slightly higher than that for the contemporary data, but the difference is not large enough to be meaningful. Moreover, the historical average is obviously slightly inflated by the correlation between the 1688 British data and the Standard Scale, which is excessively high due to a correlation of extremes. Omitting this correlation, the average correlation for the historical data drops to .72.

got half as much again as the labourer, 6d. a day to his 4d.; in the 1890's he got half as much again, 7¹/₂d. an hour to his 5d.; he got half as much again, or within a halfpenny of it, in every settled period in between. [Brown and Hopkins, 1955:202]

Finally, in our own data there is no evidence whatsoever that the industrial revolution had any impact on the relative privilege of occupational groups or on the relation between privilege and prestige. The correlations of occupational wealth levels with the Standard Scale prestige scores are equally high for the three preindustrial societies as for the three nineteenth-century cities. If industrialization had an impact, surely it would be manifest in the occupational structure of London. But there is no evidence for that in these data.

The "prestige" data for Florence and Nepal are equally striking. As would be expected, the correlation with the Standard Scale is substantially higher for Florence than for Nepal. . . . Since Florence was a major mercantile center, it is not surprising that its occupational prestige hierarchy is closer than Nepal's to the generic hierarchy of the modern world. It must be noted, however, that the Florentine hierarchy is still more idiosyncratic than are most contemporary societies regardless of their levels of industrialization. Nonetheless, as was true of the wealth hierarchy, the most striking point about the prestige hierarchy is that it is relatively stable over time.

On the basis of the theory of prestige . . . there is every reason to believe that were data available for skill hierarchies they would be even more stable over time than income or wealth hierarchies, just as is generally true in the contemporary world. This, then, provides the basis for an additional test of the theory at such time as suitable data become available for past societies. If occupational skill hierarchies for past societies can be shown to be as uniform as occupational wealth and prestige hierarchies, and, further, if the connections between skill, wealth, and prestige can be shown to be as strong for past societies as for present ones, a pure structural theory of prestige could be said to be firmly verified. However, for the present we must content ourselves with a somewhat more limited confirmation of the theory on the basis of fragmentary data. In addition to the evidence presented above, there are various impressionistic accounts of the class structure of past societies.

For example, Gideon Sjoberg's analysis of preindustrial cities includes an explicit discussion of the characteristic features of the social class systems of such societies. On the basis of data from feudal realms in traditional China, Japan, India, the Middle East, Europe, and Mesoamerica he asserts (1960: 108–109):

Preindustrial cities across cultures display strong consistency in their class structure—in the kinds of criteria that are highly valued and the manner in which these are assigned in determining class position. Thus specific kinds of occupations are rated highly, and these are closely associated with certain kinds of achievements, greater power and authority, the "desirable" possessions,

a particular kind of kinship position, and special moral and personal attributes. So too, the kinds of criteria that are devalued are very similar for cities from one culture to the next.

Sjoberg then goes on to identify the occupational groups that comprise the two major classes he sees as characteristic of preindustrial cities: a small upper class and a large lower class. He also recognizes status distinctions within each of these classes. Although his discussion is in narrative form and does not easily lend itself to a definitive rank ordering of occupational groups, I have attempted to translate Sjoberg's description (1960: 118–123) into an occupational hierarchy for the purpose of comparing it to the standard prestige hierarchy of the contemporary world. . . . The only real ambiguity in Sjoberg's account is with respect to the highest lower-class group—he may not have considered low-level government, religious, and military personnel to have higher status than other lower-class categories. . . .

Two features of this match are striking. First, there was no difficulty in effecting the matches, with the exception of large merchants. The category "general managers" is probably a poor match, both because it includes personnel who are not merchants and because it is not restricted to those involved in large enterprises. Nonetheless, it includes bankers, heads of large firms, and other titles comparable to the merchant princes Sjoberg intended to include as having equivocal upper-class status. The difficulty in effecting a match probably reflects an inadequacy of the Standard Scale more than a true lack of comparable occupational groups in preindustrial and contemporary industrial societies. Thus, once again, we have confirmation of the similarity of the occupational structure in all complex societies, industrial or preindustrial.

Second, the status hierarchies are remarkably similar. High-status occupational groups in preindustrial societies have the greatest prestige in contemporary societies, and the lowest status groups in preindustrial societies have the lowest prestige in contemporary societies. Thus, insofar as Sjoberg's assertion of uniformity in the class structures of preindustrial cities is credible, we can infer from it a uniformity of occupational hierarchies throughout the urban world, past or present.

Conclusions

The concern of this chapter has been to evaluate competing explanations for the worldwide similarity in occupational prestige hierarchies. . . .

. . . We can conclude that the data favor the pure structural theory. . . . In all complex societies, industrialized or not, a characteristic division of labor arises that creates intrinsic differences among occupational roles with respect to power; these in turn promote differences in privilege; and power and privilege create prestige. Since the same process operates in all complex societies, the resulting prestige hierarchy is relatively invariant in all such societies, past or present.

*   *   *   *

REFERENCES

Bose, C. E. (1973). *Jobs and gender: Sex and occupational prestige.* Baltimore, MD: Johns Hopkins University, Center for Metropolitan Planning and Research.

Brown, E. H. P., & Hopkins, S. V. (1955). Seven centuries of building wages. *Economics, 22* (August), 195–206.

Gunn, B. (1964). Children's conceptions of occupational prestige. *Personnel and Guidance Journal, 42* (February), 558–563.

Hicks, R. E. (1969). The relationship of sex to occupational prestige in an African country. *Personnel and Guidance Journal, 47* (March), 655–668.

Hughes, J. R. T. (1968). Industrialization: Economic aspects. In D. L. Sills (Ed.), *International Encyclopedia of the Social Sciences* (pp. 7:252–263). New York: Macmillan.

Murdock, G. P. (1937). Comparative data on the division of labor by sex. *Social Forces, 15* (May), 551–553.

Reiss, A. J., Jr. (1961). *Occupation and social status.* New York: Free Press of Glencoe.

Siegel, P. M., Hodge, R. W., & Rossi, P. H. (1974). *Occupational prestige in the United States.* New York: Academic Press.

Simmons, D. D. (1962). Children's rankings of occupational prestige. *Personnel and Guidance Journal, 41* (December), 332–336.

Sjoberg, G. (1960). *The preindustrial city: Past and present.* Glencoe, IL: Free Press.

Staley, E. (1906). *The guilds of Florence.* London: Methuen.

Wright, D. (Ed.). (1958). *History of Nepal.* (M. S. S. Singh & P. S. Guanand, trans.). Calcutta: Susil Gupta (India) Private Ltd. (First published by Cambridge University Press, 1877)

CLASS IDEOLOGY

The mode of production in material life conditions the social, political, and intellectual life processes in general. It is not the consciousness of men that determines their being, but, on the contrary, their social being that determines their consciousness.

Karl Marx
A Contribution to the Critique of Political Economy

All inequality seems natural and just to those who accept the premises upon which the stratification system is based. In feudal societies, for example, the wealth and power of rulers were justified by the belief in the "divine right of kings." The rich and powerful in caste systems justified their wealth and power by the assumption that subordinate castes were religiously or physically inferior. In modern industrial societies inequality is explained in terms of achievement and merit. Whatever the system of stratification, the unequal distribution of wealth and power will go unchallenged as long as the majority accepts the beliefs and ideology supporting the stratification system. Since ideology plays such a central role in social arrangements, it has been a particularly important issue to sociologists.

At the beginning of the last century, Georg Hegel (1770–1831) advanced the theory that societal arrangements in general and social inequality in particular were the result of ideas (the Zeitgeist) that dominate society and even whole periods of history. The ideas are a reality that exist in their own right, even outside of people. So powerful are they that they are governed by their own internal logic, which he called the dialectic. In the dialectic, every new idea (thesis) elicits its opposite (antithesis). The opposition is resolved by a transcendent idea (synthesis), which is in turn a new thesis, and the dialectic begins anew. Hegel believed that we must understand the dialectical processes that govern our ideas before we can understand our experiences.

Karl Marx took the dialectical idealism (thesis-antithesis-synthesis) of Hegel and turned it on its head. He argued that Hegel had reversed the relationship between ideas and experience. It is not ideas that make our experiences meaningful, he

said, rather it is our experience in the material world that shapes our ideas. Ideas are reflections of the material world. Our most important experiences are formed by the productive process through which material needs are satisfied. People stand in at least two different relationships to these productive forces. They may be owners or workers. The experiences of these two groups of people are so different that they see the world as fundamentally different and each develops an ideology to express this worldview.

Marx called the ideology of the owners *reactionary* because it defended the interests of the owners at the expense of the workers. The ideology of the workers he called *progressive* because it advocated sharing profits equally. These opposed ideological views (Hegel would call them the thesis and antithesis) would inevitably lead to class struggle and revolution (synthesis). Indeed, all of history can be viewed as the clash of opposed ideologies and class struggle. For the revolution to occur, workers must become aware of the progressive ideology. At first, many workers will confuse the interests of the ruling class with their own objective class interests. Friedrich Engels (1820–1895) felt that the workers possessed a false consciousness when they accepted the distorted ideas of the ruling class. Today we might consider workers who were anti-union as an example of false consciousness.

The owners of production control the economy and can promote false consciousness by controlling the creation and spread of ideas. Antonio Gramsci (1971, p. 12) claims that this gives the ruling class an ideological hegemony. The wealthy have the resources to reward those whose ideas support the dominant class. Schools that support the dominant class receive endowments, and ministers who support it are promoted. Since the owners of production control the mass media, their reactionary ideology is widely publicized, unchallenged, and accepted as the truth. They can therefore promote false consciousness.

This investigation is based on "Income and Stratification Ideology: Beliefs About the American Opportunity Structure" by Joan Huber Rytina, William Form, and John Pease, 1970, reprinted on pages 76–83.

This may account for the finding of Richard Centers (1949) that there is little class consciousness in the United States. On his national survey, only 3 percent of respondents thought of themselves as upper-class, and 1 percent as lower-class. Ninety-four percent of Americans called themselves either working- or middle-class.

One of the reasons that class consciousness has not developed in the United States as it has in Europe is the belief that everyone has an equal opportunity to achieve success. If one is poor, according to this belief, it is the failure of the individual rather than of the economic system. By contrast, Marx believed the poor are victims of an exploitative class system. Workers who believe the poor don't want to get ahead and the poor don't work as hard have a distorted or false consciousness. Until these ideas are changed, class consciousness will not develop.

Background

The American stratification ideology is based on the belief that everyone has an equal opportunity for success, that those with ability who really try have a better chance of succeeding in the United States than in any other country. Joan Rytina, William Form, and John Pease (whose research you will learn about in Reading 6) wanted to see how widely this belief was accepted, and if the rates of acceptance varied between the rich (dominant class) and the poor. In 1967 they systematically sampled 354 heads of households in Muskegon, Michigan. Their first hypothesis stated that ideological statements of a general nature would be more widely accepted than those that were more specific. The following statements illustrate general and specific questions concerning the belief in equal opportunity.

General: There is plenty of opportunity, and anyone who works hard can go as far as he or she wants.

Specific: Do you think that a boy whose father is poor and a boy whose father is rich have the same opportunity to make the same amount of money if they work hard?

[respondents were asked to answer "agree" or "disagree"]

The results of their survey indicated a great variation, and certainly no unanimity of support for the ideological beliefs under investigation. Eighty to 90 percent of the respondents in the three income groups (rich, middle, and poor) agreed with the general belief in opportunity mentioned above. The level of agreement on the specific question of the equal chances of the two boys dropped considerably. Fifty-seven percent of those in the upper class, 49 percent of those in the middle class, and 47 percent of those in the lower class agreed with the statement. Only 11 percent of poor blacks said they agreed with the specific version of this question.

Overall, the rich were more likely than the poor to believe that in the United States there is equality of opportunity, rich and poor equally influence governmental processes, the courts and laws are fair, a jail sentence is just as likely for the rich as the

poor, and the rich have more wealth as a result of more favorable personal attributes. These findings suggest great differences between rich and poor in the acceptance of capitalistic ideology. The support for beliefs comes from those who have the most to gain from the support of the ideology. Rytina et al. conclude that "there is less 'false-consciousness' than most social scientists assume. The best audience of an ideology is the audience which profits most from its repetition" (p. 82).

Replication

Rytina et al. state that two hypotheses guided their research. We will test the same two hypotheses. First, "all income strata will tend to agree more with highly generalized statements than with situationally specific statements about the operation of the American opportunity system" (p. 77). We will see if this is supported by our survey in the following hypothesis:

Hypothesis 1:

The acceptance of the ideology of educational opportunity will decrease when its tenets are viewed specifically.

Second, Rytina et al. believe that the ideology of inequality will have its strongest support among those who most profit from the inequality. Therefore, a greater proportion of the rich than the poor will agree with beliefs that support existing forms of inequality.

Hypothesis 2:

The rich will agree more than the poor with questions 24, 25, and 26 on the Student Survey (reprinted above).

You should give special attention to question 25, "Poor people don't care too much about getting ahead," Rytina et al. found that 46 percent of the rich, but only 19 percent of the poor, believed that those who are poor are so because of personal shortcomings. Compare your results with those obtained by Rytina et al. in the Investigation Results 6 table under the column titled "Poor Don't Want to Get Ahead."

The major independent variable in our investigation is income. This is taken from item 7 on the Student Survey. The three income levels have been somewhat modified from Rytina et al.'s definitions to reflect economic changes that have occurred since their 1966 study. Responses 1–2 (less than $20,000) are to be classified as poor, 4–9 ($20,000 to $149,999), as

Table 6-1

INVESTIGATION RESULTS 6
Class Ideology

Income	Equal Opportunity for College (General)		Poor as Likely to Be in College (Specific)		Poor Don't Want to Get Ahead		
	Rytina et al. Study[a]	Student Survey	Rytina et al. Study[b]	Student Survey	Rytina et al. Study[c]	Student Survey	
Poor 0-$19,999	57%	_____	38%	_____	19%	_____	$\bar{X}$poor = _____
Middle $20,000-$149,999	75%	_____	37%	_____	29%	_____	
Rich $150,000 +	96%	_____	43%	_____	46%	_____	$\bar{X}$rich = _____

Hypothesis 2 _____

| Average by ideological tenets | $\bar{X}$gen = _____ | | $\bar{X}$spec = _____ | | | | |

Hypothesis 1 _____

[a]Data in column 1 are from Table 1, page. 78, Column (c), "Whites."

[b]Data in column 3 are from Table 1, p. 78, Column (d), "Whites."

[c]Data in column 5 are from Table 4, p. 81, Column (e), "Whites."

middle income, and 10–11 ($150,000 and over) as rich. The dependent variable in the investigation is stratification ideology, and is measured by questions 24, 25, and 26 on the Student Survey. The corresponding questions asked by Rytina et al. can be found on page 79 for questions 24 and 26, and on page 82 for question 25.

Findings

Computation

The percentage agreement on each question will be computed by your instructor for each of the three economic classes.

When you have received this data, proceed as follows:

Step 1:

Enter the class results in Table 6-1, Investigation Results 6, above.

You will also need to enter row and column averages in the blank spaces indicated on the table. Four averages are called for: the average for general statement ($\bar{X}$gen), the average for specific statement ($\bar{X}$spec), the average for agreement of poor ($\bar{X}$poor), and the average for agreement of rich ($\bar{X}$rich).

Step 2:

Use these averages to test the hypotheses:

Hypothesis 1:

The acceptance of the ideology of educational opportunity will decrease when its tenets are viewed specifically.

$\bar{X}$gen _____ > _____ $\bar{X}$spec

Hypothesis 2:

The rich will agree more than the poor with questions 24, 25, and 26 on the Student Survey.

$\bar{X}$rich _____ > _____ $\bar{X}$poor

Table 6–2

SUPPORT FOR HYPOTHESES

	Significantly Supported	Partially Supported	Not Supported	Indeterminate
Hypothesis 1: General vs. specific	_____	_____	_____	_____
Hypothesis 2: Poor vs. rich	_____	_____	_____	_____

Indicate the amount of support you found for each hypothesis.

Checking Your Findings

Hypothesis 1 The Rytina et al. article states (p. 79), "A basic tenet of the ideology of opportunity is that educational resources needed for occupational mobility are equally available to all." The researchers observe that it is easier for people to test the merits of specific rather than general applications of this belief. This leads Rytina et al. to hypothesize that there will be greater support for the general rather than specific application of the belief that these is equal opportunity for everyone to go to college. Do your findings indicate there was more support for the general statement (question 24) or the specific statement (question 26)?

Hypothesis 2 Rytina et al. also hypothesized that support for an ideology will be strongest among those who have the most to gain from the system it defends; thus the rich will be more likely than the poor to agree with statements that defend the present system. Did you find this in general to be the case? More specifically, did you find the poor more likely to disagree and believe the poor want to get ahead as much as anyone else?

When you have analyzed the previous hypotheses, summarize your conclusions in Table 6–2, above.

Topics for Further Investigation

1. In 1966 the majority of the poor (57 percent) and virtually all the rich (96 percent) believed that "all young people of high ability have a fairly equal opportunity to go to college." Do the results of your survey indicate that people continue to support this belief strongly?

2. As recently as the Great Depression, people had an unshaken commitment to the belief that their problems came not from the system but from themselves: if only they worked harder, they would succeed. Do the results of your survey indicate that both rich and poor continue to accept the belief that the poor want to get ahead just as much as anyone else?

3. For class discussion, you might want to consider how widespread and extensive a belief must be in order for it to serve as an integrative force in society.

4. Conversely, how widespread must a belief be in order to serve as a *dis*integrative force in society? On page 82 Rytina et al. report that, in 1970, a majority of whites agreed with the general statement that the law and courts are fair, whereas a minority of blacks agreed with the statement. The researchers concluded that "data from such studies should provide information needed to predict the formation and activation of social movements." Do you agree with this conclusion? Do you feel that the Los Angeles riots of 1992 could have been predicted?

References and Recommended Readings

Bocock, R. (1987). *Hegemony*. New York: Methuen.

Brown, L. B. (1973). *Ideology*. Baltimore, MD: Penguin Books.

Centers, R. (1949). *The psychology of social classes: A study of class consciousness*. Princeton, NJ: Princeton University Press.

Form, W., & Rytina, J. (1969). Income and ideological beliefs on the distribution power in the United States. *American Sociological Review, 34*, 19–31.

Goldthorpe, J., Lockwood, D., Bechhofer, F., & Platt, J. (1969). The affluent worker and the thesis of embourgeoisment. *Sociology, 1*, 11–37.

Gramsci, A. (1971). *Selections from prison notes*. New York: International Publishers.

Huber, J., & Form, W. (1974). *Income and ideology*. New York: Macmillan.

Kluege, J., & Smith, E. (1986) *Beliefs about inequality*. Hawthorne, New York: Aldine de Gruyter.

Mannheim, K. (1936). *Ideology and utopia*. New York: Harcourt Brace Jovanovich.

Marx, K. (1846) *The German ideology*. New York: International Publishers.

Morris, R., & Murphy, R. (1966). A paradigm for the study of class consciousness. In J. Lopreato & L. Lewis (Eds.), *Social Stratification: A reader*. New York: Harper & Row, 1974.

Remling, G. (1967). *Road to suspicion*. New York: Appleton-Century-Crofts.

Rytina, J., Form, W., & Pease, J. (1970). Income and stratification ideology. *American Journal of Sociology, 75*, 703–716.

Smith, K., & Stone, L. (1989). Rags, riches and bootstraps: Beliefs about the causes of wealth and poverty. *Sociological Quarterly, 30*, 93–107.

Stack, S. (1978). Ideological beliefs on the distribution of power and rewards. *Sociological Focus, 11*, 221–234.

Thompson, K. (1986). *Beliefs and ideology*. New York: Methuen.

Income and Stratification Ideology: Beliefs about the American Opportunity Structure

When ideologies are stated as normative and general tenets, they tend to be accepted. This study hypothesized (1) that in an industrial community, the acceptance of the ideology of opportunity would decrease when its tenets were viewed as specific situations confronting persons of unequal economic rank, and (2) that endorsement of the tenets, expressed either in general or in situational terms, would be withheld more often by lower-income people than by those from higher-income strata. Confirmation of the hypotheses suggests that ideological adherence is greatest among those who profit most from the reiteration of the ideology.

Joan Huber Rytina
University of Notre Dame

William H. Form
Michigan State University

John Pease
University of Maryland

IDEOLOGY AND STRATIFICATION

Social stratification may be defined as the generational persistence of unequal distribution of valued rewards in a society. An ideology is a set of emotionally held beliefs and myths that account for social reality. The ideology of a stratification system explains and vindicates the distribution of rewards in an actual society or in a society believed to be possible, and contains both normative and existential statements about the way things ought to be and the way things really are. Thus, in American society a man who works hard ought to get ahead, does get ahead, and in getting ahead proves he has worked hard. By definition, then, a dominant stratification ideology justifies the distribution of power and rewards in the society. Transmitted by the communication and educational channels, this ideology becomes the "public ideology" which most social scientists study.

The integrative function of an ideology is high when all strata of the society support its tenets and concur in its mode of application. Ideologies lose this integrative character when people in various strata either reject the goals implicit in the ideology or believe that its tenets have little or no validity; that

is, when they feel that the institutions of a society are failing to implement desired societal goals.

The major assumption of this study is that all strata in the United States generally accept the normative tenets of the American ideology of equality of opportunity, the description of how things ought to be. But we expected some reservation, especially among lower strata, in accepting the idea that American institutions are effective in implementing the opportunity norms. Probably most adults in literate societies tend to test their life situations against the existing ideology. Since the symmetry between normative and existential tenets of an ideology is generally higher for upper strata, they are less inclined to test the validity of its existential tenets. The reverse situation probably is true for lower strata. In closely integrated social systems, the differences among the strata may be small, especially if the stratification ideology is buttressed by religious beliefs, as in the Indian caste system. In such cases one may indeed speak of a "theodicy of stratification," or the need to justify the suffering resulting from the inequality which God has ordained (Weber 1946, pp. 275–277). In urban-secular societies, strata will probably vary in the degree that they test the validity of an ideology's existential tenets.

Most sociologists probably assume there is wide support for the normative aspects of the ideology of equal opportunity (Smelser 1967, p. 8; Lipset 1963, p. 101), but current unrest among some segments of American society indicates that belief in some aspects may be more problematical (Miller and Rein 1966). Clearly, most studies have tested adherence to the ideology as it is expressed in general, ideal, or normative terms. It is relatively easy to obtain a consensus with regard to vague statements on how a system ought to and does operate. Such statements, especially as presented in most public opinion studies, do not concretize the tenets of an ideology. The acid test of a system which offers money as its main reward, especially from the point of view of people in lower strata, is whether a person who is poor has the same opportunities as a person who has more money. The problem for this research was to devise a technique which permitted people to respond to both (a) general statements about how the American opportunity system operates and (b) specific statements of how the system operates for persons in different economic strata.

RESEARCH DESIGN

Two major hypotheses guided this research: (1) all income strata will tend to agree more with highly generalized statements than with situationally specific statements about the operation of the American opportunity system, but (2) lower strata will show less agreement than higher strata with both types of statements. This hypothesis was based on the proposition that for most people income is the most salient stratification variable.

The major areas of ideology explored were:

1. The existence of an open opportunity structure in the United States, the equality of chances for upward and downward occupational mobility, and the relative opportunity for mobility in the United States and in Europe. These areas focus on beliefs concerning the relative openness of the economic institution.
2. The relative accessibility of educational resources to all strata as the vehicle for mobility.
3. The impartial functioning of the political and legal systems.
4. Personal or social responsibility for economic status or rank. We hypothesized that those with higher incomes support tenets of personal responsibility for a person's economic status, while the poor place greater reliance on social structural explanations, which would follow from the belief that, for the poor, the economic, educational, political, and legal institutions fail to operate in accord with democratic norms of equality of opportunity.

Annual family income was used as the major independent variable in this study for two reasons:

First, one of our research aims was to discover how poor people perceive the structure of economic opportunity; for poor people, the most salient reward of the stratification system is probably income. . . . Although the income data obtained for this study are inexact, they are sufficient to classify a respondent as rich, middle income, or poor.

The second reason for using income as the major variable is that we wanted to discover whether the rich support the tenets in the stratification ideology differently than other strata. Because they are a small part of the population and, consequently, of samples, most studies include the rich in a stratum with persons whose income is only a few thousand dollars above median family income. Yet the opinions of the rich may have disproportionate influence because they contribute great financial support to political parties. Such an assumption enables one to interpret the finding of McClosky et al. (1960, p. 416) that, on

social welfare measures, Republican followers tend to have much the same opinions as Democratic followers, while Republican leaders are far more conservative. A reasonable assumption is that the leaders reflect the views of those who support them financially, namely, the rich.

* * * *

We first presented to respondents a highly generalized statement on opportunity derived from the dominant ideology; later in the interview we presented a statement similar in logical content but specifically linking opportunity and income. All statements were worded in "either-or" form because some investigators have suggested that lower-class people tend to agree with any positive statement regardless of substantive content (Campbell et al. 1960, pp. 510–15; Christie and Jahoda 1954).

Respondents were heads of households or their spouses who . . . lived in . . . Muskegon, Michigan. . . . "Rich" . . . was the top 1 percent of the income distribution. "Poor" was defined in terms of a scale adjusted for the number of dependents. . . .

The analytic sample (N = 354) upon which this paper is based consisted of the systematic sample and the supplementary samples of rich and poor. By strata of income and race, the analytic sample included 37 poor blacks, 70 poor whites, 48 middle-income blacks, 152 middle-income whites, and 47 rich whites. . . . The sex division in each stratum was almost even. Education was associated with income: three-fifths of the respondents with 0–7 years of education were poor, and three-fifths of the college graduates were rich. We shall report black's responses separately because there is ample evidence that black and white experiences with the opportunity structure differ greatly. All findings must be regarded with great caution because of the small sample.

FINDINGS

Background findings show that about three-fourths of the respondents in all income strata liked Muskegon as a place to live and work. Respondents were also asked to identify themselves as middle, lower, working, or upper class. A little more than half identified with the working class, and a little less than half with the middle class. In a series of questions designed to tap interest in making money, blacks and poor whites showed the highest interest, and larger proportions of them reported having fewer economic opportunities than "other people." These and other data point to the importance of money to lower-income strata and their feelings of economic deprivation. These feelings are also reflected in their attitudes toward economic opportunity.

Beliefs in the Tenets of Economic Opportunity

Three tenets of the ideology of economic opportunity were explored: the importance of working hard for "getting ahead," the relevance of father's occupation to getting ahead, and

Table 1

BELIEFS ON CHANCES TO GET AHEAD AND TO GO TO COLLEGE
BY INCOME AND RACE (PERCENTAGES)

Income and Race	Plenty of Opportunity (General) (a)	Rich and Poor Have Equal Opportunity (Income-Linked) (b)	Equal Opportunity for College (General) (c)	Poor as Likely to Be in College (Income-Linked) (d)
Poor:				
Black	56	11	22	11
White	90	47	57	38
Middle:				
Black	58	21	41	28
White	80	49	75	37
Rich:				
White	93	57	96	43
Total, analytic sample:				
%	78	42	64	34
(N)	(342)	(351)	(348)	(344)
Total, systematic sample:*				
%	76	41	69	38
(N)	(177)	(184)	(184)	(181)

*For race, col. (a)—x^2 = 4.35, df = 1, p < .05; col. (b)—x^2 = 4.03, df = 1, p < .05; col. (c)—x^2 = 4.91, df = 1, p < .05.

whether occupational mobility is easier in the United States than in European countries. According to the main hypothesis, we expected more agreement with the general statements than with the specific statements, but we also expected respondents with higher incomes to show greater agreement to ideological tenets, however stated.

A general statement on economic opportunity was adopted from Campbell et al. (1954, p. 211):

Some people say there's not much opportunity in America today—that the average man doesn't have much chance to really get ahead. Others say there's plenty of opportunity and anyone who works hard can go as far as he wants. How do you feel?

From this statement we derived an income-linked specification:

Do you think that a boy whose father is poor and a boy whose father is rich have the same opportunity to make the same amount of money if they work equally hard, or do you think that the boy whose father is rich has a better chance of earning a lot more money?

In response to the general statement, over eight-tenths of the white respondents and less than six-tenths of the blacks thought that America is a land of equal opportunity (see table 1). But in response to the income-linked statement almost three-fifths of the rich, a half of middle-income and poor whites, and less than one-fifth of the blacks thought that rich and poor boys had equal opportunity (see table 1).

Since sociologists commonly use occupation of father rather than family income as the base point for studies of

occupational mobility, we decided to ask respondents about the relationship of father's occupation to mobility. Situational questions reflected significant mobility, that is, crossing a major occupational stratum boundary.

The first question pertained to upward occupational mobility:

Who do you think are more likely to become business executives and professional men: the sons of big business executives and professional men, or the sons of factory workers and small businessmen?

The second situational question pertained to downward occupational mobility:

Who do you think are more likely to become factory workers and small businessmen: the sons of factory workers and small businessmen, or the sons of big businessmen and professionals?

The questions must have appeared almost fatuous to the respondents because nine-tenths or more of all income groups felt that occupational inheritance was more likely than upward or downward occupational mobility (see table 2). Although none of the poor blacks thought that sons of fathers in lower occupational strata had more chances for upward mobility than other sons, almost one-fifth of them thought that sons of executives had more chances for downward mobility than sons of fathers in lower strata. Perhaps there is some comfort in the thought that, if one's own sons are not likely to rise, the sons of men in prestigious occupations may fall. We may well ask, if the question used in the interview situation seemed fatuous, do similar general or normative statements of the ideology re-

Table 2

BELIEFS CONCERNING GENERATIONAL MOBILITY AND OPPORTUNITY STRUCTURE IN AMERICA COMPARED WITH EUROPE, BY INCOME AND RACE (PERCENTAGE WHO AGREE)

Income and Race	Blue-Collar Son More Likely to Become Executive (a)	Executive Son More Likely to Become Blue-Collar (b)	Opportunity Better in America (c)
Poor:			
Black	0	19	16
White.	11	6	9
Middle:			
Black	4	4	7
White.	8	3	19
Rich:			
White.	9	0	30
Total, analytic sample:			
%	7	5	16
(N)	(344)	(347)	(351)
Total, systematic sample:*			
%	6	2	15
(N)	(178)	(180)	(184)

*For middle income and poor, col. (c)—x^2 = 4.95, df = 1, p < .05.

peated in everyday life also appear fatuous? Surely, people must test public ideologies against their daily life experiences.

Popular patriotic orators often proclaim that opportunity is greater in America than in European countries. Lipset and Rogoff have presented evidence casting doubt on the validity of such proclamations, but they nevertheless assumed that the belief was "traditional and universal" in the United States (Lipset and Rogoff 1954; Lipset and Bendix 1959). On the assumption that this belief is most supportive to the strata which have "made it," we predicted that the rich would be most likely to believe it and the poor least likely. Using situated class referents, we asked the respondents:

Do you believe that ambitious sons of lower class fathers are able to rise into the middle class in most European countries like Germany, France, and England, or do you think that such ambitious boys can rise only in the United States?

Unfortunately, the statement used did not call for a judgment of relative mobility rates, although some respondents (mainly, 19 percent of the rich and 32 percent of college graduates) gave a free response, indicating that mobility was possible in Europe but easier in the United States. About one-sixth of the total sample responded that mobility was possible only in the United States, or that it was easier, but three-tenths of the rich and four-tenths of the college graduates endorsed the

"myth" (see table 2). The responses obtained to this question cast some doubt on the universal acceptance of the idea that the United States has a more open opportunity structure than Europe.

In conclusion, the responses to the three statements on economic opportunity indicate considerable range and certainly no unanimity in support of the public ideology. Moreover, when family income and father's occupation are specifically mentioned in ideological statements, the degree of support for them is greatly reduced. Yet the rich consistently see greater equality of opportunity than the poor, except in the occupational structure, where the bulk of the respondents, rich and poor, white and black, see the general tendency of occupational inheritance. Even when the opportunity structure of the United States is compared with that of Europe, there is a general consensus that little or no difference exists.

Operation of Educational, Governmental, and Legal Institutions

A basic tenet of the ideology of opportunity is that educational resources needed for occupational mobility are equally available to all. Similarly, the government, the law, and the courts are supposedly blind to conditions of birth. General and situated questions involving education, government, and the law were devised to tap how different economic strata evaluated their functioning.

The general statement on education concerned the chance to go to college:

Do you feel that all young people of high ability have fairly equal opportunity to go to college, or do you feel that a large percentage of young people do not have much opportunity to go to college?

The income-specific corollary was:

Do you think that most young people in college come from families who can give them financial help or do you think that young people whose parents are poor are just as likely to be in college as anyone else?

The pattern of responses to the general question was similar to that dealing with economic opportunity, that is, greater support by the higher income strata and the whites. However, the range of responses among the strata was much greater, from one-fifth support by poor blacks to total support among the rich (see table 1). For the income-linked statement, there was a uniform decrease in support by all income groups, about one-half the proportions agreeing with the general statements. Responses to both types of statements show a much smaller degree of confidence in equal access to education in the United States than the literature suggests (Cremin 1951; Coleman 1968; Williams 1967).

Education is primarily governmentally sponsored in the United States. Does this relative lack of confidence in the ability of the educational institution to function equitably hold for government itself? A basic tenet of democratic ideology is that

Table 3

BELIEFS ABOUT LEGAL AND POLITICAL EQUALITY, BY INCOME AND RACE
(PERCENTAGE WHO PERCEIVE EQUALITY)

Income and Race	Voting Influences Government (a)	Rich and Poor Influence Government Equally (b)	Law and Courts Are Fair (c)	Jail Equally Likely for Rich or Poor (d)
Poor:				
Black	76	3	46	8
White	88	30	75	23
Middle:				
Black	89	15	27	20
White	89	30	59	20
Rich:				
White	94	55	75	22
Total, analytic sample:				
%	88	29	58	20
(N)	(303)	(345)	(340)	(343)
Total, systematic sample:*				
%	91	35	60	21
(N)	(182)	(172)	(177)	(178)

*For middle income and poor, col. (b)—x^2 = 4.34, df = 1, p < .05; col. (c)—x^2 = 4.41, df = 1, p = .05. For race, col. (c)—x^2 = 12.84, df = 1, p < .01.

the imperfections in the system are reparable—that the system is self-adjusting in response to inequities because voters are able to demand and generally get what they think the system should supply. The market analogy is clear. People who are trained to believe in political pluralism feel that all income strata should have equal influence on the operations of government and other social institutions. To explore adherence to this tenet, we prepared the following general statement on the opportunity to obtain political equality through participation in the electoral process:

> Some people think that voting is a vital part of the governmental process in this country, while others think it really doesn't make much difference who gets elected because the same people go on running things anyway. What do you think?

The income-linked specification:

> Some people say that, regardless of who gets elected, people who are rich get their way most of the time, while others say that people who are poor have just as much influence in government as people who are rich. What do you think?

Almost nine-tenths of all the respondents thought that voting was vital, the rich most of all and the poor blacks least of all (see table 3). Agreement with the specific statement shifted dramatically downward, with only three-tenths supporting it. The lower the income strata, the less the belief that wealth played no role in influencing governmental policies. Poor

whites were the exception, for their rate of support was the same as middle-income whites. Similar findings appeared for different educational levels. However, the range of differences among the educational strata was smaller than for the income strata, and this again points to the "softening effect" of the educational variable.

Equality before the law was that last institutional tenet of American ideology we examined. The general statement was:

> A number of people believe that in America everyone gets equal and fair treatment from the law, while others believe that the police and courts are basically unfair in the administration of justice. What do you think?

The income-linked corollary:

> Do you think that, if he breaks the law, a rich man is just as likely to end up in jail as a poor man, or do you think it's a lot easier for a rich man to stay out of jail?

A clear majority of the white respondents, irrespective of income, agreed to the general statement, but only a minority of the poor and middle-income blacks agreed (see table 3). In the income-linked corollary, the data clearly reveal that all income strata do not support the tenet of a fair legal system, for only one-fifth or less of the respondents in all strata felt that the courts operated equitably. When responses to the general and situated questions dealing with the legislative branch of government are compared with those dealing with the courts, there seems to be considerably less confidence in the operation of the judicial branch of government.

Table 4

PERSONAL ATTRIBUTES AS A CAUSE OF INCOME BY INCOME AND RACE (IN PERCENTAGES)

Income and Race	Wealth (a)	Poverty (b)	Being on Relief Last Six Years (c)	Poor Don't Work as Hard (d)	Poor Don't Want to Get Ahead (e)
Poor:					
Black.....................	17	17	28	3	0
White.....................	34	30	46	13	19
Middle:					
Black.....................	29	19	45	4	6
White.....................	35	41	59	30	29
Rich:					
White.....................	72	62	78	39	46
Total, analytic sample:					
%......................	37	36	54	21	23
(N)......................	(350)	(341)	(347)	(343)	(347)
Total, systematic sample:*					
%......................	31	40	57	25	25
(N)......................	(183)	(177)	(185)	(186)	(180)

Note: In the wealth column, the percentages represent those who saw favorable traits as a "cause" of wealth; in the poverty columns, unfavorable traits as a "cause" of poverty. The residual categories for the wealth column would include respondents who indicated both personal and structural responses as causal, and those who saw only structural factors as causal.

*For race, col. (b)—$x^2 = 10.29$, df = 2, $p < .01$; col. (c)—$x^2 = 9.63$, df = 2, $p < .01$; col. (d)—$x^2 = 4.85$, df = 1, $p < .05$; col. (e)—$x^2 = 7.6$, df = 1, $p < .01$.

Why Are the Rich, Rich and the Poor, Poor?

What makes some people rich and others poor? The implications of this question are political. The traditional ideology is specific. Wealth is the result of hard work, ability, motivation, and other favorable personal attributes. Wealth is earned and deserved. Poverty is the result of laziness, stupidity, and other unfavorable personal attributes, and it too is earned and deserved. People in a society get what they deserve, and the social structure is just. Since justice prevails, changes in the social structure are rarely needed. In testing support for these beliefs, we expected that those who have the most of what there is to get would be most likely to define the system as just. We therefore expected that the higher the income, the greater the tendency to assign personal factors as causes of wealth or poverty; and the lower the income, the greater the tendency to assign social structural factors as causal.

Respondents were first asked two open-ended questions, why are rich people rich, and why are poor people poor?[1] The answers were coded as pointing to personal attributes, to social structure, or to a combination of these. Only the responses which were solely in terms of personal attributes are presented in the tables. The rich are much more convinced than others that wealth is a result of favorable personal attributes; 72 percent of the rich and 17 percent of the poor blacks felt this way (see table 4). As one rich white man said, "Inheritance is the exception today. If you have to generalize, it's the self-discipline to accumulate capital and later to use that capital effectively and intelligently to make income and wealth." An opposite point of view was held by a poor black: "The rich stole, beat, and took. The poor didn't start stealing in time, and what they stole, it didn't value nothing, and they were caught with that."

The rich are also much more convinced than the poor that poverty is the result of unfavorable personal attributes. Six-tenths of the rich and 17 percent of the poor blacks supported this idea (see table 4). The same general pattern of responses to the two questions was found when the data were analyzed by the educational level of the respondents. Support for the ideology increased directly with educational level, but the differences between educational extremes were smaller than for the top and bottom income strata.

The explanation for being on relief was similar. Only about 5 percent of the total sample thought that people were on relief during the Great Depression because of personal attributes. But four-fifths of the rich and three-fifths of the middle-income whites thought that relief status in the past six years was the result of personal characteristics, while less than half of those in other strata thought so (see table 4). One rich man reported, "People on relief just don't want to work. I'm biased. I run a

---

[1] A number of respondents wanted to know the definition of "rich." Very few raised questions about the definition of "poor." Respondents were told that "rich" and "poor" meant whatever they meant to the respondent in the context of the Muskegon area.

plant where we try to hire men and they just won't stay." Another rich man said, "It's an easy way to receive their allotments. It's just too easy. Like ADC and that kind of stuff. To me, it's just criminal." In contrast, a poor black woman reported, "I've been on for six years or more and it's because I can't make enough on a job to take care of my six kids."

Hard work and motivation to get ahead are also basic tenets in the ideology of opportunity. Respondents were first asked:

> Naturally, everyone can think of exceptions, but on the whole, would you say that poor people work just as hard as rich people, or do you think that poor people generally don't work as hard as rich people?

Although only one-fifth of the total sample felt that the poor do not work as hard, two-fifths of the rich but almost no black respondents thought so (see table 4).

Respondents were then asked about the attitudes of poor people toward getting ahead:

> Do you think that poor people want to get ahead just as much as everyone else or do you think that basically poor people don't care too much about getting ahead? Please try not to think of individual exceptions you know of, but rather in terms of the group in general.

About one-fourth of the respondents thought that the poor did not want to get ahead, and the response variation was like that of the previous question (see table 4).

CONCLUSIONS

Empirical studies of ideologies are only primitively developed in the social sciences, and we hope that this research provides some suggestions about how to proceed further in this study. Obviously, national studies are sorely needed in this area, for any community study necessarily has limited generalizability. However, our hypotheses seem to be verified in the community studied. There is far from universal acceptance of the tenets of the American ideology of opportunity, even when those tenets are enunciated in the most general and vague terms. There is even less acceptance of statements in which economic inequality is made the test for accepting a tenet on equality of opportunity. The shift downward in degree of support of a tenet from its general statement to concrete specification is not a surprising finding. This phenomenon has been observed in research whenever situations are specified (Centers 1949; Prothro and Grigg 1960; Jones 1941). Our data confirm the hypothesis that the support of an ideology is strongest among those who profit most from the system which the ideology explains and defends, the rich in this case. In addition, the data reveal that people from various economic strata differ in their evaluation of the effectiveness of different institutions to implement the ideology of opportunity. Such differences are also found between blacks and whites.

We may reasonably assume that ideologies are most firmly held when they are accepted as given and not concretely tested in life situations; yet scientific analysis of ideologies cannot proceed without ascertaining how firmly the public supports them when they are enunciated in both normative and existential terms. Apparently social scientists do not know what everyone else seems to know, that people test the validity of public ideologies concretely in everyday life. We are inclined to conclude from our data that there is less "false class-consciousness" than most social scientists assume. The best audience of an ideology is the audience which profits most from its repetition. Others may not really be listening, or not listening well.

It is important for social scientists to study how firmly various segments of the community adhere to various ideological tenets, for data from such studies should provide information needed to predict the formation and activation of social movements. Clearly, such data should be gathered periodically, so that historical trends in the degree of support for old ideologies and the emergence of new ideologies can be discerned. Participation in social movements occurs when large proportions of the people in certain strata believe that institutions are not functioning to meet societal norms. They then feel that the norms must be changed or support for them must be withdrawn. In both cases, the universality of collective representations is reduced. Our data show that some people are facing a second American dilemma by questioning how they can support the ideology of opportunity in the face of massive intergenerational poverty. The dilemma is being resolved differently by people who are located differently in the social structure. We have focused on the income variable in this study, but obviously other indicators of social location are important and need to be studied. Research on ideology must become the study of the layman's sociology of the society in which he lives. Only when sociologists have this picture clearly, can they elaborate a theory on the ideology of stratification.

REFERENCES

Campbell, A., Gurin, G., & Miller, W. E. (1954). *The voter decides.* Evansville, IL: Row, Peterson.

Campbell, A., Converse, P. E., Miller, W. E., & Stokes, D. E. (1960). *The American voter.* New York: John Wiley & Sons.

Centers, R. (1949). *The psychology of social classes.* Princeton, NJ: Princeton University Press.

Christie, R., & Jahoda, M. (Eds.). (1954). *Studies in the scope and method of "the authoritarian personality."* Glencoe, IL: The Free Press.

Coleman, J. S. (1968). The concept of equality of educational opportunity. *Harvard Educational Review, 38* (Winter), 7–22.

Cremin, L. (1951). *The American common school: An historical conception.* Teachers' College Studies in Education. New York: Bureau of Publications, Columbia University.

Form, W. H., & Rytina, J. (1969). Income and ideological beliefs on the distribution of power in the United States. *American Sociological Review, 34,* 19–31.

Gross, L. (1949). The use of class concepts in sociological research. *American Journal of Sociology, 54,* 409–421.

Heard, A. (1962). *The costs of democracy.* Garden City, NY: Doubleday.

Jones, A. W. (1941). *Life, liberty and property.* Philadelphia, PA: Lippincott.

Keyserling, L. H. (1964). *Progress or poverty.* Washington, DC: Conference on Economic Progress.

Lipset, S. M. (1963). *The first new nation.* New York: Basic Books.

Lipset, S. M., & Bendix, R. (1959). *Social mobility in industrial society.* Berkeley, CA: University of California Press.

Lipset, S.M., & Rogoff, N. (1954). Class and opportunity in Europe and the United States. *Commentary, 18* (December), 562–568.

McClosky, H., Hoffman, P. J., & O'Hara, R. (1960). Issue conflict and consensus among party leaders and followers. *American Political Science Review, 54* (June), 416.

Mannheim, K. (1954). *Ideology and utopia: An introduction to the sociology of knowledge.* New York: Harcourt Brace Jovanovich.

Miller, H. P. (1965). Changes in the number and composition of the poor. In M. Gordon (Ed.), *Poverty in America.* San Francisco: Chandler.

Miller, S. M., & Rein, M. (1966). Poverty, inequality and policy. In H. S. Becker (Ed.), *Social problems: A modern approach.* New York: John Wiley & Sons.

Mosca, G. (1966). *The ruling class.* Edited by Arthur Livingston, translated by Hannah D. Kahn. New York: McGraw-Hill.

Orshansky, M. (1965). Counting the poor: Another look at the poverty profile. *Social Security Bulletin, 28* (January), 3–29.

Ossowski, S. (1963). *Class structure in the social consciousness.* Translated by Shelia Patterson. New York: The Free Press.

Parsons, T. (1953). A revised analytical approach to the theory of social stratification. In R. Bendix & S. M. Lipset (Eds.), *Class, status and power: A reader in social stratification.* Glencoe, IL: The Free Press.

Prothro, J. W., & Grigg, C. M. (1960). Fundamental principles of democracy: Bases of agreement and disagreement. *Journal of Politics, 22,* 276–294.

Smelser, N. J. (Ed.). (1967). *Sociology.* New York: John Wiley & Sons.

Weber, M. (1946). *From Max Weber: Essays in sociology.* Edited and translated by H. H. Gerth and C. Wright Mills. New York: Oxford University Press.

Westie, F. (1965). The American dilemma: An empirical test. *American Sociological Review, 30,* 527–538.

Williams, R. M., Jr. (1967). *American society.* New York: Alfred A. Knopf.

MINORITIES

> And thus the desire of liberty caused one party to raise themselves in proportion as they oppressed the other. And it is in the course of such movements of men, that in attempting to avoid fear themselves, gave others cause for fear; and the injuries which they ward off from themselves they inflict upon others, as though there were a necessity to oppress or be oppressed.
>
> Niccolò Machiavelli
> *The Prince*

Investigation 5 studied the relationship between an achieved characteristic (occupation) and social stratification. This investigation studies inequality in terms of the relationship between the ascribed characteristics of minorities (such as race and social background) and stratification. Minority groups are created when one group uses accumulated advantages to dominate and exploit other groups. The more powerful group then maintains its advantages with law (*de jure* discrimination) and/or tradition (*de facto* discrimination). The more powerful group is called a dominant group, the subordinate a minority group. Minority groups have less power but need not be smaller in numbers than the majority group. Blacks in South Africa, for example, outnumber the dominant white "majority" by more than nine to one.

Dominant groups seek to defend or advance their interests at the expense of minority groups. To do this, it is necessary that dominant groups justify and explain their discriminatory practices. They frequently do this by identifying cultural and/or racial differences between themselves and minority groups, and then branding the characteristics of minority groups as inferior.

Minority groups may be subdivided into ethnic and racial groups. Ethnic groups are disadvantaged because their national background or culture is different from that of the majority. Racial groups are minority groups that are disadvantaged by physical characteristics that are different from the majority group.

Conflict Perspective

Robert Blauner (1972) has used the conflict perspective to analyze the process by which minorities are exploited. He concludes that the exploitation of minorities is inherent in capitalism. The economic self-interest of the capitalists requires that they pay the working class as little as possible. Racism is a tool capitalists can use to explain why minority groups are in marginal, low-paying jobs. Minorities serve as a pool of surplus labor, giving capitalists a reserve army of unemployed workers. Capitalists use these surplus minority workers to depress the wage scale for *all* workers by threatening to replace employed workers with unemployed ones. Prejudice also fosters antagonism between employed and unemployed workers, thereby dividing and weakening the working class. Economic forces provide important insights into the conditions faced by many minorities, but economic factors do not readily account for some minority groups like the Quakers and Mormons.

Functional Perspective

To understand minorities one must understand the organizational requirements of society. If the society is to have social solidarity there must be a unifying basis of shared beliefs and values. This shared consciousness provides the standard by which members distinguish superior from inferior, normal from abnormal, and the natural from the foreign. William Graham Sumner (1959) considered this the basis of in-group versus out-group distinctions. He believed it was a universal tendency of in-group members to use their standards to evaluate the characteristics of the out-group. He termed this process *ethnocentrism*. Functional analysis suggests that an important function of ethnocentrism is to increase social solidarity. Equally important, though, are the dysfunctional consequences of ethnocentrism, which tend to distort perceptions of those who are different and increase intolerance of and hostility toward foreigners.

Because it performs an indispensable function in holding society together, ethnocentrism will never be completely elimi-

This investigation is based on "Bogardus Social Distance in the 1970s" by Sue R. Crull and Brent T. Bruton, 1975, reprinted on pages 91–95.

Table 7–1

A 40-YEAR RACIAL DISTANCE STUDY
Changes in Racial Distance Indices

I		II		III		IV	
Racial Distance Indices Given Racial Groups in 1926 by 1725 Selected Persons throughout the U.S.		Racial Distance Indices Given Racial Groups in 1946 by 1950 Selected Persons throughout the U.S.		Racial Distance Indices Given Racial Groups in 1956 by 2053 Selected Persons throughout the U.S.		Racial Distance Indices Given Racial Groups in 1966 by 2605 Selected Persons throughout the U.S.	
1. English	1.06	1. Americans (U.S. white)	1.04	1. Americans (U.S. white)	1.08	1. Americans (U.S. white)	1.07
2. Americans (U.S. white)	1.10	2. Canadians	1.11	2. Canadians	1.16	2. English	1.14
3. Canadians	1.13	3. English	1.13	3. English	1.23	3. Canadians	1.15
4. Scots	1.13	4. Irish	1.24	4. French	1.47	4. French	1.36
5. Irish	1.30	5. Scots	1.26	5. Irish	1.56	5. Irish	1.40
6. French	1.32	6. French	1.31	6. Swedish	1.57	6. Swedish	1.42
7. Germans	1.46	7. Norwegians	1.35	7. Scots	1.60	7. Norwegians	1.50
8. Swedish	1.54	8. Hollanders	1.37	8. Germans	1.61	8. Italians	1.51
9. Hollanders	1.56	9. Swedish	1.40	9. Hollanders	1.63	9. Scots	1.53
10. Norwegians	1.59	10. Germans	1.59	10. Norwegians	1.66	10. Germans	1.54
11. Spanish	1.72	11. Finns	1.63	11. Finns	1.80	11. Hollanders	1.54
12. Finns	1.83	12. Czechs	1.76	12. Italians	1.89	12. Finns	1.67
13. Russians	1.88	13. Russians	1.83	13. Poles	2.07	13. Greeks	1.82
14. Italians	1.94	14. Poles	1.84	14. Spanish	2.08	14. Spanish	1.93
15. Poles	2.01	15. Spanish	1.94	15. Greeks	2.09	15. Jews	1.97
16. Armenians	2.06	16. Italians	2.28	16. Jews	2.15	16. Poles	1.98
17. Czechs	2.08	17. Armenians	2.29	17. Czechs	2.22	17. Czechs	2.02
18. Indians (American)	2.38	18. Greeks	2.29	18. Armenians	2.33	18. Indians (American)	2.12
19. Jews	2.39	19. Jews	2.32	19. Japanese Americans	2.34	19. Japanese Americans	2.14
20. Greeks	2.47	20. Indians (American)	2.45	20. Indians (American)	2.35	20. Armenians	2.18
21. Mexicans	2.69	21. Chinese	2.50	21. Filipinos	2.46	21. Filipinos	2.31
22. Mexican Americans	—	22. Mexican Americans	2.52	22. Mexican Americans	2.51	22. Chinese	2.34
23. Japanese	2.80	23. Filipinos	2.76	23. Turks	2.52	23. Mexican Americans	2.37
24. Japanese Americans	—	24. Mexicans	2.89	24. Russians	2.56	24. Russians	2.38
25. Filipinos	3.00	25. Turks	2.89	25. Chinese	2.68	25. Japanese	2.41
26. Negroes	3.28	26. Japanese Americans	2.90	26. Japanese	2.70	26. Turks	2.48
27. Turks	3.30	27. Koreans	3.05	27. Negroes	2.74	27. Koreans	2.51
28. Chinese	3.36	28. Indians (from India)	3.43	28. Mexicans	2.79	28. Mexicans	2.56
29. Koreans	3.60	29. Negroes	3.60	29. Indians (from India)	2.80	29. Negroes	2.56
30. Indians (from India)	3.91	30. Japanese	3.61	30. Koreans	2.83	30. Indians (from India)	2.62
Arithmetic Mean of 48,300 Racial Reactions	2.14	Arithmetic Mean of 58,500 Racial Reactions	2.12	Arithmetic Mean of 61,590 Racial Reactions	2.08	Arithmetic Mean of 78,150 Racial Reactions	1.92
Spread in Distance	2.85	Spread in Distance	2.57	Spread in Distance	1.75	Spread in Distance	1.56

Note: From *A Forty Year Racial Distance Study* (Chart II) by E. Bogardus, 1967. Los Angeles: University of Southern California. Permission granted by Ruth Bogardus Allen.

nated. Recognizing this, many functionalists looked for ways to reduce differences between groups. One approach to reduce prejudice and discrimination was called the melting-pot theory. Its goal was to reduce differences between dominant and minority groups. The process through which these differences are blended into a common culture was called *assimilation*.

From his study of American history, Robert Park (1924) found that assimilation took place in four stages. In the first stage, contacts between native Americans and immigrants are marked by conflict. With the passage of time, the "foreignness" of the immigrants wears off and is replaced by a second stage of antagonistic cooperation, or accommodation. Increased contacts and opportunities for the discovery of mutual interests

leads to a third stage of assimilation. In the fourth stage, cooperation develops as the cultures become indistinguishable and the groups become one.

In Park's first stage, conflict is accompanied by feelings of hatred and antagonism. As conflict subsides, hostility and social distance decline. *Social distance* refers to the level of intimacy that exists between individuals and groups. Closely knit families and communities have high levels of intimacy and little social distance. Between strangers there is likely to be little intimacy or emotional closeness and considerable social distance. Elevated levels of social distance are conducive to opposition, hostility, and conflict. Park hoped to be able to measure social distance and discover how social distance could be reduced.

With this knowledge the process of cultural assimilation could be accelerated.

Emory Bogardus, in collaboration with Park, succeeded in constructing a scale of social distance. He asked respondents to use a series of increasingly intimate relationships to describe their feeling toward various groups. The relationships included in the 1933 version of the scale were as follows: (1) would marry, (2) would have as regular friends, (3) would work beside in an office, (4) would have several families in my neighborhood, (5) would have merely as speaking acquaintances, (6) would want outside my neighborhood, (7) would have to live outside of my country.

Bogardus took periodic social distance surveys to track changes in American minority relations. The results showed a trend of declining social distance (S.D.) over 40 years: in 1926, S.D. = 2.14; 1946, S.D. = 2.12; 1956, S.D. = 2.08; and 1966, S.D. = 1.92. The ratings he found for 30 racial and ethnic groups are presented in Table 7–1 on page 85.

The results of this 40-year study led Bogardus to several conclusions. Although there have been short-term reversals during World War II and the cold war, there has been a clear trend toward declining averages and spans of social distance ratings. If the trend continued, it would result in the melding of American minority groups into a composite culture that would be even more vital than it has been in the past. Bogardus was optimistic the trend would continue. He believed that unless there is some national catastrophe we could expect the trends of the previous 40 years to continue for the next 40 years. These declines in social distance have been fostered by increased opportunities for American youth to meet as equals in school and industry. Communicating as equals stimulates the discovery of what people share in common rather than the differences that set people apart.

Background

After the death of Bogardus in 1973, Sue Crull and Brent Bruton continued monitoring changes in American minority group attitudes. Their 1975 study, the results of which are reprinted in Reading 7 on pages 91–95, dealt with three questions. The first was an assessment of social distance for eight racial and ethnic groups in an attempt to replicate the Bogardus studies. The second question concerned the influence of social contact and social distance of respondents. The final question assessed the social distance of three new groups that were involved in economic or social changes at that time. To measure changes in social distance in 1975, they surveyed 395 men and 648 women in introductory sociology courses at the State University of Iowa. They did not indicate the minority or racial composition of the student raters used in the study.

Social Distance Trend   The surveys taken by Bogardus from 1926 to 1966 showed a small but steady decline in average levels of social distance. The findings of Crull and Bruton "suggest a leveling or even reversal of the long-term trend of decreasing

Table 7–2

AVERAGE SOCIAL DISTANCE TOWARD DEVIANT GROUPS

Groups (In Order of Increasing Distance)	Mean Social Distance
Intellectuals	2.0
Ex-mental patients	2.9
Atheists	3.4
Ex-convicts	3.5
Gamblers	3.6
Beatniks	3.9
Alcoholics	4.0
Adulterers	4.1
Political radicals	4.3
Marijuana smokers	4.9
Prostitutes	5.0
Lesbians	5.2
Male homosexuals	5.3

Note: From *Deviants* (Table 2, p. 33) by J. L. Simmons, 1969. Boston: Boyd & Fraser Publishing Company. Adapted by permission.

responses demonstrating less social distance" (p. 92). In following the work of Crull and Bruton, we will expect to find an increase in social distance levels.

Sex and Contact of Respondent   Crull and Bruton maintained that social contact will lower social distance. They hypothesized that "Women give more rejecting social distance responses because they have less contact with ethnic groups than do men" (p. 92). The most surprising finding of their study was the total lack of support for this hypothesis. In fact, the women in the 1975 survey at the State University of Iowa even showed more tolerance than did men. If Crull and Bruton's results are to be supported by our Student Survey findings, we should expect lower social distance ratings for women than for men.

Controversial groups   Bogardus felt that groups that are seen as politically, economically, or morally threatening will be controversial. These controversial groups will be rated higher in social distance than will noncontroversial groups. This anticipates the research findings of J. L. Simmons (1969). Simmons surveyed 280 subjects regarding their feelings towards 13 deviant groups. The results of his survey are shown in Table 7–2, above.

Simmons found that raters over 40 and the less educated tended to make the most rejecting responses. Males and females differed significantly. Males were significantly more intolerant of male homosexuals. Females were more intolerant of prostitutes and lesbians. Crull and Bruton singled out for study three controversial groups: (1) hippies, for their rejection of middle-class values, (2) Arabs, because of the energy crisis, and (3) homosexuals, for their violation of sexual mores. Crull and Bruton hypothesized that these controversial groups would have higher social distance ratings than would noncontroversial groups. We will test the validity of this hypothesis. (For the sake of maintaining consistency between our study and Crull and Bruton's, we will use the same three groups that Crull and Bruton chose to represent controversial groups.)

Replication

In order to replicate Crull and Bruton's research, we will test the following five hypotheses:

Social Distance Trend

Hypothesis 1:

There will be a leveling or even a reversal of the long-term trend toward decreasing social distance ratings.

Consistency of Social Distance

Hypothesis 2:

There will be a significant continuity in social distance ratings between the Crull and Bruton study and our survey results.

Social Contact

Hypothesis 3:

People who have had contact with minority groups will give lower social distance ratings than will those who have had no contact.

Social Distance by Sex

Hypothesis 4:

Males will give higher social distance ratings than women will.

Controversial Groups

Hypothesis 5:

Controversial groups will be rated among the highest in social distance. Hippies, Arabs, and homosexuals will have higher social distance scores than the eight noncontroversial groups.

To test these hypotheses, you will need your class's responses to questions 11–A and 11–B on the Student Survey, which will be provided to you by your instructor. In this investigation the dependent variable, social distance, is measured by question 11–A on the Student Survey. This asks for the social distance ratings of 12 groups (the rating scale has undergone some evolution since Bogardus's 1933 version). Two

---

STUDENT SURVEY QUESTION 11

11-A. Circle the number (1–7) that indicates the closest degree to which you would be willing to admit members of each of the groups listed. Make sure your reactions are to each group as a whole, not to the best or worst members you have known. Some groups you may not know personally. In such cases give your general feeling or first feeling.

(7) Exclude from my country
(6) As visitors to my country
(5) Speaking acquaintance only
(4) Work beside in an office
(3) As neighbors on my street
(2) As very good friends
(1) Close kinship by marriage

SOCIAL GROUP							
A. Arabs	1	2	3	4	5	6	7
B. Blacks	1	2	3	4	5	6	7
C. Canadians*	1	2	3	4	5	6	7
D. Chinese	1	2	3	4	5	6	7
E. Germans	1	2	3	4	5	6	7
F. Hippies	1	2	3	4	5	6	7
G. Homosexuals	1	2	3	4	5	6	7
H. Italians	1	2	3	4	5	6	7
I. Jews	1	2	3	4	5	6	7
J. Pireneans	1	2	3	4	5	6	7
K. Russians	1	2	3	4	5	6	7
L. Turks	1	2	3	4	5	6	7

11-B. Do you know anyone from these groups? Circle the letter Y or N that best describes the type of contact you have had with each group.

(Y) YES personal contact
(N) NO personal contact

A.	Arabs	Y	N
B.	Blacks	Y	N
C.	Canadians*	Y	N
D.	Chinese	Y	N
E.	Germans	Y	N
F.	Hippies	Y	N
G.	Homosexuals	Y	N
H.	Italians	Y	N
I.	Jews	Y	N
J.	Pireneans	Y	N
K.	Russians	Y	N
L.	Turks	Y	N

*If survey is taken in Canada, substitute "Americans."

---

independent variables are sex and social contact. Sex is determined by item 1 and social contact by item 11-B on the Student Survey. When you have received the class's results from your instructor, proceed as follows:

Step 1:

Turn to the social distance scale in the Student Survey. Then enter your responses to part A of question 11 in the column marked My Score in Investigation Results 7 on page 88, to simplify comparing your ratings to those of the class. To determine your average social distance, sum the ratings you gave the 11 groups listed and divide by 11.

Table 7–3

INVESTIGATION RESULTS 7
Social Distance Ratings

Group	Previous Surveys			Current Student Survey					
	1956	1966	1975	My Score	Class Average	Men	Women	Contact	No Contact
Canadians*	1.16	1.15	1.69	____	____	____	____	____	____
Germans	1.61	1.54	1.89	____	____	____	____	____	____
Italians	1.89	1.51	1.91	____	____	____	____	____	____
Jews	2.15	1.97	2.24	____	____	____	____	____	____
Blacks	2.74	2.56	2.48	____	____	____	____	____	____
Chinese	2.68	2.34	2.77	____	____	____	____	____	____
Turks	2.56	2.48	2.96	____	____	____	____	____	____
Russians	2.56	2.38	2.97	____	____	____	____	____	____
Hippies†			3.21	____	____	____	____	____	____
Arabs†			3.25	____	____	____	____	____	____
Homosexuals†			4.74	____	____	____	____	____	____
Average Social Distance			2.74	____	____	____	____	____	____

*If survey is taken in Canada, substitute "Americans."
†Controversial groups.
Note: Previous survey data are from Table 1, p. 92.

Step 2:

Fill in the rest of the Investigation Results table, using the information provided by your instructor.

Step 3:

Use the information in the Investigation Results table to fill in the blanks in the hypotheses below:

Social Distance Trend

Hypothesis 1:

There will be a leveling or even a reversal of the long-term trend toward decreasing social distance ratings.

My class's average social distance   ____ ≥ 2.74   Crull and Bruton average social distance

Consistency of Social Distance

Hypothesis 2:

There will be a significant continuity in social distance ratings between the Crull and Bruton study and our survey results.

Replication correlation   ____ ≥   Rho +.564

Social Contact

Hypothesis 3:

People who have had contact with minority groups will give lower social distance (S.D.) ratings than will those who have had no contact.

Average S.D. with contact   ____ > ____   Average S.D. without contact

Social Distance by Sex

Hypothesis 4:

Males will give higher social distance ratings than women will.

$$\bar{X}m = \text{_____} > \bar{X}w = \text{_____}$$

Controversial Groups

Hypothesis 5:

Controversial groups will be rated among the highest in social distance. Hippies, Arabs, and homosexuals ($\bar{X}c$)

Table 7–4

SUPPORT FOR HYPOTHESES

	Significantly Supported	Partially Supported	Not Supported	Indeterminate
Hypothesis 1: Social distance trend	_____	_____	_____	_____
Hypothesis 2: Rho 1975 and survey	_____	_____	_____	_____
Hypothesis 3: Contact vs. no contact	_____	_____	_____	_____
Hypothesis 4: Male vs. female	_____	_____	_____	_____
Hypothesis 5: Controversial groups	_____	_____	_____	_____

Indicate the amount of support you found for each hypothesis.

will have higher social distance scores than the eight noncontroversial groups ($\bar{X}nc$).

$$\bar{X}c = \text{_____} > \bar{X}nc = \text{_____}$$

Checking Your Findings

Hypothesis 1 generalizes national trends from the ratings of a single college class. We should not have too much confidence in this, because social distance can vary for a variety of reasons unrelated to trends. One of these reasons is regional variation. A 1977 national survey by Carolyn Owen, Howard Eisner, and Thomas McFaul (1981) regarding 30 ethnic groups (not including the high-scoring controversial groups, hippies, homosexuals, and Arabs) found average social distance varied greatly by region: West, 1.82; Midwest, 1.84; East, 2.01; South, 2.17. The highest overall score of 2.49 came from a college in the South. You must decide whether your results are representative of other American students or whether they are unique to your class. If you consider the results unique, what social characteristics would account for this (religious denomination, social class, fundamentalism, ethnic background, liberal arts versus pre-professional major)?

Hypothesis 2 asks, Is prejudice a social fact? That is, are social distance ratings consistent over time? Earlier we noted that Bogardus found social distance ratings remarkably stable over time. White Americans and Northern Europeans were rated in the top third, Eastern and Southern Europeans in the middle third, and Asian minorities in the bottom third of the social distance hierarchy. To see if this consistency is present in your data, look at the correlation between your findings and the 1975 study. A significant (.05) correlation must be larger than +.564, according to the table, "Critical Values of Rho," on page 201. After the question of rating consistency is answered,

we can look at the changes for individual minorities. Start by identifying the group or groups with the greatest changes. What do you think caused the changes?

Hypothesis 3 states that social contact will reduce prejudice. The hypothesis seems simple enough. Unfortunately, the social contact hypothesis is a little more complicated than this. If social contact reduces prejudice, why did black prejudice not decline first among Southern slave owners? Gordon Allport (1954) believed that this was because social contact only reduces prejudice when the contact is between equals. Prejudice remains high when contact occurs between unequal groups (such as master and slave). Yehuda Amir (1969) adds that even contact between equal groups may intensify prejudice if the contact is competitive. This explains the high level of prejudice between poor whites and blacks who are competing for the same manual-labor jobs. To lower prejudice, contact must be between non-competitive groups of equal status. To the extent that these factors are not operating in our study, we can expect that the differences in prejudice levels between groups with and without contact will be reduced.

Hypothesis 4 evaluates the mixed research findings regarding social distance ratings of males and females. Bogardus (1959) found women had higher social distance ratings than did men. By contrast, Crull and Bruton (Reading 7) found women had lower social distance ratings than did men. In your survey, did you find males or females to have the higher social distance ratings?

Hypothesis 5 states that deviants will be rated higher than nondeviants. Did you find that controversial groups had the highest social distance ratings? Did you find, as Simmons (1969) did, that of all groups evaluated by males, homosexuals were rated highest in social distance? If the rating of the deviant group is over 4.0, you may want to consider that Bogardus

(1967) found virtually all social distance ratings for nondeviant groups to fall between 1.0 and 3.5. Only an exceptional person used the upper limit of the scale. But this is not the case when deviant groups are rated. For homosexuals, 7.0 ("exclude from my country") is not an unusual rating; occasionally it is the most frequent rating. To avoid a ceiling effect, the scale would have to be extended beyond 7.0. What might constitute items 8.0, 9.0, and 10.0 in an extended social distance scale?

Summarize the findings of your investigation in Table 7–4 on page 89 by checking the amount of support found in this investigation for each of the five hypotheses.

Topic for Further Investigation

Eugene Hartley (1952) believed that minority group attitudes were not caused by minority group characteristics. Rather, social distance is a personal characteristic of the rater. Much like reacting to an ink blot, prejudiced individuals tend to project their feelings onto minority groups. To test this idea, he asked students to rate three nonexistent groups (Danirean, Pirenean, and Wallonian) along with 32 other minority groups. Since the social distance ratings could not be caused by characteristics of the fictitious groups, the social distance ratings would have to be the product of the individual rater. His results indicated a close correspondence between the individual's average social distance ratings of the 32 minority groups and the ratings given to the fictitious groups. To repeat this study, compare the average social distance scores of the raters with ratings of the nonexistent Pireneans. Support for Hartley's hypothesis will be provided to the degree to which you find the social distance of the rater correlated with the rating of the Pireneans.

References and Recommended Readings

Allport, G. (1954). *The nature of prejudice*. Reading, MA: Addison-Wesley.

Amir, Y. (1969). Contact hypothesis in ethnic relations. *Psychological Bulletin, 71*, 319–342.

Banton, M. (1967). Social distance. Chapter 10 in *Race relations*. New York: Basic Books.

Blauner, R. (1972). *Racial oppression in America*. New York: Harper & Row.

Bogardus, E. (1959). *Social distance*. Yellow Springs, OH: Antioch Press.

Bogardus, E. (1967). *A forty year racial distance study*. Los Angeles: University of Southern California Press.

Bonacich, E. (1972). A theory of ethnic antagonism: The split labor market. *American Sociological Review, 37*, 547–559.

Crull, S., & Bruton, B. (1979). Bogardus social distance in the 1970s. *Sociology and Social Research, 63*, 771–783.

Crull, S., & Bruton, B. (1985). Possible decline in tolerance towards minorities: Social distance on a midwest campus. *Sociology and Social Research, 70*, 57–62.

Hartley, E., & Hartley, R. (1952). *Problems in prejudice*. New York: Columbia University Press.

Klineberg, O. (1950). *Tensions affecting international understanding: A survey of research*. (Bulletin No. 62). New York: Social Science Research Council.

LaPiere, R. (1936). Type-rationalizations of group antipathy. *Social Forces, 15*, 649–652.

Owen, C., Eisner, H., & McFaul, E. (1981). A half-century of social distance research: National replication of Bogardus' studies. *Sociology and Social Research, 66*, 80–98.

Park, R. (1924). The concept of social distance. *Journal of Applied Sociology, 8*, 339–344.

Robinson, J., Rusk, J., & Head, K. (1969). Racial and ethnic attitudes. Chap. 6 in *Measures of political attitudes*. Ann Arbor, MI: Institute for Social Research.

Simmons, J. L. (1969). *Deviants*. Berkeley, CA: Boyd & Fraser.

Sumner, W. G. (1959). *Folkways*. New York: Dover.

Westie, F., & Westie, M. (1967). The social distance pyramid: Relationships between caste and class. *American Journal of Sociology, 63*, 190–196.

Bogardus Social Distance in the 1970s

Bogardus collected data over a forty-year period to assess the social distance ratings of students to various ethnic and racial groups. Generally, over time, Bogardus found the social distance scores slowly decreased.

In 1975, a social distance scale was administered to 1043 college students. Eight ethnic groups from the original Bogardus studies and three new groups were included in the study. Analysis shows that the social distance scores in 1975 for comparable ethnic groups were slightly higher than the scores for the 1950s and 1960s. Also the 1975 scores for female respondents were lower (reflecting less social distance) than the scores for the males, which is a reversal of the previous Bogardus studies. Students who have had contact with a group averaged lower social distance scores than did the students who had not had personal contact with the ethnic group. This latter finding is consistent with previous Bogardus studies. The three new groups (Arabs, "hippies," and homosexuals) received much higher social distance scores than did any of the eight groups involved in the previous social distance studies.

Sue R. Crull
Brent T. Bruton
Iowa State University

INTRODUCTION

Emory S. Bogardus analyzed social distance, the feelings of acceptance or rejection for different racial and ethnic groups for over forty years, using the social distance scale. The last study done by Bogardus was in 1966. The purpose of the study was to continue the social distance analysis and consider social distance ratings in the 1970s. Bogardus found that generally over time (1926, 1946, 1956, and 1966) social distance ratings of students to various ethnic and racial groups decreased. Bogardus (1967) believed that his findings over time represented social trends and perhaps a general social movement. He also found that men generally gave lower social distance scores than did women and that the social distance scores of women were decreasing. He believed that if they continued to decrease as they had from 1956 to 1966, the difference between men's and women's reactions would eventually disappear. One wonders what Bogardus would have hypothesized in the 1970s with ERA and the women's liberation movement.

The goals in this study were three-fold. The first was to replicate the Bogardus studies in order to assess change in the social distance ratings of eight racial and ethnic groups in 1975.

The second was to assess the social distance ratings of three new groups that were involved in economic or moral issues of the times. The third goal was to analyze the influence of the sex of the respondents and the contact of the respondents with the ethnic groups on their social distance responses. Three hypotheses were developed for the latter goal.

Social Distance Trend:

Bogardus used the same social distance scale in all four studies. Also each study involved a similar sample of college students from many areas of the U.S. Although the social distance responses to specific groups varied because of issues and feelings of the times, arithmetic means of the reactions toward all racial and ethnic groups showed a decline in distance reactions from 1926 to 1966, with the greatest decline coming in the 1956 to 1966 period (Bogardus: 1958, 1967). Studies done by Payne et al. (1974) and Warheit et al. (1975) also give some support to the idea that social distance scores have decreased over time.

Controversial Groups:

In 1958, Bogardus suggested that a specific racial or ethnic group's social distance rating may be high if situations develop that arouse an awareness of insecurity, a sense of fear, or a loss of status between the specific group and the respondents. Examples given by Bogardus (1958) were that the cold war raised the social distance score for the Russians in 1956 from the allies situation in 1946, and the high social distance scores for Japanese decreased in 1956 after World War II and Japan's shift

Reprinted with permission from *Sociology and Social Research, 63*, 1979, pp. 771–783.

toward democracy. In this study, Arabs were included because of their involvement in the economics of the energy crisis; "hippies" were included because of their contrast to traditional values and the work ethic, and the homosexuals were included because of their conflict with conventional mores. All three groups were considered to be involved in controversial issues of the 1970s, and, based on Bogardus' ideas, one would expect the three groups to have the highest social distance ratings.

Sex and Contact of Respondent:

Hypothesis 1:

Women make more rejecting social distance responses to various ethnic groups than do men.

Numerous studies have found women to hold more prejudicial attitudes than men. Both Bogardus (1958) and Ames et al. (1968) found that women showed greater social distance than men. Triandis and Triandis (1972) provide support for this hypothesis in their study of social distance in the 1960s, and Pettigrew's (1972) study in 1955 on racial attitudes also lends support.

Hypothesis 2:

People who have had contact with ethnic groups give lower social distance responses than do those who have had no contact.

Hypothesis 3:

Fewer women than men have contact with people of other racial and ethnic groups.

Both Bogardus (1958) and Ames et al. (1968) discuss the sex difference in social distance responses in terms of contact with racial and ethnic groups. They both assumed that contact lowered prejudicial feelings. Amir (1972) admits that the contact and positive attitude assumption is popular, but feels that the generalization is naive and that contact could produce negative attitudes under certain circumstances. Warheit et al. (1975) addressed the negative aspect in terms of forced busing and school integration. Bogardus (1958) used the contact assumption to suggest the hypothesis: "The greater racial distance expressed by women than by men may be accounted for in part on the ground that men have more racial contacts than women have" (p. 441). According to Ames et al. (1968), Bogardus pointed out that women had less contact with people of other races than men because of restricted movement and lack of work contacts.

If hypotheses 1, 2, and 3 are supported, the following generalization based on Bogardus' rationale would seem appropriate:

Women give more rejecting social distance responses because they have less contact with ethnic groups than do men. No empirical study has included an analysis of the relationship of sex and contact of the respondent to social distance responses.

Table 1

MEANS AND STANDARD DEVIATIONS FOR SOCIAL DISTANCE RESPONSES TO SELECTED RACIAL AND ETHNIC GROUPS

	1956 Bogardus Total Sample Mean	1966 Bogardus Total Sample Mean	1975 College Student Sample Mean	1975 College Student Sample Std. Dev.
Canadians	1.16	1.15	1.69	1.11
Germans	1.61	1.54	1.89	1.27
Italians	1.89	1.51	1.91	1.23
Jews	2.15	1.97	2.24	1.26
Blacks	2.74	2.56	2.48	1.22
Chinese	2.68	2.34	2.77	1.51
Turks	2.56	2.48	2.96	1.71
Russians	2.56	2.38	2.97	1.85
Hippies	—	—	3.21	1.66
Arabs	—	—	3.25	1.82
Homosexuals	—	—	4.74	1.57
N	2053	2383	1043	

METHODOLOGY

An availability sample of 1043 introductory sociology students responded to the request to provide information for this study. The Bogardus social distance scale was presented as follows:

1. close kinship by marriage
2. very good friends
3. as my neighbors
4. same work group
5. speaking acquaintance only
6. as visitors only to my country
7. exclude from my country

Each respondent was asked to designate the groups with which he or she had had personal contact.

While the sample has limitations, the 1043 students in a required core course are quite representative of lower division students at a major midwestern state university. Thus, the sample is roughly comparable to the sample in the Bogardus studies. It must be remembered that Bogardus used college student respondents from 32 well-distributed areas over the U.S.; therefore, to provide comparability it is appropriate to again take a college sample. Analysis of variance was the major technique used in the analysis of the mean social distance scores. Chi-square was used to test the sex and contact proportions. Results from multiple regression with dummy variables were also considered.

FINDINGS

Social distance trend: The data in Table 1 suggest a leveling or even reversal of the long-term trend of decreasing responses demonstrating less social distance. With the exception of blacks,

Table 2

MEANS AND STANDARD DEVIATIONS FOR SOCIAL DISTANCE RESPONSES TO SELECTED RACIAL AND ETHNIC GROUPS CLASSIFIED BY SEX OF THE RESPONDENT

	Male		Female	
	Mean	Std. Dev.	Mean	Std. Dev.
Canadians*	1.80	1.19	1.62	1.05
Germans*	2.08	1.42	1.77	1.15
Italians*	2.15	1.42	1.77	1.07
Jews*	2.49	1.47	2.10	1.10
Blacks*	2.65	1.35	2.38	1.12
Chinese*	3.16	1.68	2.53	1.35
Turks*	3.25	1.84	2.78	1.60
Russians*	3.12	1.92	2.88	1.81
Hippies	3.29	1.75	3.15	1.61
Arabs*	3.54	1.93	3.08	1.72
Homosexuals*	5.10	1.60	4.51	1.53
N	395		648	

*Means significantly different at the .05 level.

Table 3

MEANS AND STANDARD DEVIATIONS FOR SOCIAL DISTANCE RESPONSES TO SELECTED RACIAL AND ETHNIC GROUPS CLASSIFIED BY CONTACT

	% of 1043 students who had contact with the group	Contact		No contact	
		Mean	Std. Dev.	Mean	Std. Dev.
Canadians*	70%	1.61	1.03	1.88	1.24
Germans*	76%	1.72	1.10	2.45	1.56
Italians*	72%	1.78	1.11	2.26	1.43
Jews*	75%	2.10	1.15	2.68	1.48
Blacks	94%	2.47	1.21	2.68	1.31
Chinese*	49%	2.51	1.41	3.02	1.56
Turks*	13%	2.36	1.49	3.05	1.72
Russians*	14%	2.54	1.59	3.04	1.88
Hippies*	73%	2.93	1.62	3.96	1.55
Arabs*	31%	2.97	1.78	3.38	1.82
Homosexuals*	25%	4.01	1.70	4.98	1.46

*Means significantly different at the .05 level.

the mean social distance scores found in the present study exceed that of the Bogardus studies in 1966 and even 1956.

It is not likely that this apparent reversal is simply an artifact of the sample. The present study covers only one area of the U.S.—the upper middle west. This area, referred to by Bogardus as the North Middle region, was characterized by a relative high level of tolerance compared to other regions (Bogardus 1959a). Since Bogardus did present regional data, the evidence strongly suggests that this reversal of social distance trends is not due to sample selection. The trend is quite consistent through the groups considered, and merits further investigation in other regions. Apparently the data reflect a new conservative exclusive ethos among college students in the mid-1970s.

Controversial groups: The three controversial groups added for consideration in the present study were regarded with attitudes involving a rather high degree of exclusiveness (see Table 1, p. 92). The vague referent "hippies" received a comparatively high mean social distance response of 3.21. Arabs received an almost identical score of 3.25. Homosexuals received the highest or most exclusive social distance scores of any of the groups considered (4.74). Bogardus's idea was generally supported. Arabs (with political and economic differences) and "hippies" (with value differences) received higher scores than any group differing merely in terms of ethnicity, while homosexuals (with clear differences at the level of social mores) received the scores reflecting greatest social distance. Although blacks may be considered a controversial group by individuals deeply involved in issues such as affirmative action and busing, blacks were not defined as controversial in this study because they are a part of the traditional American social

structure, not deviant by choice, and do not per se threaten the political, moral or economic values of our society.

Sex and contact of the respondent: The most surprising finding in the present study was the total lack of support for the conclusions of earlier studies with regard to the differences in responses by sex (see Table 2, above). In complete contrast to the findings of earlier research, females in the present study had consistently and generally significantly lower social distance scores than males. That is, female respondents displayed more tolerance for the groups considered than did their male counterparts.

Given the sample size and the consistency of this tendency through the groups considered, it seems highly unlikely that this reversal is a chance occurrence. It appears that as women now enter college in great numbers, enter male-dominated fields, and have increased awareness of discrimination on the basis of sex, they become more tolerant of ethnic and life style differences.

Hypothesis 2: Clearly and generally to a statistically significant degree respondents who had had contact with an ethnic or other minority group tended to have greater tolerance than those who had not had such social contact (see Table 3, above). The one exception is in the case of blacks. Here the relationship is reversed, but not significantly.

The data offer limited support for the contact hypothesis. However, there is no attempt here to infer causality, even though that may have been the attempt of some earlier studies. For example, certainly those who are more tolerant of homosexuals are more likely to allow themselves to come into social contact with homosexuals. The six percent of the sample who claimed to have had no contact with blacks in such a university setting

Table 4

MEANS FOR SOCIAL DISTANCE RESPONSES TO SELECTED RACIAL AND ETHNIC GROUPS FOR RESPONDENTS CLASSIFIED BY SEX AND CONTACT

	% of 395 males who had contact		% of 648 females who had contact	Contact		No Contact	
				Males Mean	Females Mean	Males Mean	Females Mean
Canadians[a]	73%	*	68%	1.74	1.52	1.96	1.84
Germans[b]	80%	*	74%	1.84	1.62	3.00	2.20
Italians[b]	73%		71%	1.95	1.67	2.69	2.00
Jews[b]	77%		74%	2.35	1.94	2.94	2.53
Blacks[b]	96%	*	92%	2.60	2.39	3.87	2.30
Chinese[b]	54%	*	46%	2.89	2.24	3.46	2.78
Turks[b]	17%	*	10%	2.48	2.23	3.41	2.84
Russians	17%	*	12%	2.74	2.37	3.19	2.95
Hippies	78%	*	70%	3.04	2.85	4.17	3.87
Arabs[b]	44%	*	23%	3.18	2.71	3.82	3.19
Homosexuals[b]	30%	*	22%	4.44	3.64	5.38	4.77

[a]Means significantly different at the .05 level comparing males with contact and females with contact.
[b]Means significantly different at the .05 level comparing males without contact and females without contact.
*Proportions differ significantly at the .05 level.

would almost have had to make a deliberate attempt to avoid such contact.

Hypothesis 3: Fewer females reported contact with other ethnic groups than did males. This finding was consistent throughout the groups considered, and proportions differed significantly for 9 of the 11 groups. In most cases the male-female social distance differences in relation to contact were significant (see Table 4, above). Thus the findings of the present study support the propositions 2 and 3 advanced earlier by studies with regard to sex of respondent and contact with other ethnic groups. To better understand the relationship of contact to social distance, the measure should contain indications of the nature (positive or negative) and frequency and/or intensity of the contact.

However, since Hypothesis 1 was not supported, the generalization that women give more rejecting social distance responses because they have less contact with ethnic groups than do men becomes moot. Contact did seem to lower the social distance responses, and proportionally fewer women than men had contact with the minority groups. But generally the men gave the more rejecting social distance responses. Contact with an ethnic or other minority group was associated with less social distance for both males and females; however, with or without control for contact, female respondents were characterized by lower or more inclusive social distance scores than were male respondents.

Although the means were significantly different, the differences do not have to be great to be significantly different with such a large sample. To assess the extent to which gender and contact explained the variation of social distance scores, regression analysis was run for each of the 11 racial and ethnic groups. The r^2s of the regression analysis of social distance with

contact, gender of the respondent, and the interaction between gender of the respondent and contact ranged from .01 for Russians to .11 for homosexuals. The regression for each minority group was significant at the .05 level. Both the sex of the respondent and the contact of the respondent with the minority group were significant, individual, independent variables in most cases. The interaction variable was generally insignificant. Although sex and contact of the respondent did not generally explain much variance in the social distance scores, they were significant and consistent variables and should be included in future studies.

SUMMARY

Bogardus collected data over a 40-year period to assess college students' social distance ratings to various ethnic and racial groups. Bogardus found that over time social distance scores slowly decreased. Only groups involved in controversial issues of the times appeared to have increasing social distance scores. Eight racial and ethnic groups from the original Bogardus studies were included in this study, and all but one of the groups averaged higher social distance scores than they did in 1966 or even 1956. While it is recognized that social distance deals with only one facet of racial attitudes, this increase in social distance scores likely is an indication of more conservatism in racial and ethnic attitudes in the mid-1970s.

New groups were included in the study to assess the social distance ratings of groups involved in controversial issues of the 1970s. All three groups (Arabs, "hippies" and homosexuals) received much higher social distance scores than did any of the eight groups involved in the previous social distance studies.

Results of previous social distance studies revealed that female respondents generally gave more rejecting social distance responses than did males. Bogardus and others generalized that the higher social distance responses of females might be accounted for in part on the ground that males had more racial and ethnic contacts than females.

Findings in this study support the assumption of Bogardus that respondents who have had contact with ethnic and racial groups do give lower social distance responses than do those who have not had contact. Also, the results give support to Bogardus' speculation that more men than women have contact with minority groups. However, the results undermine the rationale of the Bogardus generalization. The social distance scores for female respondents were lower (reflecting less social distance) than were the scores for the male respondents, which is a reversal of the previous studies. Therefore, contact does not appear to be the underlying dimension in determining differences in social distance scores of male and female respondents. Possibly the women of the 1970s are more tolerant of minorities than men because they, the "new" minority of the 1970s, are more conscious of the effects of discrimination.*

---

*Preliminary analysis of a comparable 1978 sample indicates verification of male-female reversal in social distance scores and a continuation of the upward trend in social distance scores overall.

REFERENCES

Ames, R. G., & Sakuma, A. F. (1969). Criteria for evaluation of others: A re-examination of the Bogardus social distance scale. *Sociology and Social Research, 54,* 5–24.

Ames, R. G., Moriwaki, S. Y., & Basu, A. K. (1968). Sex differences in social distance: A research report. *Sociology and Social Research, 52,* 280–289.

Amir, Y. (1972) Contact hypothesis in ethnic relations. In J. Brigham & T. Weissbach (Eds.), *Racial attitudes in America: Analysis and findings of social psychology.* New York: Harper & Row.

Bogardus, E. S. (1925a). Measuring social distance. *Journal of Applied Sociology, IX,* 299–308.

Bogardus, E. S. (1925b). Social distance and its origins. *Journal of Applied Sociology, IX,* 216–225.

Bogardus, E. S. (1933). A social distance scale. *Sociology and Social Research, 17,* 265–271.

Bogardus, E. S. (1951). Measuring changes in ethnic reactions. *American Sociological Review, 16,* 48–53.

Bogardus, E. S. (1958). Racial distance changes in the United States during the past thirty years. *Sociology and Social Research, 43,* 127–135.

Bogardus, E. S. (1959a). Racial reactions by regions. *Sociology and Social Research, 43,* 287–290.

Bogardus, E. S. (1959b). Race reactions by sexes. *Sociology and Social Research, 43,* 439–441.

Bogardus, E. S. (1967). *A forty year racial distance study.* Los Angeles: University of Southern California Press.

Payne, M. C., Jr., York, C. M., & Fagen, J. (1974). Changes in measured social distance over time. *Sociometry, 37,* 131–136.

Pettigrew, T. F. (1972). Regional differences in anti-Negro prejudice. In J. Brigham and T. Weissbach (Eds.), *Racial attitudes in America: Analysis and findings of social psychology.* New York: Harper & Row.

Triandis, H. C., & Triandis, L. M. (1972). Some studies of social distance. In J. Brigham and T. Weissbach (Eds.), *Racial attitudes in America: Analysis and findings of social psychology.* New York: Harper & Row.

Warheit, G. J., Swanson, E., & Schwab, J. J. (1973). A study of racial attitudes in a southeastern county: A confirmation of national trends. *Phylon, 36,* 395–406.

RELIGION

> I remember my buddies of years ago, in the hallways still, frozen on the needle; and my brother saying to me once, "If Harlem didn't have so many churches and junkies, there'd be blood flowing in the streets."
>
> James Baldwin
> *The Fire Next Time*

All United States coins and bills proclaim "In God We Trust." The highest legislative bodies in the country begin their business with a prayer. Teams gather together in locker rooms for pre-game prayer. Athletic events often begin with an invocation. Among all industrial nations, Americans are a uniquely religious people. In view of the pervasiveness of religion, it would be easy to suppose that Americans also agree about the supernatural, and what constitutes appropriate religious practice. Such a conclusion would be quite contrary to a growing body of evidence. Research indicates that there is a rich diversity of religious practice and belief even within small and apparently homogeneous American communities.

In community studies by A. B. Hollingshead (1949) and W. Lloyd Warner (1949), indices of social class were devised that allowed the researchers to identify and place families in social classes. They found that there was a close connection between class and church membership. Characteristically, working-class people were members of Baptist and sectarian denominations, while the upper class affiliated with Presbyterian and Episcopalian denominations. Hollingshead's study of "Elmtown," a small town in northern Illinois, found working-class people less likely to be church members. When they were, they were members of blue-collar churches. A strong connection between social class and religious affiliation has been repeatedly found in national surveys. Results of the General Social Survey from 1975 to 1984 indicate the upper-class tendency to join Episcopalian and Presbyterian churches, while the lower class tend to join sectarian and Baptist churches (see Table 8–1, p. 97).

Since it is unusual to have an opportunity to visit a cross section of churches in a community and discover their diversity, Liston Pope's book *Millhands and Preachers* (1942) gives us an informative and frequently surprising insight into religious differences in a small textile mill town in Gastonia, North Carolina. A group of investigators revisited Gastonia in the 1970s and updated Pope's study in *Spindles and Spires* (Earle, Knudsen, & Shriver, 1976). Although great changes had obviously occurred in the interval, the underlying connection between social class and religion remained evident. Earle et al. identified five strata of religious groups in Gastonia: uptown, transitional, middle-class, sectarian, and black. Their book provides a guided tour of the five religious groups. We will follow part of their tour and visit three of the groups.*

The Uptown Church The uptown church traces its origins back to the beginning of Gastonia. The church facilities are extensive and its buildings imposing. Two full-time ministers are employed on its staff. They are well educated and are charged with the intellectual instruction of the members. The congregation is mostly made up of those employed in professional, managerial, and proprietary occupations. A large proportion of the congregation has either college or advanced degrees. The intellectual background of the ministers and church members gives the church a distinctly formal quality. Furthermore, the positions that are taken on spiritual issues tend to find compromise and accommodation with the secular world. Earle et al. now begin our tour by walking up

> concrete stairs flanked by neatly sculptured shrubbery. [You are] greeted at the door by an usher and escorted to a seat. The sanctuary has stained glass windows, carpeted floor, padded pews, and elaborately decorated pulpit furniture. About 500 people, most of whom are middle-aged or older, all well attired, are present for the prelude, written by a classical composer and skillfully played on a pipe organ. The printed bulletin indicates the order of service, but also lists a large number of board meetings

---

This investigation is based on "Faith, Hope OR Charity: A Look at Church Sermons and Social Class," by Bart Dredge, 1986, reprinted on pages 105–109.

*Passages from *Spindles and Spires,* 1976, by John Earle, Dean D. Knudsen, and Donald W. Shriver, Jr., used by permission.

Table 8–1

RELIGIOUS MEMBERSHIP BY SOCIOECONOMIC STATUS
(in percent)

Membership	Socioeconomic Status				Total N
	Upper Class	Middle Class	Working Class	Lower Class	
Catholic	25.2	26.2	26.1	22.5	4,262
Jewish	51.8	21.8	14.7	11.7	394
Baptist	14.9	18.2	29.0	37.8	3,595
Methodist	26.2	25.1	25.1	23.6	2,031
Lutheran	22.6	28.7	26.8	21.9	1,324
Presbyterian	40.2	24.3	21.8	13.7	786
Episcopal	51.5	21.6	16.2	10.7	439
Sectarian	20.8	23.3	24.7	31.2	2,211

Note: From General Social Surveys, 1975–1984, by the National Opinion Research Center, University of Chicago. Reprinted by permission.

and interest groups, scheduled for the coming week. During a processional hymn, the robed choir enters, followed by the ministers. The service follows the printed program without introduction and is conducted with great dignity and formality. The atmosphere of the service is suffused with a sense of stability, permanence, and devotion to time-honored truth.

The Transitional Church   This church is transitional in that it stands between the formality of the uptown church and the sectarian churches of the mill village workers. Members of the transitional church are drawn largely from upper blue-collar occupations that vary considerably in income and educational requirements. The church is probably Baptist or Methodist. As we approach from a paved parking lot, we are

greeted by several people at the door, and . . . directed to a seat by an usher. The decor of the sanctuary indicates the moderate prosperity of the congregation. In addition to an organ, there is carpeting, a divided chapel, unpretentious but attractive stained glass windows, overhead medieval-style lights, and modern, simple, pulpit furniture. Present are about 250 well-dressed persons, mostly in their 30's and 40's. The mimeographed bulletin describes a rather formal structure for the service, with written and pastoral prayers, public affirmation of faith and scripture reading. In spite of the formal character of the order of service, it is frequently interrupted for announcements or other concerns. The sermon is well prepared and delivered with enthusiasm by the pastor.

The Sect   Rodney Stark (1972) believes that the poor participate most fully in sectarian activities that meet emotional needs and provide answers to problems deriving from deprivation. Here emphasis is given to membership within a small and more exclusive community of believers. Sect members are more likely to view themselves as the "elect" and deny pleasures of the flesh and the importance of material wealth. In comparison

with churches like the uptown church, their beliefs are more literal and absolute. Through sectarian involvement, those with little worldly power can find compensation and comfort. In the sect, material possessions and wealth in this world are condemned, with spirituality to be rewarded in another world. Such beliefs reverse the secular status order: the first become last and the last become first. The poor, for example, can take comfort in the belief that it is harder for a rich man to get into Heaven than for a camel to pass through the eye of a needle. Similarly, they can find comfort in the hymn by B. B. McKinney:

Have you failed in your plan of your storm-tossed life?
Place your hand in the nail-scarred hand;
Are you weary and worn from its toil and strife?
Place your hand in the nail-scarred hand;
Are you walking alone thro' the shadows dim?
Place your hand in the nail-scarred hand.

Liston Pope (1942) claims that the mill owners founded the sects in order to create a more compliant labor pool. Pope notes that the Gastonia sects are almost entirely in the mill villages. Furthermore, they attract only the unskilled mill workers and the poor. The services are led by preachers who have only an elementary school education, or possibly have taken some correspondence courses from a Bible institute. Few members of the congregation have much formal education. The goal of the service is not to communicate an intellectually insightful message but to provide a religious experience. On our visit with Earle et al. to the Gastonia sect, we climb three wooden or cinder-block steps that lead into

a small, bare room which has old, unmatched pews seating 150 people. On one Thursday night in the middle of a week-long revival, about 60 people—including 10 children—are present at the time the service is scheduled to begin. Drums, a guitar, a piano, and an electronic organ are being played, the songs having pronounced rhythms which involve the audience almost involuntarily in clapping of hands, tapping of feet, or movement of the body. The mood of those in attendance is informal. A dozen teenagers sit together and talk, while the older people move more freely about the room to talk to others.
    A crudely constructed pulpit and a speaker's pew are on the platform at front. . . . The preacher and his two associates move to the platform from the audience where they have been talking and shaking hands, and the service begins. After announcing the song, one of the men moves about, all the time singing into the microphone which he holds close to his face. The beat of the music is pronounced, and the people present respond with rhythmic clapping. A prayer follows, accompanied by shouts of "Hallelujah," "Praise the Lord," "Yes Jesus," "Glory," and is followed by another hymn, and then another. . . .
    The sermon begins with the preacher describing the "foolishness of the people in the world" and their careless disdain of the "fact that Jesus died for them, to deliver them from Hell." Certain themes appear repeatedly in his sermon: "salvation," "punishment from the evil in these days," "the danger of giving into the world," "God will see you through," "open your heart to Jesus." The

faithful of God are pictured as being free from the bonds of religious tradition, and willing to "let God go," by shouting, clapping, dancing, and singing.

Functional Perspective

To explain the diversity of religious belief and practice, functionalists begin with the questions: How does religion fit into society, and what is the role of the church in the operation of social order? Functionalists answer these questions by identifying at least four functions that are fulfilled by religion: First, religion answers the most profound questions of humanity: Is there purpose in life? Is there a supernatural order, and what is it? Why are we here? Second, religion integrates society around a shared set of moral norms and creates solidarity through the establishment of a community of believers. Both collective and individual identity is created by religious membership. Participation in the ritual order of the sacred sustains and supports this identity. Third, religion provides social control by reinforcing existing social arrangements. In a legitimate social order, people are asked to trust and cooperate with other members of society. Finally, religion provides a theodicy. A theodicy is a religious explanation of an unjust condition that exists within the social order. Theodicy addresses the questions, Why does God allow evil to exist? Why do the good suffer while those who are evil flourish? James Baldwin, for example, wondered, "If He loved all His children, why were we, the blacks, cast down so far?" (1963, p. 90). As we saw in Gastonia, North Carolina, members of sects tend to have a theodicy of suffering to explain their lack of power and wealth, whereas members of churches, by contrast, tend to have theodicies that accommodate the existing social arrangements and are more likely to accept and legitimate the possession of worldly power and wealth.

Conflict Perspective

Conflict theorists are more critical than functionalists are of religion in general and theodicy in particular. Karl Marx began his analysis of religion from a radically different perspective. According to him, the nature of society could best be explained by discovering which groups are economically dominant and subordinate. According to this approach, other institutions, like religion, can be seen as weapons used to advance the interests of the dominant economic group. Marx argued that the dominant religion will be the religion of the dominant class. Members of that religion would legitimate their power and privilege while simultaneously oppressing the subordinate classes. He pointed out that in ancient societies religion legitimated slavery. During feudal times, the dominant religion sanctified the divine right of kings. Currently, Protestantism accepts capitalistic economic arrangements and the unequal distribution of wealth and privilege.

According to Marx, capitalists use religion as a tool to justify the exploitation of workers or subordinate classes. Worker discontent and suffering are defused with promises of compensation in the afterlife and the belief that the meek shall inherit the earth. To Marx, religion was a form of false consciousness that siphons off discontent and preserves existing economic arrangements. "Religion is the sign of the oppressed creature," he wrote, "the heart of a heartless world, just as it is the spirit of a spiritless situation. It is the opium of the people" (1957/1964, p. 42). Inspired by these ideas, the labor activist, Joe Hill, wrote "Pie in the Sky," to be sung to the music of the hymn "In the Sweet Bye and Bye." One illustrative stanza is as follows:

> You will eat bye and bye,
> In that glorious land above the sky;
> Work and pray, live on hay,
> You'll get pie in the sky when you die.

The ideas of the conflict theorists have also inspired some important research on the question of whether religion is an opiate or an inspiration to change. Gary T. Marx (1967) investigated the effect of religious devotion on black participation in the civil rights movement. Using a national survey of blacks, he measured three elements of religious involvement: subjective importance of religion, orthodoxy of religious belief, and frequency of attendance at worship services. He then measured civil rights militancy on an eight-item scale. He found the evidence supported the Marxist view. Religious involvement of blacks resulted in an "accommodative opiate" that tended to produce an other-worldly focus with little concern for civil rights change.

Concerned by these findings, Larry and Janet Hunt (1976) reanalyzed Marx's data. They arrived at some surprising conclusions. They found that the difference between church and sect beliefs was critical in understanding the relationship between religiosity and civil rights militancy. They found that only sectarian beliefs were inversely correlated with civil rights militancy, while orthodox church beliefs were positively associated with militancy.

Background

The research of Bart Dredge in *Faith, Hope OR Charity* (1986) carried the investigation done by Larry and Janet Hunt further, by looking into the question of whether religion challenges the social order or consoles its victims. Dredge's research material came from 40 Sunday morning sermons that were delivered to white-collar and blue-collar congregations. He analyzed the content of each sermon for the number of "this-worldly" and "other-worldly" references (that is, references to the material or the spiritual world). Dredge's findings are consistent with those of Hunt and Hunt: because he found that white-collar sermons tended to contain a greater number of this-worldly references and that blue-collar sermons tended to contain a greater number of other-worldly references, Dredge concluded that upper-class congregations search for *justification,* whereas lower-class congregations search for *consolation.*

Replication

To investigate whether or not Dredge's conclusion is valid, we first need to see if we find the same differences that he did between the contents of white-collar and blue-collar sermons. We will do this by testing two hypotheses that sum up Dredge's findings:

Hypothesis 1:

White-collar sermons will have a greater number of this-worldly references than will blue-collar sermons.

Hypothesis 2:

Blue-collar sermons will have a greater number of other-worldly references than will white-collar sermons.

For our investigation, which will be on a much smaller scale than Dredge's, we will compare the content of one white-collar sermon to the content of one blue-collar sermon. Read Dredge's article "Faith, Hope OR Charity" (Reading 8, on pages 105–109) before you undertake selecting and coding sermons. As you read the article, note his examples and illustrations of "this-worldly" versus "other-worldly" categories.

Selecting Sermons

Dredge transcribed taped recordings of 40 sermons. Transcribing sermons would take more time and work than you probably have available for this investigation. Fortunately, there are a good number of published sermons that are available. You may be able to find a book of sermons in the school or public library. Look in the card catalog under "sermons," and for blue-collar sources look for topic references to "fundamentalism," "evangelism," and "holiness." There are also inexpensive paperbacks of sermons at bookstores specializing in the sale of religious material. Church libraries and church bookstores provide another good source of published sermons.

From these sources we want to select two sermons: one representative of a white-collar church and one representative of a blue-collar or sect church. Since Dredge found both white- and blue-collar churches among Baptists, it is clear that denominations are not homogeneous. If you obtain your sermons directly from a church, you must be able to have enough information to judge the social class of the church. If you do not have enough information to determine the social class of the church you will have to use the following guidelines to determine whether the church is white-collar or blue-collar. *Blue-collar* sermons will most likely not be published by a major university press or major secular publisher. The author of the blue-collar sermon is most likely Pentecostal, evangelical, charismatic, or fundamentalistic. The author may acknowledge his or her religious affiliation on the dust cover, or it may be cited in the card catalog, or it may be indicated by the publisher. For blue-collar sermons, look for a sect affiliation such as The

Assembly of God, The Church of God, The Church of Christ, The Church of the Nazarene, The Foursquare Gospel Church, Independent Tabernacle, Jehovah's Witnesses, and Holiness churches.

White-collar sermons may be published by major university presses (Harvard, Yale, Oxford, Cambridge) or secular establishment presses (Prentice-Hall, Doubleday, Harper-Collins). The author may acknowledge affiliation with an upper-class church (such as Episcopalian, Presbyterian, or Methodist). When the author is a member of a church with a heterogeneous membership and publishes with a major university press, it is likely the sermon is white-collar. When the Baptist Harvey Cox publishes through the Yale University Press, it is probable that he is expressing a white-collar view. A listing of anthologies of white-collar and blue-collar sermons appears at the end of this investigation, on pages 103–104. There are, of course, many more sources of sermons available and these are only illustrative.

Avoid choosing sermons that are written for special occasions such as graduations, weddings, or holy days.

Analyzing the Content of Sermons

Your analysis will be easier to perform and the results will be more consistent if you work with printed copies of the sermons. Mark on these copies with a highlighting pen to identify words or phrases that have "worldly" references. Do not highlight entire paragraphs or themes, as they require more subjective judgments and are less reliable indicators of sermon content.

Words or terms referring to something natural that one experiences through the senses should be considered *this-worldly*. Words that deal with the supernatural or those things known through faith, intuition, or spirituality should be considered *other-worldly*.

Step 1:

Go through the sermon and highlight each important "worldly" term. Do NOT include prayers that are part of the sermon.

Step 2:

To classify each term, look over the 25 categories that follow and get a feel for the type of words that illustrate each category. Do not try to memorize the words in each category. The list is not exhaustive, nor is it meant to be used without considering the intent or meaning of the word in the sermon. The word *law,* for example, might refer to Caesar's law (this-worldly) or God's law (other-worldly). The intention of the minister is usually clear.

When you feel you understand the meaning of each category, determine to which of the 16 this-worldly or 9 other-worldly categories each highlighted word belongs. For each one, enter a tally, or slash (/), in the appropriate category in Table 8–2, the Sermon Analysis Worksheet, on the following page. Use one sermon analysis worksheet for each sermon you analyze. Make up additional analysis forms as you need them by using Table 8–2 as a guide.

Table 8–2

SERMON ANALYSIS WORKSHEET

NAME OF CODER _____

WHITE-COLLAR OR BLUE-COLLAR: WC   BC   DATE CODED _____

MINISTER _____ DENOMINATION _____

SERMON TITLE _____

PUBLISHER _____ LOCATION _____ DATE _____

This-Worldly References

	Tally	Total
War		
Child Abuse		
Crime		
Drugs		
Economic Problems		
Education		
Environment		
Marriage		
Freedom		
Meaninglessness		
Hunger		
Racial Injustice		
Political-Social Disorder		
Poverty		
Career		
Other		
	Total this-worldly references =	

Other-Worldly References

	Tally	Total
Heaven		
Hell		
Eternal Life		
Salvation		
Satan		
God		
Holy Spirit		
Jesus		
Other		
	Total other-worldly references =	

Note: Based on Tables 1 and 2 in "Faith, Hope OR Charity: A Look at Church Sermons and Social Class" by B. Dredge, 1986, *Sociological Inquiry, 56,* p. 531, Tables 1 & 2. Copyright 1990 by the University of Texas Press. Adapted by permission.

This-Worldly Categories

This-worldly references include the 15 categories that were identified in the original article (see p. 107), plus a final category, "Other." In the following, these categories are listed along with terms that are usually included:

(1) War: ambush, army, assault, atrocity, attack, blitz, bomb, casualties, clash, combat, conflagration, fight, genocide, guerrilla, invasion, marines, navy, onslaught, pillage, raid, sabotage, slaughter, soldiers, terrorism, warfare, warriors, weapons

(2) Child abuse: abuse, brutalize, corrupt, degrade, hurt, incest, molest, pedophilia, pervert, pornography, statutory rape, victimize

(3) Crime: arrest, assault and battery, burglary, con, delinquency, execution, FBI, felony, graft, homicide, homosexuality, hustle, illegal, imprison, killer, law, lawyer, Mafia, murder, organized crime, parole, police, prison, prostitution, punishment, racket, rape, rip-off, sodomy, steal, sting, vice

(4) Drugs: addiction, alcoholism, barbiturates, cocaine, crack, dealer, dope, grass, heroin, ice, LSD, marijuana, narcotics, opium, pot, pusher, valium

(5) Economic problems: bankrupt, bills, broke, business, cost, credit, debt, embezzle, finance, fired, indigent, insolvent, scam, swindle, unemployed

(6) Education: books, certification, classes, college, courses, credentials, examination, experience, instruction, learn, research, scholarship, schooling, study, teach, university

(7) Environment: atmosphere, climate, habitat, nature, niche, pollution

(8) Marriage: alimony, bride, children, child support, commitment, conjugal, divorce, family, father, fidelity, husband, liaison, love, marriage, matrimony, mother, parents, separation, wedding, wife

(9) Freedom: independence, liberty, rights

(10) Meaninglessness: alone, bewildered, confused, disconnected, disoriented, distant, estranged, foreign, futility, helplessness, hopeless, pessimism, purposeless

(11) Hunger: famine, food, malnourished, starvation

(12) Racial injustice: discrimination, exploit, harm, inequity, injure, oppress, persecute, prejudice, torture, unfair, victimize

(13) Political-social disorder: anarchy, chaos, collapse, commotion, confusion, corruption, debauchery, depraved, disarray, disturbance, favoritism, havoc, immoral, mayhem, nepotism, pandemonium, revolution, riot, ruination, tumult

(14) Poverty: broke, destitute, dirt poor, down and out, homeless, impoverished, needy, poor, unfortunate, welfare

(15) Career: business, calling, employment, job, labor, livelihood, occupation, profession, task, trade, vocation, work

(16) Other: includes references to or quotations from famous people (athletes, politicians, military personnel, businessmen, secular writers, artists, musicians, entertainers, and the like).

Other-Worldly Categories

Eight categories of other-worldly references were identified by Dredge. These, along with a category for "Other," include the following topics:

(1) Heaven: abode of bliss, abode of God, abode of the blessed, Celestial City, City of Light, Eden, God's Throne, Heavenly Kingdom, hereafter, Holy City, New Jerusalem, nirvana, paradise, rapture, world to come

(2) Hell: abyss, damnation, eternal fire, eternal punishment, Hades, inferno, perdition, the pit, sulphurous, torment, underworld

(3) Eternal life: deathless, endless, enduring, everlasting, immortal, imperishable, limitless, perpetual, timeless, undying, unending

(4) Salvation: atonement, deliverance, expiation, forgiveness, purgatory, redemption, repentance, savior

(5) Satan: Antichrist, archfiend, Beelzebub, devil, demon, evil, fallen angel, foe of God, Lucifer, prince of darkness, satanic, spirit

(6) God: Absolute Deity, Adonai, All-Knowing, Almighty, Creator, Divine One, Divinity, Eternal Being, Infinite Being, Jehovah, King of Kings, Light of the World, Lord of Lords, Master Workman, Most High, Omnipotent, Providence, Supreme Soul, Yahweh

(7) Holy Spirit: angelic, blessed, consecrated, divine, divine grace, hallowed, holy, Living Presence, pious, righteous, sacred, sanctified, sanctity, spiritual

(8) Jesus: Christ, Glorified One, Good Shepard, Holy One, Immanuel, Infinite One, King of Kings, Lamb of God, Lion of Judah, Lord, The Messiah, The Nazarene, Only Begotten Son, Prince of Peace, The Risen One, Savior, Son of God, Word Made Flesh, Word of God

(9) Other: includes sacred people, writings, and topics.

Sacred people are persons with qualities of divinity, such as apostles, bishops, cardinals, disciples, martyrs, ministers, popes, priests, rabbis, saints, and vicars.

Sacred writings include Acts, Bible, encyclicals, Epistles, Genesis, Good Book, Gospels, Holy Writ, parables, psalms, Revelation, Ten Commandments, the Word of God.

Sacred Topics include anointed, ascension, baptism, covenant, creation, creed, crucifixion, ecstasy, exodus, faith, idols, Last Judgement, prayer, preach, prophecy, rapture, repent, resurrection, revival, sabbath, soul, spirit, spiritual love, tithe, transfiguration, transubstantiation, worship, and witness.

Table 8–3

INVESTIGATION RESULTS 8
Investigation Summary Table

Social Class of Denomination	Sermon Orientation	
	This-Worldly	Other-Worldly
White-Collar Sermon		
Blue-Collar Sermon		

$d_{xy} =$ Total N $=$

Enter the totals from your tally sheets in the summary table above. These individual summary results will be collected and combined into a class summary table.

Note: Adapted from Table 3, p. 109.

Step 3:

When you are done coding the first sermon, count the number of tallies in Table 8–2 and enter the totals in each category. Then add the total tallies for this-worldly and other-worldly references. When you are done, attach the copy of the sermon to the analysis worksheet. Analyze the second sermon in the same way and attach it to a separate analysis worksheet.

Step 4:

When an analysis worksheet has been completed for each sermon, your instructor will collect the worksheets, total the tallies for the entire class, and provide you with the results. Enter the results in the Investigation Summary table, Table 8–3, above.

With the results entered in Table 8–3, you may test the hypotheses by filling in the blank spaces below:

Hypothesis 1:

White-collar sermons will have a greater number of this-worldly references than will blue-collar sermons.

White-collar   Blue-collar
This-worldly   ——— > ———   This-worldly

Hypothesis 2:

Blue-collar sermons will have a greater number of other-worldly references than will white-collar sermons.

White-collar   Blue-collar
Other-worldly   ——— < ———   Other-worldly

Checking Your Findings

We will test the statistical significance of these hypotheses with the contingency table provided by your instructor. If Dredge's hypothesis is supported, d_{xy} will be positive and greater than 0. If it is not supported, d_{xy} will be negative. The probability that our results could occur by chance will be determined by the analysis program. If the results would not happen 5 times in 100 by chance, we will conclude our findings are significant.

Dredge found that white-collar sermons tended to have a greater number of this-worldly references than blue-collar sermons did. Was this also true for your class?

Dredge also found that blue-collar sermons contained a greater number of other-worldly references than white-collar sermons did. Do the results of your class's sermon analyses indicate that this is still true? Summarize your conclusions in Table 8–4 on page 103, labeled "Support for Hypotheses."

If your class's findings match Dredge's, does this validate his view that "lower class church members search for consolation while upper class congregations search for justification for and continuation of their elevated social status"? Do you feel, like Dredge, that religion serves to both "console and sanction" class, depending upon the membership of the particular church?

Topics for Further Investigation

1. When you have completed your analysis, you may want to consider a number of related research questions. You may want to compare the other- and this-worldly emphases by particular

Table 8–4

SUPPORT FOR HYPOTHESES

			Significantly Supported	Partially Supported	Not Supported	Indeterminate
Hypothesis 1:						
White-collar This-worldly	>	Blue-collar This-worldly	_____	_____	_____	_____
Hypothesis 2:						
White-collar Other-worldly	<	Blue-collar Other-worldly	_____	_____	_____	_____

Indicate the amount of support you found for each hypothesis.

Protestant denominations. You might also consider the following questions:

   a. Are there significant differences between Protestant, Roman Catholic, and Jewish sermons?

   b. Are there regional (North, South, East, West) differences?

   c. Are there differences between the sermons of men and women ministers?

   d. Are there differences in ways of knowing God (emotionally versus intellectually, through faith versus reason)?

   e. Are there differences in the complexity and word difficulty of the sermons?

   f. Are there differences in the level of tolerance, ethnocentrism, or in- versus out-group references?

2. Another set of questions concerns the social conditions that have influenced the content of the sermons. As Ludwig Feuerbach asserted, "The more empty life is, the fuller, the more concrete is God. The impoverishing of the real world and the enriching of God is one act" (quoted in Tucker, 1961, p. 89).

   a. Do blue-collar sermons describe God in more concrete terms?

   b. Are blue-collar sermons more alienated from the material order?

   c. Under what conditions are people most likely to be attracted to sermons focusing on other-worldly issues?

   d. Are other-worldly concerns of more immediate interest to individuals or groups facing unemployment, poverty, downward mobility, minority status, social isolation, rapid social change, or cultural disorganization?

Illustrative Collections of Blue-Collar Church Sermons

Biederwolf, W. (1949). *Evangelistic sermons*. Grand Rapids, MI: W. B. Eerdmans.

Carter, C (1959). *Road to revival*. Butler, IN: Higley Press.

DeLong, R. (1956). *Evangelistic sermons of the great evangelists*. Grand Rapids, MI: Zondervan.

Finney, C. (1965). *The guilt of sin: Evangelistic sermons*. Grand Rapids, MI: Kregel.

Finney, C. (1966). *Victory over the world: Revival messages*. Grand Rapids, MI: Kregel.

Finney, C. (1967). *True submission: Revival messages*. Grand Rapids, MI: Kregel.

Ford, W. (1954). *Simple sermons on saints and sinners*. Grand Rapids, MI: Baker Book House.

Ford, W. (1955). *Simple sermons on salvation and service*. Grand Rapids, MI: Baker Book House.

Ford, W. (1969). *Simple sermons for Sunday morning*. Grand Rapids, MI: Baker Book House.

Ford, W. (1972). *Simple sermons on conversion and commitment*. Grand Rapids, MI: Baker Book House.

Freeman, C. (1951). *Evangelism in action through Christ-centered messages*. Wheaton, IL: VanKampen Press.

Fuller, E. (1953). *Evangelistic sermons*. Nashville, TN: Broadman Press.

Henry, C. (1948). *The evangelical pulpit*. Grand Rapids, MI: W. B. Eerdmans.

Jones, B. (1969). *Ancient truths for modern days*. New York: Loizeaux Bros.

Jones, B. (1944). *Things I have learned: Chapel talks at Bob Jones College*. Murfreesboro, TN: Sword of the Lord Publishers.

Kernahan, A. (1934). *Great sermons on evangelism*. Nashville, TN: Cokesbury Press.

Lawrence, J. (1950). *Kindling for revival fires*. Old Tappan, NJ: Fleming H. Revell.

Lee, R. (1944). *Be ye also ready: Evangelistic sermons*. Grand Rapids, MI: Zondervan.

Martin, G. (1969). *Great Southern Baptist evangelistic preaching*. Grand Rapids, MI: Zondervan.

Martinez, A. (1956). *Revival at midnight*. Grand Rapids, MI: Zondervan.

Murray, A. (1952). *The best of Andrew Murray*. Grand Rapids, MI: Baker Book House.

Robinson, H. (1989). *Biblical sermons*. Grand Rapids, MI: Baker Book House.

Sunday, W. (1965). *The best of Billy Sunday*. Murfreesboro, TN: Sword of the Lord Press.

Sweeting, G. (1965). *Special sermons for evangelism*. Chicago, IL: Moody Press.

Torrey, R. (1956). *Soul-winning sermons*. Old Tappan, NJ: Fleming H. Revell.

Wallis, C. (1964). *88 evangelistic sermons*. Westwood, NJ: Harper & Row.

Wesberry, J. (1973). *Evangelistic sermons*. Nashville, TN: Broadman Press.

Wirt, S. (1970). *Great preaching: Evangelical messages by contemporary Christians*. Waco, TX: World Books.

Illustrative Collections of White-Collar Church Sermons

Coffin, W. (1985). *Living the Truth in a world of illusions*. New York: Harper & Row.

Marshall, C. (Ed.). (1951). *A man called Peter*. New York: McGraw-Hill.

Marshall, C. (Ed.). (1983). *The best of Peter Marshall*. Grand Rapids, MI: Zondervan.

Marshall, P. (1949). *Mr. Jones, meet the Master*. Old Tappan, NJ: Fleming H. Revell.

Maynard, D. (1987). *Episcopalians: Following in the way of Jesus*. Greenville, SC: Christ Episcopal Church.

Maynard, D. (1988). *The Christ Church PULPIT*. Greenville, SC: Christ Episcopal Church.

Neibuhr, H. R. (1974). *Justice and mercy*. New York: Harper & Row.

Tillich, P. (1955). *The new being*. New York: Charles Scribner's & Sons.

References and Recommended Readings

Avery, W. S., & Gobbel, R. (1980). The words of God and the words of the preacher. *Review of Religious Research, 22,* 41–53.

Bainbridge, W. S., & Stark, R. (1980). Sectarian tension. *Review of Religious Research, 22,* 105–124.

Baldwin, J. (1963). *The fire next time*. New York: Dial Press.

Dredge, B. (1986). Faith, hope or charity: A look at church sermons and social class. *Sociological Inquiry, 56,* 523–534.

Earle, J., Kudsen, D., & Shriver, D. (1976). *Spindles and spires*. Atlanta, GA: John Knox Press.

Eckhart, K. W. (1970). Religiosity and civil rights militancy. *Review of Religious Research, 11,* 197–203.

Hill, J. (n.d.). Pie in the sky (hymn). Ft. Lauderdale, FL: Plymouth music.

Hollingshead, A. B. (1949). *Elmtown's youth*. New Haven, CT: Yale University Press.

Hunt, L., & Hunt, J. (1976). Black religion as both opiate and inspiration of civil rights militance: Putting Marx's data to the test. *Social Forces, 56,* 1–14.

Johnson, B. (1971). Church-sect revisited. *Journal for the Scientific Study of Religion, 510,* 124–137.

Marx, G. T. (1967). Religion: Opiate or inspiration of civil rights militancy among Negroes? *American Sociological Review, 32,* 64–73.

Marx, K., & Engels, F. (1957). *Marx and Engels on religion*. Moscow: Foreign Languages Publishing House. Reprint. New York: Schocken, 1964.

McKinney, B. B. (1956). The nail-scarred hand (hymn). In W. H. Sims (Ed.), *Baptist Hymnal* (no. 231). Nashville, TN: Convention Press.

Pope, L. (1942). *Millhands and preachers*. New Haven, CT: Yale University Press.

Stark, R. (1985). Church and sect. In P. Hammond (Ed.), *The sacred in a secular age* (pp. 139–149). Berkeley, CA: University of California Press.

Stark, R. (1972). The economics of piety: Religious commitment and social class. In G. Thielbar & A. Feldman (Eds.) *Issues in Social Inequality* (pp. 483–503). Boston: Little, Brown.

Tucker, R. (1961). *Myth and philosophy in Karl Marx*. New York: Cambridge University Press.

Warner, W. L. (1949). *Social class in America*. New York: Harper Torchbook.

Faith, Hope OR Charity: A Look at Church Sermons and Social Class

This paper reports a content analysis of church sermons in terms of social class distinctions in the memberships of two Southern Baptist churches. The major finding is that there is a relationship between social class and sermon content. The data for this analysis was obtained by the transcription of forty Sunday morning sermons. The results are interpreted as suggesting that lower class church members search for consolation while upper class congregations search for justification for and continuation of their elevated social status.

Bart Dredge
University of North Carolina, Chapel Hill

Despite Karl Marx's hostility toward religion and his failure to treat it systematically, he did recognize some of its social functions and, in doing so, foreshadowed the work of others (Yinger, 1970; Leuba, 1969). This analysis of religion in society is found in various places in Marx's works. Perhaps the most often cited of all of Marx's comments is his assertion (1972:54) that religion is "the sigh [sic] of the oppressed creature, the sentiment of a heartless world, and the soul of soulless conditions. It is the opium of the people." This statement implies that religion has palliative and consolatory functions in society and that the consolatory function is primarily reserved for a narrowly-focused set of social ills imposed on one social class by another. In addition to the suggestion that religion serves as "the general ground of consolation," Marx explicitly asserted (1967:250) that religion functions as the "moral sanction of the world." That is, religion functions conservatively in a class society by justifying the particular moralities and interests of the dominant class.

Marx, of course, was not alone in pointing out the consolatory functions of religion. Lenin (1981:264) later agreed in writing that religion is "perpetuated by the oppression of social forces. It is used by the exploiting class to justify their rule and to drug the exploited masses into submission." Non-Marxists such as H. Richard Neibuhr (1957:31) have also expressed similar hypotheses. Neibuhr wrote that the church of the poor provides a salvation that is "the salvation of the socially disinherited. Intellectual naivete and practical need combine to create a marked propensity toward millenarianism, with its promise of tangible goods and the reversal of all present social systems of rank."

Likewise, others have noted that religion functions to sanction and justify the status of the upper or dominant class. This justification is essentially discovered in the temporal orientation of upper class religion which is primarily directed towards the solution to problems of this world, not the promises of the next. Lenin, again, wrote (1958:208) that "(I)n order to make existing conditions palatable, priests were dispatched to identify God with the authorities, to sacrilize ruling class policies, and to prove that serfdom was approved by the Most High and ratified by Holy Writ." Religion is, at least in part, a form of self-deception for the poor. It provides for an identification with the dominant social class and through this identification the lower class person supports interests that are not in accordance with his own objective self-interests. At the same time religion serves as a powerful device whereby the ruling class justifies its status while at the same time manipulating the working class. It is an "ideological screen" to support the status quo (Bonino, 1976:124).

Religion provides a consolatory service for the lower classes in that it promises an eternal salvation to those who despair of material salvation in this life. To the upper classes, religion provides, in the various forms of Christian charity and social concern, a justification for their current and future elevated social status. Lenin wrote (1958:658), "To him who toils and suffers want all his life religion teaches humility and patience on earth, consoling him with the hope of reward in heaven. And to those who live on the labor of others religion teaches charity on earth, offering them a very cheap justification for their whole existence as exploiters and selling them at a suitable price tickets for admission to heavenly bliss." The clear distinction between these two functions of religion has provided fertile ground for much sociological analysis regarding social class and religious participation. As will be described below, much of this work bears directly on this study which attempts a content analysis of church sermons to explore further the correlation between church activity, in this case exposure to Sunday sermons, and the class status of the different congregations.

Reprinted with permission from *Sociological Inquiry,* 56, 1986, pp. 523–534. Copyright 1990 by The University of Texas Press.

REVIEW OF THE LITERATURE

Few articles exist in the sociological literature specifically analyzing church sermons. Pargament and Silverman (1982) have attempted to evaluate the general impact sermons have on church members in terms of various members' demographic variables, background variables, and listener's perceptions of the sermons themselves. Another study (Avery and Gobbel, 1980) questioned the degree to which the church laity comprehends the relationship between the words of the preacher and the Word of God. And a final study generally explored the effect church sermons have on a sample of lay Catholics (Newman and Wright, 1980). No studies were found which explicitly discuss class and the content of church sermons.

Much has been written, however, by sociologists concerned with social class and religious participation. Perhaps the most important study that contributes to an understanding of the association between religion and social stratification was Liston Pope's (1942) classic analysis of the Gastonia, North Carolina textile mill workers, entitled Millhands and Preachers. This study, which was later replicated (Earle, et al. 1976), largely informed the direction of this current project. Other articles and books have broadly addressed the composition of religious groups with regard to social status. For example, differences of denominations in terms of percentages of each representative social class were reported by Schneider (1973). Further, according to Robertson (1970) and others, religious doctrinal orthodoxy tends to appear in the religions of the socially and materially deprived. The frequency of church attendance itself, in terms of member social class, has been examined (Argyle, 1959:130; Stark, 1964). Finally, several studies (Bell, 1957; Laserwitz, 1961) found that church attendance is highly correlated with social status regardless of the indicators used to measure social class.

Several community studies have also demonstrated that social class and religion are linked. In the famous Elmtown study, for example, Warner and Lunt (1941) demonstrated the existence of this linkage. In another, Lynd and Lynd (1929), it was shown that the upper classes of society are more likely to be members of a church. This is supported by Cantril (1943) who suggests that members of the middle class are more likely to join religious groups than are manual laborers. And this has held true when several midwestern towns, ranging in size from a few hundred to several thousand, were studied (Schroeder and Oberhaus, 1964).

Admittedly, no single dimension of religious experience, such as church attendance, can be relied upon as an indicator of overall religious intensity. Several studies have examined the various dimensions of religiosity relative to social stratification (Fukayama, 1961; Demerath, 1961). Stark (1972) reported not only the difference in the extent of individual religiosity, but also the difference in the form of religiosity which included, among other categories, attendance of church services and type of religious beliefs held. Other studies have investigated the choice of religion type in terms of member socioeconomic status measured by education, occupation and income (Goldstein,

1969; Crespi, 1963). Further articles reveal the relationship between religious preference and worldly success in both the Detroit area (Mayer and Sharp, 1962) and in national surveys (Glenn and Hyland, 1967).

Various relationships, then, between social class and church activity have been consistently and empirically demonstrated. It appears that individuals do tend to find churches which meet their needs whether this involves a search for consolation for the working classes or a search for justification for the middle classes. The lower or working classes find promises of eternal bliss and heavenly reward for their faithful patience through the misery and deprivation in this life. The middle classes are directed to temporal, earthly problems. The attention to matters of this world serves to justify their continued elevated social status and guarantee salvation after death. The purpose of this study is to examine the relationship between social class of church memberships and the consoling or sanctioning functions expressed in the church sermons at each church. When the membership of a church is primarily composed of working class people, it is expected that the sermons will present a message of predominantly transcendent or otherworldly concerns. When the membership of a church is predominantly middle class in composition, church sermons are expected to emphasize temporal, this-worldly matters.

RESEARCH DESIGN

The churches chosen for this study are both of the Southern Baptist denomination. This denomination was selected because of the democratic, congregational nature of the church polity. These churches generally have "pulpit committees" which operate as search committees for the hiring of new pastors. Once a pastor is selected, he is subject to the vote of the entire church membership before appointment. In this way, the selection of each pastor can be thought of as reflecting the conscious choice of the church membership, not merely an appointment by a distant and perhaps ill-informed or unresponsive hierarchy. The membership chooses the pastor, and in effect, the type of sermons that he preaches.

The two Southern Baptist churches selected in this case are both located in the Greenville-Spartanburg, South Carolina Standard Metropolitan Statistical Area (SMSA). The population of the region, part of the southern "Bible Belt," is numbered in excess of half a million people, and Southern Baptists are the predominant Protestant denomination in the region. Both churches are members of the National Southern Baptist Convention, the South Carolina Baptist Convention, and the local Southern Baptist association. Both are large churches with regular memberships in excess of fifteen hundred people, and both are well established in their respective communities. Additionally, both churches have an annual budget of approximately one million dollars which supports the church physical plants, affiliated Christian schools, radio and television ministries, and ministers of Education, Music, Youth, and Visitation in addition to the pastor and his staff. It appears that the only major difference between these churches is the social class of their respective memberships. In order to respect the anonymity of each church, the popular images of White Collar and Blue Collar will be used to suggest middle and working class memberships. The churches will hereinafter be referred to as White Collar Baptist Church and Blue Collar Baptist Church.

Several interrelated methods were utilized to establish the social class of each church body. Admittedly the least reliable but perhaps the most instructive involved an interview with the primary pastor of each church. When asked for their subjective opinions as to the social class of their congregations, both pastors were quick to express their personal impressions. The pastor of White Collar Baptist placed his church membership in the upper or middle class and complained that in the summer months he had a great deal of trouble getting his members to church as they preferred to "stay at their condominiums on Hilton Head Island." At Blue Collar Baptist, on the other hand, the pastor was just as quick to ascribe social class to his congregation and only requested that he be allowed to use slightly different terms. He said that he was reluctant to use the term *poor* to describe his congregation, but would "definitely classify them as *working class*." In both cases, the pastors were willing informants who expressed their views of the broad social class structures of their own congregations.

For a second measure of membership social class, we examined a random sampling ($N = 110$) of members' home addresses taken from complete membership lists provided by each church secretary. These addresses were selected and then located on Block Statistics maps from the 1980 Department of Commerce Census of Population and Housing for the Greenville-Spartanburg, South Carolina SMSA (PHC80-1-177). This procedure provided a direct comparison between the memberships of each church in several categories including the average number of rooms and average value of each home owned. In this way we determined a quantitative measure which suggested social class status of the individual members of each group. The sample of Blue Collar Baptist Church members revealed that of the block addresses selected and located, the homes had an average of 3.9 rooms and, while only twenty-seven percent of the membership reported owning their homes, the average house value was listed as $23,000. Most of the houses were located clearly within the boundaries of textile mill communities and, in the past, had been constructed and owned by the textile mill companies themselves. On the other hand, the sample of homes of members of White Collar Baptist Church showed that the houses had an average of 6.7 rooms and, with 71.1 percent of the members indicating ownership of their homes, an average house value of approximately $83,400 was discovered. These figures are consistent with the subjective evaluations of the pastors of the two churches.

Finally, a third measure was employed to indicate the relative social status of the church congregations. The memberships were examined to discover what categories of occupations are represented within each group. This information, it was thought, might shed some further light on the occupational makeup of the memberships and therefore assist in determining the social class of each church body. Examining the membership

Table 1

THIS-WORLDLY REFERENCES

Indicator	White Collar Baptist	Blue Collar Baptist
War	43	0
Child Abuse	4	7
Crime	44	22
Drug Abuse	31	8
Economic Problems	23	2
Educational Problems	22	4
Environmental Issues	68	0
Marital Problems	136	9
Political Freedom	135	1
Meaninglessness	312	21
World Hunger	26	2
Racial Injustice	31	0
Political-Social Disorder	296	2
Poverty	23	0
Career Problems	71	11
	N = 1265	N = 89
	(93.4%)	(6.6%)

lists of Blue Collar Baptist Church, we found several plumbers, carpenters, electricians, police officers, and auto mechanics. The predominant occupation, however, was that of textile mill worker or worker in textile-related industries. At White Collar Baptist Church, on the other hand, we found a church membership that included at least eighty physicians, twenty-five local attorneys, at least fifteen college professors, three local bank presidents, one Federal Circuit Court judge, three current or retired United States' attorneys, one state senator, and one former United States Congressman. Clearly the occupational makeup of these church members suggests a difference in social class with middle class members represented heavily in one church and the working or lower-middle class members represented in the other. It is our contention that, although not perfect, the combination of pastor's subjective opinion regarding the congregational social status, the housing statistics of each membership, and the occupational analysis support characterization of these church bodies into the broad middle class and working class divisions used throughout this paper.

Our unit of analysis in this project was that of the specific words found in church sermon transcripts. A total of forty sermons, twenty from each church, was obtained on cassette tape and subsequently transcribed. Each set of sermons was restricted to only that of the primary church pastor who presented the sermons during regularly scheduled Sunday morning services. No special event sermons such as Christmas, Easter, or Mother's Day were included. The final set of transcripts consisted of approximately sixty-seven thousand words of sermon content for each church.

Once transcribed, each sermon was analyzed by three observers, two of whom were unaware of the theoretical and conceptual framework of this study. Each observer read all of the transcripts independently and coded them according to

Table 2

OTHER-WORLDLY REFERENCES

Indicator	White Collar Baptist	Blue Collar Baptist
Heaven	61	131
Hell	5	25
Eternal Life	15	131
Salvation	32	169
Satan	37	101
God	368	747
Holy Spirit	3	103
Jesus	216	396
	N = 737	N = 1803
	(29%)	(71%)

predetermined scoring units or indicators. Words or phases in each sermon that indicated "this-worldly" or "other-worldly" emphasis were identified and coded. Acceptance of each classification depended upon unanimous agreement between all three readers. If this agreement was not reached, the particular indicator was deleted for the purposes of this paper. In this way indicator reliability was enhanced.

Throughout the coding process, care was taken to ensure that each indicator was contextually valid. For example, if the problem of street crime was discussed in a sermon, on the surface an indicator of this-worldly orientation, but was mentioned only in terms of criminal activity being defined as sin that jeopardizes entry to heaven, then crime in this instance was not counted as an object of this-worldly concern. Only crime emphasized as a social problem that required temporal attention and concern was considered to be an indicator of this-worldly orientation. The same held true if, for example, proper stewardship and care of the natural environment was mentioned as a requirement for heavenly reward. In this case, the issue of the environment did not clearly express a this-worldly perspective. At the same time, the remarks about heavenly rewards could not be shown to precisely refer to other-worldly concerns. Both indicators were subsequently omitted from further consideration. Each indicator was required to represent, in the context presented, either a clear temporal or a clear transcendent orientation.

Finally, it should be mentioned that the words and phases coded and counted in this study were often collapsed for the purposes of final expression in Tables 1 and 2. For instance, an often discussed concept in the sermons at White Collar Baptist Church was that of the "alienation" or "normlessness" that plagues the lives of people living in a modern secular society. In these cases in which several different words were used to express essentially the same idea, the words were collapsed into one central word most often chosen to reflect the spirit of the issue. In this case, for example, the several terms for personal alienation are simply referred to as "meaninglessness." The same is true in regards to the many references to Jesus Christ. He is referred to alternately as Christ, Jesus, Savior, the Son of

God, etc. Here this is simplified by the consistent reference to "Jesus" alone. As in the problem of original coding of indicators themselves, these reductions of terms were only done in the event that there was unanimous agreement among the three readers of the sermon transcripts. Otherwise, the word or phrase was simply left out. Tables 1 and 2 are the result of the unanimous reduction of terms into meaningful indicators that are at least intuitively understandable as being suggestive of either this-worldly or other-worldly matters.

FINDINGS

As the contingency table (Table 3, p. 109) strongly suggests, the analysis of church sermons by social class indicates that a strong correlation exists between the social status of a particular group and this-worldly or other-worldly orientation of the sermons the congregation regularly hears. Simple common sense might lead one to believe that churches of the same denomination are typically exposed to essentially the same message from the pulpit. It is our contention that each congregation, although members of the same denomination, in the same city, and at precisely the same time in history, directly influence the particular type of sermon they receive in regular church services. In each case, this choice of sermon content is an expression of a particular shared need. In the working class church, the church members express their need for a promise of eternal heavenly salvation in the face of despair in the search for material happiness and salvation in this life. Thus the sermons, as the figures indicate, consistently speak of clearly other-worldly matters and only speak to the smallest degree to the social, educational, economic, and political matters of this world.

The middle class church members, on the other hand, do not depend upon religion to ease their passage through this life by a promise of eternal life. Instead the upper class appeals to their religion to ensure the continuation and justification of the material life they enjoy in this world. Much less in the middle class sermons are references to other-worldly matters found. To the extent that Marx was correct in suggesting that religion is what it does, it seems plausible that much of its function is expressed through its formal, regularly scheduled weekly messages. It serves to both console and sanction, then, depending upon the church membership, social class, and the specific individual needs of each social class. This function is accomplished through the orientation expressed in the church sermons.

Finally, it should be mentioned that this study is primarily exploratory in nature, suggests further empirical research, and is flawed in several ways. For example, further study of the issue of church participation and social class by the analysis of specific sermons should include churches from different geographical regions and should contrast the sermons between different denominations. Additionally, the social class of the church congregations should be determined with more precision. Self-reports, for instance, would allow for precise consideration of income, educational levels, and occupations of all the church membership. Finally, continued work could examine the orientation of evening services, revivals, Bible-study classes, and other special events which also comprise the potential body of events presented to the members of each church group. Part of this research could then address the issue of church participation itself by taking into account reasons for church attendance separate from the need for specific types of sermon messages. To the extent that these things are accomplished, a better analysis will be available to determine the relationship between social class and church participation. This paper serves to suggest the direction of that correlation and to indicate areas of further research.

Table 3

SERMON ORIENTATION

Social Class	This-Worldly	Other-Worldly	
White Collar Baptist	1265 (63%)	737 (36%)	2002 (100%)
Blue Collar Baptist	89 (4%)	1803 (96%)	1892 (100%)
	1354	2540	N = 3894

Note: Each cell figure represents one explicit this-worldly or other-worldly indicator as discussed above.

Chi-square = 1466.8477
$p = {}^1/_4 .0001$
n = 3894

REFERENCES

Argyle, M. (1959). *Religious behavior.* Glencoe, NY: The Free Press.

Avery, W. O., & Gobbel, A. R. (1980). The word of God and the words of the preacher. *Review of Religious Research, 22* (September), 41–53.

Bell, W. (1957). Anomie, social isolation and the class structure. *Sociometry, 20,* 105–116.

Bonino, J. M. (1976). *Christians and the Marxists: The mutual challenge to revolution.* Grand Rapids, MI: Eerdmans Publishers.

Cantril, H. (1943). Educational and economic composition of religious groups. *American Journal of Sociology, 48,* 574–579.

Crespi, I. (1963). Occupational status and religion [letter to the editor]. *American Sociological Review, 28,* 131.

Demerath, N. J., III. (1961). Social stratification and church involvement. *Review of Religious Research, 2* (Spring), 146–154.

Earle, J., Knudsen, D., & Shriver, D. (1976). *Spindles and spires.* Atlanta, GA: John Knox Press.

Fukayama, Y. (1961). The major dimensions of church membership. *Review of Religious Research, 2* (Spring), 154–161.

Glenn, N. D., & Hyland, R. (1967). Religious preference and worldly success: Some evidence from national surveys. *American Sociological Review, 32,* 73–85.

Goldstein, S. (1969). Socioeconomic differentials among religious groups in the United States. *American Sociological Review, 32,* 73–85.

Laserwitz, B. (1961). Some factors associated with variations in church attendance. *Social forces, 34,* 301–309.

Lenin, V. I. (1958). *Collected works.* Moscow: Foreign Languages Publishing House.

Lenin, V. I. (1981). Atheism and materialism. In A. F. McGovern, *Marxism: An American Christian perspective.* Maryknoll, NY: Orbis Books.

Leuba, J. (1969). *A psychological study of religion: Its origin, function and future.* New York: AMS Press.

Lynd, R., & Lynd, H. (1929). *Middletown.* New York: Harcourt, Brace.

Marx, K. (1967). Reflections of a youth on choosing an occupation. In L. D. Easton & K. H. Guddat (Eds.), *Writings of the young Marx on philosophy and society.* New York: Doubleday and Company.

Marx, K. (1972). Contribution to the critique of Hegel's philosophy of right: Introduction. In R. C. Tucker (Ed.), *The Marx-Engels reader.* New York: W. W. Norton.

Mayer, A. J., & Sharp, H. (1962). Religious preferences and worldly success. *American Sociological Review, 27,* 218–227.

Neibuhr, H. R. (1957). *The social sources of denominationalism.* New York: New American Library.

Newman, W. A. & Wright, S. A. (1980). The effects of sermons among lay Catholics: An exploratory study. *Review of Religious Research, 22* (September), 54–59.

Pargament, C., & Silverman, W. H. (1982). Exploring some correlates of sermon impact in Catholic parishioners. *Review of Religious Research, 24* (September), 33–39.

Pope, L. (1942). *Millhands and preachers.* New Haven, CT: Yale University Press.

Robertson, R. (1970). *The sociological interpretation of religion.* New York: Schocken Books.

Schneider, H. W. (1973). *Religion in twentieth century America.* Cambridge, MA: Harvard University Press.

Schroeder, W. W., & Oberhaus, V. (1964). Church participation patterns. In *Religion in American culture* (pp. 32–54). New York: The Free Press.

Stark, R. (1964). Class, radicalism and religious involvement in Great Britain. *American Sociological Review, 24,* 698–706.

Stark, R. (1972). The economics of piety: Religious commitment and social class. In H. P. Chalfant et al., *Religion in Contemporary Society* (p. 389). Sherman Oaks, CA: Alfred Publishing Company.

Warner, W. L., & Lunt, P. S. (1941). *The social system of a modern community.* New Haven, CT: Yale University Press.

Yinger, J. M. (1970). *The scientific study of religion.* London: The Macmillan Company.

POLITICS

Society has no justification if it does not bring a little peace to men—peace in their hearts and peace in their mutual intercourse.

Émile Durkheim
Professional Ethics and Civic Morals

With a modem and a few keystrokes a skilled investigator can obtain an astonishingly detailed list of information about your personal life. This includes, but is not limited to, your complete medical history, the items you have purchased by check and credit card, your credit rating, state and federal tax records, court records, traffic tickets, phone numbers you have called over the last few months, and even the books you have checked out of the library. Ultimately, the only reason this private information is not used by employers, market researchers, schools, friends, and enemies is because of civil liberties protected by the Bill of Rights.

The protection of the Bill of Rights cannot, however, be taken for granted, nor can its support among the American public. This was illustrated by an Associated Press article of February 3, 1980, which reported that a civics teacher in Vassalboro, Maine, who decided to dramatize the freedoms in the Bill of Rights for his high school students, assigned students to go into the streets with a petition. The petition urged the repeal of 10 laws that "coddled criminals." These untitled laws were word-for-word reproductions of the text of the first 10 amendments to the United States Constitution (see next page). To the surprise and dismay of the students, 74 percent of the people who listened to the students' request signed the petition for the repeal of these laws. Less than 8 percent of the respondents recognized the petition's text as the Bill of Rights. More recent surveys by Strasser (1991) and DeBenedictis (1991) suggest that there is still mixed knowledge of and support for the Bill of Rights.

The low level of support for the Bill of Rights should come as a surprise to functionalists. They argue that in the long run, laws must develop from a general consensus in order for laws to represent the larger interests of society. On the other hand, the findings would not be surprising to many conflict theorists.

They are consistent with the conflict theorists' view that society is divided into competing groups, each of which has its own interests that are, in turn, advanced or threatened by laws.

Conflict Perspective

According to Marx, as primitives worked to overcome their poverty they gradually began to produce a surplus of wealth. With wealth came ideas about property and how it should be distributed. Classes formed to advance their claims for the biggest share. In the ensuing struggle over property rights, the natural community disintegrated. Civil law developed to impose ways of behavior upon those who would no longer spontaneously accept the rules of their masters. The state was born in this class struggle, and is controlled by the class most successful in the struggle for power. In modern society this leads to the state becoming a virtual "machine" of the capitalists. The goal of Marx and Engels was to bring an end to class distinctions: if all classes disappeared, there would no longer be any need for the state or its bourgeois laws. Civil laws and government would wither and disappear. People would become truly free upon the disappearance of laws and the state.

Functional Perspective

Durkheim rejected the notion that people were necessarily oppressed by the state. He believed that individual liberty and dignity are protected, not destroyed, by the state. Democratic states have passed much notable legislation that safeguards minorities against discrimination, protects societal diversity, and ensures the rights of individuals. Durkheim believed that the classless society envisioned by Marx would destroy these protective laws, and thereby threaten the rights of the individual by creating a compulsory fraternity and fusing of state and society.

Functionalists maintain that the state performs a number of essential societal functions. According to Parsons and Bales (1953), all effective governments fulfill four functions:

This investigation is based on "Support of Civil Liberties Among College Students" by Clyde Z. Nunn, 1973, reprinted on pages 118–124.

Table 9-1

BILL OF RIGHTS OF THE UNITED STATES

AMENDMENT I.	Congress shall make no law respecting an establishment of religion, or prohibiting the free exercise thereof; or abridging the freedom of speech, or of the press; or the right of the people peaceably to assemble, and to petition the Government for a redress of grievances.
AMENDMENT II.	A well regulated Militia, being necessary to the security of a free State, the right of the people to keep and bear Arms, shall not be infringed.
AMENDMENT III.	No Soldier shall, in time of peace, be quartered in any house, without the consent of the Owner, nor in time of war, but in a manner to be prescribed by law.
AMENDMENT IV.	The right of the people to be secure in their persons, houses, papers, and effects, against unreasonable searches and seizures, shall not be violated, and no Warrants shall issue, but upon probable cause, supported by Oath or affirmation, and particularly describing the place to be searched, and the persons or things to be seized.
AMENDMENT V.	No person shall be held to answer for a capital, or otherwise infamous crime, unless on a presentment or indictment of a Grand Jury, except in cases arising in the land or naval forces, or in the Militia, when in actual service in time of War or public danger; nor shall any person be subject for the same offence to be twice put in jeopardy of life or limb, nor shall be compelled in any criminal case to be a witness against himself, nor be deprived of life, liberty, or property, without due process of law; nor shall private property be taken for public use without just compensation.
AMENDMENT VI.	In all criminal prosecutions, the accused shall enjoy the right to a speedy and public trial, by an impartial jury of the State and district wherein the crime shall have been committed, which district shall have been previously ascertained by law, and to be informed of the nature and cause of the accusation; to be confronted with the witnesses against him; to have compulsory process for obtaining witnesses in his favor, and to have the Assistance of Counsel for his defence.
AMENDMENT VII.	In Suits at common law, where the value in controversy shall exceed twenty dollars, the right of trial by jury shall be preserved, and no fact tried by a jury shall be otherwise reexamined in any Court of the United States, than according to the rules of common law.
AMENDMENT VIII.	Excessive bail shall not be required, nor excessive fines imposed, nor cruel and unusual punishments inflicted.
AMENDMENT IX.	The enumeration in the Constitution, of certain rights, shall not be construed to deny or disparage others retained by the people.
AMENDMENT X.	The powers not delegated to the United States by the Constitution, nor prohibited by it to the States, are reserved to the States respectively, or to the people.

1. *Determining goals.* The government must establish a priority from among competing goals. For example, which has priority: industrial modernization, space exploration, or social welfare?
2. *Developing resources.* The government may draft personnel in time of war, electrically develop the Tennessee Valley, control the money supply, or regulate vital resources.
3. *Distributing resources.* Through taxation, issuance of contracts, or provision of welfare benefits, the government is responsible for the distribution of wealth.
4. *Maintaining social order.* The government is ultimately responsible for protecting individuals from external dangers, as well as for internally enforcing norms and adjudicating differences between individuals, and between individuals and the state.

Individual liberties guaranteed in the Bill of Rights are ultimately anchored in the moral order. Courts cannot enforce for long any laws that lack social support. As society changes, so do the priorities accorded to the rights of the individual and society. This tension is expressed in the balance between laws that protect the collective order and laws that protect individual freedoms. By protecting the rights of the individual, for instance, the Bill of Rights can be seen as "coddling criminals."

This often results in an ambivalence toward the freedoms guaranteed by the Bill of Rights. On the one hand, people support the abstract principles of the Bill of Rights (such as freedom of speech); but on the other hand, many reject specific application of these rights (such as allowing communists to speak on college campuses).

In 1970, CBS commissioned a survey to measure the support for individual liberties. They translated a general right provided in Amendment V in the Bill of Rights into a question concerning its specific application. The amendment, with the relevant passage underlined, and the CBS poll question are given below.

> Amendment V. No person shall be held to answer for a capital, or otherwise infamous crime, unless on a presentment or indictment of a Grand Jury, except in cases arising in the land or naval forces, or in the Militia, when in actual service in time of war or public danger; nor shall any person be subject for the same offense to be twice put in jeopardy of life or limb, nor shall be compelled in any criminal case to be a witness against himself, nor be deprived of life, liberty, or property, without due process of law; nor shall private property be taken for public use without just compensation.

Table 9–2

AGREEMENT WITH THE BILL OF RIGHTS
(N = 560)

Amend-ment	Provision	Percent of Respondents		
		Yes	No	No Opin-ion
I	Freedom of speech, press	82.5	14.0	3.2
I	Freedom of religion	77.1	13.6	9.3
I	Peaceable assembly	56.8	35.7	7.5
II, III	Bear arms, quartering troops	63.6	20.3	16.1
IV	Search and seizure	81.8	14.6	3.6
V	Self-incrimination	56.1	33.2	10.7
V	Due process	70.0	25.7	4.3
V	Double jeopardy	23.6	71.8	4.6
VI	Public trial	54.3	34.3	11.4
VI	Confront accuser	23.9	67.5	8.6
VI	Informed of accusation	94.8	2.3	2.9
VI, VII	Trial by jury	89.6	9.3	1.1
VIII	Excessive bail and punishment	61.4	32.2	6.4
IX, X	Reserved rights of people	44.3	51.1	4.6

Note: From "Do We Really Believe in the Bill of Rights?" by Ray Mack. Copyright 1956 by the Society for the Study of Social Problems. Reprinted by permission from *Social Problems, 3,* No. 4, April 1956, p. 267.

CBS POLL QUESTION: If a man is found innocent of a serious crime, but new evidence is uncovered later, do you think he should be tried again for the same crime?

In answer to this question, only 58 percent of Americans thought a person should be protected against double jeopardy. Many analysts found in these responses a disturbing lack of support for the rights of individuals.

Samuel Stouffer (1955) found the greatest support for civil liberties among those with the greatest social and cultural diversity. Specifically, he found those who were most supportive of civil liberties were young, urban, male, and non-Southern. Education is consistently and positively related to tolerance. But even among presumably tolerant college students, Ray Mack (1956, p. 268) found a "considerable body of disagreement and indecision regarding what have been considered basic civil rights." He also found an "impressive ignorance of educated people regarding the Constitutional provisions for these rights." In his student survey, fewer than one in ten recognized the provisions of the Bill of Rights. The level of student support for individual civil liberties is indicated in Table 9–2 above.

On a more positive note, Stouffer argued that support for civil liberties would grow stronger as time passed. He claimed

that social, economic, and technological forces will foster greater levels of social and political tolerance. "The rising level of education and accompanying decline in authoritarian child-rearing practices increase independence of thought and respect for others whose ideas are different" (1955, p. 236). A replication of Stouffer's study by J. Allen Williams et al. (1976) suggested that levels of tolerance had, in fact, increased from 1954 to 1973. Associated with more tolerance were city size, occupational status, region (West, high; South, low), sex (male, high; female, low), and education.

National research based on NORC (National Opinion Research Center) surveys led Davis (1975) and Lawrence (1976) to conclude that Stouffer was correct in his optimism. Davis found tolerant answers had increased 22 percent from Stouffer's 1954 survey to the 1971 NORC survey. He estimated that 4 percent of the increased tolerance was due to higher levels of education, 5 percent to generational changes, and 13 percent to increased levels of tolerance among all generations and educational groups.

Analysis of a later 1977 NORC survey by Nunn, Crockett, and Williams (1978) shows levels of tolerance continuing to rise significantly throughout the 1970s. From 1954 to 1977, tolerant responses to the Stouffer questions rose dramatically from 25 to as much as 35 percent. Based on this evidence and the societal trends that they identified, Nunn et al. concluded that "given the substantial increase in public support for democratic principles, the risk of demagogic takeover or the undermining of civil liberties is less now than it once was" (p. 158).

Sullivan, Pierson, and Marcus (1979) do not share the optimistic conclusions expressed by these researchers. Their skepticism is based on two problems. The first is that the majority of the Stouffer questions concern tolerating communists, socialists, and atheists. Sullivan et al. note that the Stouffer research was carried out during and after the Army-McCarthy hearings. This was a unique period in American history when the threat posed by communism was perceived as being of crisis proportions. With détente, glasnost, perestroika, and the collapse of the communist empire, it has become easy to tolerate, and even accept, nonthreatening communists, socialists, and atheists. Thus, changes that have occurred may be explained as change in the target group rather than as changes in tolerance. Secondly, previous studies focused on the toleration of left-wing but not right-wing target groups (such as anti-abortionists, white supremacists, the Aryan League, the Ku Klux Klan, and Posse Comitatus). When Sullivan et al. asked respondents to select either liberal or conservative groups that they disliked, the researchers found little change in tolerance levels from Stouffer's 1954 survey. Furthermore, the researchers concluded that education played less of a role in increasing tolerance than had been previously thought. Subsequent research by Bobo and Licari (1989) indicates there is a connection between education and political tolerance when the target group is "merely disliked." Education is not, however, found to be associated with greater tolerance of "extraordinarily disliked groups" (extremist groups perceived as law-breaking and/or violent).

Background

Clyde Z. Nunn's research (Reading 9, pp. 118–124) focuses upon the relationship between support for the Bill of Rights and education. His survey shows great variability in student support of the Bill of Rights. Only one-third of students were termed highly supportive of civil liberties (libertarian). Least supportive of the Bill of Rights were women planning to marry, active Protestant church attenders, upperclassmen, and non–liberal arts majors. While the impact of college education was not as strong as expected, Nunn concludes that college attendance did significantly increase support for the Bill of Rights. Our investigation seeks to update these findings. Specifically, we will reexamine Nunn's hypotheses concerning (1) the level of support for civil liberties, and (2) the impact of background characteristics on the support for civil liberties.

Replication

Our investigation will use three independent variables from the Student Survey. Sex is determined by question 1, education by question 4, and religious attendance by question 8. You may consider "trend" as a fourth independent variable. The trend is indicated by comparing changes from 1957 and 1971 to your libertarianism results. Libertarianism, the dependent variable, is measured by questions 19–23. These five items are adapted from the fifteen used in Nunn's study of civil liberties. They appear in the Student Survey in the form shown in the box to the right, which also indicates which responses are considered libertarian.

Support of Civil Liberties

In Table 1 on page 120, "Attitudes Toward Principles of the Bill of Rights," Nunn found (1) no item from the Bill of Rights was universally accepted (this will be tested by hypothesis 1), and (2) there was great variability in the support of civil liberties (this will be tested by hypothesis 2). The least-supported civil right concerned the government's right to withhold evidence (question 19 in our survey). This was supported by only 31 percent of the students. Of the five questions used in our Student Survey, greatest support was given to the rights of a suspect: 75 percent of the students believed that to detain a suspect, police must have sufficient evidence to indict him or her (question 20 in our survey). Nunn's findings show that libertarian support for the five questions we are examining ranged from 31 to 75 percent. If this variability persists, we should find a range of 44 percent or more between the most- and least-supported items. We will also investigate whether or not support for the Bill of Rights is increasing over time.

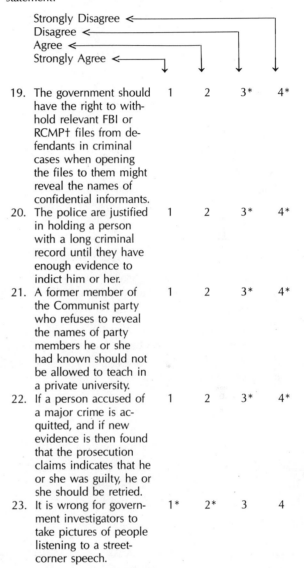

Support of Civil Liberties

Hypothesis 1: Universality

No item in the Bill of Rights is accepted by everyone. (We will consider 95+ percent agreement as acceptance by virtually everyone.)

Hypothesis 2: Variability

There is great variability in the support of items in the Bill of Rights.

Table 9–3

INVESTIGATION RESULTS 9
Support for Civil Liberties

Item	Percent Giving Libertarian Response		
	Nunn's (1971) Study	Student Survey	My Response (L or NL)
The police are justified in holding a person with a long criminal record until they have enough evidence to indict him or her. (Question 20)	75%	_____ %	_____
A former member of the Communist party who refuses to reveal the names of Party members he or she had known should not be allowed to teach in a private university. (Question 21)	65%	_____ %	_____
It is wrong for government investigators to take pictures of people listening to a street-corner speech. (Question 23)	50%	_____ %	_____
If a person accused of a major crime is acquitted, and if new evidence is then found that the prosecution claims indicates that he or she was guilty, he or she should be retried. (Question 22)	34%	_____ %	_____
The government should have the right to withhold relevant FBI or RCMP (Royal Canadian Mounted Police) files from defendants in criminal cases when opening the files to them might reveal the names of confidential informants. (Question 19)	31%	_____ %	_____
Nebraska variability =	44%		
Investigation variability (Hypothesis 2) =	=	_____ %	
My libertarianism score =			_____
SLIGHT Libertarian (0–1)			
MODERATE Libertarian (2–3)			
HIGH Libertarian (4–5)			

Note: Nunn's data are from Table 1, p. 120.

Hypothesis 3: Trend

The support for the Bill of Rights is increasing.

Background Characteristics of Respondents

To determine the importance of the respondent's background characteristics to the support of civil rights, Nunn compared respondents by sex, religious attendance, and year in college. The influence of these background characteristics is indicated by the proportion of students falling in the high libertarian category (that is, those who supported four or five items from the Bill of Rights). This proportion is used to evaluate hypotheses 4, 5, and 6.

Hypothesis 4: Sex

Males are more libertarian than females.

Hypothesis 5: Religion

Low religious attendance is positively associated with libertarianism. (For religious attendance, low is "almost never" and high is "weekly attendance.")

Hypothesis 6: Education

The more education a person has, the greater will be that person's support of civil liberties.

To test these hypotheses, we will first need to know the percentages of students in your class that gave libertarian

Table 9–4

SUPPORT FOR BILL OF RIGHTS
BY YEAR

	Libertarianism		
	Slight (0–1)	Moderate (2–3)	High (4–5)
Previous Samples*			
California (1957)	20%	46%	34%
Nebraska (1971)	17%	45%	38%
Student Survey	_____	_____	_____
	Hypothesis 3 _____↑		

*California and Nebraska data are from Table 2, p. 121.

Table 9–5

SUPPORT FOR BILL OF RIGHTS
BY SEX

	Libertarianism		
	Slight (0–1)	Moderate (2–3)	High (4–5)
Sex*			
Female	_____ (29%)	_____ (48%)	_____ (32%)←
Male	_____ (15%)	_____ (41%)	_____ (44%)←
	Hypothesis 4 _____		

*Data in parentheses are from Table 3, p. 121.

responses to Student Survey questions 19 through 23. We then need to analyze the levels of libertarian response (low, medium, or high) in terms of the independent variables of year, sex, religious attendance, and education. All of these data will be compiled by your instructor and provided to you. When you have received the data, proceed as follows:

Step 1:

Fill in the responses you gave to Student Survey question 19 through 23 in the right-hand column in Table 9–3, under the heading My Response. This will help you compare your responses to the class's.

Step 2:

Fill in the class's responses to questions 19 through 23 in the column in Table 9–3 under the heading Student Survey. Also fill in the blank spaces in tables 9–4 through 9–7 with the information provided by your instructor. Arrows in these tables will indicate where to find the data to test hypotheses 3 through 6.

Step 3:

To test hypothesis 1, find the highest libertarian response for questions 19 through 23. You might note that the highest support found by Nunn for these five items was 75 percent. Enter the highest percent libertarian response from your class in the blank provided in hypothesis 1 below.

Hypothesis 1: Universality

No item in the Bill of Rights is accepted by everyone.

Support for highest item _____ < 95%

Step 4:

Next, locate "Investigation variability" at the bottom of Table 9–3. To test hypothesis 3, compare the variability in the responses to the five questions to the variability that Nunn found (44%).

Hypothesis 2: Variability

There is great variability in the support of items in the Bill of Rights.

Replication variation _____ ≥ 44% (Nunn variation)

Step 5:

To test hypothesis 3, compare the percentage of those giving a high libertarianism response (that is, supporting four or five items in the Bill of Rights) to the percentage who did so in a 1957 California study cited by Nunn (p. 121).

Hypothesis 3: Trend

The support for the Bill of Rights is increasing. (Use Table 9–4, above left)

Student Survey libertarianism _____ > 34% (1957 libertarianism)

Step 6:

To test hypothesis 4, compare the percentage of males who gave a high libertarian response on the Student Survey to the percentage of females who did so.

Hypothesis 4: Sex

Males are more libertarian than females. (Use Table 9–5, above right.)

Males _____ > _____ Females

Step 7:

To test hypothesis 5, compare the percentage of those with low religious attendance ("almost never") who gave a high libertarian response to the percentage of those with high religious attendance ("every week") who did so.

Table 9–6

SUPPORT FOR BILL OF RIGHTS BY RELIGIOUS ATTENDANCE

	Libertarianism		
	Slight (0–1)	Moderate (2–3)	High (4–5)
Religious Attendance*			
Every week (3 and 4)	_____ (20%)	_____ (48%)	_____ (32%)
1 to 2 times per month (2)	_____ (24%)	_____ (52%)	_____ (24%)
Sporadically (1)	_____ (15%)	_____ (45%)	_____ (40%)
Almost never (0)	_____ (9%)	_____ (34%)	_____ (57%)

Hypothesis 5 _____

*Data in parentheses are from Table 3, p. 121.

Table 9–7

SUPPORT FOR BILL OF RIGHTS BY EDUCATION

	Libertarianism		
	Slight (0–1)	Moderate (2–3)	High (4–5)
College Year*			
Freshman	_____ (21%)	_____ (53%)	_____ (26%)
Sophomore	_____ (15%)	_____ (48%)	_____ (37%)
Junior	_____ (17%)	_____ (36%)	_____ (47%)
Senior	_____ (13%)	_____ (39%)	_____ (48%)

Hypothesis 6 _____

*Data in parentheses are from Table 4, p. 123.

Hypothesis 5: Religion

Low religious attendance is positively associated with libertarianism. (Use Table 9–6, above left.)

Low _____ > _____ High

Step 8:

To test hypothesis 6, compare the percentage of seniors (or "upperclassmen") who gave a high libertarian response to the percentage of freshmen who did so.

Hypothesis 6: Education

The more education a person has, the greater will be that person's support of civil liberties. (Use Table 9–7, above right.)

Seniors _____ > _____ Freshmen

Checking Your Findings

In Investigation 1 we reported that Christenson found considerable agreement that personal freedom was the most important value. Functionalists would point out that such agreement is necessary for the effective operation of laws. But freedom is an abstract value, and may not always be consistent with specific beliefs. Conflict theorists emphasize the discrepancies that exist between the support of abstract freedoms guaranteed in the Bill of Rights and the lack of support for the specific protections of these rights. The hypotheses we are investigating here will help us determine if there are discrepancies between the importance we attach to freedom and specific applications of that value. We will then look at what role education can play in bringing about a greater consistency between values and applications.

Hypothesis 1 is concerned with determining the level of support for the Bill of Rights. It asks if any right is accepted by virtually everyone. Which right did you find to have the most widespread support? Was it supported by more than 95 percent of the students?

Hypothesis 2 examines the variability in the support of these rights. Which item had the least support? How much difference is there between the most and least supported rights?

Hypothesis 3 deals with the controversy about whether or not there is a rising level of tolerance and support of the Bill of Rights. Did you find more or less than 34 percent (the percent in the 1957 California survey) to be in the high libertarian group?

Hypothesis 4 examines the effect of one's sex on libertarianism. Did you find males or females to have the greatest support for the Bill of Rights?

Hypothesis 5 explores the effect of religious attendance on libertarianism. Does religious attendance adversely affect support for the Bill of Rights?

Hypothesis 6 Nunn's central finding was that the greater the level of education, the greater the support for the Bill of Rights. Do your findings support those of Nunn?

After studying the results, summarize your findings in Table 9–8 on the next page by indicating the amount of support for each hypothesis.

Table 9–8

SUPPORT FOR HYPOTHESES

	Significantly Supported	Partially Supported	Not Supported	Indeterminate
Hypothesis 1: Most support < 95%	_____	_____	_____	_____
Hypothesis 2: Variation > = 44%	_____	_____	_____	_____
Hypothesis 3: Student Survey > 34%	_____	_____	_____	_____
Hypothesis 4: Males > females	_____	_____	_____	_____
Hypothesis 5: Religion low > high	_____	_____	_____	_____
Hypothesis 6: Seniors > freshmen	_____	_____	_____	_____

Indicate the amount of support you found for each hypothesis.

Topics for Further Investigation

1. We traditionally speak of the Bill of Rights as an almost sacred document representing the most basic values of American democracy. Does your survey indicate that any right guaranteed in the Bill of Rights is accepted by virtually everyone?

    a. How would you describe the level of support for the Bill of Rights expressed by your class?

    b. If the level of support has changed since Nunn's survey, do you feel it represents a trend?

2. Studies consistently find the support for civil rights increases with the level of education. Was this supported in your survey? If that is not the case, do you feel it is because your school is conservative? Or do you feel education in general is no longer a liberalizing experience?

3. We began the investigation with the question, Would Americans repeal the Bill of Rights? After analyzing the results of your survey, how would you answer this question? How confident are you of your answer?

References and Recommended Readings

Associated Press. (1980, February 3). Students find citizens would kill Bill of Rights. *Los Angeles Times,* part IV, p. 2.

Bobo, L., & Licari, F. (1989). Education and political tolerance: Testing the effects of cognitive sophistication and target group affect. *Public Opinion Quarterly, 53,* 285–308.

Chandler, R. (1972). *Public opinion.* New York: R. R. Bowker Company.

Davis, J. A. (1975). Communism, conformity, cohorts, and categories: American tolerance in 1954 and 1972–73. *American Journal of Sociology, 81,* 491–513.

DeBenedictis, D. (1991). Legal literacy: Californians get a C– on Bill of Rights quiz. *ABA Journal* (July), 77, 19.

Durkheim, E. (1962). *Socialism.* New York: Collier Books.

Durkheim, E. (1965). *Montesquieu and Rousseau.* Ann Arbor, MI: Ann Arbor Paperbacks.

Feiffer, J. (1978, July). Love-hate and the First Amendment. *Nation,* pp. 19–20.

Lawrence, D. (1976). Procedural norms and tolerance: A reassessment. *American Political Science Review, 70,* 80–100.

Mack, R. (1956). Do we really believe in the Bill of Rights? *Social Problems, 3,* 264–269.

McClosky, H., & Brill, A. (1983). *Dimensions of tolerance.* New York: Russell Sage Foundation.

Nunn, C. Z. (1973). Support of civil liberties among college students. *Social Problems, 20,* 200–210.

Nunn, C. Z., Crockett, H., & Williams, J. A. (1978). *Tolerance for nonconformity.* San Franciso: Jossey-Bass.

Parsons, T., & Bales, R. (1953). *Working papers in the theory of action.* New York: The Free Press.

Robin, S., & Story, F. (1963). Ideological consistency of college students: The Bill of Rights and attitudes toward minority groups. *Sociology and Social Research, 48,* 187–196.

Selvin, H., & Hagstrom, W. (1960). Determinants of support for civil liberties. *British Journal of Sociology, 11,* 51–73.

Strasser, F. (1991). Americans are fuzzy on rights. *National Law Journal* (December 23), *14,* 6.

Stouffer, S. (1955). *Communism, conformity and civil liberties,* New York: John Wiley & Sons.

Sullivan, J., Piereson, J., & Marcus, G. (1979). An alternative conceptualization of political tolerance: Illusory increases 1950's–1970's. *American Political Science Review, 73,* 781–794.

Sullivan, J., Piereson, J., & Marcus, G. (1982). *Political tolerance and American democracy.* Chicago: University of Chicago Press.

Williams, J. A., Nunn, C. Z., & St. Peter, L. (1976). Origins of tolerance: Findings from a replication of Stouffer's communism, conformity and civil liberties. *Social Forces, 55,* 394–418.

9

Support of Civil Liberties Among College Students

Modeled after the Selvin and Hagstrom study of Berkeley students in 1957, the present study compared the extent and consistency of civil liberties support in a Nebraska college sample to Berkeley. Results at the two schools were highly similar. Support of civil liberties depended in large part on the particular principle involved, but generally about a third of the students could be called highly libertarian. Sources of support were also explored. Those who were female (especially females with early marriage plans), active church attenders (especially Protestant), underclassmen, non-liberal arts majors, and those who reported little or no impact from their college life, were least supportive of civil liberties. It was concluded that extensive civil liberties support on the college campus was far less than an accomplished fact; yet there is evidence that college has a significant impact generally and on civil liberties support in particular.

Clyde Z. Nunn
Center for Policy Research, New York

Several conclusions are apparent from a survey of the literature on support of civil liberties: (1) When civil liberties are situation specific rather than clichés about the Bill of Rights, there is a lack of consensus on the extent to which civil liberties should be extended to all Americans. (2) A relatively low level of support for such liberties exists, and support in this sphere is not increasing but may even be declining. (3) Education is the most persistently powerful predictor of support for the individual, though support among the highly educated is far from overwhelming.

Surveys of national samples and those drawn from local communities attest to the general lack of consensus on the extent civil liberties should protect nonconformists. In the most extensive national study of civil liberties undertaken, Stouffer (1955) found marked variation in the degree of tolerance of nonconformity. While tolerance varied depending on how extreme the nonconformist was perceived to be, an index of responses to different nonconformists indicated 19 percent of a probability sample were low in tolerance, 50 percent were moderate, and 31 percent were highly tolerant. In particular, academic freedom for the admitted communist high school teacher got less than ten percent support (Stouffer, 1955). More recently in a review of national poll results on freedom of speech, Erskine (1970) found the maximum percentage believing in freedom of speech for

extremists never exceeded 50 percent. Estimates of changes over the decades by Erskine (1970), though the data have limited comparability, found support of freedom of speech for extremists regressing from a maximum support of 49 percent before 1950 to 29 percent during the 1950's to 21 percent after 1960.[1] The lack of consensus observed in national samples was also observed at local levels in surveys of Midwestern and Southern communities (Prothro and Grigg, 1960; Lenski, 1961).

While tolerance of nonconformity and support of civil liberties were found to be consistently and positively associated with educational level in a wide variety of studies, extent of support or tolerance remains conditional and limited to a considerable degree even among the most educated (Stouffer, 1955; Dynes, 1967; Prothro and Grigg, 1960; Erskine, 1970). Among college students, tolerance and support were prominent but still lacking definitive consensus. For instance, during the early 1950's at Cornell University, Goldsen and others (1960) found civil liberties got less than overwhelming support when couched in situational statements. Only 58 percent disagreed that religion which preached unwholesome ideas should be suppressed. Similarly, only 59 percent unconditionally supported academic freedom. Lipset (1953) found at Berkeley in the 1950's that only 39 percent were unwilling to exclude a communist from a teaching post, while 64 percent opposed loyalty oaths for faculty. Selvin and Hagstrom (1960) found support of the Bill of Rights at Berkeley in the late 1950's fluctuated from principle to principle; and their index of these 15

Reprinted with permission from *Social Problems, 20*, No. 3, Winter 1973, pp. 300–310. Copyright 1973 by the Society for the Study of Social Problems.

1. From a national survey of high school students, Remmers (1963) observed between 1951 and 1960 either a decline in or relatively unchanged support for Bill of Rights principles.

situationally paraphrased principles resulted in only 34 percent of the students being classified as "highly libertarian," 46 percent "moderately libertarian," and 20 percent "slightly libertarian." Academic freedom issues received at least majority support; three-fourths disagreed that a high school teacher who pleads the Fifth Amendment while being questioned by a congressional committee should be fired. Less support (60 percent) was reported for academic freedom when the subject was a professor at the university level.

In addition to the concern with the extent of support of civil liberties, a central issue in college studies has been the effects of college experience on these democratic attitudes. Again the findings appeared unequivocal; the move from freshman to senior years was usually accompanied by greater support of civil liberties issues (Selvin and Hagstrom, 1960; Lipset, 1953; Kosa and Nunn, 1965). The only longitudinal data available (Finney, 1971) showed a net increase in libertarianism of 16 percent between 1959 and 1961. Even though a net increase was found during this time span, 21 percent became less libertarian. Hence, the impact of college is not always unidirectional. In addition there are those who argue that the reported positive impact of college on students' attitudes and values has been exaggerated and may even be nonexistent (Jacob, 1957). The issue of college impact is not settled and deserves added attention. Furthermore it has been over a decade since the last appraisal of college influence on civil liberties support, and the widely reported campus ferment would make additional estimates of what is taking place now appear essential.

The relation of religion and religiosity to libertarian attitudes is another unsettled issue. Studies of college populations in the 1950's found little or only moderate differences between Protestants and Catholics (Lipset, 1953; Selvin and Hagstrom, 1960). On the other hand, the data were much more convincing about religiosity and libertarianism; the most active and religious students proved to be least libertarian (Selvin and Hagstrom, 1960; Goldsen, et al., 1960). One study of high school students using the Selvin-Hagstrom index of libertarianism found no association between this index and either religious preference or church attendance (Alonzo and Kinch, 1964). At the community level, Lenski (1961) claimed Protestants were more libertarian than Catholics, while at the national level Erskine's (1970) review of opinion poll evidence showed little or only moderate differences between Catholics and Protestants. Both religious affiliation differences and religiosity or church attendance differences will be considered in the present study.

The present study was primarily modeled after the Selvin and Hagstrom (1960) study at Berkeley, and most of the same issues explored then will be considered here. In addition to an estimate of the extent and consistency of support of civil liberties and the impact of educational and religious institutions on libertarianism, the present study attempts to specify additional sources of support or nonsupport in this area, taking account of such variables as sex, major subject of student, and size of community where the student was reared. General libertarianism and support of academic freedom in particular will be the focus.

SAMPLE AND DATA COLLECTION

Data were collected by structured questionnaires from 437 undergraduates of the University of Nebraska. While random sampling procedures were not followed, the sample, obtained from a cross-section of sociology courses in the University, closely approximates the University population in several important respects. With the exception of the proportion of females, who were overrepresented by 14 percent, the sample showed approximately the same proportions of freshmen, sophomores, juniors, and seniors as found in the entire student body, and a close similarity of proportions of different majors (Note the wide distribution of majors in Table 4 on page 123).[2] It is assumed that the sample represents a fairly typical middle-of-the-road college population.

The questionnaire contained only items pertaining to the civil liberties issue and necessary social and attitudinal information. The dependent variable, support of civil liberties, was measured by the same procedures used by Selvin and Hagstrom (1960). They derived an index from 15 paraphrased statements of the Bill of Rights, which they took to reflect an accurate measure of the student's general sentiments of fairness or "libertarianism." From the index, the sum of libertarian responses for each student, three major categories of libertarianism were composed: 0–7 libertarian responses = "slightly libertarian," 8–11 libertarian responses = "moderately libertarian," and 12–15 libertarian responses = "highly libertarian." The index was not intended to make fine distinctions, but to classify subjects along the broad, and perhaps multi-dimensional, content area of willingness to permit others optimal levels of individual liberties. More detailed measurement rationale can be found in Selvin and Hagstrom (1960).

RESULTS

General Description and Comparisons

One of the most important findings in the Selvin-Hagstrom study in 1957 (1960) was the wide variation in support of different principles of the Bill of Rights, from 87 percent to 24 percent. A very similar phenomenon occurred in the 1971 Nebraska sample; the range in this case was from 90 percent to 31 percent. Selvin and Hagstrom's contention that support of civil liberties cannot be taken simply as a neat package of similar responses on all issues was strongly supported by the Nebraska data in Table 1 [p. 120]. While there was no clear clustering of issues that got most or least support, questions dealing with free speech, freedom of public gatherings, and free press received greatest support; by contrast, items dealing with rights of accused criminals claimed the least support. These

---

2. Confidence in the representativeness of our sample is supported by similar data from a study relying on a randomly selected sample. In this survey, 66 percent of Nebraska students expressed a willingness to permit a communist to teach in the University (Welch and Carlson, forthcoming). In the present study the libertage on a comparable question was 65 percent.

Table 1

ATTITUDES TOWARD PRINCIPLES OF THE BILL OF RIGHTS

Item	% Giving Libertarian Response
1. The Government should have the right to prohibit any group of persons who disagrees with our form of government from holding public meetings.	90%
2. The circulation of Russian or Chinese newspapers in this country should be restricted to scholars.	85
3. State governments should have the power to pass laws making it illegal to speak against racial or religious groups.	85
4. A high-school teacher who 'pleads the Fifth Amendment' while being questioned by a Congressional Committee should be fired at once.	85
5. Large-scale police round-ups of 'undesirables' are proper as long as they are restricted to people with known criminal records.	83
6. The police are justified in holding a man with a long criminal record until they have enough evidence to indict him.	75
7. The government is acting properly in refusing a passport to a Socialist.	75
8. It unduly hampers the police in their efforts to apprehend criminals when they have to have a warrant to search a house.	74
9. It is reasonable to suspect the loyalty of a lawyer who represents accused Communists before a Congressional Committee.	72
10. A former member of the Communist party who refuses to reveal the names of party members he had known should not be allowed to teach in a private university.	65
11. 'Crime' comic books should be screened by some government agency before publication.	64
12. Legislative committees should not investigate the political beliefs of university faculty members.	59
13. It is wrong for government investigators to take pictures of people listening to a streetcorner speech.	50
14. If a person accused of a major crime is acquitted, and if new evidence is then found that the prosecution claims indicates that he was guilty, he should be retried.	34
15. The government should have the right to withhold relevant FBI files from defendants in criminal cases, when opening the files to them might reveal the names of confidential informants.	31

data also appear to give governmental investigators a rather broad range of freedom to find or withhold information on citizens. Overall, rankings of support for the different principles were quite similar at California and Nebraska; the Coefficient of Concordance for the rankings at the two schools was .95.

There were also strong similarities in results at the two campuses on the Index of Libertarianism, a measure composed of summations of libertarian responses to the 15 items. In Table 2 [see next page] the proportions who were slightly, moderately, and highly libertarian were nearly identical at the two universities. In both instances approximately a third were highly libertarian. Whether these data mean that there have been insignificant shifts in civil liberties support on college campuses over the past decade and a half or that Nebraska continues to enjoy cultural lag in this area is not certain. However, the Stouffer (1955) data comparing regions on tolerance of nonconformity suggest the cultural lag explanation as most applicable. In that study, there were 10 to 15 percentage point differences in those "more tolerant" among college graduates in the West and Midwest. Nevertheless, the Nebraska data raise an interesting question about changes in civil liberties support in this country, particularly among the highly educated. Has there, in fact, been a significant shift in tolerance levels over the past decade or

two? While national sample data are needed to unambiguously answer this and other questions regarding tolerance of nonconformity, the fact that war protest movements, urban riots, and most other forms of nonconformity occur with recognizable regularity and intensity in the Midwest, as well as the West and East Coasts, suggests that at least at the college level, tolerance might be comparably distributed in these regions.

Background Characteristics and Libertarianism

Sex roles, even though changing, have long been distinguishable by a conservatism or traditionalism, with females much more cautious and guarded than males in entertaining new or different ideas (Maccoby, 1966). While it can be assumed that females attracted to higher education might be different from their non-college counterparts, the college experience remains for many females an opportunity to improve marital aspirations rather than a training ground for non-family careers. Hence, traditional sex role differences might still be observable in attitudes such as tolerance of nonconformity. This is apparently the case, judging from data in Table 3 [right], which show males to be significantly more likely to be "highly" libertarian and less likely to be "slightly" libertarian than females. Again the results

Table 2

RESPONSES ON THE INDEX OF LIBERTARIANISM AT CALIFORNIA (1957) AND NEBRASKA (1971)

Libertarianism	California	Nebraska
Slightly Libertarian	20%	17%
Moderately Libertarian	46	45
Highly Libertarian	34	38
	N = 894	N = 437

parallel those of the Berkeley study, where females were consistently more anti-libertarian than males. Derived percentages from data in the Selvin-Hagstrom study indicated 27 percent of the females and 36 percent of the males were highly libertarian. In the Nebraska study, the comparable percentages were 32 and 44, respectively, for females and males.

The argument that sex differences in tolerance of nonconformity, which seemingly persist even at the college level, are rooted in the traditional orientation of females toward home and family (or at least traditional sex role orientation and intolerance vary concomitantly) finds even more convincing support in the data of Table 3. The earlier females expected to marry, the more likely they were to be anti-libertarian; the later they expected to marry, if at all, the more highly libertarian they were.

Another enduring and notably traditional institution in American society is religion. Given Selvin and Hagstrom's (1960) findings that non-churchgoers were more often highly libertarian than churchgoers, findings which were similar to Stouffer's (1955), it may well be that the constricting influence of religious institutions is still felt by college students. This expectation is further supported by Goldsen, *et al.* (1960), who in a survey of 11 universities in 1952, found the more religious student more willing to constrict and control others, particularly if others were perceived to be deviant in some manner such as expressing unconventional opinions or holding unorthodox views.

Table 3

BACKGROUND CHARACTERISTICS AND LIBERTARIANISM

Characteristic	Libertarianism			N
	Slightly	Moderately	Highly	
Sex				
Female	29%	48	32	(234)
Male	15%	41	44	(203)
$x^2 = 7.16$, p = .02				
Marriage plans (females)				
Before graduation	28%	52	20	(56)
3 yrs. or less after graduation	19%	51	30	(111)
4 yrs. or more after graduation or never	13%	41	46	(32)
$x^2 = 8.62$, p = .07				
Religious attendance				
Every week	20%	48	32	(118)
Once or twice monthly	24%	52	24	(95)
Sporadically	15%	45	40	(140)
Never	9%	34	57	(80)
$x^2 = 24.44$, p = .0004				
Religious Affiliation and Attendance				
Protestant	24%	54	22	(124)
Active				
Nonactive	14%	49	37	(106)
Catholic	21%	39	40	(77)
Active				
Nonactive	6%	59	35	(17)
x^2 for Protestant vs. Catholic (actives) = 8.11, p < .02				
x^2 for Protestant (actives vs. nonactives) = 7.71, p < .05				
x^2 for Catholic (actives vs. nonactives) = 3.09, p < .20				
*Hometown Size**				
2500 or less	23%	40	37	(146)
2501–100,000	15%	50	35	(135)
More than 100,000	14%	45	41	(155)
$x^2 = 5.62$, p = .23				

*Community lived in the longest

Precisely what it is about those who are religious that makes
them less tolerant of nonconformity remains a question which
cannot be answered here, but the data in Table 3 again argue
persuasively for the claim that more active participation in
religion is clearly associated with anti-libertarianism and inactivity
with strong libertarianism. The proportion who were slightly
libertarian among every-week attenders was 20 percent, while
among the nonattenders the figure was only nine percent. On
the other hand, 32 percent of every-week attenders are highly
libertarian, and 57 percent of the nonattenders are so classified.

This same tendency for the active churchgoer to be less
libertarian than the less active attender was also found among
Protestants (Table 3). However, the pattern for Catholics was
not so linear. Among Catholics, the active attenders were more
likely to be slightly libertarian than the nonactives, and slightly
more likely than nonactives to be highly libertarian. Finally,
while differences between inactive Protestants and inactive
Catholics were negligible, active Catholics were significantly
more likely to be highly libertarian than active Protestants, who
are more likely to be either moderately or slightly libertarian.
These last data were the only data noticeably different from the
Selvin-Hagstrom (1960) data. In that study, it was the nonattend-
ing Catholics and Protestants that were found to differ in their
support of civil liberties. On the other hand, like Lenski's
(1961), our results indicated small differences between Catholic
and Protestant inactives, but significant differences for the
active members of those faiths. However, the direction of
results among the actives was different; it was the active
Catholics who were most supportive of civil liberties, rather
than the Protestants, as Lenski (1961) found in his Detroit
sample; but the small number of nonactive Catholics (17) in this
study does not invite confidence in our conclusions. Those other
than Protestant or Catholic were not considered here because of
insufficient numbers.

A last background variable considered here, size of community in which the student was reared, was not included in the
Selvin-Hagstrom (1960) study, but it was in Stouffer's (1955)
national survey. He found that even with region taken into
consideration, tolerance of nonconformity increased with community size. However, Fischer (1971) recently reported results
indicating that as successive controls (race, religion, region, and
occupation) were introduced, the correlation between community size and tolerance of racial differences approached zero. In
this study (see Table 3) community size was not significantly
associated with libertarianism. The association was positive,
but weak. Certainly the racial, regional, and occupational
homogeneity of this sample suggests that Fischer's conclusions,
even though tolerance of racial difference may not be the same
as tolerance of nonconformity, might well be extended to the
Nebraska results.

The College Experience and Libertarianism

One of the variables most consistently and strongly associated
with libertarianism in the Stouffer study was education. Regardless of the control variables considered, education remained a

powerful predictor of tolerance of nonconformity. Even within
the four-year range of the college career, Selvin and Hagstrom
(1960) found a strong and positive association between year in
school and libertarianism. At Berkeley the percent highly
libertarian was 21 in the first year in contrast to 40 in the last
year. In the Nebraska sample, the results reported in Table 4
were again comparable to those from Berkeley. There was a
statistically significant and positive association between college
year and libertarianism. In fact, the percentage shift in highly
libertarians from the first to the last year of college was almost
the same as in the Berkeley sample; for Nebraska the change
was from 26 percent to 48 percent. At first consideration it
appears that the college experience continues to have a marked
impact on such attitudes as libertarianism. These findings
certainly go counter to the claim by some social scientists, such
as Jacob (1957), that the increasing scale and bureaucratization
of especially state universities has minimized the impact of these
institutions even in those areas purported to involve their
primary goals. In addition, these data are contrary to the
argument that Newcomb's (1943) results apply only to the small
college with a liberal reputation and are not be expected in
larger institutions.

Additional support for the claim that college life still has
considerable impact on students in attitudinal areas is reflected
in Table 4 [right], which reports data bearing on libertarianism
and the self-estimated impact that college had in general. A
strong and positive association was found; the more important
the reported impact, the more likely the student to be highly
libertarian, and conversely, the less significant the reported
impact, the more likely to be only slightly libertarian. Furthermore, if these data accurately reflect what is going on, whether
the impact of college was reported to be extremely important or
just fairly important did not make much difference in support of
civil liberties. It was those who reported insignificant or no
impact that were distinctly different in level of support. Precisely what it is about college life that produces such results is
not clear. Academic learning, peer culture influences, social
contacts with a wide variety of people, disengagement from
parents and binding adult ties, and subtle social structural
effects all apparently contribute to this impact. How each of
these effects produce changes is still an important research
problem.

Finally the student's major subject is a central concern of
his academic and post-college life; and while cause and effect
are again not clear, there is a strong association between
academic major and libertarianism. Probably the best guess is
that the two interact with each other. That is, those predisposed
to be libertarian are likely to be attracted to subject areas where
these attitudes are supported and encouraged; and as they are
exposed to more of the same, libertarianism is likely to increase.
Selvin and Hagstrom (1960) found a definite association between major and libertarianism, and results in Table 4 indicate
that subjects in the Nebraska sample responded in much the
same manner. The social science majors were clearly the most
likely to be highly libertarian. Those least likely to support civil
liberties majored in agriculture, engineering, and education

Table 4

COLLEGE EXPERIENCE AND LIBERTARIANISM

College Experience	Libertarianism			N
	Slightly	Moderately	Highly	
College year				
Freshmen	21%	53	26	(151)
Sophomores	15%	48	37	(92)
Juniors	17%	36	47	(110)
Seniors	13%	39	48	(82)
$x^2 = 18.45$, $p = .01$				
*College Impact**				
Extremely important	15%	45	40	(209)
Fairly important	19%	43	38	(191)
Insignificant or none	35%	52	13	(23)
$x^2 = 12.43$, $p = .02$				
*From Question: "All things considered, what impact would you say college has had on you?"				
Major Subject				
Social Science	6%	40	54	(96)
Humanities	12%	45	43	(42)
Natural Science	24%	33	42	(45)
Business Administration	13%	57	30	(56)
Education	22%	54	24	(108)
Engineering	27%	49	24	(33)
Agriculture	46%	27	27	(11)
Other	19%	36	45	(31)
$x^2 = 41.61$, $p = .0001$				

areas. Humanities and natural sciences fell close to the social sciences, and business administration between the extremes. With few modifications, these results are the same as those from the Berkeley study. And as indicated in the Berkeley results, those students who majored in the area that trained them for elementary and secondary school teaching were among the lowest in support of civil liberties. This particular lack of support for civil liberties becomes even more curious when academic freedom issues are considered apart from the general index. For these academic freedom questions (Table 1, items 4 and 10), only 51 percent of the education majors gave the libertarian response on the first question and 52 percent on the second question, the lowest percentage support among the different majors.

DISCUSSION AND SUMMARY

The most outstanding feature of the results is that both opinions about civil liberties and social characteristics associated with support of civil liberties are very similar to those found by Selvin and Hagstrom (1960) in Berkeley 15 years ago. While a reasonably strong argument can be generated to account for this similarity by assuming a cultural lag in Nebraska, the consistently comparable data from the two schools does raise a question about how much change in values has occurred on college campuses. Is the college campus becoming more libertarian, or does the much vaunted new college liberalism fail to include civil libertarianism? The present study certainly suggests need for additional and more extensive research on the subject.

The study also indicated that while growing up in a small community failed to have the constricting effect expected, those who were active participants in Catholic or Protestant faiths, especially Protestants, and those who were females, particularly if early marriage plans were endorsed, were less supportive of civil liberties than the religiously inactive and males. College life might reduce participation in institutional religion, but it apparently fails to extinguish the effects of some of our most enduring institutions and roles for those who retain their identities and participation.

On the other hand, nearly half of the students reported "extremely important" college impact on themselves, and the force of this influence is clearly associated with increased libertarianism. The college campus, even the large state university, is apparently a significant change agency in the task of developing greater confidence in and support for civil liberties both on and off campus. The continued presence of college influence may be encouraging for civil libertarians; but the data also indicate that some aspects of the college scene, particularly teacher and engineering colleges, may be something other than "hotbeds of democracy" in regard to encouragement of support for civil liberties, even those pertaining to academic freedom. The task of democratizing American college students is clearly an unfinished task.

REFERENCES

Alonzo, A. A., & Kinch, J. W. (1964). Education level and support of civil liberties. *Pacific Sociological Review, 7,* 89–93.

Dynes, W. (1967). Education and tolerance: An analysis of intervening factors. *Social Forces, 46,* 22–33.

Erskine, H. (1970). The polls: Freedom of speech. *Public Opinion Quarterly, 34,* 483–496.

Finney, H. C. (1971). Political libertarianism at Berkeley: An application of perspectives from the new student left. *Journal of Social Issues, 27,* 35–61.

Fischer, C. S. (1971). A research note on urbanism and tolerance. *American Journal of Sociology, 76,* 847–856.

Goldsen, R., Rosenberg, M., Williams, R., Jr., & Suchman, E. (1960). *What college students think.* New York: Van Nostrand.

Jacob, P. E. (1957). *Changing values in college.* New York: Harper & Row.

Kosa, J., & Nunn, C. Z. (1965). Race, deprivation and attitude toward communism. *Phylon, 25,* 337–346.

Lenski, G. (1961). *The religious factor.* New York: Doubleday.

Lipset, S. M. (1953). Opinion formation in a crisis situation. *Public Opinion Quarterly, 17,* 20–46.

Maccoby, E. E. (1966). *The development of sex differences.* Stanford, CA: Stanford University Press.

Newcomb, T. M. (1943). *Personality and social change.* New York: Dryden.

Prothro, J. W., & Grigg, C. M. (1960). Fundamental principles of democracy: Bases of agreement and disagreement. *Journal of Politics, 22,* 276–294.

Remmers, H. H. (1960) *Anti-democratic attitudes in American schools.* Evanston, IL: Northwestern University Press.

Selvin, H. C., & Hagstrom, W. O. (1960). Determinants of support for civil liberties. *British Journal of Sociology, 11,* 51–73.

Stouffer, S. A. (1955). *Communism, conformity and civil liberties.* New York: John Wiley & Sons.

Welch, S., & Carlson, E. (forthcoming). The public and the campus: A view from two communities. *Social Science Quarterly.*

MARRIAGE

> Men are not gentle creatures who want to be loved . . . ; they are, on the
> contrary, creatures among whose instinctual endowments is to be reckoned a
> powerful share of aggressiveness. As a result, their neighbor is for them not
> only a potential helper or sexual object, but also someone who tempts them
> to satisfy their aggressiveness on him, to exploit his capacity for work
> without compensation, to use him sexually . . . to seize his possessions.
>
> Sigmund Freud
> *Civilization and Its Discontents*

The anthropologist Ralph Linton (1936) cynically observed that "all societies recognize that there are occasional violent, emotional attachments between persons of the opposite sex, but [the] present American culture is practically the only one which has attempted to capitalize on these, and make them the basis for marriage" (p. 175). With the benefit of hindsight, we can see that Linton's conclusion was exaggerated. His observation does, however, draw our attention to industrialization's impact on the formation of marriage: changing it from traditional contractual agreements to romantically based ones. Conflict theorists view the rise in romanticism as ultimately produced by the struggle between men and women. Functionalists see the increase in romanticism as fulfilling the needs of modern industrial societies. In the following investigation we will look at Zick Rubin's efforts to define and measure romantic love. We will then look at three hypotheses that deal with the different ways men and women view love.

Conflict Perspective

The best that Freud could say of human nature was "Homo homini lupus" (Man is a wolf to man). Because of our predatory nature, our emotions—even love—are ultimately rooted in conflict. We love out of fear, not selflessness. Freud deduced that "it is precisely because your neighbor is not worthy of love, and is on the contrary your enemy, that you should love him as yourself" (1930/1961, p. 58). Randall Collins believes that Freud saw more clearly than anyone else that conflict in family life forms around the struggle for sex and power between men and women as well as adults and children.

He holds that all humans are highly motivated by sex and that they may use violence or coercion to obtain sexual gratification. Since males are physically larger, Collins postulates, men are more likely to prevail in the struggle over property rights in general and sexual property in particular. He states (1982, p. 123) that "this sexual property is the key to family structure; it is the hinge on which everything turns." The ability of males to transform women into sexual property, he theorizes, underlies the development of sexual stratification.

The structure of sexual stratification changes with economic and societal development. The decline of feudalism and the emergence of a market economy permitted women greater freedom to negotiate sexual contracts. Viewed in this light, the love contract was a weapon women could use to take advantage of the freer market structure. Collins (1975) states that romantic love used in courtship "creates male deference; after marriage it expresses and reinforces women's attempt to control the sexual aggressiveness of their husbands" (p. 244). Furthermore, it enhances the "sexual bargaining power of the wife, since she is the only available sex object." These and other struggles between men and women result in the reduction of inequalities both in and out of marriage.

Functional Perspective

The family is presumably the oldest human institution. It endures not because it advances the interest of a dominant group, but because it performs at least five indispensable societal functions:

1. *Regulation of sexual behavior.* Although standards vary greatly, all societies regulate sexual behavior. Incest and jealousy, for example, are important concerns in most societies.

This investigation is based on "Measurement of Romantic Love" by Zick Rubin, 1970, reprinted on pages 132–136.

2. *Reproduction.* Fertility rates must equal or exceed mortality rates or the society will eventually disappear (as did the Shaker colonies).
3. *Socialization.* Children must be trained to assume responsible roles in society.
4. *Support of dependents.* Parents have both moral and legal responsibility for the material needs of their children.
5. *Social and emotional support.* The family provides a portable primary group that offers a haven in an otherwise impersonal and competitive industrial society.

Robert Goode argues that extended family structures function more efficiently in feudal societies, whereas nuclear families function better in industrial societies. He observes that as nuclear families become more widespread, romantic love plays an increasingly important role in family formation. Goode (1959) defines love as "a strong emotional attachment, a cathexis, between adolescents or adults of opposite sexes, with at least components of sex, desire, and tenderness" (p. 41). He found romantic love to be almost completely absent in villages in India. India would, therefore, be placed at the nonromantic end of a romantic love continuum. Hellenic Greece and Rome of the Republic would be in the center of the continuum. The United States, a society that greatly emphasizes romantic love, would be found at the most romantic end of the love continuum. Both social and psychological factors are involved in romantic love.

Social Factors   Because love often leads to marriage, Goode argues that families are concerned that it lead to socially desirable marriage. Bernard Barber (1957) claims that "all societies tend to disapprove not only of all marriage between people from different social classes but also of social relations between them that could lead to marriage" (p. 123). To ensure that socially desirable results occur, love is controlled by such practices as (1) arranging child marriages before love can intervene, (2) segregating women from men (in all-male or all-female schools and institutions), (3) maintaining supervision (through chaperons), and (4) supplying informal group pressure.

Goode notes that the effects of love are very different when viewed from the family of orientation (the family in which we are born) and the family of procreation (the family created when you marry and have children). Love can threaten the stability of the family of orientation if it leads to a "bad marriage" (for example, a member of the royal family marrying a gypsy). On the other hand, for the family of procreation, love provides an emotional bond necessary for family stability. In view of the declining number of functions for which the family is directly responsible (in areas like education, health care, and economic production), love has become virtually the only basis of marriage and family solidarity in American society.

The expression of love is governed by cultural rules that specify acceptable and unacceptable mates. Some rules restrict love and marriage to people of a particular social class, income, ethnic and racial background, age, and sex (endogamous rules). When these limitations have been used to sift through a population, few serious candidates remain for romantic interest.

Geographic limitations and the "likes marry likes" tendency (homogamy) further limit mate selection and the possibility of finding the few remaining candidates with romantic potential.

Personal Factors   Within this small circle of socially acceptable mates we may consider personal qualities that may lead to love. Jack Horn (1976) found that people who came from families that placed greater emphasis on love than upon material things were more likely to give and receive love as adults. Better-adjusted persons with higher self-esteem proved most capable of establishing love relationships. James Coleman (1984) found that personal qualities that foster the development of intimate relationships (effective communication, mutual self-disclosure, and conflict resolution skills) foster the development of romantic relationships as well. Love is most likely to succeed when based on effective interpersonal skills, rather than upon idealized hopes for the future. Coleman's view is consistent with Eric Fromm's (1956) belief that love is an art: Once you rationally understand the basic principles involved, it is necessary to work at applying them as an artist would and construct an enduring relationship of love.

Background

Zick Rubin (1970) believed that love could be measured with a questionnaire, as other attitudes are. He began by defining love as "an *attitude* held by a person toward a particular person, involving predispositions to think, feel, and behave in certain ways toward that other person" (Reading 10, p. 132). This definition of love contains no researchable elements. Its generality excludes few attitudes, even aggression. Rubin's definition of *romantic* love, however, is more specific and ultimately researchable. He defines it as "love between unmarried opposite-sex peers, of the sort which could possibly lead to marriage."

Love Scale   From his review of theoretical material and research on interpersonal attraction, Rubin constructed a 13-item scale of love. These items measure three basic qualities of romantic love. The first is *attachment,* which grows from affiliative and dependency needs, such as parent-child relationships. It involves the personal need to receive emotional support and/or to possess another person. Attachment was measured by questions like "If I could never be with _____, I would feel miserable" and "It would be hard for me to get along without _____."

The second quality of romantic love is an active *caring* to help the other person grow and better themselves. This care for the other person is so great that the lover is selflessly and altruistically concerned with the other's security and satisfaction. This self-surrender is close to what the Greeks called *agape.* Scale items related to caring include "If _____ were feeling bad, my first duty would be to cheer him (her) up" and "I would do almost anything for _____."

Lastly, there is a special *intimacy* that gives the lovers a distinctive exclusiveness and absorption. This gives the rela-

STUDENT SURVEY QUESTION 34

Circle the number opposite each of the following 26 items that best represents your feelings toward the OPPOSITE-SEX peer whom you are dating or with whom you are romantically involved. If you are not presently romantically involved, imagine an opposite-sex partner with whom you would desire to be romantically involved.

Agree   Disagree

A. If _____ were feeling bad, my first duty would be to cheer him (her) up. 9 8 7 6 5 4 3 2 1
B. I feel that I can confide in _____ about virtually everything. 9 8 7 6 5 4 3 2 1
C. I find it easy to ignore_____'s faults. 9 8 7 6 5 4 3 2 1
D. I would do almost anything for _____. 9 8 7 6 5 4 3 2 1
E. I feel very possessive toward _____. 9 8 7 6 5 4 3 2 1
F. If I could never be with _____, I would feel miserable. 9 8 7 6 5 4 3 2 1
G. If I were lonely, my first thought would be to seek _____ out. 9 8 7 6 5 4 3 2 1
H. One of my primary concerns is _____'s welfare. 9 8 7 6 5 4 3 2 1
I. I would forgive _____ for practically anything. 9 8 7 6 5 4 3 2 1
J. I feel responsible for _____'s well-being. 9 8 7 6 5 4 3 2 1
K. When I am with _____, I spend a good deal of time just looking at him (her). 9 8 7 6 5 4 3 2 1
L. I would greatly enjoy being confided in by _____. 9 8 7 6 5 4 3 2 1
M. It would be hard for me to get along without _____. 9 8 7 6 5 4 3 2 1
N. When I am with _____, we are almost always in the same mood. 9 8 7 6 5 4 3 2 1
O. I think that _____ is unusually well-adjusted. 9 8 7 6 5 4 3 2 1
P. I would highly recommend _____ for a responsible job. 9 8 7 6 5 4 3 2 1
Q. In my opinion, _____ is an exceptionally mature person. 9 8 7 6 5 4 3 2 1
R. I have great confidence in _____'s good judgment. 9 8 7 6 5 4 3 2 1
S. Most people would react very favorably to _____ after a brief acquaintance. 9 8 7 6 5 4 3 2 1
T. I think that _____ and I are quite similar. 9 8 7 6 5 4 3 2 1
U. I would vote for _____ in a class or group election. 9 8 7 6 5 4 3 2 1
V. I think that _____ is one of those people who quickly wins respect. 9 8 7 6 5 4 3 2 1
W. I feel that _____ is an extremely intelligent person. 9 8 7 6 5 4 3 2 1
X. _____ is one of the most likable people I know. 9 8 7 6 5 4 3 2 1
Y. _____ is the sort of person whom I would like to be. 9 8 7 6 5 4 3 2 1
Z. It seems to me that it is very easy for _____ to gain recognition. 9 8 7 6 5 4 3 2 1

After completing these ratings for your opposite-sex peer, use the same scales to rate your best SAME-SEX friend. Put an "X" through the appropriate response that best expresses your feelings toward your best same-sex friend.

tionship its unusually strong bond. Intimacy is measured by such questions as "I would feel very possessive toward _____" and "I feel that I can confide in _____ about virtually everything."

Rubin believed liking and loving are related but different. To study this difference he devised a similar 13-question "liking scale." The scale measures two qualities of liking: affection and respect. If he was correct, these scales should be able to measure differences between friends and lovers. Both scales were administered to couples at the University of Michigan who were dating but not engaged. They were instructed to rate on a scale from 1 to 9 their dating partner and their same-sex best friend on each of the 13 items on the love and liking scales. Thus, the scores for each could range from a low of 13 to a high of 117.

Validation To check the validity of the scales, Rubin correlated the amount of time that couples spent gazing into each other's eyes with ratings on the love and liking scales. He found "strong love" couples spent more time gazing into each other eyes than the "weak love" group. There is also evidence that the scales can discriminate between loving and liking. The respondents provided such evidence by estimating their chances of marrying their partner. For both men and women the correlation between their estimated probability of getting married and the love scale was +.59. The correlation between the probability of getting married and the liking scale, however, fell to only +.35 for men and +.32 for women. It seems reasonable to conclude from the foregoing that loving and liking are different. While liking helps a relationship endure, the bond provided by love is more than just intense liking.

Findings   There was little difference between men (with an average score of 89.37) and women (average score of 89.46) in the love reported for their dating partners. But women (88.48) liked their boyfriends more than the boyfriends (84.65) liked them in return. The reported liking of same-sex friends was virtually identical for men (79.10) and women (80.47). The amount of love reported for the same-sex friend was, however, significantly higher for women (65.27) than for men (55.07). Rubin believes this reflects cultural norms that discourage men from freely expressing affection.

Replication

In following Rubin's research, we will investigate whether or not his findings hold true for your class by testing the following hypotheses:

Hypothesis 1:

Women like their boyfriends more than their boyfriends like them.

Hypothesis 2:

Women love their same-sex friends more than men do.

Hypothesis 3:

Whereas both men and women like their dating partners only slightly more than they like their same-sex friends, they love their dating partners more than they love their friends.

We will test these hypotheses by using the class's responses to questions 1 and 34 on the Student Survey (reproduced on page 127) as our data source. Question 1 provides the respondent's sex (the independent variable). Question 34 has two scales to measure the dependent variables, loving and liking. The love scale consists of questions lettered from A through M. The liking scale consists of questions N through Z. Each set of 13 questions is summed to determine the amount of love and liking. As you will recall, you were asked to answer questions A through Z once in terms of how you feel about the opposite-sex peer with whom you are romantically involved, and once in terms of your feelings toward your best same-sex friend. This yields four different measurements necessary to our investigation: love for dating partner, liking for dating partner, love for friend, and liking for friend. The class totals on these four scales, by sex of the respondent, will be tabulated by your instructor and handed out to you. When you have received this information, proceed as follows:

Step 1:

To determine your own personal scores, turn to item 34 in the Student Survey (p. 198) and sum the values you circled or crossed out in the love and liking scales. Love for an opposite-sex peer, for example, would be the total of the circled ratings for items A through M. When you compute them, enter the four scores in the Investigation Results table on the opposite page, in the far right column titled My Score.

Step 2:

Enter the class's results for this investigation in cells 1 through 12 in the Investigation Results table.

Step 3:

Test the validity of the three hypotheses by filling in the blank spaces below. For hypothesis 1, for example, locate cell 4 in the Student Survey section and enter the score in the blank provided next to "Women like date," below. Locate cell 5 and enter that score for "Men like date." Fill in hypotheses 2 and 3 in similar fashion.

Hypothesis 1:

Women like their boyfriends somewhat more than their boyfriends like them.

Women like date ____ > ____ Men like date
                 (cell 4)   (cell 5)

Hypothesis 2:

Women love their same-sex friends more than men do.

Women love   ____ > ____ Men love friends
friends
                 (cell 7)   (cell 8)

Hypothesis 3:

Whereas both men and women like their dating partners only slightly more than they like their same-sex friends, they love their dating partners more than they love their friends.

Women + Men   ____ > ____ Women + Men
like date   like friends
                 (cell 6) (cell 12)

Women + Men   ____ > ____ Women + Men
love date   love friends
                 (cell 3) (cell 9)

Checking Your Findings

Hypothesis 1 replicates Rubin's finding that women *liked* their boyfriends (88.48) somewhat more than their boyfriends liked them (84.65). He states that "the data do not support the conclusion that men are generally more likable than women, but only that they are more liked in the context of the dating relationship" (p. 135). Do your findings support Rubin's?

Table 10–1

INVESTIGATION RESULTS 10
The Measurement of Romantic Love

| | Rubin's Findings | | Student Survey | | | My Score |
	Women	Men	Women	Men	Average	
Love for Dating Partner	89	89	Cell (1)	Cell (2)	Cell (3)	————
Liking for Dating Partner	88	85	(4)	(5)	(6)	————
Love for Same-Sex Friend	65	55	(7)	(8)	(9)	————
Liking for Same-Sex Friend	80	79	(10)	(11)	(12)	————

Note: Data in columns 1 and 2 are from Table 2, p. 135.

Sample size: _____

Number of males: _____

Number of females: _____

Hypothesis 2 states that women tend to love their same-sex friends (65.27) more than men do (55.07). Rubin explains this as consistent with the cultural stereotypes that make it more socially acceptable for females than males to speak of affectionate relationships with same-sex friends. Are your findings consistent with the previous study?

Hypothesis 3 concerns Rubin's finding that "whereas both women and men *liked* their dating partners only slightly more than they liked their same-sex friends, they *loved* their dating partners much more than their friends" (p. 135). Do your results indicate this is correct? Can the scales discriminate between loving and liking?

Summarize the findings by checking the amount of support found in this investigation for each of the hypotheses in Table 10-2, page 130.

Topics for Further Investigation

1. Six months after the original survey, Rubin (1973) did a follow-up study of the 182 involved couples. The results showed only a slight correlation (men +.19, women +.20) between previous romantic love and how intense the relationship had become. To find out why the correlation was not higher, Rubin divided the couples into those who had idealized notions of love and marriage (romantics) and those who had practical concerns about economic security and marriage (nonromantics). Romantic individuals with high love scores generally became more intensely involved. There was no correlation between love and the progress or intensity of relationships for nonromantic indi-

Table 10–2

SUPPORT FOR HYPOTHESES

	Significantly Supported	Partially Supported	Not Supported	Indeterminate
Hypothesis 1: Like date	_____	_____	_____	_____
Hypothesis 2: Love friend	_____	_____	_____	_____
Hypothesis 3: Like date > friend	_____	_____	_____	_____
Love date > friend	_____	_____	_____	_____

Indicate the amount of support you found for each hypothesis.

viduals. In fact, where both partners were nonromantics, there was a slight negative correlation ($-.10$ men, $-.16$ women) between love and the development of the relationship.

These findings appear related to Goode's theory that the greater the importance of kinship and financial arrangements, the less free the young will be to select their mates romantically. Since wealthy families have more at stake economically in the marriage of their children, one should find greater controls placed on their marriageable children, such as sending them to finishing schools, exclusive colleges, or expensive social and recreation clubs. This leads us to expect that more upper-class students will be nonromantic (that is, they will consider economic, family, and rational issues more important than love). Overall, were the love ratings in your class higher or lower than those found by Rubin? If the ratings were different from Rubin's, could this be explained by social class?

2. Research by Charles Hill, Zick Rubin, and Letitia Peplau (1976) indicates that women are less romantic and more reluctant to become committed romantically. Women were also less accepting of such romantic notions as "love conquers all" and "love at first sight." Women were more likely to take the initiative in breaking up an unsatisfactory romance. Collins might interpret these findings as indicating women are less likely to be romantically involved because they are more aware of love as a bargaining resource. This would also explain why women would be the last in and the first out of romantic relationships. Are there differences between Rubin's findings and your class's concerning liking and loving by sex? Could this be related to changes in sex role expectations? Could these differences be explained by a gender gap (discussed in Investigation 2)?

3. Will those who fall in love and marry live happily ever after? Paul Popenoe (1950) called it "romantic infantilism" to hold an unrealistic belief that romantic love would never die. His skepticism that romantic love could provide a solid basis for establishing an enduring marriage seems well founded. Richard

Cimbalo, Virginia Falling, and Patricia Mousaw (1976) found that the longer a couple is married, the lower they score on the love scale, suggesting that romantic love is likely to fade. If the marriage is to remain stable and rewarding, romantic love must be replaced by a more durable form of companionate love.

References and Recommended Readings

Barber, B. (1957). *Social stratification.* New York: Harcourt, Brace and World.

Baron, R., & Byrne, D. (1977). *Social psychology: Understanding human interaction.* Boston: Allyn & Bacon.

Benson, L. (1971). Love, myth and reality. Chapter seven in *The family bond: Marriage, love and sex in America.* New York: Random House.

Cimbalo, R., Falling, V., & Mousaw, P. (1976). The course of love: A cross-sectional design. *Psychological Reports, 38,* 1292–1294.

Coleman, J. (1984). *Intimate relationships, marriage, and family.* Indianapolis, Indiana: Bobbs-Merrill.

Collins, R. (1975). *Conflict sociology.* New York: Academic Press.

Collins, R. (1982). *Sociological insight.* New York: Oxford University Press.

Engels, F. (1884). The origin of the family, private property and the state. In R. Tucker (Ed.), *The Marx-Engels reader* (2nd ed.). New York: W. W. Norton, 1978.

Freud, S. (1930). *Civilization and its discontents.* Reprint. New York: W. W. Norton, 1961.

Fromm, E. (1956). *The art of loving.* New York: Harper & Row.

Goode, R. (1959). The theoretical importance of love. *American Sociological Review, 24,* 38–47.

Goode, R. (1963). *World revolution and family patterns.* New York: The Free Press.

Harlow, H. (1958). The nature of love. *American Psychologist, 13,* 673–685.

Hendrick, S., & Hendrick, C. (1992). *Romantic love.* Newbury Park, CA: Sage.

Hendrick, S., Hendrick, C., & Adler, N. (1988). Romantic relationships: Love satisfaction and staying together. *Journal of Personality and Social Psychology, 54,* 980–988.

Hill, C., Rubin, Z., & Peplau, L. (1976). Breakups before marriage: The end of 103 affairs. *Journal of Social Issues, 32,* 147–168.

Horn, J. (1976, July). Love: The most important ingredient is happiness. *Psychology Today,* pp. 98–102.

Linton, R. (1936). *The study of man.* New York: Appleton-Century-Crofts.

Mathes, E., & Serva, N. (1981). Jealousy, romantic love and liking. *Psychological Reports, 49,* 23–31.

Popenoe, P. (1950). *Marriage is what you make it.* New York: Macmillan.

Reiss, I. (1960). Toward a sociology of the heterosexual love relationship. *Journal of Marriage and Family Living, 22,* 139–145.

Reiss, I. (1980). The sociological explanation of heterosexual love relationships. Chapter seven in *The family system in America* (3rd Ed.). New York: Holt, Rinehart & Winston.

Rubin, Z. (1970). Measurement of romantic love. *Journal of Personality and Social Psychology, 16,* 265–73.

Rubin, Z. (1973). *Liking and loving: An invitation to social psychology.* New York: Holt, Rinehart & Winston.

Rubin, Z. (1980, February). My love-hate relationship with the media. *Psychology Today,* pp. 7, 12–13.

Sternberg, R., & Grajek, S. (1984). The nature of love. *Journal of Personality and Social Psychology, 47,* 312–329.

Tennov, D. (1979). *Love and limerence.* New York: Stein & Day.

Thompson, B., & Borello, G. (1987). Concurrent validity of a love relationship scale. *Educational Psychological Measurement, 47,* 985–995.

Walster, E. (1971). Passionate love. In B. Murstein (Ed.), *Theories of attraction and love.* New York: Springer.

Walster, E., & Bernscheid, E. (1971, June). Adrenaline makes the heart grow fonder. *Psychology Today,* pp. 46–50.

Measurement of Romantic Love

This study reports the initial results of an attempt to introduce and validate a social-psychological construct of romantic love. Starting with the assumption that love is an interpersonal attitude, an internally consistent paper-and-pencil love scale was developed. The conception of romantic love included three components: affiliative and dependent need, a predisposition to help, and an orientation of exclusiveness and absorption. Love-scale scores were only moderately correlated with scores on a parallel scale of "liking," which reflected a more traditional conception of interpersonal attraction. . . .

Zick Rubin
Harvard University

Love is generally regarded to be the deepest and most meaningful of sentiments. It has occupied a preeminent position in the art and literature of every age, and it is presumably experienced, at least occasionally, by the vast majority of people. In Western culture, moreover, the association between love and marriage gives it a unique status as a link between the individual and the structure of society.

In view of these considerations, it is surprising to discover that social psychologists have devoted virtually no attention to love. Although interpersonal attraction has been a major focus of social-psychological theory and research, workers in this area have not attempted to conceptualize love as an independent entity. For Heider (1958), for example, "loving" is merely intense liking—there is no discussion of possible qualitative differences between the two. Newcomb (1960) does not include love on his list of the "varieties of interpersonal attraction." Even in experiments directed specifically at "romantic" attraction (e.g., Walster, 1965), the dependent measure is simply a verbal report of "liking."

The present research was predicated on the assumption that love may be independently conceptualized and measured. In keeping with a strategy of construct validation (cf. Cronbach & Meehl, 1955), the attempts to define love, to measure it, and to assess its relationships to other variables are all seen as parts of a single endeavor. An initial assumption in this enterprise is that love is an *attitude* held by a person toward a particular other person, involving predispositions to think, feel, and behave in certain ways toward that other person. This assumption places love in the mainstream of social-psychological approaches to interpersonal attraction, alongside such other varieties of attraction as liking, admiration, and respect. (cf. Newcomb, 1960).

The view of love as a multifaceted attitude implies a broader perspective than that held by those theorists who view love as an "emotion," a "need," or a set of behaviors. On the other hand, its linkage to a particular target implies a more restricted view than that held by those who regard love as an aspect of the individual's personality or experience which transcends particular persons and situations (e.g., Fromm, 1956). As Orlinsky (1970) has suggested, there may well be important common elements among different varieties of "love" (e.g., filial love, marital love, love of God). The focus of the present research, however, was restricted to *romantic love,* which may be defined simply as love between unmarried opposite-sex peers, of the sort which could possibly lead to marriage.

The research had [two] major phases. First, a paper-and-pencil love scale was developed. Second, the love scale was employed in a questionnaire study of student dating couples. . . .

DEVELOPING A LOVE SCALE

The development of a love scale was guided by several considerations:

1. Inasmuch as the content of the scale would constitute the initial conceptual definition of romantic love, its items must be grounded in existing theoretical and popular conceptions of love.
2. Responses to these items, if they are tapping a single underlying attitude, must be highly intercorrelated.
3. In order to establish the discriminant validity (cf. Campbell, 1960) of the love scale, it was constructed in conjunction with a parallel scale of liking. The goal was to develop internally consistent scales of love and of liking which would be conceptually distinct from one another and which would, in practice, be only moderately intercorrelated.

The first step in this procedure was the assembling of a large pool of questionnaire items referring to a respondent's

Reprinted by permission of the author from *Journal of Personality and Social Psychology, 16,* 1970, pp. 265–273.

attitude toward a particular other person (the "target person"). Half of these items were suggested by a wide range of speculations about the nature of love (e.g., de Rougemont, 1940; Freud, 1955; Fromm, 1956; Goode, 1959; Slater, 1963). These items referred to physical attraction, idealization, a predisposition to help, the desire to share emotions and experiences, feelings of exclusiveness and absorption, felt affiliative and dependent needs, the holding of ambivalent feelings, and the relative unimportance of universalistic norms in the relationship. The other half of the items were suggested by the existing theoretical and empirical literature on interpersonal attraction (or liking; cf. Lindzey & Byrne, 1968). They included references to the desire to affiliate with the target in various settings, evaluation of the target on several dimensions, the salience of norms of responsibility and equity, feelings of respect and trust, and the perception that the target is similar to oneself.

To provide some degree of consensual validation for this initial categorization of items, two successive panels of student and faculty judges sorted the items into love and liking categories, relying simply on their personal understanding of the connotations of the two labels. Following this screening procedure, a revised set of 70 items was administered to 198 introductory psychology students during their regular class sessions. Each respondent completed the items with reference to his girlfriend or boyfriend (if he had one), and also with reference to a nonromantically viewed "platonic friend" of the opposite sex. The scales of love and of liking which were employed in the subsequent phases of the research were arrived at through factor analyses of these responses. Two separate factor analyses were performed—one for responses with reference to boyfriends and girlfriends (or "lovers") and one for responses with reference to platonic friends. In each case, there was a general factor accounting for a large proportion of the total variance. The items loading highest on this general factor, particularly for lovers, were almost exclusively those which had previously been categorized as love items. These high-loading items defined the more circumscribed conception of love adopted. The items forming the liking scale were based on those which loaded highly on the second factor with respect to platonic friends. Details of the scale development procedure are reported in Rubin (1969, ch. 2.)

The items forming the love and liking scales are listed in Table 1 [p. 134]. Although it was constructed in such a way as to be factorially unitary, the content of the love scale points to three major components of romantic love:

1. *Affiliative and dependent need*—for example, "If I could never be with _____, I would feel miserable"; "It would be hard for me to get along without _____."
2. *Predispositon to help*—for example, "If _____ were feeling badly, my first duty would be to cheer him (her) up"; "I would do almost anything for _____."
3. *Exclusiveness and absorption*—for example, "I feel very possessive toward _____"; "I feel that I can confide in _____ about virtually everything."

The emerging conception of romantic love, as defined by the content of the scale, has an eclectic flavor. The affiliative and dependent need component evokes both Freud's (1955) view of love as sublimated sexuality and Harlow's (1958) equation of love with attachment behavior. The predisposition to help is congruent with Fromm's (1956) equation of love with attachment behavior. The predisposition to help is congruent with Fromm's (1956) analysis of the components of love, which he identifies as care, responsibility, respect, and knowledge. Absorption in a single other person is the aspect of love which is pointed to most directly by Slater's (1963) analysis of the social-structural implications of dyadic intimacy. The conception of liking, as defined by the liking-scale items, includes components of favorable evaluation and respect for the target person, as well as the perception that the target is similar to oneself. It is in reasonably close accord with measurers of "attraction" employed in previous research (cf. Lindzey & Byrne, 1968).

QUESTIONNAIRE STUDY

The 13-item love and liking scales, with their component items interspersed, were included in a questionnaire administered in October 1968 to 158 dating (but nonengaged) couples at the University of Michigan, recruited by means of posters and newspaper ads. In addition to the love and liking scales, completed first with respect to one's dating partner and later with respect to a close, same-sex friend, the questionnaire contained several personality scales and requests for background information about the dating relationship. Each partner completed the questionnaire individually and was paid $1 for taking part. The modal couple consisted of a junior man and a sophomore or junior woman who had been dating for about 1 year.

Each item on the love and liking scales was responded to on a continuum ranging from "Not at all true; disagree completely" (scored as 1) to "Definitely true; agree completely" (scored as 9), and total scale scores were computed by summing scores on individual items. Table 1 presents the mean scores and standard deviations for the items, together with the correlations between individual items and total scale scores. In several cases an inappropriate pattern of correlations was obtained, such as a love item correlating more highly with the total liking score than with the total love score (minus that item). These inappropriate patterns suggest specific revisions for future versions of the scales. On the whole, however, the pattern of correlations was appropriate. The love scale had high internal consistency (coefficient alpha was .84 for women and .86 for men)* and, as desired, was only moderately correlated with the liking scale (r = .39 for women and .60 for men). The finding that love and liking were more highly correlated among men than among women ($z = 2.48$, $p < .02$) was unexpected. It provides at least suggestive support for the notion that women discriminate more

_____
*Coefficient alpha of the liking scale was .81 for women and .83 for men.

Table 1

MEANS, STANDARD DEVIATIONS, AND CORRELATIONS WITH TOTAL SCALE SCORES
OF LOVE-SCALE AND LIKING-SCALE ITEMS

Love-scale Items	Women				Men			
	$\bar{X}$	SD	r^a Love	r Like	$\bar{X}$	SD	r^a Love	r Like
1. If _____ were feeling badly, my first duty would be to cheer him (her) up.	7.56	1.79	.393	.335	7.28	1.67	.432	.304
2. I feel that I can confide in _____ about virtually everything.	7.77	1.73	.524	.274	7.80	1.65	.425	.408
3. I find it easy to ignore _____'s faults.	5.83	1.90	.184	.436	5.61	2.13	.248	.428
4. I would do almost anything for _____.	7.15	2.03	.630	.341	7.35	1.83	.724	.530
5. I feel very possessive toward _____.	6.26	2.36	.438	−.005	6.24	2.33	.481	.342
6. If I could never be with _____, I would feel miserable.	6.52	2.43	.633	.276	6.58	2.26	.699	.422
7. If I were lonely, my first thought would be to seek _____ out.	7.90	1.72	.555	.204	7.75	1.54	.546	.328
8. One of my primary concerns is _____'s welfare.	7.47	1.62	.606	.218	7.59	1.56	.683	.290
9. I would forgive _____ for practically anything.	6.77	2.03	.551	.185	6.54	2.05	.394	.237
10. I feel responsible for _____'s well-being.	6.35	2.25	.582	.178	6.67	1.88	.548	.307
11. When I am with _____, I spend a good deal of time just looking at him (her).	5.42	2.36	.271	.137	5.94	2.18	.491	.318
12. I would greatly enjoy being confided in by _____.	8.35	1.14	.498	.292	7.88	1.47	.513	.383
13. It would be hard for me to get along without _____.	6.27	2.54	.676	.254	6.19	2.16	.663	.464

Liking-scale Items	Women				Men			
	$\bar{X}$	SD	r Love	r^b Like	$\bar{X}$	SD	r Love	r^b Like
1. When I am with _____, we are almost always in the same mood.	5.51	1.72	.163	.270	5.30	1.77	.235	.294
2. I think that _____ is unusually well-adjusted.	6.36	2.07	.093	.452	6.04	1.98	.339	.610
3. I would highly recommend _____ for a responsible job.	7.87	1.77	.199	.370	7.90	1.55	.281	.422
4. In my opinion, _____ is an exceptionally mature person.	6.72	1.93	.190	.559	6.40	2.00	.372	.609
5. I have great confidence in _____'s good judgment.	7.37	1.59	.310	.538	6.68	1.80	.381	.562
6. Most people would react very favorably to _____ after a brief acquaintance.	7.08	2.00	.167	.366	7.32	1.73	.202	.287
7. I think that _____ and I are quite similar to each other.	6.12	2.24	.292	.410	5.94	2.14	.407	.417
8. I would vote for _____ in a class or group election.	7.29	2.00	.057	.381	6.28	2.36	.299	.297
9. I think that _____ is one of those people who quickly wins respect.	7.11	1.67	.182	.588	6.71	1.69	.370	.669
10. I feel that _____ is an extremely intelligent person.	8.04	1.42	.193	.155	7.48	1.50	.377	.415
11. _____ is one of the most likable people I know.	6.99	1.98	.346	.402	7.33	1.63	.438	.514
12. _____ is the sort of person whom I myself would like to be.	5.50	2.00	.253	.340	4.71	2.26	.417	.552
13. It seems to me that it is very easy for _____ to gain admiration.	6.71	1.87	.176	.528	6.53	1.64	.345	.519

Note: Based on responses of 158 couples. Scores on individual items can range from 1 to 9, with 9 always indicating the positive end of the continuum.
[a]Correlation between item and love scale total *minus that item.*
[b]Correlation between item and liking scale total *minus that item.*

Table 2

LOVE AND LIKING FOR DATING PARTNERS AND SAME-SEX FRIENDS

Index	Women $\bar{X}$	SD	Men $\bar{X}$	SD
Love for partner	89.46	15.54	89.37	15.16
Liking for partner	88.48	13.40	84.65	13.81
Love for friend	65.27	17.84	55.07	16.08
Liking for friend	80.47	16.47	79.10	18.07

Note: Based on responses of 158 couples.

Table 3

INTERCORRELATIONS AMONG INDEXES OF ATTRACTION

Index	1	2	3	4
Women				
1. Love for partner				
2. Liking for partner	.39			
3. "In love"[a]	.59	.28		
4. Marriage probability[b]	.59	.32	.65	
5. Dating length[c]	.16	.01	.27	.46
Men				
1. Love for partner				
2. Liking for partner	.60			
3. "In love"[a]	.52	.35		
4. Marriage probability[b]	.59	.35	.62	
5. Dating length[c]	.04	−.03	.22	.38

Note: Based on responses of 158 couples. With an N of 158, a correlation of .16 is significant at the .05 level and a correlation of .21 is significant at the .01 level (two-tailed values).
[a]Responses to question, "Would you say that you and _____ are in love?", scored on a 3-point scale ("No" = 0, "Uncertain" = 1, "Yes" = 2).
[b]Responses to question, "What is your best estimate of the likelihood that you and _____ will marry one another?" Scale ranges from 0 (0%–10% probability) to 9 (91%–100% probability).
[c]The correlation across couples between the two partners' reports of the length of time they had been dating (in months) was .967. In this table, "dating length" was arbitrarily equated with the woman's estimates.

sharply between the two sentiments than men do (cf. Banta & Hetherington, 1963).

Table 2 [above] reveals that the love scores of men (for their girlfriends) and women (for their boyfriends) were almost identical. Women *liked* their boyfriends somewhat more than they were liked in return, however ($t = 2.95$, $df = 157$, $p < .01$). Inspection of the item means in Table 1 indicates that this sex difference may be attributed to the higher ratings given by women to their boyfriends on such "task-related" dimensions as intelligence, good judgment, and leadership potential. To the extent that these items accurately represent the construct of liking, men may indeed tend to be more "likable" (but not more "lovable") than women. Table 2 also reveals, however, that there was no such sex difference with respect to the respondents' liking for their same-sex friends. The mean liking-for-friend scores for the two sexes were virtually identical. Thus, the data do not support the conclusion that men are generally more likable than women, but only that they are liked more in the context of the dating relationship.

Table 2 also indicates that women tended to *love* their same-sex friends more than men did ($t = 5.33$, $df = 314$, $p < .01$). This result is in accord with cultural stereotypes concerning male and female friendships. It is more socially acceptable for female than for male friends to speak of themselves as "loving" one another, and it has been reported that women tend to confide in same-sex friends more than men do (Jourard & Lasakow, 1958). Finally, the means presented in Table 2 show that whereas both women and men *liked* their dating partners only slightly more than they liked their same-sex friends, they *loved* their dating partners much more than their friends.

Further insight into the conceptual distinction between love and liking may be derived from the correlational results presented in Table 3. As expected, love scores were highly correlated both with respondents' reports of whether or not they were "in love" and with their estimates of the likelihood that they would marry their current dating partners. Liking scores were only moderately correlated with these indexes.

Although love scores were highly related to perceived marriage probability, these variables may be distinguished from one another on empirical as well as conceptual grounds. As

Table 3 indicates, the length of time that the couple had been dating was unrelated to love scores among men, and only slightly related among women. In contrast, the respondents' perceptions of their closeness to marriage were significantly correlated with length of dating among both men and women. These results are in keeping with the common observations that although love may develop rather quickly, progress toward marriage typically occurs only over a longer period of time.

The construct validity of the love scale was further attested to by the findings that love for one's dating partner was only slightly correlated with love for one's same-sex friend ($r = .18$ for women, and $r = .15$ for men) and was uncorrelated with scores on the Marlowe-Crowne Social Desirability Scale ($r = .01$ for both women and men). These findings are consistent with the assumption that the love scale was tapping an attitude toward a specific other person, rather than more general interpersonal orientations or response tendencies. Finally, the love scores of the two partners tended to be moderately symmetrical. The correlation across couples between the woman's and the man's love was .42. The corresponding intracouple correlation with respect to liking was somewhat lower ($r = .28$). With respect to the partners' estimates of the probability of marriage, on the other hand, the intracouple correlation was considerably higher ($r = .68$).

* * * *

CONCLUSION

"So far as love or affection is concerned," Harlow wrote in 1958, "psychologists have failed in their mission. The little we know about love does not transcend simple observation, and the little we write about it has been written better by poets and novelists [p. 673]." The research reported in this paper represents an attempt to improve this situation by introducing and validating a preliminary social-psychological conception of romantic love. A distinction was drawn between love and liking, and its reasonableness was attested to by the results of the questionnaire study. It was found, for example, that respondents' estimates of the likelihood that they would marry their partners were more highly related to their love than to their liking for their partners. In light of the culturally prescribed association between love and marriage (but not necessarily between liking and marriage), this pattern of correlations seems appropriate. Other findings of the questionnaire study, to be reported elsewhere, point to the value of a measurable construct of romantic love as a link between the individual and social-structural levels of analysis of social behavior.

Although the present investigation was aimed at developing a unitary conception of romantic love, a promising direction for future research is the attempt to distinguish among the patterns of romantic love relationships. One theoretical basis for such distinctions is the nature of the interpersonal rewards exchanged between partners (cf. Wright, 1969). The attitudes and behaviors of romantic love may differ, for example, depending on whether the most salient rewards exchanged are those of security or those of stimulation (cf. Maslow's discussion of "Deficiency Love" and "Being Love," 1955). Some of the behavioral variables which might be focused on in the attempt to distinguish among such patterns are in the areas of sexual behavior, helping, and self-disclosure.

REFERENCES

Banta, T. J., & Hetherington, M. (1963). Relations between needs of friends and fiancees. *Journal of Abnormal and Social Psychology, 66,* 401–404.

Campbell, D. T. (1960). Recommendations for APA test standards regarding construct, trait, and discriminant validity. *American Psychologist, 15,* 546–553.

Cronbach, L. J., & Meehl, P. E. (1955). Construct validity in psychological tests. *Psychological Bulletin, 52,* 281–302.

de Rougemont, D. (1940). *Love in the western world.* New York: Harcourt, Brace.

Exline, R. V. (1963). Explorations in the process of person perception: Visual interaction in relation to competition, sex, and need for affiliation. *Journal of Personality, 31,* 1–20.

Exline, R., Gray, D., & Schuette, D. (1965). Visual behavior in a dyad as affected by interview content and sex of respondent. *Journal of Personality and Social Psychology, 1,* 201–209.

Freud, S. (1955). Group psychology and the analysis of the ego. In, *The standard edition of the complete psychological works of Sigmund Freud.* Vol 18. London: Hogarth.

Fromm, E. (1956) *The art of loving.* New York: Harper & Row.

Goode, W. J. (1959). The theoretical importance of love. *American Sociological Review, 24,* 38–47.

Harlow, H. F. (1958) The nature of love. *American Psychologist, 13,* 673–685.

Heider, F. (1958). *The psychology of interpersonal relations.* New York: John Wiley & Sons.

Jourard, S. M., & Lasakow, P. (1958). Some factors in self-disclosure. *Journal of Abnormal and Social Psychology, 56,* 91–98.

Lindzey, G., & Byrne, D. (1968). Measurement of social choice and interpersonal attractiveness. In G. Lindzey & E. Aronson (Eds.), *Handbook of social psychology.* Vol 2. (2nd ed.) Reading, MA: Addison-Wesley.

Maslow, A. H. (1955). Deficiency motivation and growth motivation. *Nebraska Symposium on Motivation, 2.*

Newcomb, T. M. (1960). The varieties of interpersonal attraction. In D. Cartwright & A. Zander (Eds.), *Group dynamics.* (2nd ed.) Evanston, IL: Row, Peterson.

Orlinsky, D. E. (1970). Love relationships in the life cycle: A developmental interpersonal perspective. Unpublished manuscript, University of Chicago.

Rubin, Z. (1969). *The social psychology of romantic love.* Ann Arbor, MI: University Microfilms, No. 70–4179.

Slater, P. E. (1963). On social regression. *American Sociological Review, 28,* 339–364.

Strodtbeck, F. L., & Mann, R. D. (1956). Sex role differentiation in jury deliberations. *Sociometry, 19,* 3–11.

Wallach, M. A., & Kogan, N. (1959). Sex differences and judgment processes. *Journal of Personality, 27,* 555–564.

Walster, E. (1965). The effect of self-esteem on romantic liking. *Journal of Experimental Social Psychology, 1,* 184–197.

Wright, P. H. (1969). A model and a technique for studies of friendship. *Journal of Experimental Social Psychology, 5,* 295–309.

ALIENATION

Turning and turning in the widening gyre
The falcon cannot hear the falconer;
Things fall apart; the centre cannot hold;
Mere anarchy is loosed upon the world,
The blood-dimmed tide is loosed, and everywhere
The ceremony of innocence is drowned;
The best lack all conviction, while the worst
Are full of passionate intensity.

W. B. Yeats
The Second Coming

Alienation has always been part of the human condition. But there is a growing concern that the Industrial Revolution destroyed a way of life that held society together and gave meaning and purpose to life. The revolution signaled the end of an understandable, sacred order, consisting of traditions that had been so firmly established in feudal society that they had been accepted unquestioningly as natural, timeless, and even divinely ordained. The Industrial Revolution lacked a moral center that could hold the hearts and minds of people. As its hold has loosened, disenchantment with the world has grown, and levels of alienation have reached epidemic proportions.

Not only did the Industrial Revolution separate people from their past but also from God, nature, and community. Howard Becker (1957) saw in the accelerating force of secularization the displacement of religion by science and the domination of nature by technology. And Georg Simmel found, as people moved from rural to urban settlements, that the mentality required to survive in the city would not support the personal, social, and tribal bonds of the village. People could no longer depend on their neighbors. They were not even sure they understood the purpose of life and death. Separated from God and home, without a past or future, their hold on the present became precarious. Comparisons to 1871–1875 statistics collected by Henry Morselli (1882) show a tripling, quadrupling, even quintupling of suicide rates in European countries in less than 50 years. In the United States, suicide has become one of the 10 leading causes of death, and in some colleges ranks second only to automobile deaths. For increasing numbers of

people, the loneliness and meaninglessness of modern life have become crises of unbearable proportions.

Alienation is one of the central and most studied concepts in sociology. An unfortunate result of this has been a proliferation of meanings attached to the concept. Some distinguish between the psychological state of alienation and the societal condition of anomie. Others use the terms interchangeably. The conventional meanings of alienation, according to *The American Heritage Dictionary* (1976 New College Edition), are "1. The condition of being an outsider; a state of isolation. 2. A state of estrangement between the self and objective world, or between different parts of the personality." The concept has been expanded in its use in the social sciences to mean more than separation. According to Melvin Seeman (1959, 1983) the term now has at least five distinct dimensions:

1. *Powerlessness:* the sense of being overwhelmed and being incapable of influencing important events.
2. *Meaninglessness:* the inability of the individual to understand his or her part in a complex productive process.
3. *Normlessness:* the cynical belief that socially disapproved behaviors like force and fraud are required to achieve goals.
4. *Isolation:* the feeling that the individual is cut off from others and is not a part of an integrated social unit.
5. *Self-estrangement:* the result when a job or activity is not fulfilling or a means of self-expression.

Sources of Alienation

Psychological Dimensions Herbert McClosky and John Schaar (1965) define anomie as "the feeling that the world and oneself are adrift, wandering, lacking clear rules and stable

This investigation is based on "Social Integration and Certain Corollaries: An Exploratory Study" by Leo Srole, 1956, reprinted on pages 144–148.

moorings. The anomic feels literally *de*-moralized; for him, the norms governing behavior are weak, ambiguous, and remote" (p. 19). They argue that three personality factors make individuals susceptible to anomie: (1) inadequate *cognitive* skills; (2) *emotional* problems that reduce the ability to cope with change; and (3) extreme and rigid *substantive beliefs.* Survey findings from national and Minnesota samples supported their expectations. Those who had high anomie scores had lower educational levels, had less information on social and political events, and were more likely to believe in mysticism. They were more rigid, obsessive, cynical, pessimistic, anxious, and hostile, and felt more political futility. They also expressed more "contempt for human weakness," were less trusting of people, and were more authoritarian.

Social Dimensions   If psychological factors were solely responsible for anomie, it would be distributed uniformly throughout society. But anomie is clustered in certain groups: the poor; the uneducated; those in low-prestige occupations; the downwardly mobile; those who are divorced, separated, or widowed; the elderly; and blacks. This suggests that conditions within society create special problems for these groups. Both Karl Marx and Émile Durkheim believed that the source of these problems could be traced to changes in the division of labor. The division of labor created by the Industrial Revolution set people apart from their friends and neighbors and made life a lonely, alien experience. Marx and Durkheim, however, were in basic disagreement as to how this could be set right.

Functional Perspective

In preindustrial and feudal societies, people lived together in groups that had little division of labor. People were born to yeomanry, serfdom, or nobility, and followed basically the same roles as their parents. In these small, tightly knit groupings, individual differences were minimal. Thought and action were governed by a common set of traditions. After the nineteenth-century revolutions, the homogeneity of the village gave way to the moral heterogeneity of the city. The simple division of labor became more technically specialized and elaborate. As the social order grew more heterogeneous, a new basis of social integration was needed.

Durkheim believed that even as we specialize, we can produce a social bond through our increasing dependence upon other specialists. Through this interdependence, social solidarity is possible even in large, complex, and impersonal societies. But he was concerned that amoral economic forces threatened to overwhelm and dominate modern life. This would lead to moral anarchy and to two pathological forms (forms that do not increase moral solidarity) of the division of labor: anomic and forced. In the *anomic* form workers are either replaced by or subordinated to machines, and are relegated to repetitive and meaningless work. If such amoral economic processes go unchecked, social life will disintegrate. Symptomatic of this disintegration are unstable family life, opposition between workers and capital, and conflict between social classes. The second pathological form Durkheim called the

forced division of labor. This occurs when individuals are forced to (1) take roles that do not fit their talents, and (2) take less than fair compensation for their work. While this may occur in premodern societies—for example, caste systems—it occurs in industrial societies when one group or social class gains unfair advantages over others. Durkheim believed that if these pathological conditions are to be avoided, amoral economic interests must not be allowed to dominate society.

Conflict Perspective

To Marx the focal point of the social order was the workplace. People come together not because they share values or because they desire a life in common, but because they are useful to each other. From work experiences we develop an understanding of ourselves, and of our connection to others and the natural world. Alienation occurs when there is a breakdown in the natural relationships that exist between people and their work. In *The Communist Manifesto,* Marx (1972) claimed that capitalism destroyed this relationship because it had "pitilessly torn asunder the motley feudal ties that bond man to his 'natural superiors,' and has left no other nexus between man and man than naked self-interest, than callous 'cash payment' " (p. 337). Under capitalism, workers can no longer choose their craft or calling. They can only sell their labor to a capitalist who determines the nature of the work they will do. Workers lose control of both the economic value of their work and what is produced. Capitalists then use machines produced by workers to increase their control and regulation of workers. Thus, the machines and assembly lines created by the workers are turned against them, making work an ever more alienating experience. To the extent that monotonous, uncreative jobs increase as one descends the occupational ladder, Marx would expect workers to be increasingly alienated. Our first hypothesis looks at this relationship between social class and alienation.

Background

Leo Srole (1956; reprinted in Reading 11) uses the word *anomia* (not anomie) rather than *alienation* simply "for semantic neatness." He views anomia as "an individual's generalized, pervasive sense of social malintegration or self-to-others alienation"; conversely, *eunomia* refers to self-to-other belongingness. Anomia and eunomia form a continuum, anomia representing disordered or disintegrated conditions and eunomia representing ordered conditions. To measure anomia, Srole constructed a five-item scale. Each item was developed to measure one aspect of anomia. The items are opinion statements, and respondents are asked whether they agree or disagree. Agreement indicates anomia and disagreement its opposite, eunomia. In these questions, only those statements receiving "agree" are scored. The possible range of scores is, therefore, 0–5. The scale is also cumulative. That is to say, if you have a score of 1, you probably endorsed the first statement, or "Anomia 1," but not the other four statements. If you had a score of 3, you probably endorsed

Figure 11–1

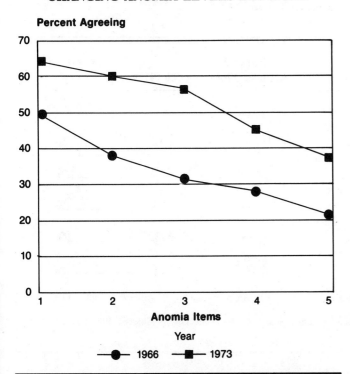

CHANGING ANOMIA LEVELS 1966 to 1973

Percent Agreeing

Anomia Items

Year

——●—— 1966   ——■—— 1973

Note: 1966 data are from "Anomia and Eunomia: A Methodological Evalua-tion of Srole's Anomia Scale" by C. Miller and E. Butler, 1966, *American Sociological Review, 31,* pp. 400–406. 1973 data are from General Social Surveys, 1972–1988, by the National Opinion Research Center, University of Chicago, 1988. Used by permission.

Figure 11–2

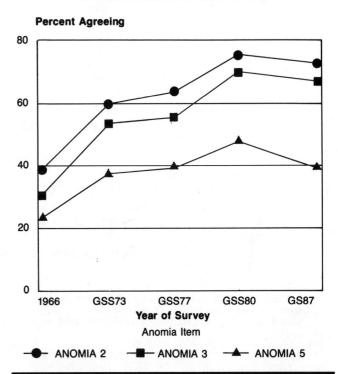

ANOMIA SURVEYS 1966 to 1987

Percent Agreeing

Year of Survey

Anomia Item

——●—— ANOMIA 2   ——■—— ANOMIA 3   ——▲—— ANOMIA 5

Note: 1966 data are from "Anomia and Eunomia: A Methodological Evalua-tion of Srole's Anomia Scale" by C. Miller and E. Butler, 1966, *American Sociological Review, 31,* pp. 400–406. 1973 data are from General Social Surveys, 1972–1988, by the National Opinion Research Center, University of Chicago, 1988. Used by permission.

Anomia 1, Anomia 2, and Anomia 3, but not Anomia 4 or Anomia 5. The five-item scale follows (you will notice they were presented, in a different order, as questions 13 through 17 on the Student Survey):

Anomia 1: These days a person doesn't really know whom he or she can count on.

Anomia 2: There's little use writing to public officials because they often aren't really interested in the problems of the average person.

Anomia 3: In spite of what some people say, the lot of the average person is getting worse, not better.

Anomia 4: Nowadays a person has to live pretty much for today and let tomorrow take care of itself.

Anomia 5: It's hardly fair to bring children into the world with the way things look for the future.

In 1956 Srole surveyed 401 Springfield, Massachusetts, transit riders aged 16–69 and found they agreed, on average, with 2.1 items. In 1966 Curtis Miller and Edgar Butler surveyed 981 adults in Los Angeles and found a lower level (1.7) of anomia. In 1973 the five Srole items were included in the General Social Survey (GSS), a national sample of 1,504

people. The results shown in Figure 11-1, "Changes in Anomia Levels, 1966 to 1973" (above left), indicate consistent and substantial increases in anomia in the 1973 GSS. In three later surveys (1977, 1980, and 1987) the GSS included only three of the anomia items. Figure 11-2, "Anomia Surveys 1966 to 1987" (above right), portrays the results and suggests a continued trend of rising anomia levels.

Srole maintains that individuals who experience conditions of anomia will feel a greater distance between themselves and others. It is also expected that anomia will be associated with a decline in the individual's identification with and attachment to others. Survey findings supported Srole's hypothesis that an-omia is positively associated with self-to-other distance. The correlation between anomia and negative attitudes toward mi-norities was +.43. Anomia was found to be inversely related to social class (r = −.30). The association between anomia and negative attitudes toward minorities held even when controlling for the effects of social class.

Robert Angell's (1962) survey of Detroit residents also found significant negative correlations between anomia and occupational status (r = −.25), income (r = −.19), and education (r = −.25). He found some evidence that anomia tended to increase with age (r = +.16) and was higher for

Table 11–1

INVESTIGATION RESULTS 11
Agreement With Anomia Items

Five Items on Srole Anomia Scale	Miller & Butler 1966[a]	GSS 1973[b]	Class Survey
13. There's little use writing to public officials because they often aren't really interested in the problems of the average man.	39%	60%	____%
14. Nowadays a person has to live pretty much for today and let tomorrow take care of itself.	29%	44%	____%
15. In spite of what some people say, the lot of the average man is getting worse, not better.	33%	56%	____%
16. It's hardly fair to bring children into the world with the way things look for the future.	23%	37%	____%
17. These days a person doesn't really know whom he or she can count on.	50%	65%	____%

[a]Miller & Butler data are from "Anomia and Eunomia: A Methodological Evaluation of Srole's Anomia Scale" by C. Miller & E. Butler, 1966, *American Sociological Review, 31*, pp. 400–406.
[b]GSS data are from General Social Surveys, 1972–1988, by the National Opinion Research Center, University of Chicago, 1988. Used by permission.

blacks than for whites (r = +.25). Subsequent research suggests that social attachment is inversely related to anomia. Wendell Bell (1957) found that measures of social isolation positively related to anomia. Dorothy Meier and Wendell Bell (1959) and Arnold Rose (1962) report that participation in formal and informal organizations is inversely related to anomia.

Replication

Three variables will be measured in this investigation. The first two deal with socioeconomic status (SES). In Srole's study, this was an index value based on the respondent's education and the occupational level of the head of the household. Using these two items as an index of social class, Srole found a negative correlation of r = −.30 between socioeconomic status and anomia.

When Angell separated income from education, however, he found the correlation between income and anomia to be r = −.19. This replication will use family income (Student Survey question 7) as a variable, to simplify the fairly complex job of classifying and weighting occupations. In accordance with Angell's findings, we should expect a small negative correlation between income and anomia.

The second variable is education. We will compare the anomia average from the Student Survey (questions 13–17) with the average that Srole found in his survey of Massachusetts mass-transit riders.

The third variable is social distance. The items on the original scale have become dated; for example, "Refugees from Nazi Germany should be kept out of the United States and sent to Palestine instead." In view of this, we will use the Bogardus Social Distance Scale. This was used in Investigation 7, and consists of the responses to item 11–A in the survey (p. 194).

Both Angell and Srole found that anomia was inversely related to socioeconomic status. We will therefore hypothesize that this relationship continues.

Hypothesis 1:

The relationship between socioeconomic status and anomia will be an inverse one, similar to that found by Angell (1962).

Hypothesis 2 follows from Angell's (1962) finding that there is an inverse relationship between education and anomia. If we can assume the educational level of Srole's survey of mass-transit riders drawn from Springfield, Massachusetts, is lower than that of a sample of college students, then we should expect the anomia level to be lower for college students than for Srole's survey.

Hypothesis 2:

The anomia level of college students will be lower than the anomia level of Srole's (1956) mass-transit riders.

The third hypothesis holds that anomia is positively associated with social distance toward outgroups in general and

Table 11–2

ANOMIA BY INCOME

Family Income	Anomia	Number
Under $15,000	_____	_____
15,000–19,000	_____	_____
20,000–24,999	_____	_____
25,000–29,999	_____	_____
30,000–39,999	_____	_____
40,000–49,999	_____	_____
50,000–59,999	_____	_____
60,000–74,999	_____	_____
75,000–99,999	_____	_____
100,000–149,999	_____	_____
150,000 and over	_____	_____

Average   Average
Income $ _____   Anomia = _____

Correlation Between Income and Anomia (Rho) = _____

Table 11–3

COMPARATIVE DISTRIBUTION OF ANOMIA

Anomia		Anomia (Springfield, Mass.)[a]	Anomia (Los Angeles)[b]	Class Survey
(low)	0	16%	29%	_____%
	1	25	24	_____
	2	20	17	_____
	3	21	14	_____
	4	13	9	_____
(high)	5	5	7	_____
		100%	100%	100%
Average Anomia		2.1	1.7	_____

[a]Springfield data are from Table 1 on page 146.
[b]Los Angeles data are from "Anomia and Eunomia: A Methodological Evaluation of Srole's Anomia Scale" by C. Miller and E. Butler, 1966, *American Sociological Review, 31,* pp. 400–406.

minority groups in particular. We will test this by correlating anomia with social distance as measured by the Bogardus scale.

Hypothesis 3:

The relationship between social distance and anomia will be a positive one, similar to that found by Srole (1956).

In order to test these hypotheses, we will need the class's responses to questions 7 (income), 13 through 17 (anomia), and 11A (social distance). These will be tabulated by your instructor and provided to you. When you have received these data, proceed as follows:

Step 1:

Fill in tables 11-1, 11-2, and 11-3 with the class's data provided by your instructor.

Step 2:

To test hypothesis 1, use the data presented in Table 11-2, above. At the bottom of the table is a blank space in which you are asked to enter the correlation between income and anomia in your Student Survey findings. Your instructor may provide you with this correlation or may ask you to calculate it on your own. When you have obtained the correlation, enter it in the blank space in hypothesis 1 below.

Hypothesis 1:

The relationship between socioeconomic status and anomia will be an inverse one, similar to that found by Angell (1962).

Correlation   _____ = −.19   Correlation
between SES   found by Angell
and anomia

Step 3:

To test hypothesis 2, use the data presented in Table 11-3, above. Enter the average anomia found in your class's survey in the blank space below.

Hypothesis 2:

The anomia level of college students will be lower than the anomia level of Srole's (1956) mass-transit riders.

Average college   _____ < 2.1   Average Srole
anomia   anomia

Step 4:

To test hypothesis 3, calculate the correlation between the class's responses to Student Survey questions 11A (social distance scale) and 13 through 17 (anomia scale). Enter the correlation in the blank space below.

Hypothesis 3:

The relationship between social distance and anomia will be a positive one, similar to that found by Srole (1956).

Correlation   _____ ≥ +.43   Correlation
between social   found by Srole
distance and
anomia

Checking Your Findings

We began our investigation with the broad theoretical issues raised by Marx and Durkheim. Both were concerned that the revolutionary changes that occurred in the nineteenth century could result in alienation reaching epidemic proportions in the modern world. To subject these ideas to scientific study, Srole

Table 11–4

SUPPORT FOR HYPOTHESES

	Significantly Supported	Partially Supported	Not Supported	Indeterminate
Hypothesis 1: *Negative* correlation between class and anomia.	_____	_____	_____	_____
Hypothesis 2: The level of anomia will be *lower* for college students than for a random sample of adults.	_____	_____	_____	_____
Hypothesis 3: *Positive* correlation between anomia and social distance.	_____	_____	_____	_____

Indicate the amount of support you found for each hypothesis.

developed a scale to measure anomia. Our first job was then to see how widespread anomia is. Compare the class results to those of Miller and Butler's 1966 findings in Table 11–1 (p. 140). Do you still find half the respondents agreeing with item 17, "These days a person doesn't really know whom he or she can count on"? How much agreement is there for the other four indicators of anomia? Table 11–3 (p. 141) compares surveys done in Springfield (Srole, 1956) and Los Angeles (Miller and Butler, 1966). Are your results similar to these studies? Is the average level of anomia higher, lower, or the same?

The first hypothesis deals with the idea that alienation is related to the division of labor or the oppression of the working class. In both cases the expectation is that alienation will be greater in the lower class. Compare average income with average anomia in Table 11–2 (p. 141). Did you find anomia inversely related with income?

The second hypothesis assumes the educational level of mass-transit riders drawn from Springfield, Massachusetts, is lower than that of a sample of college students. We should, therefore, expect the anomia level to be lower for college students than Srole's survey. Does the information in Table 11–3 support this hypothesis?

The third hypothesis asserts that there is a positive relationship between anomia and the amount of distance that we feel is separating us from others. Using the anomia and social distance scales, did you find these two variables to be positively correlated?

After analyzing the findings, summarize your conclusions in Table 11–4, above. Indicate the amount of support you found for each hypothesis.

Topics for Further Investigation

Alienation is not new to the human experience. Many are concerned, however, that the levels of alienation have been steadily increasing because of disruptions that were created or accelerated by the Industrial Revolution. The following four approaches illustrate the diversity of perspectives to the question of modern alienation.

1. The first approach is expressed by many Christians who believe that secularization has separated the individual from God. If this is true, it would seem that those who are more religious would be less alienated. Is this true?

2. A second approach is taken by some philosophers who believe that self-consciousness brings with it a separation of the self into subjective and objective elements. Alienation is the result of the growing levels of consciousness that separate objective and subjective selves. If this is true, we would expect that the more educated would be more self-conscious and, therefore, more alienated. Is this the case?

3. Marx offered a third approach when he expressed alarm about machine and factory production separating workers from the products of their work. Factory labor thus becomes an alienating experience to humans. If this is true, those who have the least control (such as blue-collar workers) should feel more alienation than those with more control (such as managers and owners) over their work. Is this correct?

4. Lastly, Durkheim believes that people will be alienated to the degree they see the division of labor as being forced or unfair. Investigation 6 looked at support for existing ideologies. If Durkheim is correct, those who are most alienated would least support the dominant ideology. One can also consider Investigation 3 in terms of alienation. Are those who are most attached to groups the least alienated? In Investigation 10 we might go on to see if those who have indicated the highest levels of love and liking are also those with the lowest alienation. What other questions might be investigated, and how could we undertake the research?

References and Recommended Readings

Angell, R. (1962). Preference for moral norms in three areas. *American Journal of Sociology, 67*, 650–660.

Becker, H. (1957). Current sacred-secular theory and its development. In H. Becker & A Boskoff (Eds.), *Modern Sociological Theory* (pp. 133–185). New York: Holt, Rinehart & Winston.

Bell, W. (1957). Anomie, social isolation and the class structure. *Sociometry, 20*, 105–116.

Clinard, M. (Ed.). (1964). *Anomie and deviant behavior.* New York: The Free Press.

Dean, D. (1961). Meaning and measurement of alienation. *American Sociological Review, 26*, 185–189.

Erikson, K. (1986). On work and alienation. *American Sociological Review, 51*, 1–8.

Jaspers, K. (1957). *Man in the modern age.* Garden City, New York: Anchor.

Kohn, M. (1976). Occupational structure and alienation. *American Sociological Review, 82*, 111–130.

Marx, K. (1972). The communist manifesto. In R. Tucker (Ed.), *The Marx-Engels reader.* New York: W. W. Norton.

McClosky, H., & Schaar, J. (1965). Psychological dimensions of anomy. *American Sociological Review, 30*, 14–40.

Meir, D., & Bell, W. (1959). Anomia and differential access to achievement of life goals. *American Sociological Review, 24*, 189–202.

Meszaros, I. (1970). *Marx's theory of alienation.* New York: Harper Torchbook.

Miller, C., & Butler, E. (1966). Anomia and eunomia: A methodological evaluation of Srole's anomia scale. *American Sociological Review, 31*, 400–405.

Morris, W. (Ed.). (1976). *The American Heritage dictionary: New college edition.* Boston: Houghton-Mifflin.

Morselli, H. (1882). *Suicide: An essay on comparative statistics.* New York: Appleton.

Orru, M. (1987). *Anomie: History and meaning.* Winchester, MA: Allen & Unwin.

Rose, A. (1962). Alienation and participation. *American Sociological Review, 27*, 834–838.

Schact, R. (1984). *Alienation.* Lanham, MD: University Press of America.

Schmitt, R. (1983). *Alienation and class.* New York: Schenkman.

Seeman, M. (1959). On the meaning of alienation. *American Sociological Review, 24*, 783–791.

Seeman, M. (1983). Alienation motifs in contemporary theorizing: The hidden continuity of the classic themes. *Social Psychology Quarterly, 46*, 171–184.

Shoham, S., & Grahame, A. (Eds.). (1982). *Alienation and anomie revisited.* Tel Aviv: Ramot.

Simmel, G. (1964). The metropolis and mental life. In K. Wolff (Ed.), *The Sociology of Georg Simmel* (pp. 409–424). New York: The Free Press.

Srole, L. (1956). Social integration and certain corollaries. *American Sociological Review, 21*, 709–716.

Tiryakian, E. (1962). *Sociologism and existentialism.* Englewood Cliffs, NJ: Prentice Hall.

Social Integration and Certain Corollaries:
An Exploratory Study

Leo Srole
Cornell University Medical College

This article has evolved from a preliminary report of a study conducted in Springfield, Massachusetts, in 1950. Although the study was originally conceived as applied rather than pure research, the attitude-type scale devised afforded an operational formulation of the anomie concept. This formulation was broader, however, than that specified by Durkheim.

The writer felt the need for further conceptualization in the light of theoretical developments centering on the concept of "social integration," and in 1952 it became possible to apply the writer's version of the anomie concept to research in New York City in connection with a large scale study of mental health and its social corollaries. This paper benefits from the findings of the New York research, although it is substantively based on the earlier research.

CONCEPTS, HYPOTHESES AND RESEARCH DESIGN

The objective of the Springfield study was the measurement and assessment of the impact of a series of ADL card advertisements (anti-discrimination and American Creed messages) that were posted under controlled conditions in vehicles of the public transit system. The applied character of this research imposed a different research design than would have been developed if the study had exclusively focused on the anomie concept.

The "target" audience studied was the Springfield transit riding population, defined arbitrarily as individuals of age 16 and over who paid four or more fares in the average week. Because available resources limited us to a relatively small sample, heterogeneity in the sample was reduced. . . .

Differential audience "penetration" effects of the test transit cards were expected to be mediated by a number of

Reprinted with permission from *American Sociological Review, 21,* 1956, pp. 709–716.

intervening variables, e.g., prior attitudinal set toward minority groups. Accordingly, respondents were classified by degree of attitudinal acceptance or rejection of minority groups in general, on the basis of two different kinds of data in combination:

1. Responses to five structured social distance questionnaire items referring by indirection to Negroes, Jews, foreigners, etc.
2. Spontaneous comments revealing underlying attitudes toward minority groups. These were unexpectedly elicited in many cases by the projective nature of the special versions of the posted car cards (text converted into hieroglyphics) used in the interview to test message recall.

* * * *

Considerations of questionnaire design compelled placement of our structured attitudes-to-minorities items early in the instrument. Moreover, in order to divert respondent attention from their common, underlying element, these items were scattered among questions of quite different content. These diversionary items afforded a "hitch hike" opportunity to test hypotheses centering on Durkheim's concept of anomie. These hypotheses center on a pair of antinomic Greek terms, "eunomia" and "anomia." The former originally denoted a well ordered condition in a society or state, the latter its opposite. The two terms can be adapted with some license to refer to the continuum of variations in the "integratedness" of different social systems or sub-systems, viewed as molar wholes. They can also be applied to the parallel continuum of variations seen from the "microscopic" or molecular view of individuals as they are integrated in the total action fields of their interpersonal relationships and reference groups.

Although research employing the macroscopic approach to the phenomena of integration in large social systems has appeared in recent years, it still presents formidable operational problems. On the other hand, the molecular approach has the advantage of being readily fitted to the established operational apparatus of the sample survey. With the molecular approach, the immediate analytical objective would be to place individuals on a eunomia-anomia continuum representing variations in interpersonal integration with their particular social fields as "global" entities. More concretely, this variable is conceived as referring to the individual's generalized, pervasive sense of "self-to-others belongingness" at one extreme compared with "self-to-others distance" and "self-to-others alienation" at the other pole of the continuum. For semantic neatness the terms eunomia-anomia are here used to refer specifically to this socio-psychological continuum.

It may clarify this conception of the eunomia-anomia dimension on the molecular level to note the likelihood that in the individual adult it covers more than the cumulative consequences of his particular integrations in his current social roles and groups. Specifically, three more inclusive sets of forces are also seen as operating in this contemporary situation.

1. Reference groups beyond his immediate field of action, within which acceptance and ultimate integration are sought.
2. Generalized qualities of the molar society penetrating his contemporary action field, as these affect (a) his life-goal choices, (b) his selection of means toward these goals, and (c) his success or failure in achieving these goals.
3. The socialization processes of his interpersonal relationships during childhood and adolescence, as these have conditioned the interpersonal expectations, value orientations, and behavioral tendencies of his current personality structure.

Accordingly, individual eunomia-anomia is viewed as a variable contemporary condition having its origin in the complex interaction of social[1*] and personality factors, present and past. In short, the condition is regarded as a variable dependent on both sociological and psychological processes. As such, it warrants direct attack in the wide-ranging strategy of research.[2]

This is not the place to explore systematically the relationship of the concept of anomia, under the definition here proposed, to cognate concepts. But two clarifying observations may be offered. First, in the writer's view "self-to-others alienation" may be regarded as the common element[3] in Durkheim's conceptualization of *anomie, egoisme, altruisme,* and *fatalisme* as different but often overlapping forms of suicide. Second, there has been reflected among some social scientists a sense of the limited utility of Durkheim's specification of anomie as referring to the breakdown of those moral norms that limit desires and aspirations (a breakdown which he tended to associate with rather special "change of role" circumstances). This development has been accompanied by diversification in the usage of the term, in one direction toward convergence with the broader concepts of dysfunction and malintegration in molar social systems.[4] The convergence most closely approximating the definition proposed here is to be seen in (1) MacIver's definition of anomie as "the breakdown of the individual's sense of attachment to society"[5] and (2) Lasswell's reading of the

concept as referring to the "lack of identification on the part of the primary ego of the individual with a 'self' that includes others. In a word, modern man appeared to be suffering from psychic isolation. He felt alone, cut off, unwanted, unloved, unvalued."[6]

The hypothesis within our framework that lent itself to testing in the Springfield study was this: social malintegration, or anomia, in individuals is associated with a rejective orientation toward out-groups in general and toward minority groups in particular.[7] To test this hypothesis it was necessary to devise a measure of interpersonal alienation or "anomia." This, we reasoned, could be constructed in opinion-poll format to represent, directly or indirectly, the respondent's definition or perception of his own interpersonal situation. To this end, we set down the ideational states or components that on theoretical grounds would represent internalized counterparts or reflections, in the individual's life situation, of conditions of social dysfunction. Five components from the larger series were selected for inclusion in the study. For each, "opinion" type statements of the simple agree-disagree type were framed and pretested (for verbal clarity and response distributions) in fifty interviews. From the pretest experience we selected one item which, with subsequent revisions, finally represented each anomia component in the Springfield questionnaire.

The first of these postulated components was the individual's sense that community leaders are detached from and indifferent to his needs, reflecting severance of the interdependent bond within the social system between leaders and those they should represent and serve. The item selected to represent this component was the agree-disagree statement, "There's little use writing to public officials because often they aren't really interested in the problems of the average man."

The second hypothesized element of anomia was the individual's perception of the social order as essentially fickle and unpredictable, i.e., orderless, inducing the sense that under such conditions he can accomplish little toward realizing future life goals. The item that seemed to come closest to this facet of anomia was the Epicurean statement, "Nowadays a person has to live pretty much for today and let tomorrow take care of itself."

Closely related to this aspect of anomia was a third element: the individual's view, beyond abdication of future life goals, that he and people like him are retrogressing from the goals they have already reached. The item chosen to represent this component was the statement rejecting the American Creed doctrine of progress: "In spite of what some people say, the lot of the average man is getting worse, not better."

The fourth component postulated, and the one perhaps most closely approximating Durkheim's particular definition of anomie, was the deflation or loss of internalized social norms and values, reflected in extreme form in the individual's sense of the meaninglessness of life itself. Standing for this element was the item proposition: "It's hardly fair to bring children into the world with the way things look for the future."

The final anomia component was hypothesized as the individual's perception that his framework of immediate personal relationships, the very rock of his social existence, was no longer predictive or supportive, and was expressed by the item worded: "These days a person doesn't really know whom he can count on."

* * * *

After deciding on the inclusion of the five anomia items in the Springfield questionnaire, it became clear to us that we would also have to control analytically for the authoritarian personality factor, as measured in the California Study,[8] if we were to test adequately the hypothesis that orientation toward minority groups is related to the factor assumed to be reflected in our measure of anomia. For this specific purpose we incorporated into the questionnaire a shortened five-item version of the California F scale of authoritarianism. Replication of the California study was not intended.

In the interview, the fifteen items of the anomia, authoritarianism, and attitudes-to-minorities measures were all presented to the respondent as "opinion statements" with which he could either agree or disagree. As was expected and provided for in the precoded list of possible replies available to the interviewer for checking, some respondents gave qualified or "can't decide" answers. In the scoring system, we applied the severe criterion that only an unequivocal "agree" (score values, 1) to an item was to be counted in the score of its particular measure. Thus, for the anomia (A) and authoritarianism (F) measures, the respondent's score falls in a range from zero to five.

The three-way minority attitudes classification, designated the "M" measure, is based, as noted earlier, on scored replies to five structured questionnaire items in combination with revealing spontaneous comments elicited by the textually masked test cards used in the interview. The final score range for this classificatory scheme is zero to two.

FINDINGS

The distributions of the Springfield sample on the A, F, and M measures appear in Table 1. . . . It was found that they satisfy the criteria of unidimensionality, i.e., comprise one latent continuum. It is relevant to add that from New York City data gathered by the Cornell community mental health study, the writer's associate, Thomas Langner, has established that the same five anomia items satisfy the requirements of a Guttman-type scale. On two sets of evidence, therefore, we have grounds for referring to the anomia item series as a scale.

* * * *

The hypothesis motivating the construction and inclusion of the A scale in the Springfield study was that anomia is a factor related to the formation of negative rejective attitudes toward minority groups. The Pearson correlation actually found in the Springfield data between A scores and M was +.43, supporting the hypothesis.

The F scale was introduced into the study design to control for the factor of authoritarian personality trends, known previ-

Table 1

DISTRIBUTION OF THE SPRINGFIELD SAMPLE (N = 401) ON THE THREE MEASURES OF A, F, AND M, IN PER CENT

Score	Anomia (A)	Authoritarianism (F)
0	16	18
1	25	17
2	20	20
3	21	23
4	13	13
5	5	9
Total	100	100

Score		Attitudes toward Minorities (M)
0	Positive ("Tolerant")	44
1	Ambivalent ("Borderline")	36
2	Negative ("Prejudiced")	20
	Total	100

ously to be associated with attitudes to minorities. In Springfield, we found a Pearson correlation of +.29 between F scores and M.

As to the significance of the difference between the A-M correlation of .43 and the F-M correlation of .29, application of the "t"-test of significance produces a "t" value of 3.11. To meet the requirements of the .05 level of confidence, the "t" value should be 3.18. For all practical purposes, therefore, we can accept the difference between the two correlations as being statistically significant.

Although lacking any basis for hypothesizing about the expected relationship of anomia scores and M when F scores are controlled, we were interested in the direction of this relationship. By the method of partial correlation, we have found that the correlation of .43 between A and M is negligibly reduced to .35 when F scores are partialled out. Thus, we can conclude that in our sample population anomia scores are related to attitudes toward minorities *independently* of the personality trends measured by the authoritarianism scale.

We next faced the question of the relationship of F scores and M when A scores are held constant. Again by the method of partial correlation, we find that when A scores are partialled out, the correlation of .29 between F and M is reduced to .12. We could conclude, therefore, that in our sample the correlation between authoritarian personality trends and attitudes toward minorities is partially accounted for by the anomia factor, i.e., F scores do *not* stand in a close relationship to M *independently* of the anomia factor.

We had originally hypothesized that the anomia factor would be significantly related in an inverse direction to socioeconomic status. In the Springfield interview, we accordingly asked for respondent's education and occupation of head of household, in order to combine them, equally weighted, into a composite status score. On the basis of the score distribution the

Table 2

PEARSON PRODUCT MOMENT CORRELATIONS OF A AND M, F AND M IN THREE SES STRATA

	Low (N = 139)	Middle (N = 163)	High (N = 97)
A and M	.44*	.42*	.47*
F and M	.20†	.34*	.29*

*Significant at or beyond .01 level of confidence.
†Significant at .02 level of confidence.

sample was classified into three SES strata. Applying this measure of socioeconomic status, we find a Pearson correlation between A scores and SES of $-.30$, supporting the hypothesis. The corresponding correlation of F scores and SES is $-.22$; and of M and SES, $-.14$. Apparently then, in our sample population attitudes toward minority groups are to only a small degree a function of the status variable, whereas anomia is to a moderate degree, and authoritarian personality tendencies to an extent intermediate between A and M.

For each SES stratum separately we have computed first the Pearson correlation of A and M and next the correlation of F and M. These coefficients are presented in Table 2. In the separate correlations of A and F with M, we find almost identical coefficients in the Middle stratum, but appreciable differences in the two extreme strata.

* * * *

DISCUSSION

In an exploratory study such as this, caution dictates that the findings be weighed principally on the scale of their suggestive potentialities. Space does not permit us to define and evaluate the many questions inherent in the concepts, hypotheses and data presented in this paper.[9] However, several brief observations may be offered.

Recent unpublished research by others, and by the writer and his Cornell associates, in applying the A scale or adaptations of it have established significant connections between this measure of individual anomia and such diverse phenomena as social isolation among the aged, certain specific forms of psychopathology among metropolitan adults, the life threat represented by the exogenous condition of rheumatic heart disease, adolescents living in areas marked by different rates of drug addiction, etc.

These studies, by their cumulative weight, support the general hypothesis of an interactive process linking the individual state of anomia and interpersonal dysfunction in the social realm.

Of special interest in the Springfield data is the isolation of anomic states and authoritarian personality trends as relatively discrete dimensions that are closely related to each other, a

finding corroborated by our current New York City study. It could be predicted of course that a personality with authoritarian tendencies bred in the family of origin would tend to be a "misfit" in a democratic social system, thereby generating the conditions both in itself and in the interpersonal milieu, that give rise to one type of self-to-others alienation.

On the other hand, we would follow Fromm and Merton[10] in hypothesizing a second kind of developmental sequence. To Fromm, among personalities basically "fitted" for a democratic society, escape reactions from socially generated "aloneness" and "helplessness" (i.e. individual anomia) may issue either in authoritarianism or "compulsive conformity." For Merton, individual "modes of adaptation" to dysfunctional "contradictions in the cultural and social structure" are differentiated on the basis of a more systematic and comprehensive typology of deviancy, including "ritualism" hypothesized as a dominant type. To freely paraphrase both writers, social dysfunction is the independent variable, the individual's state of self-to-group alienation is the intervening variable, and change in personality (Fromm) or adaptive modes (Merton) is the dependent variable.

As a closing note, there appears to be a trend among social scientists toward convergence of interest in the phenomena of social integration. Equipped with the advances of the past decade in theory and research technology, this trend gives promise of accelerating the scientific attack, powerfully and single-handedly launched by Émile Durkheim more than a half-century ago, on one of the most pervasive and potentially dangerous aspects of Western society, namely, the deterioration in the social and moral ties that bind, sustain and free us.

1. Under the influence of the Cornell mental health investigation, the notion of the sociogenesis of individual anomia was refined to include the self-generated or psychogenic type of alienation from others. This, of course, extends the sociogenic time perspective to earlier states of the life history when more narrowly localized social processes of a malintegrating kind set in motion pyschopathological processes of alienation from self and others. Remaining of central interest, however, are the individuals entering adulthood as "normal" personalities but in whom anomia develops in response to objective conditions of stressful malintegration in their social worlds.
2. Operationally speaking, Robin Williams (*op. cit.*, p. 537) appears to take a dissenting position: "Anomie as a social condition has to be defined independently of the psychological states thought to accompany normlessness and normative conflict. . . . The basic model for explanatory purposes is: normative situation → psychological state → behavioral item or sequence." But in an interesting footnote he adds: "Strictly speaking, of course, the arrows should be written ← →: the relations are reciprocal." If the relations are reciprocal, as we concur,then the explanatory model is significantly altered. With such alterations, considerations of operational efficiency, rather than of a unidirectional causal theory, may dictate to the investigator at what point his research should break into a chain. Clearly, verbalizable psychological states of individuals and their situational concomitants are more readily accessible to the instruments of the researcher than is the operationally complicated cultural abstraction that Williams calls the "normative structure" and seems to predicate as the researcher's *necessary* point of first attack.
3. This general point of view has been expressed by Ivan Belknap and Hiram J. Friedsam, "Age and Sex Categories as Sociological Variables in the Mental Disorders of Later Maturity," *American Sociological Review*, 14 (June, 1949), p. 369: "Ultimately, *suicide altruiste* may also be an anomic phenomenon, since the group actually extrudes the particular individual,

providing no further 'place' for him. *Egoisme,* another of Durkheim's type of suicide is also perhaps significant only as a cause of *anomie."*

4. An outstanding example is provided in Robert K. Merton's "Social Structure and Anomie: Revisions and Extensions" in his *Social Theory and Social Structure,* Glencoe, Illinois: The Free Press, 1949.

5. Robert M. MacIver, *The Ramparts We Guard,* New York: The Macmillan Co., 1950, pp. 84–92.

6. Harold Lasswell, "The Threat to Privacy" in Robert M. MacIver (editor), *Conflict of Loyalties,* New York: Harper and Bros., 1952.

7. Williams (*op. cit.,* p. 536) independently arrived at substantially the same hypothesis: "It is enough to note here one possible connection between anomic conditions and problems of intergroup, or intercategory, relations. . . . [Anomie] is a context highly favorable to rigidly categorical definition of out-groups."

8. T. W. Adorno, E. Frenkel-Brunswik, Daniel J. Levinson, and R. Nevitt Sanford, *The Authoritarian Personality,* New York: Harper and Bros., 1950.

9. It is hoped that further research will yield answers to these questions. The five A scale items employed in both the Springfield and New York investigations, together with the five new anomia items constructed for the latter study, will be made available by the writer to social scientists who may wish to undertake such research.

10. *Escape from Freedom,* New York: Rinehart and Co., 1941, pp. 136–206; Merton, *op. cit.*

DETECTING SOCIAL FACTS

> While the individual man is an insoluble puzzle, in the aggregate he becomes a mathematical certainty. You can, for example, never foretell what any one person will do, but you can say with precision what an average member will be up to. Individuals vary, but percentages remain constant.
>
> Sherlock Holmes, in
> Sir Arthur Conan Doyle's
> *The Sign of Four*

Émile Durkheim (1858–1917) is regarded as a founder of modern sociology. To him, two issues were central to sociology: establishing a scientific basis to study society and diagnosing the breakdown of modern society. He traced this breakdown to the declining capacity of groups such as the family, church, and community to bond individuals to the social order. As a rule, the more the individual is attached to groups, the more the individual can draw upon the groups for support and strength. Detachment for the individual means personal isolation and anomie. Isolated and lonely individuals find adversity increasingly frustrating and life emptied of purpose. As their despair deepens, suicide correspondingly begins to seem an increasingly reasonable alternative. Durkheim predicted, for example, that those who are married (more attached) will have lower suicide rates than those who are divorced (less attached). Durkheim investigated these and other ideas with percent and rate tables. In the following section we will see how Durkheim used tables for his research, how tables are organized, how to read one- and two-variable tables, and, lastly, how to infer causal connections.

The Organization of Tables

A good table quickly tells you what it is trying to communicate. It does this by including the following elements: title, notes, headings, stub, and cells. Table 1 on the next page illustrates how these elements appear in a well-organized table.

1. Title The title introduces the reader to the subject the table is presenting. In Table 1, the title states that the table is explaining suicide rates for selected countries (the assumed effect) by age and sex (assumed causes).

2. Footnote This information appears below the bottom table rule. In Table 1 the asterisk that follows the title refers us to the foot of the table. This note indicates that the original table can

be found in *The Statistical Abstract of the United States 1990* on page 838.

3. Headnotes This information immediately follows the title and is essential to a correct interpretation of the statistics that are presented in the table. Our headnote tells us that the definition of suicide that the table uses comes from the *International Classification of Diseases* (ICD). The ICD definition of suicide includes lethal injuries that are either directly or indirectly self-inflicted.

4. Headings and Stub The table is divided with lines, called rules, into blocks of columns and rows. The column headings in Table 1 identify the seven countries and years being described. The stub identifies the information in the rows. In this table, it consists of the suicide rate by age group for males and females.

5. Cells The cells provide more specific information. These are found in the stub where the rows and columns intersect. To interpret cells we need to know if they consist of raw or transformed numbers. Raw number tables may or may not specify if the cells contain simple frequency counts. Tables that have transformed numbers into averages, indices, percents, rates, or ratios *must* identify the values in the cells. The unit indicator (just below the table title) provides this information. In Table 1, the unit indicator tells us that the numbers given are numbers of suicides per 100,000 population.

Table Reading

After discovering the table's organization, the interpretation of its information can begin. With Table 1 we can consider the question of what, if any, relationship exists between suicide, sex, and age. Our analysis of the table begins by noting that overall suicide rates have a range of 123.9 (from 1.3 for Italian females aged 15–24 to 125.2 for Austrian men 75 years of age and older). Both variables—sex and age—play central roles in understanding the variation in suicide rates. The ranges for men (28.5, or 40.1 minus 11.6) and women (15.4, or 19.9 minus 4.5) reveal a relationship between sex and suicide. Age, however, has an even larger range of 96.0 (29.2 for Austrian men aged 15–24 versus 125.2 for Austrian men aged 75 and older), indicating that

This chapter is based on *Reading Tables* by Alan G. Hill, Delta College, 1983 (unpublished manuscript). Adapted by permission.

Table 1

SUICIDE RATES FOR SELECTED COUNTRIES ◄──────────────── **Table Title**
BY SEX AND AGE GROUP* ◄──────────────── **Footnote Indicator**
(Rates per 100,000 population) ◄──────────────── **Unit Indicator**

[Includes deaths resulting indirectly from self-inflected injuries. Except as noted, deaths classified
according to the ninth revision of the *International Classification of Diseases*] ◄── **Headnote**

Sex and Age	United States 1986	Australia 1986	Austria 1987	Denmark 1986	Italy 1985	Nether- lands 1986	United Kingdom 1987
MALE							
Total	20.6	19.1	40.1	35.6	12.2	13.9	11.6
15–24 yrs. old	21.7	21.2	29.2	16.5	5.2	8.1	9.3
25–34 yrs. old	25.5	28.3	42.9	33.2	9.2	15.2	14.6
35–44 yrs. old	23.0	23.5	44.8	50.6	10.1	15.3	14.6
45–54 yrs. old	24.4	23.1	54.9	54.3	14.8	19.6	15.0
55–64 yrs. old	26.7	24.6	48.5	62.2	22.0	22.6	17.8
65–74 yrs. old	35.5	27.1	68.1	52.9	33.7	25.5	15.8
75 and older	56.0	36.8	125.2	65.5	50.0	42.8	20.0
FEMALE							
Total	5.4	5.6	15.7	19.9	4.7	8.2	4.5
15–24 yers. old	4.4	5.4	8.1	5.2	1.3	3.6	2.1
25–34 yrs. old	5.9	6.3	10.7	14.0	2.7	9.1	3.8
35–44 yrs. old	7.6	7.5	15.9	24.6	4.3	10.9	4.6
45–54 yrs. old	8.8	10.8	16.8	36.7	5.9	13.6	7.6
55–64 yrs. old	8.4	8.3	22.9	44.2	8.8	13.5	7.3
65–74 yrs. old	7.3	7.6	33.8	29.3	11.9	12.5	8.1
75 and older	6.8	6.2	35.4	26.0	12.4	13.0	6.9

◄── **Column Heads**, **Table Stub**

Note: From World Health Organization, Geneva, Switzerland, *1988 World Health Statistics Annual.* ◄── **Sourcenote**
*From *Statistical Abstract of the United States 1990* (110th ed., p. 838), 1990, Washington, D.C.: U.S. Government Printing ◄── **Footnote**
Office.

age plays an important part in explaining suicide. In addition to the connections between age and sex, it is equally clear that great differences in suicide rates exist between the seven countries. The suicide rates of Austria, for example, are three to four times as large as those of the United Kingdom. This difference tends to hold true across both age and sex boundaries.

Conclusions   Our study of Table 1 allows several conclusions: men have much higher suicide rates than women; suicide rates generally increase with age for men but not necessarily for women; and suicide rates vary greatly from one country to another. We may conclude that a very important connection exists between suicide, age, sex, and country.

One- and Two-Variable Tables

One-Variable Tables

All tables try to describe or explain variables. A variable is simply a category (for example, religion) that has more than one value. Variables must be divided into values that may be qualities (such as Roman Catholic or Protestant) or quantities

(such as ranks or numbers). A one-variable table or array merely presents those values and the frequency of each. Table 2, on the next page, is a one-variable table.

To read Table 2 most effectively, identify the variable presented. In this case, the variable is Cause of Death or Selected Cause of Death. The same variable may be given different names. Do not let this mislead you. The variable is measured by an indicator. An *indicator* indicates the presence (or, better, the degree of presence) of a given variable. Cause of Death might be indicated by the entry on death certificates. While such entries may not always be perfectly accurate, they are probably valid (that is, actually indicate what we think they indicate) and reliable (give the same value in instances that are the same and different values in instances that are different) enough for our purposes.

Be careful not to confuse values with variables. Remember all variables must vary; they must have at least two values (otherwise they would not be variables, but constants). In Table 2, the variable Cause of Death has three values—Homicide, Suicide, and Accidents. These values are nominal; that is, they have names instead of quantities. Values often are quantities like 1, 2, 3, or 4. A sequence of values, such as 1st, 2nd, 3rd, or 4th, is called a rank order.

Table 2

SELECTED CAUSES OF DEATH PER 100,000 IN THE UNITED STATES, 1986*

Cause of Death	Frequency
Homicide	9.0
Suicide	12.8
Accidents	39.5

*Compiled from *Statistical Abstract of the United States 1990* (110th ed., Table 118), 1990, Washington, D.C.: U.S. Government Printing Office; and U.S. Center for Health Statistics, *Vital Statistics of the United States,* annual and unpublished data.

Having identified the variable and the values, we then want to know what the table tells us about the variable. To learn that, we look at the figures listed next to the values. We see that next to the value Homicide the rate is 9.0. That means that there were 9.0 murders in the United States in a single year for every 100,000 persons. Why is this figure used? Why not simply list the total number of murders in the United States? The reason is that using a rate (which this is) or a percentage (a kind of rate that always is given per 100—the number out of 100—allows us to compare frequencies in different-sized groups, samples, or nations without being misled. For example, there are hundreds of murders (and suicides) each year in a large city like New York City, while there are only a few in most small towns. Yet this does not necessarily mean that the small town is safer than the big city. The rates (or percentages) might be the same in both places. Therefore, we use rates or percentages so that we can know if the frequencies of phenomena are really similar or different without being misled by the difference in the size of the population or sample from which our data are drawn. Of course, more people die from all causes in large cities than in small towns. But that does not mean that the rate is necessarily greater.

In sociology, percentages are the most commonly used form of rate. If a percentage had been used in Table 2, the right column heading would have read Percentage rather than Frequency. Percentages could have been used in this table, but because percentage means number per 100, the resulting figures would have been inconvenient to use because they would involve so many decimal places (for example, expressed as a percentage, the homicide rate of 9.0 per 100,000 would be written 0.009%).

If we compare the frequencies shown in the table, we learn that in the United States a person is about twice as likely to die in an accident than to be killed intentionally through homicide or suicide (39.5 is about twice the total of 9.0 + 12.8). Furthermore, if a person is killed intentionally, it is more likely to be a case of suicide than a homicide (the homicide rate of 9.0 is less than the suicide rate of 12.8). This fact may surprise some people, since we do not often realize that we are in greater danger from ourselves than from others. Actually, if we put this information together with other data (not shown in this table),

we see that most murder victims knew their murderer either as a friend, acquaintance, or relative before the crime: one must conclude that we are fairly unlikely to be killed by a stranger.

We can learn, as you can see, quite a bit from a one-variable table. A detective who discovered a person shot to death, and who had seen these data, would first ask if the shooting could have been an accident (most likely) or a suicide (next most likely) before suspecting murder. And with the additional information mentioned above, even if it were a murder, the detective would be well advised to check the victim's friends and relatives before looking for a homicidal maniac who was a stranger to the victim. This method of investigation would be the one most likely to solve the case quickly and efficiently, despite what some popular murder stories may have led us to believe.

Two-Variable Tables

As useful as one-variable tables are, sociologists use them only marginally in their work. We are not interested in frequencies alone. We want to know how variables relate to one another. We seek associations and, ultimately, causes of social behavior. But studying just a single variable will not allow us to find associations or causes; it will show us only results (or effects). A univariate (one-variable) table such as Table 2 tells us only that people do kill themselves and others, and how frequently. Sociologists, however, usually want to know *why*—not only in this area of behavior but in all human action.

To learn why, to seek associations and causes, we need a table showing at least two variables. This kind of table (a bivariate table) is shown below as Table 3.

As before, the first questions to ask about this table are, how many variables are presented and what are they? Then one should ask how many values does each variable have and what the values are. In Table 3, one variable is Cause of Death, as in Table 2. How many values does it have in Table 3? Not three as in Table 2, but only two. Accidental deaths have been omitted. Investigators often omit possible values to focus on those that are more important to the questions they are asking. Here we are focusing on intentional killing—suicide and homicide. The

Table 3

CAUSE OF DEATH PER MILLION BY RELIGION (EUROPE)

Religion	Cause of Death	
	Suicide	Homicide
Protestant	326.3	3.8
Catholic	86.7	32.1

Note: Reprinted with permission of The Free Press, a division of Macmillan, Inc., from Émile Durkheim, *Suicide* (pp. 154, 353), translated by John A. Spaulding and George Simpson. Copyright © 1951, renewed 1979 by The Free Press.

title of this table is "Cause of Death per Million by Religion." The word *by* often links variables in a title. The second variable is Religion. How many values does it have? Again, the answer is two: Protestant and Catholic.

Table 3 is the simplest kind of two-variable table—a "two-by-two" table. It is called two-by-two because each of the two variables has two values. Depending on the number of variables and the number of values each variable has, tables can become very complex. A two-by-two table has four cells. The intersection of Suicide and Protestant gives us the rate of suicide among Protestant Europeans. In other words, in the upper left cell of this table one finds the rate 326.3. Be sure you can find all four cells and understand the figures in them before reading further. (Note that now we are using rates per 1,000,000 population.)

Association

Discovering Relationships With the Diagonal Rule

Our main interest in looking at Table 3 is to discover if the two variables are related or associated. What tends to go with what? If we knew the value of one variable, could we guess with a better-than-even chance of being right the value of the other variable? If so, we would be well on our way to understanding (and predicting) this sort of human behavior.

To see if a table shows an *association* between variables, we compare the figures (usually rates or percentages) in the cells of the table. Table 3 organizes information so we can test Durkheim's belief that there is an association between religion and suicide. At the intersection of Protestant and Suicide, we note the rate of 326.3 per million. At the intersection of Catholic and Homicide, we find 32.1 (the lower right cell). In the upper right cell (Homicide and Protestant) and in the lower left cell (Catholic and Suicide) we find 3.8 and 86.7 respectively. How are we to interpret these figures? It seems that Protestants are more likely to commit suicide than are Catholics, whereas Catholics are more likely to be murdered than are Protestants. We would say that the variables, Cause of Death and Religion, are associated. We know this because the numbers that make up the greatest proportion of each column form a diagonal set of cells. In this table, the numbers in the upper left and lower right cells are each the largest in their columns, and they can be linked by a diagonal line. This rule of thumb, called the "diagonal rule," is one handy way of seeing if variables in a table are associated—that is, tend to "go together." Put into other words, the diagonal rule says that in a two-variable table, if the proportions (percentages, rates, or absolute numbers) on one diagonal are much greater than the proportions on the other diagonal, then the variables are probably associated with each other.

In Table 3, we have found an association between religion and cause of death. We know this by following the diagonal rule. This rule is not a precise measure of association, but it

Table 4

VARIATIONS OVER TIME OF THE RATE OF MORTALITY BY SUICIDE AND THE RATE OF GENERAL MORTALITY*

| Year | Mortality Rate | |
	Suicides (Per 100,000)	General Mortality (Per 1,000)
1849–1855	10.1	24.1
1856–1860	11.2	23.2

Note: Reprinted with permission of The Free Press, a division of Macmillian, Inc., From Émile Durkheim, *Suicide* (p. 49, Table II), translated by John A. Spaulding and George Simpson. Copyright © 1951, renewed 1979 by The Free Press.

does give us a first approximation—an idea of what goes with what. (More exact measures of association, discussed later, can also be used.) In this case, we would say that religion seems to be somehow related to certain kinds of behavior—murder and suicide. Protestant Europeans were found to have higher suicide rates than Catholic Europeans. Religion and suicide seem to be associated in some way. (Note that having shown only an association, we cannot speak accurately of cause.)

Now, you might ask if tables always show associations between variables. No! They do not. But what would a table showing no association be like? The answer is that it would usually be the opposite of Table 3. Instead of numbers piling up on the diagonal, the cells would have very similar numbers in the rows and/or columns. Table 4 is an example of a "no association" table.

There is no clustering on the diagonal in Table 4. Instead, the cells show rates that are much the same. There were 10–11 suicides (per 100,000 people) and 23–24 deaths (per 1,000 people) during the time from 1849 to 1860. Here we would say that there is no association between time period and cause of death. By knowing the time period, you gain little ability to predict either the suicide or death rate. One could do about as well by flipping a coin—pure guess. Although there are other table distributions that also show no association, this kind is probably the most common. (If one does much social research, one realizes just how common findings of no association really are!)

Durkheim turned his "no finding" into an important discovery. In a more detailed study of these rates over time, he found mortality, as stable as it was, fluctuated more than suicide did. Durkheim's discovery suggested that some feature of society was responsible for the remarkable stability of suicide rates. He understood that the individual plays a part in the decision to commit suicide, but individuals cannot determine the suicide rates across generations. He concluded that suicide rates could not be understood as a psychological fact. They must be understood as a new order of fact—as social facts. Social facts (such as the rates of crime, birth, literacy, and poverty) cannot be explained by psychological facts but only by other social facts (such as religion, family, industry, or urban life). Thus, as Durkheim demonstrated, scientific results that report no findings can be just as important as those that report significant findings.

With real data, one is unlikely to find such obvious cases as shown in Tables 3 and 4. But the general principles of table reading apply: the more the numbers tend to pile up on the diagonal, the greater the level of association. The more evenly the numbers are distributed among the cells, the less the association.

The same principles of table reading apply to tables that are larger than two-by-two. If there are more cells, but still only two variables, one can apply the diagonal rule. For example, if in Table 4 we had included the value Accidental Deaths under Mortality Rate and added 1870–1879 as another time period under investigation, we would have produced a table with nine cells (a three-by-three table). The two variables would then have three values each. If we had not included Accidental Deaths but had included 1870–1879, we would produce a table with six cells. The structure of tables with two variables can grow rather complex when the number of values shown is increased. Nevertheless, as long as there are only two variables, the principles of reading are much the same.

Three-variable tables are more complex still, but most of them are really a set of two-variable tables. For example, we might show cause of death by time period and religion. Then we might show tables like those in Table 3 and 4, but one table would be only Protestants, while the other would be only Catholics. Such three-variable tables are common when one wishes to control for other variables. But remember that each component two-variable table may be read as we have described.

The principles of reading two-variable tables may be presented as follows:

LARGER	smaller
smaller	LARGER

This would show an association between the variables.

smaller	LARGER
LARGER	smaller

This would also show an association between the variables.

about the same	about the same
about the same	about the same

This would show no association between the variables.

Now look at Table 5.

Table 5

LEVEL OF ANXIETY BY RELIGION*

Religion	Anxiety Level		
	High	Low	
Catholic	25%	75%	100%
	(175)	(525)	(700)
Protestant	65%	35%	100%
	(520)	(280)	(800)
		N = 1,500	

*Fictitious data

Table 5 introduces a new variable, Anxiety Level. This variable could be indicated by a series of questions (indicators) forming an anxiety index. (A typical question might be, "How worried are you about the future?") Such an index could have many values from lowest to highest. But for the sake of simplicity, we will present this variable "dichotomously"—having only two values (High and Low). If one reduces the number of values in a variable by combining values together, this is called *collapsing*. Collapsing causes the loss of some information but may make the table easier to understand.

Note that Table 5 uses percentages that are based on row totals. The actual ("absolute") numbers for each cell are given in parentheses under the percentages. This is a very common practice. The total number studied or sampled is called the "N" of the study or table. Here it is 1,500. (Remember that these are fictitious data.)

Once we have located the variables and the variables' values as we did before, we can ask if this two-variable table shows an association between the variables. Apply the diagonal rule. Are the numbers (percentages) greater on one diagonal (not row or column) than on the other diagonal? In the lower left we find the figure 65%. In the upper right we find 75%. Note that it does not matter whether the percentages are based on the row totals, column totals, or total N; the diagonal rule can still be used as a guide. In the other diagonal set of cells, we read 25% and 35%. There is indeed a piling up of these cases on the first diagonals. The variables are associated. That means, in terms of substance, that Catholics tend to be less anxious than Protestants. Although we note that 25% of the Catholics and 35% of the Protestants do not follow this tendency, that does not mean that the tendency or association does not exist. There are few perfect associations to be found in science.

We could interpret our finding to mean that either anxious people tend to become Protestants or that Protestants have a greater likelihood of becoming anxious. Or there could be some combination of these interpretations. How can we know which interpretation is the correct one? In addition to association, we must also know the time order of the variables. A *cause* (what sociologists call an independent variable) must always come earlier in time than an *effect* (called a dependent variable). Time order is usually easy to establish when you compare ascribed or inherited characteristics (such as race, sex, or age) with achieved or earned characteristics (for example, social class, education, occupation, or crime). It would not make sense to say education causes people to be male or female, since one is male or female from birth; sex is determined prior to education. Time order becomes more difficult to determine in situations like that which exists between religion and anxiety. In such cases we must often, like Durkheim, rely upon a theory to establish causal order.

If we could show that religion does come first, we could propose that the religion is the cause of anxiety. We might establish prior occurrence by asking in what religion subjects were raised. Then we might assume that a person's current anxiety level comes after the religion acquired in childhood. If this was our interpretation (and we would still need to control for other factors or variables before we could accurately speak of causes), how might it relate to the suicide rates shown earlier?

In his book *Suicide* (1897) Durkheim reasoned as follows: Suicide rates are functions of unrelieved anxieties and stresses to which persons are subjected. Catholics have lower levels of anxiety than do Protestants; therefore, there will be lower suicide rates among Catholics than among Protestants. This is exactly what he found to be true. Protestants do have higher suicide rates. If Table 5 were not fictitious, it would lend further support to Durkheim's hypothesis relating religion, anxiety, and suicide. But why should Protestants experience greater anxiety? To understand that, Durkheim introduced another variable, social cohesion. The anxiety may come from lower social cohesion (social support) among Protestants. Protestantism puts more emphasis on the individual's responsibility before God for his or her sins. On the other hand, the Catholic church mediates to a greater extent between God and man. It could be, then, that the Catholic facing stress does not feel quite so alone or individually culpable as does the Protestant. The Catholic has greater social support in dealing with stress than does the Protestant, who is more likely to put the blame for difficulty directly on him- or herself. If this line of reasoning is correct, one could understand higher anxiety among Protestants leading to a higher suicide rate. The causal chain would be as follows: religion leads to greater or less social cohesion, which leads to greater or less unrelieved anxiety, resulting in different suicide rates. Note that anxiety is the only psychological variable, and it is treated socially in terms of rate. This is a social explanation of social facts.

Of course, more data are needed before Durkheim's theory can be fully accepted. (For example, can you think how one might try to measure group attachment or shared values?) One must also control for other relevant variables, such as age and marital status. These variables might affect the associations we have found. We know, for example, that single people have a higher suicide rate than do married people. Is it possible that Catholics are more likely to get married early and stay married

longer than Protestants? If so, how might that affect the association between religion and suicide rates?

In order to state accurately that one variable causes another, we must have all three elements we have mentioned:

1. An association between the variables;
2. A time order, in which cause is prior to effect; and
3. A way to control for other relevant variables.

Table analysis is one way of showing the first of these elements, and we have just discussed the importance of the other two. All causal analysis must begin with association. If there is no association, there can hardly be causality. You should now be able to discover associations in tables. (For more information on associations, causality, and controlling for the other relevant variables, see the sociology texts that have been recommended at the end of this section.)

Now you know of Durkheim's methods. Try them in the following exercises.

Exercise 1: Table Reading

Durkheim believed that the origins of homicide and suicide lie in different social conditions. Where the constraint of the moral order is weakest, isolation produces despair, depression, and suicide. Where it is strongest, homicidal retribution is permitted or even expected for violations of the moral order (which includes the ideas of personal or family honor and patriotic duty). Durkheim (1897/1951, p. 351) speculated that "where homicide is very common it confers a sort of immunity against suicide." This explains the inverse relationship between homicide and suicide in Table 3. Table 6 uses information from the *Statistical Abstract of the United States 1990* (Table 122) to describe homicide and suicide statistics for a typical community of 100,000 people. Let's use that information to investigate Durkheim's idea.

Table 6

VIOLENT MALE DEATHS PER 100,000 BY RACE

		Cause of Violent Death		
		Suicide	Homicide	Total
Race	White	221	79	300
	Black	116	533	649
Total		337	612	949

Note: From *Statistical Abstract of the United States 1990* (110th ed., Table 122), 1990, Washington, D.C.: U.S. Government Printing Office.

1. How many variables are shown in this table? _____

2. How many values are there for each variable? _____

3. How many black males died violently? _____

4. How many white males died violently? _____

5. What racial group had the greatest percentage die violently? Group_____ Percent_____

6. How many men died from homicide? N =_____

7. What racial group had the greatest percentage of homicides? Group_____ Percent_____

8. What racial group had the greatest percentage of suicides? Group_____ Percent_____

9. Is there an association shown in this table? _____

   Explain your reasoning: _____

   _____

   _____

10. Which is the independent variable? _____ Why?

11. Does homicide confer an immunity against (that is, reduce) suicide? Discuss the significance of these data.

   _____

   _____

   _____

Exercise 2: Multivariate Table Reading

As a final exercise in table reading, study the table below. With more than two variables, this table is more complex than the table in Exercise 1. Remember to follow the principles of table reading. Read the title and identify the variables in the table. Look in the cells and see if the data cluster on a diagonal. If there is no diagonal, is there another pattern that describes the relationships between the variables?

Now answer these questions:

1. How many variables are shown in this table? _____
   Variable names:

2. Identify the dependent variable. _____

3. Identify the independent variable(s). _____

   _____

Table 7

1986 SUICIDE RATES BY SEX, RACE, AND AGE GROUP
(Rates are per 100,000 population. Excludes deaths of nonresidents of the United States.)

Age	Total[a]	Male White	Male Black	Female White	Female Black
All Ages[b]	12.8	22.3	11.1	5.9	2.3
10–14	1.5	2.4	1.5	.7	.4
15–19	10.2	18.2	7.1	4.1	2.1
20–24	15.8	28.4	16.0	5.3	2.4
25–34	15.7	26.4	21.3	6.2	3.8
35–44	15.2	23.9	17.5	8.3	2.8
45–54	16.4	26.3	12.8	9.6	3.2
55–64	17.0	28.7	9.9	9.0	4.2
65+	21.5	45.6	16.2	7.5	2.4

[a]Includes other races not shown separately.
[b]Includes other age groups not shown separately.
Note: From *Statistical Abstract of the United States 1990* (110th ed.), 1990, Washington, D.C.: U.S. Government Printing Office. Adapted from Table 125.

4. In the United States in 1986, how many suicides were there per 100,000 population? _____

5. What group had the highest suicide rate? _____

   _____

6. What group had the lowest suicide rate? _____

   _____

7. What relationship exists between age and suicide?

   _____

   _____

8. What relationship exists between sex and suicide?

   _____

   _____

9. What is the most important relationship that exists between or among the variables? Explain how you reached your conclusion and what the association or lack of association means.

   _____

   _____

   _____

   _____

   _____

References and Recommended Readings

Bart, P., & Frankel, L. (1986). *The student sociologist's handbook* (4th ed.). Glenview, IL: Scott, Foresman & Company.

Bogue, G. (1981). *Basic sociological research design.* Glenview, IL: Scott, Foresman & Company.

Cole, S. (1980). *The sociological method* (3rd ed.). Chicago: Rand McNally.

Davis, J. A., & Jacobs, A. (1966). Tabular presentation. In D. Sills (Ed.), *International encyclopedia of the social sciences* (Vol. 16, pp. 497–508). New York: Macmillan & The Free Press.

Durkheim, E. ([1897] 1951). *Suicide.* Reprint. New York: The Free Press.

Encyclopedic dictionary of sociology (4th ed.). (1991). Guilford, CT: The Dushkin Publishing Group.

Huff, D. (1954). *How to lie with statistics.* New York: W. W. Norton.

Labovitz, S., & Hagedorn, R. (1981). *Introduction to social research* (3rd ed.). New York: McGraw-Hill.

Merton, R. K. (1967). *Theoretical sociology.* New York: The Free Press.

Saunders, W. B. (1976). *The sociologist as detective: An introduction to research methods* (2nd ed.). New York: Praeger.

Sommer, R., & Sommer, B. (1986). *A practical guide to behavioral research* (2nd ed.). New York: Oxford University Press.

Wallis, W. A., & Roberts, H. V. (1956). How to read a table. In *Statistics: A new approach* (pp. 279–289). New York: The Free Press.

Zeisel, H. (1985). *Say it with figures* (6th ed.). New York: Harper & Row.

For More Advanced Reading

Babbie, E. (1989). *The practice of social research* (5th ed.). Belmont, CA: Wadsworth.

Blalock, A., & Blalock, H. (1982). *An introduction to social research* (2nd ed.). Englewood Cliffs, NJ: Prentice Hall.

Rosenberg, M. (1968). *The logic of survey analysis.* New York: Basic Books.

STATISTICAL TOOLS FOR DESCRIPTION AND COMPARISON

Society is not a mere sum of individuals. Rather, the system formed by their association represents a specific reality which has its own characteristics. . . . The group thinks, feels, and acts quite differently from the way in which its members would were they isolated. If, then, we begin with the individual, we shall be able to understand nothing of what takes place in the group.

Émile Durkheim
The Rules of Sociological Method

Descriptive Statistics

Averages: Mode, Median, Mean

Comparisons: Percentages and Rates

Correlation: Scattergrams, Meaning, Significance, Rho

Averages and Comparisons

When asked to explain our behavior, our first response is to look inward and offer a set of unique individual motives. In fact, the cause of most of our social behavior is a reaction to forces external to us. To detect social forces and understand how they shape our behavior, we must take advantage of the tools that have been developed by statisticians. As we have seen, prior to Durkheim many believed suicide was a psychological fact. By looking at individual cases, they failed to see the social patterns that were distinctive of groups and societies. Their research should have begun with *descriptive* statistics, through which they could have summarized what were normal numbers (averages) of suicides in a society, made comparisons (through percents and rates) between societies and groups and investigated whether social facts such as divorce and suicide were associated (correlated). In the following section, we will review three of the descriptive tools that are necessary to discover and understand the nature of social facts.

Averages

Just as it is often difficult to see the forest for the trees, it may be difficult to see the group for the individuals. So many and so interesting are the differences that set individuals apart, we often fail to note the similarities between them. To discover these similarities, we must determine what is typical or normal. A statistical answer to this is the average. Averages are usually expressed as a mode, median, or mean.

The **mode** is the most frequent observation. If there is only one mode, the distribution is unimodal. If two observations are equally frequent, the distribution is bimodal. If you have a bimodal distribution, check to see if there are two distinct groups that have been combined. This might happen, for example, if males and females were aggregated into a common distribution of height. The result would be a bimodal distribution, composed of the modal height for males and the modal height for females.

The **median** is the middle number in an array of scores. An array refers to the arrangement of scores in ascending or descending order. The median is the middle location in an array of scores. It does not consider score values but score ranks. The median is valuable when trying to represent extremely uneven scores. For example, we may wish to describe the average income of people working in a small business. Assume their monthly income is as listed on the top of the next page:

```
$500
  500    MODE = $500
  500
  500
  700    MEDIAN  = (N + 1)/2 = (10 + 1)/2 = 5.5 OR $750
  800
1,000
1,250
1,750    MEAN
10,000
```
Sum X = 17,500

Note that if the number of scores in an array is odd, the median will actually be the middle number of the array. If there is an even number in the array, the median will be between the two middle scores. In the illustration above the two middle scores are $700 and $800. The midpoint between these two scores is $750.

The **mean** is the sum of the values of a set of scores, divided by the number of scores in that set. This is expressed by the formula:

$$\bar{X} = \frac{\text{Sum } X}{N} = \frac{\$17,500}{10} = \$1,750$$

Where
$\bar{X}$ = Mean
X = Score
N = Number of scores

Since the mean uses the actual values of the scores, it is responsive to extreme values. Note in the illustration of monthly income the considerable difference between the mode ($500), median ($750), and mean ($1,750). They are all averages, but with different assumptions. The mode identifies the most frequently occurring score, the median identifies the middle-ranking score, and the mean identifies the average value of the scores. Which one value correctly describes an array may be as much a matter of perspective as a technical question. In labor relations, management would probably prefer the mean wage, to bolster their claim of how good wages are, and the workers would prefer the median wage, to support their claim of low wages. Thus, the facts do not "speak for themselves." As producer and consumer of statistical evidence, you must actively involve yourself in the interpretation of statistical data.

Comparisons

Percentages   In our investigations we will need to compare groups. Are there differences in suicide rates between blacks and whites? Between men and women? Between rich and poor? If groups are of equivalent size, direct comparisons can be made (such as between 50 males and 50 females). But when there are great differences in size (such as between 87 blacks and 13

whites) direct comparison is difficult. Percentages standardize results of unequally sized groups by the frequency per 100 cases. This is expressed by the formula:

$$\% = \frac{f}{N}(100)$$

Where
f = Frequency
N = Number of cases

Assuming 9 out of 20 students in a class were Catholic, for example, we would describe the class as 45 percent Catholic. Since the purpose of percentages is to simplify comparisons, round decimals off to the nearest tenth.

$$\% = \frac{f}{N}(100) = \frac{9}{20}(100) = .45(100) = 45\%$$

To make accurate comparisons, it is important to know the numbers involved in computing the percentages. To help the reader interpret the meaning of a percentage table, report the total number of cases upon which the percentages are computed. If the number of cases is less than 30, it is preferable to simply report the number of cases and omit percentage comparisons. Unless the number of cases upon which the percentage is based is over 50, do not attach too much significance to small percentage differences.

Rates   When the number of occurrences of an event falls below 1 in 100, it is often easier to use a rate instead of a percent. In such cases rates allow you to compare whole numbers instead of fractions of a percent. Rates are typically based on the number of occurrences per 1,000, 100,000, or 1,000,000 people. On the top of the next page, for example, is a computation of general mortality death rates (per thousand) and suicide rates (per hundred thousand).

Correlation

"The principal difficulty in your case," remarked Holmes in his didactic fashion, "lay in the fact of there being too much evidence. What was vital was overlaid and hidden by what was irrelevant. Of all the facts which were presented to us we had to pick just those which we deemed to be essential, and then piece them together in their order, so as to reconstruct this very remarkable chain of events."

Sir Arthur Conan Doyle
The Naval Treaty

When we investigate the characteristics of groups and societies we are often faced with vast amounts of data. Discovering

$$\text{1986 U.S. general mortality rate} = \frac{\text{Number of deaths}}{\text{U.S. population}}(1,000) = \frac{2,105,400}{241,107,000}(1,000) = 8.7$$

$$\text{1986 U.S. suicide rate} = \frac{\text{Suicides}}{\text{Population}}(100,000) = \frac{30,904}{241,107,000}(100,000) = 12.8$$

Note: From *Statistical Abstract of the United States 1990* (110th ed.), 1990, Washington, D.C.: U.S. Government Printing Office. Compiled from Tables 116 and 124.

social facts and connections embedded in these numbers requires both theory and statistical tools to see the meaning that underlies the complexity of the data. Durkheim, for example, was faced with making sense out of the French Bureau of Legal Statistics' records of 26,000 suicides. These records were further classified by, among other things, sex, marital status, age, presence or absence of children in the family, and religion. Even with a good theory to show where to look, it was only because of his use of statistics that he could clearly see relationships his predecessors had failed to see.

Earlier we used percent tables to organize data and discover associations. The correlation coefficient allows us to go further and specify the strength of the association. This is important for explanation and prediction. With strongly correlated variables, a knowledge of one variable lets us predict the value of the other variable. In Table 8 on the next page, for example, you can see that as age increases, so does the suicide rate. People who are over 40 years old are more likely to commit suicide (in this case over three times more likely) than people aged 16–21.

Graphs help to visualize correlations. We can take information from Table 8 and represent the values for four groups (A, B, C, D) as points on a graph called a *scattergram*. In Scattergram 1 below Table 8, the independent variable (X) is located on the baseline and the dependent variable (Y) on the vertical line. Group A is at the intersection of X (age 16–21) and Y (suicide rate 45.9). Group B is at the intersection of X (age 21–30) and Y (suicide rate 97.9). In Scattergram 2 next to it, Group A is at the intersection of X (few Roman Catholics) and Y (suicide rate 192). Group B is at the intersection of X (mixed) and Y (suicide rate 135).

Visual inspection of the points plotted on Scattergram 1 shows that as the age increases, so does the suicide rate. Since these variables fluctuate together in Scattergram 1, we describe this as a positive (+) association. In Scattergram 2, the relationship between the variables is reversed. As the proportion of Roman Catholics increases, the suicide rate declines. Since the change in X results in an opposite change in value for variable Y, this is described as an inverse or negative (−) relationship. Earlier, in Exercise 1 (pp. 154–155), we saw a negative relationship between suicide and homicide (the lower the homicide rate, the higher the suicide rate).

Interpretation   In percentage tables, the diagonal rule told us to look for relationships between variables by the way data clustered in cells along a diagonal. In a more precise manner,

the rank order correlation measures how much clustering there is on the diagonal. A perfect positive association would be described by a diagonal line running from the bottom left to the top right of Scattergram 1. A perfect negative relationship would be described by a line running from the top left to the bottom right of Scattergram 2. If there is no association between X and Y, the plotted points are randomly distributed on the scattergram, and there is no clustering around a diagonal line. The rank order correlation is then zero. The variation in Y is not simply (or linearly) related to changes in X. Our knowledge of a score on X will give us no information on score Y.

The closer the paired observations cluster together, the stronger the correlation. We are going to look at two ways to measure the strength of the association. The first method was devised by Karl Pearson (1857–1936) and measures the association between scores. His coefficient is symbolized by the letter r. The second method measures the association between ranks. The procedure was created by Charles Spearman to approximate r when one is dealing with small samples like the ones we will probably have in our investigations. It is called **rank order correlation** or **Rho** and is symbolized by the letter r with a subscript s (r_s). Both measures are limited to detecting linear or straight-line relationships.

When all the paired observations fall on a diagonal line, the correlation is perfect (either r = +1.0 or r = −1.0). When this happens, all the values of one variable Y can be perfectly predicted by a knowledge of the other value (X). In both Scattergrams 1 and 2, we can predict exactly the suicide rate by our knowledge of the age or proportion of Roman Catholics. Thus, our correlation coefficients would be a perfect +1.0 (for age) and a perfect −1.0 (for proportion of Roman Catholics). Since many factors are usually involved and almost all studies have errors, it is important to have a coefficient that expresses the strength of the association. As a rule of thumb, the strength of the rank order correlation may be described in the following terms:

+1.00 perfect positive correlation
+ .75 strong positive correlation
+ .50 moderate positive correlation
+ .25 weak positive correlation
  .0 no correlation
− .25 weak negative correlation
− .50 moderate negative correlation
− .75 strong negative correlation
−1.00 perfect negative correlation

Table 8

SUICIDE RATE PER MILLION BY AGE

Group	Age	Suicide Rate
A	16–21	45.9
B	21–30	97.9
C	31–40	114.5
D	41–50	164.4

Note: Reprinted with permission of The Free Press, a division of Macmillan, Inc., from Émile Durkheim, *Suicide* (p. 172), translated by John A. Spaulding and George Simpson. Copyright © 1951, renewed 1979 by The Free Press.

Scattergram 1

SUICIDE RATE PER MILLION BY AGE

Suicide Rate per Million				
150–199				D
100–149			C	
50–99		B		
0–49	A			
	16–21	21–30	31–40	41–50
			Age	

Positive Association

Table 9

SUICIDE RATE PER MILLION BY PERCENT ROMAN CATHOLIC

Group	Percent Catholic	Suicide Rate
A	Less than 50%	192
B	Mixed (50%–90%)	135
C	Catholic (over 90%)	75

Note: Reprinted with permission of The Free Press, a division of Macmillan, Inc., from Émile Durkheim, *Suicide* (p. 152), translated by John A. Spaulding and George Simpson. Copyright © 1951, renewed 1979 by The Free Press.

Scattergram 2

SUICIDE RATE PER MILLION BY PERCENT ROMAN CATHOLIC

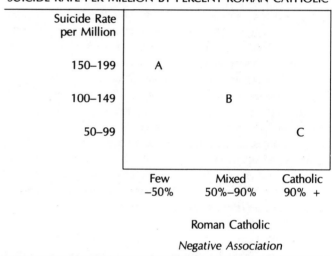

Suicide Rate per Million			
150–199	A		
100–149		B	
50–99			C
	Few −50%	Mixed 50%–90%	Catholic 90% +

Roman Catholic

Negative Association

Significance We have established that an association exists between age, proportion of Roman Catholics, and the suicide rate. But could this association be a coincidence? To answer that question we need to consult a table of correlation confidence levels. The table "Critical Values of Rho," found at the end of this book (p. 201) provides the correlation values that must be exceeded if we want to be sure our correlation is not an accident. When the chances of such a correlation are only 5 in 100 (.05) or 1 in 100 (.01), we can pretty confidently conclude that our results were not accidental.

To find out if your correlation could be produced by chance less than 5 times in 100, turn to the "Critical Values of Rho" table on page 201. Then determine the number of pairs used to compute your correlation. Take that number and look at the left-hand column (N) in the Rho table. Read the correlation values in the two columns to the right to determine the size of the correlation needed to be significant at the .05 and .01 levels. One study of Durkheim's we will look at investigated the relationship between divorce and suicide rates for 15 countries. Since the abbreviated table for the critical values of Rho does not have 15, we will use the more conservative entry for 14.

Where N = 14 we need a correlation of +.456 to be significant at the .05 level. A correlation of +.645 would be needed to reach the .01 level of significance. If we exceed these correlation values, we can conclude that this association is no accident; a relationship really exists between divorce and suicide rates.

Caveat Emptor "Let the buyer beware!" The statistical tools we have do not eliminate the need for caution and some skepticism. Only after we become familiar with our subject matter and the strengths and weaknesses of our data can we interpret our results with any level of confidence. Be careful not to forget that correlation is *not* causation. In studying complex social issues, it is safer to speak of how the variables influence one another. Durkheim argued that a straightforward connection existed between Protestantism and suicide (X → Y). But maybe other factors are involved. Are those who are of a suicidal mentality selectively attracted to the Protestant church (Y → X)? Could the relationship between Protestantism and suicide be influenced by a third variable, like climate? If Protestants live disproportionately in colder northern countries and Catholics live predominantly in the warmer southern countries, perhaps it is not religion but climate that produces the

Scattergram 3

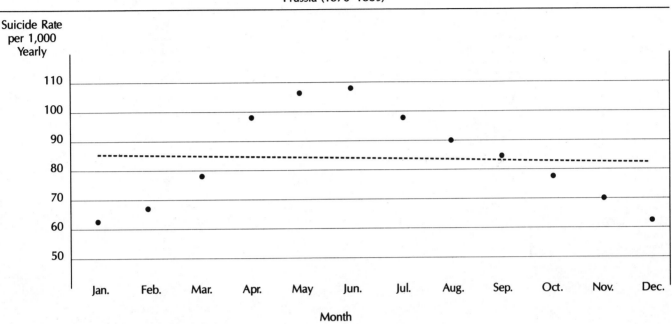

MONTHLY SUICIDE RATES
Prussia (1876–1889)

Note: Reprinted with permission of The Free Press, a division of Macmillan, Inc., from Émile Durkheim, *Suicide* (p. 112), translated by John A. Spaulding and George Simpson. Copyright © 1951, renewed 1979 by The Free Press.

different suicide rates between Protestants and Catholics. If we denote our third variable (climate) by "T," then our connection might look like this: X ← T → Y. Or maybe a third factor was industrialization, which supported Protestantism, which, in turn, influenced higher suicide rates (T → X → Y)? Could the variables be mutually interrelated and influencing (X ← → Y)?

While these possibilities may seem to offer a confusing number of alternatives, they only suggest some of the possible relationships that exist. This does not mean that the possible explanations are infinite. By investigating the most plausible rival explanations first and rejecting them, we grow increasingly confident in our conclusions. As Sherlock Holmes observed: "When you have eliminated all which is impossible, then whatever remains, however improbable, must be the truth. It may well be several explanations remain, in which case one tries test after test until one or the other of them has a convincing amount of support" (Doyle, 1927, p. 1011).

It can be just as great a mistake to assume that no correlation means there is no relationship between the variables. In Scattergram 3, above, the number of monthly suicides per 1,000 yearly is represented with a point (.). You can see from this that in January the suicide rate starts at 61, rises to 105 in June, and then falls back to 61 in December.

The rank order correlation for these data is virtually zero (Rho = −.009). The reason for this goes back to the diagonal rule.

The diagonal around which our observations cluster is shown in the diagram by the dotted line. Obviously this straight line does not fit the U-shaped relationship that exists between month and suicide rate. The rank order correlation measures only straight-line relationships, so it does not detect nonlinear relationships. While statistics provide important tools for detecting connections, a thorough investigator must never forget Holmes's warning: "One should always look for a possible alternative and provide against it" (Doyle, 1927, p. 567).

Rank Order Correlation   Spearman's rank order correlation coefficient (Rho) is a measure of association proper for most ranked data. All the earlier mentioned characteristics about association apply to Rho. It varies between +1.0 and −1.0. Critical values for Rho are supplied in Table A on page 201. The value of Rho is determined by the following formula:

$$Rho = 1 - \frac{6 \,(Sum \; D^2)}{N \,(N^2 - 1)}$$

Where
Rho = rank order correlation coefficient
D = rank difference between X and Y variables
N = total number of cases

To illustrate the calculation of Rho, let us return to the question of the relationship between suicide and divorce that was

Table 10

COMPARISON OF EUROPEAN STATES FROM THE POINT OF VIEW OF BOTH DIVORCE AND SUICIDE

Country	Column 1 Divorces per 1,000 marriages	Column 2 Rank	Column 3 Suicides per Million	Column 4 Rank	Column 5 D	Column 6 D²
Norway	0.5	1	73.0	7	6	36
England-Wales	1.3	2	68.0	5	3	9
Russia	1.6	3	30.0	1	2	4
Italy	3.1	4	31.0	3	1	1
Finland	3.9	5	30.8	2	3	9
Bavaria	5.0	6	90.5	9	3	9
Belgium	5.1	7	68.5	6	1	1
Holland	6.0	8	35.5	4	4	16
Sweden	6.4	9	81.0	8	1	1
Baden	6.5	10	156.6	11	1	1
France	7.5	11	150.0	10	1	1
Wurttemberg	8.4	12	162.4	12	0	0
Saxony	26.9	13	229.0	15	2	4
Denmark	38.0	14	258.0	14	0	0
Switzerland	47.0	15	216.0	13	2	4

Sum D² = 96.0

$$\text{Rho} = 1 - \frac{6\,(96.0)}{15\,(15^2 - 1)} = 1 - \frac{576}{15\,(224)} = 1 - \frac{576}{3360} = 1 - .17 = +.83$$

Note: Reprinted with permission of The Free Press, a division of Macmillan, Inc., from Émile Durkheim, *Suicide* (p. 259), translated by John A. Spaulding and George Simpson. Copyright © 1951, renewed 1979 by The Free Press.

raised by Durkheim. As a rule, he said, "suicide varies inversely with the degree of integration in domestic society" (Durkheim, 1897/1951, p. 208). Since those who are married are more integrated into domestic life than those who are divorced, one would expect the suicide rate to increase for those who are divorced. To test this hypothesis Durkheim compared the divorce and suicide rates of European countries. These data are shown in the table above.

Computing Rho in Three Steps

Step 1: Ranking   We must first convert the divorce rates (column 1) and suicide rates (column 3) into ranks (columns 2 and 4). If there had been any tied rates, all the tied ranks would be assigned the average of the tied ranks. For example, in column 1, if Bavaria and Belgium both had divorce rates of 5.0 they would have tied for ranks 6 and 7. If that had been the case we would add the ranks together (6 + 7 = 13) and divide by the number of cases (2). This yields an average rank of 6.5, which would be assigned to both countries. If the top three countries had tied, the rank would be determined as follows:

$$\text{Rank} = \frac{1 + 2 + 3}{3} = \frac{6}{3} = 2$$

If the top three countries had tied and were assigned a rank of 2, the next country, Italy, would be assigned the rank of 4 because the ranks of 1, 2 and 3 had been used in figuring the previous three tied ranks.

Step 2: Rank difference   Next we take the difference in ranks between columns 2 and 4 for each of the countries and enter the rank difference (D) in column 5. Norway, for example, ranked 1st in divorce and 7th in suicide, a difference of 6 ranks. Positive and negative signs are unimportant because the difference is squared. The square of 6 is 36 and is entered in column 6. When this is completed for all the countries, all the squared differences are added. Since there are 15 countries with 15 pairs of ranks N = 15. This is all the information we need to compute Rho.

Step 3: Significance.   Our rank order correlation of +.83 tells us there is a strong positive correlation in these 15 European countries between the suicide rate and the divorce rate. While the correlation does not imply causality, it does establish an important piece of evidence that supports Durkheim's argument. To decide whether or not our Rho is explainable by chance we need to consult Table A (p. 201). A Rho of .645 obtained from 14 pairs would happen less than 1 time in 100 by chance. Since our Rho (+.83) exceeds this value (.645), we can conclude that chance does not explain this association.

Exercise 3: Correlation

The determining cause of a social fact should be sought among the social facts preceding it and not among the states of individual consciousness.

Émile Durkheim
The Rules of Sociological Method

At the turn of the century, it was widely believed the individual was the final and most complex of all subjects. Many believed that society, institutions, and groups were nothing more than the sum total of what individuals brought into those groups. The laws governing the character of society would be found in human character. Durkheim rejected this argument. He believed there was a level of social facts beyond psychological facts.

Durkheim said that social facts are external to the individual and are shared in the conscious thoughts of other members of society. Psychological facts exist only in the mind of an individual. He also claimed that social facts influence and shape the behavior of individuals, and constrain the behavior of individuals who violate expectations and traditions. Rules are appealed to in order to change the individual's unacceptable behavior. And finally, he said that social facts exist before and after the individual. Social facts persist across generations and through time, while individuals die and are replaced. Thus, social facts are identifiable because (1) they are *external* to individuals, (2) they *constrain* individual behavior, and (3) they persist through *time*. Durkheim's critics countered that social facts were nothing more than the sum of the characteristics of the individuals who made up the group. They asserted that Durkheim's social facts were social fictions. In response to this challenge, Durkheim undertook the first scientific study in sociology.

Durkheim claimed that many psychological facts were really created by social conditions. Loneliness, divorce, drugs, alienation, murder, and suicide, he said, are all symptoms of the prevailing social conditions in a society. By studying rates within groups, individual differences are canceled and group uniformities appear. These rates will show that social conditions such as societal cohesion are directly connected to individual behavior. Specifically, cohesion is inversely related to the suicide rate; that is, high cohesion is associated with low suicide rates, and low cohesion with high suicide rates. Cohesion is a social condition that endures across generations. It creates an environment that encourages or discourages suicide. The social conditions that encourage suicide affect the consciousness of the individual increasingly from youth to maturity. If the number of suicides next year is already fixed, then current social conditions are now preparing the individuals who will commit suicide next year.

If Durkheim is correct, individuals are or are not disposed to suicide on the basis of social integration and regulation. These are social facts that should not vary greatly from year to year. If the national suicide rates varied greatly from year to

Table 11

RATE OF SUICIDES FOR INHABITANTS OF FOURTEEN EUROPEAN COUNTRIES: 1870–1970 (Per 100,000)

Country	Period 1870	Period 1970
Ireland	1.5	3.8
Spain	1.7	4.0
Finland	2.9	24.1
Netherlands	3.6	9.4
Belgium	6.0	16.2
United Kingdom	6.6	7.8
Austria	7.2	22.7
Norway	7.6	10.8
Sweden	8.5	19.4
Italy	9.0	5.8
West Germany	14.8	20.9
France	15.0	15.4
Switzerland	19.6	22.0
Denmark	25.8	23.9

Note: Data from *ShowCase: Social Change,* version 2.0 [computer software] by R. Stark, 1987. Seattle, WA: Cognitive Development. Used by permission.

year, they would be of no value in explaining suicide rates by cultural differences. To test this, Durkheim (1897/1951) compared suicide rates for European countries for the periods 1866–1870, 1871–1875, and 1874–1878. As he expected, he found the rates to be highly correlated. Using data collected by Rodney Stark (1987), we can measure the stability of suicide rates over the 100-year period. The rates for 14 countries are presented in Table 11, above.

To compute Rho for these rates, follow these four steps in Table 12:

Step 1. Rank the suicide rates for 1870 and then for 1970.

Step 2. Find the rank differences (D) between 1870 and 1970.

Step 3. Square the rank differences (D^2) and sum the total.

Step 4. Enter the appropriate values and compute the Rho formula.

Exercise 4: Investigation Report

The Research Problem

In Exercise 3, we considered Durkheim's theory that social facts are a separate, measurable reality. They are recognizable by their (1) externality, (2) constraint, and (3) persistence over time. If suicide rates describe social facts for European coun-

Table 12

COMPUTATION OF RHO FOR SUICIDE RATES SHOWN IN TABLE 11

Country	1870 Rank	1970 Rank	D	D²
Ireland	_____	_____	_____	_____
Spain	_____	_____	_____	_____
Finland	_____	_____	_____	_____
Netherlands	_____	_____	_____	_____
Belgium	_____	_____	_____	_____
United Kingdom	_____	_____	_____	_____
Austria	_____	_____	_____	_____
Norway	_____	_____	_____	_____
Sweden	_____	_____	_____	_____
Italy	_____	_____	_____	_____
West Germany	_____	_____	_____	_____
France	_____	_____	_____	_____
Switzerland	_____	_____	_____	_____
Denmark	_____	_____	_____	_____
			Sum D² =	_____

$$\text{Rho} = 1 - \frac{6 \,(\text{Sum } D^2)}{N \,(N^2 - 1)} = $$

tries, the rates should be stable over time. To test this belief, we ranked the suicide rates for 14 countries from 1870 to 1970. Durkheim treated suicide rates as the dependent variable. He treated persistence over time as an independent variable, indicating the existence of a social fact.

Hypothesis

State briefly and precisely a hypothesis that is consistent with Durkheim's argument about social facts.

_____

_____

_____

Discussion

What correlation did you obtain?

Rho = _____

To decide if your correlation is statistically significant, determine the number of paired observations upon which the correla-

tion was based. Do this by determining the number of countries reported for periods 1870 and 1970.

N pairs = _____

Using this information, look up Table A on page 201. To determine the critical values of Rho, find in the column titled "N" the number that comes closest to the number of pairs in your study. If you do not find the exact number, you should select the next smaller N. In doing this you will obtain a slightly larger significance level.

   a. At .05 level Rho must be > _____

   b. At .01 level Rho must be > _____

How likely is it that this correlation is a result of chance? (Circle the correct answer.)

   a. It is not statistically significant.

   b. It exceeds the .05 significance level.

   c. It exceeds both the .05 and .01 significance levels.

Does your correlation show that rank order of suicide rates for the 14 countries is stable over the 100-year period?

Explain:_____

_____

_____

_____

_____

While the size and significance of the correlation are important, to understand the results you also need to look closely at the original data. Look at individual observations for exceptions and surprises. What impression do you get of trends, patterns, and consistencies? For example, how many countries changed more than two ranks relative to the other countries?

Countries changing more than 2 ranks:_____

_____

Median suicide rate in 1870 = _____

Median 1970 rate = _____

Does this indicate a trend?_____

_____

_____

Conclusion

This section draws your research to a close. You need to decide if the evidence you have gathered answers the question that started the investigation. Do Durkheim's social facts exist or are they really social fictions? The question can only be partly answered, because suicide rates are only one of many indicators of social facts. Recognizing this limitation, what do you conclude? (See next page.)

Circle the correct answers:

(1) For the 100-year period I studied, the ranked suicide rates for 14 European countries:

    a. showed remarkable rank persistence between countries.
    b. showed remarkable rank instability between countries.
    c. provided too little information draw a conclusion.
    d. were explainable by chance or coincidence.

(2) The best conclusion that I can draw from this correlation is that:

    a. suicide is a psychological fact.
    b. suicide is a social fact.
    c. suicide is a fiction.
    d. too little information is available to draw a conclusion.

A balanced report of your findings must note any evidence that is inconsistent with Durkheim's theory. Even if there is little or no evidence contrary to the hypothesis, other variables may be related to suicide and call for further investigation. If more factors are identified, suggest how research might be carried out (for example, through surveys, experiments, and analysis of government documents) to clarify the relationship.

Can you accept Durkheim's argument that suicide is a social fact? Write a fair and objective conclusion based upon the evidence.

_____

_____

_____

_____

_____

_____

References and Recommended Readings

Bainbridge, W. S., & Stark, R. (1981). Suicide, homicide and religion: Durkheim reassessed. *Annual Review of the Social Sciences of Religion, 5,* 33–56.

Danigelis, N., & Pope, W. (1979). Durkheim's theory of suicide as applied to the family: An empirical test. *Social Forces, 57,* 1081–1106.

Doyle, A. C. (1927). *The complete Sherlock Holmes.* Garden City, New York: Doubleday.

Durkheim, E. ([1895] 1964). *The rules of sociological method.* Reprint. New York: The Free Press.

Durkheim, E. ([1897] 1951). *Suicide.* Reprint. New York: The Free Press.

Gibbs, J. (Ed.). (1968). *Suicide.* New York: Harper & Row.

Johnson, B. (1965). Durkheim's one cause of suicide. *American Sociological Review, 30,* 875–886.

Katzer, J., Cook, K., & Crouch, W. (1978). *Evaluating information.* Reading, MA: Addison-Wesley.

Leedy, P. (1989). *Practical research* (4th ed.). New York: Macmillan.

Lester, D. (1987). The stability of national suicide rates in Europe. *Sociology and Social Research, 71,* 208.

Madge, J. (1962). Suicide and anomie. Chapter 2 in *The origins of scientific sociology.* New York: The Free Press.

Pope, W. (1976). *Durkheim's suicide.* Chicago: University of Chicago Press.

Sanders, W. (1976). *The sociologist as detective: An introduction to research methods* (2nd ed.). New York: Praeger.

Schmid, C. (1966). Graphic presentation. In D. Sills (Ed.), *International Encyclopedia of the Social Sciences* (Vol. 6, pp. 243–253). New York: Macmillan and The Free Press.

Stack, S. (1983). Religion and suicide. *Journal for the Scientific Study of Religion, 22,* 239–252.

Stack, S. (1978). Suicide: A comparative analysis. *Social Forces, 57,* 644–653.

Stark, R. (1987). ShowCase: Social change, version 2.0 [computer software]. Seattle, WA: Cognitive Development, Inc.

Wainer, H. (1984). How to display data badly. *The American Statistician, 38,* 137–147.

HOW TO WRITE INVESTIGATION REPORTS

"I am lost without my Boswell."*

Sherlock Holmes, in
Sir Arthur Conan Doyle's
A Scandal in Bohemia

When a case is solved, the detective is expected to complete a report. The purpose of the report is to document how the crime was solved and close the case. While this may appear to be a simple task, even Sherlock Holmes wrote only two reports of the hundreds of cases in which he was involved. There was probably more truth than he cared to allow in his admission that he was lost without Watson's reports. Unfortunately, neither you nor I will have a Watson or a Boswell at our disposal. You will have to explain your theory carefully, summarize your findings, and defend your conclusions. This is no easy task, as Holmes would surely attest. The following guidelines are suggested to help overcome the obstacles and inertia that make it difficult to report investigation results. Each investigation report will, however, be unique, because each deals with a different question and uses specially designed research procedures for that particular question.

Composition

Your first thought will be to direct your report to the instructor who will read and evaluate it. In doing so, you risk omitting basic parts of the investigation that you presume your instructor already knows. If you address your report to nonspecialists, you must include and systematically organize all the essential information. By writing to a general audience, you will better organize your thoughts and understand the investigation results. As Sherlock Holmes has observed, "Nothing clears up a case so much as stating it to another person" (*Silver Blaze*). Directing your report to a general audience requires modifications in (1) vocabulary, (2) sentence complexity, (3) style, and (4) precision.

1. Vocabulary Your ideas should guide your choice of words. Don't let words dominate your thoughts. If a technical or an unusual term suits the idea you want to express, use it. But avoid writing sentences that are affected with jargon and are pretentious in style. If there is no clear reason to use a complicated term, use the simpler term. Sociologists have frequently been criticized for saying the obvious in a way that can't be understood by anyone.

It is widely thought both inside and outside academic circles that sociologists do not express themselves well. The editor of Fowler's *Modern English Usage,* in an entry on 'sociologese' (p. 570), says that

> sociology is a new science concerning itself not with esoteric matters outside the comprehension of the layman, as the older sciences do, but with the ordinary affairs of ordinary people. This seems to engender in those who write about it a feeling that the lack of any abstruseness in their subject demands a compensatory abstruseness in their language. . . . There are of course writers on sociological subjects who express themselves clearly and simply; that makes it the more deplorable that such books are often written in a jargon which one is almost tempted to believe is deliberately employed for the purpose of making what is simple appear complicated, exhibiting in an extreme form the common vice . . . of preferring pretentious abstract words to simple concrete ones.

In "Politics and the English Language" George Orwell shared the concerns expressed by Fowler. To illustrate the problem, he translated a passage from *Ecclesiastes* (9:11, King James Version) into sociologese. The original reads:

> I returned, and saw under the sun, that the race is not to the swift, nor the battle to the strong, neither yet bread to the wise, nor yet riches to men of understanding, nor yet favor to men of skill; but time and chance happeneth to them all.

Orwell's translation into sociologese is rendered as:

*James Boswell (1740–1795) wrote the *Life of Samuel Johnson* (1791). Some consider this to be the most brilliantly written biography in the English language.

Objective consideration of contemporary phenomena compels the conclusion that success or failure in competitive activities exhibits no tendency to be commensurate with innate capacity, but that a considerable element of the unpredictable must invariably be taken into account. (Orwell & Angus, 1968, p. 133)

2. Sentence Structure Use simple rather than complex sentences. Reading comprehension is associated with sentence length. Sentences longer than 28 words are very difficult for the average reader to understand. Reduce complexity when it is possible to break sentences into distinct thoughts. Compound sentences with *ands* and *buts* cause the average reader little difficulty. Complex sentences with *if, because,* and *as* are the ones that can often be divided up and improved.

3. Style It is rare that double negatives are included in reports. The use of a simple negation is, however, a common practice. While thoughts expressed in the negative are understandable, such ideas take longer to comprehend. For example:

Negative: The data revealed the perception of the crime rate was not inversely correlated with the amount of television viewing.

Positive: Television viewing is positively correlated to the perceived crime rate.

Negative statements are often incorrectly used to obscure or hide ambiguous findings. Positive statements are easier to understand and are more forceful.

Reports are written in either the first person ("I have discovered . . .") or the third person ("It was discovered . . ."). There is no consensus as to which form is preferable. There is a growing usage of the active ("The data indicate . . .") rather than the passive ("It is indicated . . .") voice. The active voice is a livelier form of expression that results in more reader interest and involvement.

4. Precision Holmes advises: "Never trust to vague impressions . . . but concentrate yourself on details" (*A Case of Identity*). Avoid vague generalities. The more detail you are able to include in your report, the more effective it will be.

Imprecise/ General: Marx found that religion was an opiate of political activism.

Precise/Specific: Marx found scores on civil rights militancy decreased with frequency of church attendance.

Since only two pages are provided for each investigation report, you must use the space carefully. Revising your draft report will make it more succinct. In the revision you should eliminate any unnecessary words, phrases, or sentences. Reorganizing sentences may also make your ideas clearer and briefer. For additional information you may wish to refer to Strunk and White's *The Elements of Style*.

The Friend Reading Test: Nothing is more important to the researcher than the ability to organize and communicate ideas in writing. This is perhaps the most important aspect of your entire college experience, augmented by a broadened curiosity, willingness to withhold judgment, and some familiarity with research resources, such as the literature in sociology. The following process is a useful method to check the effectiveness of your communication: after you have finished your first draft of your report, give a copy to a friend whose opinion you value. Ask your friend to tell you what you are trying to communicate. If your friend's version of your ideas is confused or incomplete, chances are you need to rewrite all or part of your work, either elaborating or shortening until you can pass the friend reading test. You might find a second friend for the second reading. Chances are, if your friends can't understand what you are trying to say, neither can anyone else.

Report Format

The purpose of this report format is to standardize and simplify reporting your results. The report format can be organized into five major topics or sections: (1) Statement of the Research Problem and Review of the Literature, (2) Research Hypotheses, (3) Research Methods, (4) Discussion and Findings, and (5) Summary.

Section I. Research Problem

The introduction to your report should be "funnel-shaped." It should begin with a general overview and survey of relevant literature. Then, by systematically eliminating the irrelevant, you should increasingly narrow the focus of your discussion until you reach the specific research question. Place your research in a larger context to develop the reader's understanding and appreciation of the significance of the research. Note that in this book we give primary importance to the theoretical rather than the practical significance of the research. The goal of these investigations is enhanced student understanding rather than immediate application.

Variables The research hypothesis often, though not always, states a cause-and-effect relationship. If this is the case, identify the variables involved and the nature of their relationship. The *independent variable* (X) is the presumed cause of changes in the dependent variable. The *dependent variable* (Y) is influenced by or depends upon some other factor or combination of factors. Pay special attention to the title of the original research article, because it probably contains all of this information.

Section II. Hypotheses

This is the culmination of the preceding section. That is, the hypotheses should be explained by and develop from the discussion of the research problem. The resulting hypotheses should be precise statements of the questions that you intend to test. The direction of the hypothesized relationship between the variables should be specified as positive (+) or negative (−), more (>) or less <).

Durkheim (1897, p. 209) began his investigation with the theoretical view that "suicide varies inversely with the degree of integration of the social groups of which the individual forms a part." From this he deduced the following propositions:

Suicide varies inversely with the degree of integration in religious society.
Suicide varies inversely with the degree of integration in domestic society.

Then Durkheim translated these propositions into researchable questions. The research questions became his hypotheses. In the first proposition he hypothesized that suicide would be greater for Protestants (low integration) than for Catholics (high integration). In the second proposition he hypothesized that suicide would be greater for those who were single or divorced (low integration) than for those who were married (high integration).

All the investigations have the hypotheses stated in the investigation report form. Some may ask that you form your own hypotheses. If you do develop your own research hypothesis, you should state it *before* you look at and analyze the data. Hypotheses should develop logically from your theory, and be stated so that they can be disproven. Hypotheses developed after studying the data are called *ex post facto* hypotheses—explanations created to fit the facts.

Section III.   Research Methods

Measurement   How the variables are translated into operational definitions and are measured can significantly affect the outcome of the research. If we use a subjective method to measure social class and ask people to what class they belong, over 90 percent will say working or middle class. If we use a reputational method and ask judges to place people in classes, the proportion in the upper middle and lower middle class declines to 38 percent. It is, therefore, critical to indicate how variables are measured, what other methods are available, and why you chose this method.

Research Procedures   Explain the methods you will be using to answer your research question. Why should the reader be compelled to accept your answer by the evidence you collect? Is your data obtained from existing documents, experimental methods, or a survey? Is it a cross-sectional or a longitudinal design? Do you propose to analyze your findings by comparing group averages, by percent tables, or by correlation? When this section is completed, ask yourself how easily someone else could duplicate your research on the basis of this description.

Section IV.   Discussion and Findings

Statistical Evidence   This introduces the reader to statistical results that are essential to the investigation. Avoid unnecessary

details and defer discussion of your results to the next section of the report. Be sure to do three things in this section:

1. Identify the important findings. Several of our investigations will produce a great amount of statistical information that will require your interpretation. Holmes reminds us that "It is of the highest importance in the art of detection to be able to recognize out of a number of facts which are incidental and which are vital" (*The Reigate Squires*).
2. Explain the decision rules. State exactly how large the similarities or differences must be before you think that it is unreasonable to say your results are explainable by chance, accident, or coincidence.
3. Compare your research with your decision rules. If your research findings exceed the limits you set, you should conclude that your findings are significant.

Interpretation   This section is given over to a close reading of your research results. At the very least, you should describe the data and interpret it for the reader. Begin by organizing data and evaluating its importance to the research project. Then compare and contrast your results with the original research findings. Always give an objective and honest interpretation of your results. Holmes gave Watson good advice on the importance of objectivity in reporting: "Detection is, or ought to be, an exact science and should be treated in the same cold unemotional manner" (*The Sign of Four*).

One symptom of a biased report is the discounting of significant data with a casual comment that the results were produced by some unique or vague characteristics of the class. Experimental errors and imprecision almost invariably work against your hypothesis by reducing measurable differences between variables (such as education and prejudice) and groups (such as Catholics and Protestants). The results you obtained, in all probability, were in spite of errors (mistakes in filling out the questionnaire, misunderstood questions, and errors in recording the data), rather than caused by them. You will find an interesting example of how errors can influence findings in Reading 4 on page 55: in the second footnote to their Table 1, Rossi et al. point out that one item was accidentally repeated on a questionnaire and, surprisingly, received two different ranks by respondents. From this discovery Rossi et al. concluded that rankings on their survey could vary as much as .185 due to "response unreliability." Other factors to be aware of are sample size and makeup: if your class is small and homogeneous, the class will have little attitudinal variation in comparison to the general population. The differences among subgroups within the class are, therefore, likely to be small. Don't discount the significance of your results unless you can offer a better alternative explanation. To do this you should identify other variables and clearly show how these variables can explain the findings.

After you have given the reader an objective interpretation of both positive and negative findings, conclude by relating your findings to the theory and hypotheses from which you started your investigation. Do your results add information to the original study? Do they challenge some or all of the earlier findings? Do they raise new questions?

Section V. Summary

In a sentence or two, summarize the answer to your research question. Is there a generation gap? Is there a battle between the sexes? Are women more romantic than men? Is religion declining? Do Americans accept the Bill of Rights? Pay special attention to the title of the original research article. It probably poses the basic question you want to answer here. An article by Gary T. Marx, for example, was entitled "Religion: Opiate or Inspiration of Civil Rights Militancy?" If this article had been the subject of our investigation, we would now want to answer the question of whether or not religion is an opiate.

Following these comments, you may offer a personal assessment of the findings and implications of the research results. These comments should always, in some manner or other, be researchable. If you feel the results are valid, indicate whether these trends are desirable (and how they might be accelerated) or undesirable (and how they might be retarded).

On the other hand, you may feel the results are invalid. In such a case you should identify the shortcomings of the research and suggest ways these problems can be avoided in future research. If you are skeptical of the research findings, think of other factors that might explain your findings. For example, if you think the correlation between the amount of time spent watching television and the amount of crime people perceive is spurious, you should suggest another variable that might explain this correlation. Urbanism might be such a variable. You might point out that people watch less television in rural areas, where there are also lower crime rates. People watch more television in urban areas, where there are higher crime rates. You could then argue that it is not television but living in the city that causes people to believe crime rates are higher. You may find it useful to review a methods text on multivariate analysis at this time. In any case, don't conclude with the cliché "It is clear that more research is needed." It is hard to imagine a circumstance when this would not be true, but it is of little value to say so unless you can offer specific suggestions that would result in research to clarify the situation.

We have reached the point in our report where we can conclude with Holmes that ". . . when [our] original intellectual deduction is confirmed [or disproven] point by point by quite a number of independent incidents, then the subjective becomes objective and we can say confidently we have reached our goal" (*The Adventure of the Sussex Vampire*).

References and Recommended Readings

Agnew, N., & Pyke, S. (1987). *The science game.* Englewood Cliffs, NJ: Prentice-Hall.

American Psychological Association. (1983). *Publication manual of the American Psychological Association* (3rd ed.). Washington, DC: Author.

Bart, P., & Frankel, L. (1986). *The student sociologist's handbook* (4th ed.). New York: Random House.

Becker, H. (1986). *Writing for social scientists.* Chicago: University of Chicago Press.

Becker, L., & Gustafson, C. (1976). *Encounter with sociology: The term paper* (2nd ed.). Boston: Boyd & Fraser.

DiLeonardi, J., & Curtis, P. (1988). *What to do when the numbers are in.* Chicago: Nelson-Hall.

Durkheim, E. (1897). *Suicide.* Reprint. New York: The Free Press, 1951.

Fowler, H. (1965). *A dictionary of modern English usage* (2nd ed.). New York: Oxford University Press.

Friedman, S., & Steinberg, S. (1989). *Writing & thinking in the social sciences.* Englewood Cliffs, NJ: Prentice-Hall.

Katzer, J., Cook, K., and Crouch, W. (1978). *Evaluating information.* Reading, MA: Addison-Wesley.

Leedy, P. (1989). *Practical research* (4th ed.). New York: Macmillan.

Orwell, S., & Angus, I. (Eds.). (1968). *The collected essays, journalism, and letters of George Orwell* (Vol. 4). New York: Harcourt Brace Jovanovich.

Richlin-Konsky, J., & Strenski, E. (Eds.). (1968). *A guide to writing sociology papers.* New York: St. Martin's Press.

Sommer, R., & Sommer, B. (1986). *A practical guide to behavioral research* (2nd ed.). New York: Oxford University Press.

Strunk, W., & White, E. B. (1979). *The elements of style* (3rd ed.). New York: Macmillan.

True, J. (1989). *Finding out.* Belmont, CA: Wadsworth.

REPORT CHECKLIST

Composition

1. Vocabulary
   a. Use definite, specific, concrete terms
   b. Use appropriate, unpretentious concepts
   c. Strive for simplicity and clarity

2. Sentence structure
   a. Edit needless words
   b. Avoid unnecessary complexity
   c. Avoid long sentences

3. Style
   a. Put statements in positive form
   b. Use active voice
   c. Either first or third person acceptable

4. Precision
   a. Avoid vague generalizations
   b. Strive for precision and detail

Format

Section I. Research Problem
   1. Introduction
      a. Theoretical relevance
      b. "Funnel-shaped" discussion
   2. Variables
      a. Identify independent and dependent variables
      b. Specify other variables

Section II. Hypotheses
   1. State prior to evaluating data
   2. State hypotheses clearly
   3. Specify direction of hypothesized relationship
   4. Avoid *ex post facto* explanations

Section III. Research Methods
   1. Measurement: How variables are measured
   2. Research Procedures

Section IV. Discussion and Findings
   1. Statistical evidence
      a. Identify the most important findings
      b. State decision rule
      c. Compare results to decision rule
   2. Interpret results objectively

Section V. Summary
   1. Organize and evaluate findings
   2. Give personal interpretation of results
   3. Speculate on research implications
   4. Suggest improvements to research methods
   5. Identify other relevant variables
   6. Suggest future research

INVESTIGATION REPORT 1

Values

NAME _____ COURSE _____ DATE _____

Research Problem

_____

_____

_____

_____

_____

_____

_____

_____

_____

_____

_____

_____

_____

_____

Hypotheses

Hypothesis 1:

Moral integrity		Highest other social value
Men	_____ > _____	Men
Women	_____ > _____	Women

Hypothesis 2:

Personal freedom		Highest other personal value
Men	_____ > _____	Men
Women	_____ > _____	Women

Hypothesis 3:

Correlation Social values		Correlation Personal values
Men	_____ > _____	Men
Women	_____ > _____	Women

Research Methods

_____
_____
_____
_____
_____
_____
_____
_____

Discussion and Findings

_____
_____
_____
_____
_____
_____
_____
_____

Summary

_____
_____
_____
_____
_____
_____
_____
_____

REPORT STATUS   **L**   **—**   **OK**   **+**

INVESTIGATION REPORT 2

Social Roles

NAME _____ COURSE _____ DATE _____

Research Problem

_____
_____
_____
_____
_____
_____
_____
_____
_____
_____
_____
_____
_____
_____
_____
_____

Hypotheses

Gender Gap Hypotheses

Hypothesis 1: $\bar{X}ff$ _____ > $\bar{X}fm$ _____
Hypothesis 2: $\bar{X}M$ _____ > $\bar{X}F$ _____

Generation Gap Hypotheses

Hypothesis 3: $\bar{X}fm$ _____ > $\bar{X}F$ _____
Hypothesis 4: $\bar{X}ff$ _____ > $\bar{X}M$ _____

Gender-Generation Gap Hypotheses

Hypothesis 5: $\bar{X}ff$ _____ > $\bar{X}F$ _____
Hypothesis 6: $\bar{X}ff$ _____ > $\bar{X}fm$ _____
                                $\bar{X}M$ _____
                                $\bar{X}F$ _____

Research Methods

_____
_____
_____
_____
_____
_____
_____

Discussion and Findings

_____
_____
_____
_____
_____
_____
_____

Summary

_____
_____
_____
_____
_____
_____
_____
_____

REPORT STATUS   **L**   **—**   **OK**   **+**

INVESTIGATION REPORT 3

Primary Groups

NAME _____ COURSE _____ DATE _____

Research Problem

_____

_____

_____

_____

_____

_____

_____

_____

_____

_____

_____

_____

_____

_____

_____

_____

_____

_____

_____

Hypotheses

Hypothesis 1:

Correlation
1966 to present   ____ ≥   Rho + .504

Hypothesis 2:

Primary groups   ____ > ____   Secondary groups

Hypothesis 3:

United States   Next highest ranked
rank   ____ > ____   secondary group

175

Research Methods

_____
_____
_____
_____
_____
_____
_____
_____

Discussion and Findings

_____
_____
_____
_____
_____
_____
_____

Summary

_____
_____
_____
_____
_____
_____
_____
_____

REPORT STATUS   **L**   **—**   **OK**   **+**

INVESTIGATION REPORT 4

Deviance

NAME _____ COURSE _____ DATE _____

Research Problem

_____

_____

_____

_____

_____

_____

_____

_____

_____

_____

_____

_____

_____

_____

Hypotheses

Hypothesis 1:

Crimes against
police ____ > ____

Crimes against
strangers

Hypothesis 2:

Crimes against
strangers ____ > ____

Crimes against
spouse

Hypothesis 3:

Crimes against
others ____ > ____

Crimes against
property

Hypothesis 4:

Crimes against
others ____ > ____

White-collar
crimes

____ > ____ Victimless crimes

____ > ____

Crimes against
order

Hypothesis 5:

Rho between men
and women
ratings = ____ $\geq$ + .377

.05 level of
significance

Hypothesis 6:

Rho between 1974
and present
ratings = ____ $\geq$ + .377

.05 level of
significance

Research Methods

_____

_____

_____

_____

_____

_____

_____

Discussion and Findings

_____

_____

_____

_____

_____

_____

_____

Summary

_____

_____

_____

_____

_____

_____

_____

_____

REPORT STATUS   **L**   **—**   **OK**   **+**

INVESTIGATION REPORT 5

Social Stratification

NAME _____ COURSE _____ DATE _____

Research Problem

_____

_____

_____

_____

_____

_____

_____

_____

_____

_____

_____

_____

_____

_____

_____

Hypotheses

Hypothesis 1:

Correlation 1947 to present	____ $\geq$	Rho + .399
Correlation 1963 to present	____ $\geq$	Rho + .399

Hypothesis 2:

Current study and U.S. Census	____ $\geq$	Rho + .399
Current study and another school	____ $\geq$	Rho + .399

Hypothesis 3:

Current study and New Zealand	____ $\geq$	Rho + .399
Current study and International Standard	____ $\geq$	Rho + .399

Research Methods

_____
_____
_____
_____
_____
_____
_____
_____

Discussion and Findings

_____
_____
_____
_____
_____
_____
_____
_____

Summary

_____
_____
_____
_____
_____
_____
_____
_____

REPORT STATUS   **L**   **—**   **OK**   **+**

INVESTIGATION REPORT 6

Class Ideology

NAME _____ COURSE _____ DATE _____

Research Problem

_____
_____
_____
_____
_____
_____
_____
_____
_____
_____
_____
_____
_____
_____
_____
_____
_____
_____
_____

Hypotheses

Hypothesis 1:

$\bar{X}$gen _____ > _____ $\bar{X}$spec

Hypothesis 2:

$\bar{X}$rich _____ > _____ $\bar{X}$poor

181

Research Methods

_____

_____

_____

_____

_____

_____

_____

Discussion and Findings

_____

_____

_____

_____

_____

_____

_____

Summary

_____

_____

_____

_____

_____

_____

_____

REPORT STATUS   **L**   **—**   **OK**   **+**

INVESTIGATION REPORT 7

Minorities

NAME _____ COURSE _____ DATE _____

Research Problem

_____

_____

_____

_____

_____

_____

_____

_____

_____

_____

_____

_____

_____

_____

_____

Hypotheses

Hypothesis 1:

My class's social
distance   ____ ≥ 2.74 Crull & Bruton
                                                    social distance

Hypothesis 2:

Replication Rho   ____ $\geq$ Rho + .564

Hypothesis 3:

With contact   ____ > ____   Without contact

Hypothesis 4:

Men   ____ > ____ $\bar{X}$ Women

Hypothesis 5:

Controversial
groups   ____ > ____   Noncontroversial
                                                    groups

Research Methods

_____

_____

_____

_____

_____

_____

_____

Discussion and Findings

_____

_____

_____

_____

_____

_____

_____

Summary

_____

_____

_____

_____

_____

_____

_____

_____

REPORT STATUS　　　　　**L**　　　　**—**　　　　**OK**　　　　**+**

INVESTIGATION REPORT 8

Religion

NAME _____ COURSE _____ DATE _____

Research Problem

_____

_____

_____

_____

_____

_____

_____

_____

_____

_____

_____

_____

_____

_____

_____

_____

_____

_____

_____

Hypotheses

Hypothesis 1:

White-collar		Blue-collar
This-worldly	___ > ___	This-worldly

Hypothesis 2:

White-collar		Blue-collar
Other-worldly	___ < ___	Other-worldly

Research Methods

_____

_____

_____

_____

_____

_____

_____

Discussion and Findings

_____

_____

_____

_____

_____

_____

_____

Summary

_____

_____

_____

_____

_____

_____

_____

_____

REPORT STATUS   **L**   **—**   **OK**   **+**

INVESTIGATION REPORT 9

Politics

NAME _____ COURSE _____ DATE _____

Research Problem

_____

_____

_____

_____

_____

_____

_____

_____

_____

_____

_____

_____

_____

_____

_____

_____

_____

Hypotheses

Hypothesis 1:

    Support for
highest item ____ <   95%

Hypothesis 2:

    Replication   Nunn 1971
variation ____ ≥   44%   variation

Hypothesis 3:

    Present   1957
libertarianism ____ >   34%   libertarianism

Hypothesis 4:

            Males ____ > ____ Females

Hypothesis 5:

    Low religion   High religion
High libertarianism ____ > ____ Low libertarianism

Hypothesis 6:

           Seniors ____ > ____ Freshmen

Research Methods

_____
_____
_____
_____
_____
_____
_____
_____

Discussion and Findings

_____
_____
_____
_____
_____
_____
_____
_____
_____

Summary

_____
_____
_____
_____
_____
_____
_____
_____
_____

REPORT STATUS   **L**   **—**   **OK**   **+**

INVESTIGATION REPORT 10

Marriage

NAME _____ COURSE _____ DATE _____

Research Problem

_____

_____

_____

_____

_____

_____

_____

_____

_____

_____

_____

_____

_____

_____

_____

_____

_____

_____

_____

Hypotheses

Hypothesis 1:

Women like date   _____ (cell 4)   >   _____ (cell 5)   Men like date

Hypothesis 2:

Women love friends   _____ (cell 7)   >   _____ (cell 8)   Men love friends

Hypothesis 3:

Women + men like date   _____ (cell 6)   >   _____ (cell 12)   Women + men like friends

Women + men love date   _____ (cell 3)   >   _____ (cell 9)   Women + men love friends

189

Research Methods

_____

_____

_____

_____

_____

_____

_____

_____

Discussion and Findings

_____

_____

_____

_____

_____

_____

_____

_____

Summary

_____

_____

_____

_____

_____

_____

_____

_____

_____

REPORT STATUS   **L**   **—**   **OK**   **+**

INVESTIGATION REPORT 11

Alienation

NAME _____ COURSE _____ DATE _____

Research Problem

_____

_____

_____

_____

_____

_____

_____

_____

_____

_____

_____

_____

_____

_____

_____

_____

Hypotheses

Hypothesis 1:

| Correlation between SES and anomia | ____ | = | $-.19$ | Correlation found by Angell |

Hypothesis 2:

| Average college anomia | ____ | < | 2.1 | Average Srole anomia |

Hypothesis 3:

| Social Distance anomia correlation | ____ | ≥ | $+.43$ | Correlation found by Angell |

Research Methods

_____

_____

_____

_____

_____

_____

_____

_____

Discussion and Findings

_____

_____

_____

_____

_____

_____

_____

_____

Summary

_____

_____

_____

_____

_____

_____

_____

_____

_____

REPORT STATUS   **L**   **—**   **OK**   **+**

STUDENT SURVEY

COMPLETE THIS SECTION BEFORE READING ADDITIONAL MATERIALS IN THE BOOK

The survey will take about 40 minutes to complete. The information you provide will form the data base for the investigations, so it is vital to answer every question. Some may ask for information you are not sure of. In such cases, make your best estimate or guess. In other cases, where indicated in the instructions, you may enter an "X" or select "DK" (Don't Know) when you cannot make even an informed guess.

In order to preserve anonymity, you are requested to identify your survey with a code, such as your Social Security or Social Insurance number. After the data have been collected, you will be asked to reclaim this survey, as you will need to refer to it in completing the investigations.

Student code: _____

SECTION 1: BACKGROUND INFORMATION

1. Sex: 1. Male
        2. Female

2. Which do you consider yourself to be?
    1. Black
    2. White
    3. Native American
    4. Mexican American
    5. Asian American
    6. Other: _____

3. Your age: _____

4. Your present class standing:
    1. Freshman
    2. Sophomore
    3. Junior
    4. Senior
    5. Graduate
    6. Other: _____

5. Your present major:
    1. Social Science
    2. Humanities
    3. Natural Science
    4. Business Administration
    5. Education
    6. Engineering
    7. Agriculture
    8. Other _____

6. Your marital status:
    1. Single
    2. Divorced
    3. Separated
    4. Married
    5. Widowed

7. Estimate your family income last year before taxes:
    1. Under $15,000
    2. $15,000 to $19,999
    3. $20,000 to $24,999
    4. $25,000 to $29,999
    5. $30,000 to $39,999
    6. $40,000 to $49,999
    7. $50,000 to $59,999
    8. $60,000 to $74,999
    9. $75,000 to $99,999
    10. $100,000 to $149,999
    11. $150,000 and over

8. How often do you attend religious services?
    4. More than once a week
    3. Once a week
    2. Once to several times a month
    1. Less than once a month
    0. Less than once a year

9. Please indicate your religious preference:
    1. United Church of Christ
    2. Methodist
    3. Episcopalian/Anglican
    4. Disciples of Christ
    5. Presbyterian
    6. American Lutheran
    7. American Baptist
    8. Missouri Lutheran
    9. Southern Baptist
    10. Other Protestant
    _____
    11. Roman Catholic
    12. Jewish
    13. Other _____
    14. None

SECTION 2: GROUP ATTACHMENTS

10. Study the list that follows. Think carefully of ALL the organizations and informal groups to which you belong. Then rate these organizations by circling the number that most nearly expresses your feeling toward the group or organization. Enter an "X" next to any group that does not apply to you. If you belong to two or more groups or organizations of a single type (such as if your parents were separated and remarried), evaluate the one for which you have the greatest positive feeling.

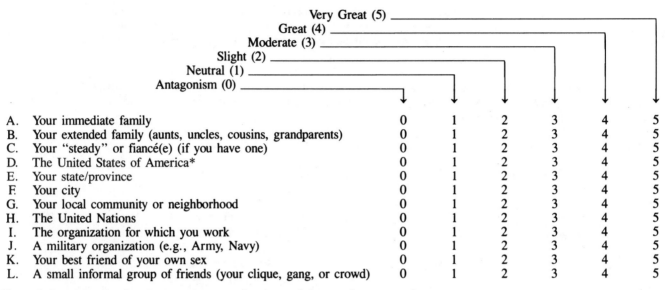

FEELING OF ATTACHMENT

Very Great (5)
Great (4)
Moderate (3)
Slight (2)
Neutral (1)
Antagonism (0)

A.	Your immediate family	0	1	2	3	4	5
B.	Your extended family (aunts, uncles, cousins, grandparents)	0	1	2	3	4	5
C.	Your "steady" or fiancé(e) (if you have one)	0	1	2	3	4	5
D.	The United States of America*	0	1	2	3	4	5
E.	Your state/province	0	1	2	3	4	5
F.	Your city	0	1	2	3	4	5
G.	Your local community or neighborhood	0	1	2	3	4	5
H.	The United Nations	0	1	2	3	4	5
I.	The organization for which you work	0	1	2	3	4	5
J.	A military organization (e.g., Army, Navy)	0	1	2	3	4	5
K.	Your best friend of your own sex	0	1	2	3	4	5
L.	A small informal group of friends (your clique, gang, or crowd)	0	1	2	3	4	5

If you belong to several such groups, answer in terms of the one that means the most to you.

*If survey is taken in Canada, substitute "Canada."

11-A.   On the left-hand scale below, circle the number (1–7) that indicates the closest degree to which you would be willing to admit members of each of the groups listed. Make sure your reactions are to each group as a whole, not to the best or the worst members you have known.

11-B.   Do you know anyone from these groups? On the right-hand scale below, circle the letter Y or N that best describes the type of contact you have had with each group.

Exclude from my country (7)
As visitors to my country (6)
Speaking acquaintance only (5)
Work beside in an office (4)
As neighbors on my street (3)
As very good friends (2)
Close kinship by marriage (1)

SOCIAL GROUP								PERSONAL CONTACT Yes	No
A.	Arabs	1	2	3	4	5	6	7	Y	N
B.	Blacks	1	2	3	4	5	6	7	Y	N
C.	Canadians†	1	2	3	4	5	6	7	Y	N
D.	Chinese	1	2	3	4	5	6	7	Y	N
E.	Germans	1	2	3	4	5	6	7	Y	N
F.	Hippies	1	2	3	4	5	6	7	Y	N
G.	Homosexuals	1	2	3	4	5	6	7	Y	N
H.	Italians	1	2	3	4	5	6	7	Y	N
I.	Jews	1	2	3	4	5	6	7	Y	N
J.	Pireneans	1	2	3	4	5	6	7	Y	N
K.	Russians	1	2	3	4	5	6	7	Y	N
L.	Turks	1	2	3	4	5	6	7	Y	N

†If survey is taken in Canada, substitute "Americans."

SECTION 3: SOCIAL AND POLITICAL VALUES

12. Below are listed some commonly expressed American values. How important are each of these to you?

IMPORTANCE OF THIS TO YOU
(circle your response)

VALUE	Slight	Moderate	Great	Very Great
A. Achievement (getting ahead)	1	2	3	4
B. Moral integrity (honesty)	1	2	3	4
C. Being practical and efficient	1	2	3	4
D. National progress	1	2	3	4
E. Individualism (nonconformity)	1	2	3	4
F. Personal freedom	1	2	3	4
G. Material comfort	1	2	3	4
H. Equality (racial)	1	2	3	4
I. Equality (sexual)	1	2	3	4
J. Patriotism (to country)	1	2	3	4
K. Political democracy	1	2	3	4
L. Work	1	2	3	4
M. Leisure	1	2	3	4
N. Helping others	1	2	3	4

Here are a number of social issues about which there is some disagreement. We would like to know how you feel about these issues. Please circle the number that indicates your response.

13. There's little use writing to public officials because often they aren't really interested in the problems of the average person.
    1. I agree
    2. I disagree

14. Nowadays a person has to live pretty much for today and let tomorrow take care of itself.
    1. I agree
    2. I disagree

15. In spite of what some people say, the lot of the average person is getting worse, not better.
    1. I agree
    2. I disagree

16. It's hardly fair to bring children into the world with the way things look for the future.
    1. I agree
    2. I disagree

17. These days a person doesn't really know whom he or she can count on.
    1. I agree
    2. I disagree

Answer questions 18–26 by circling the response (1–4) that indicates how strongly you agree or disagree with the statement.

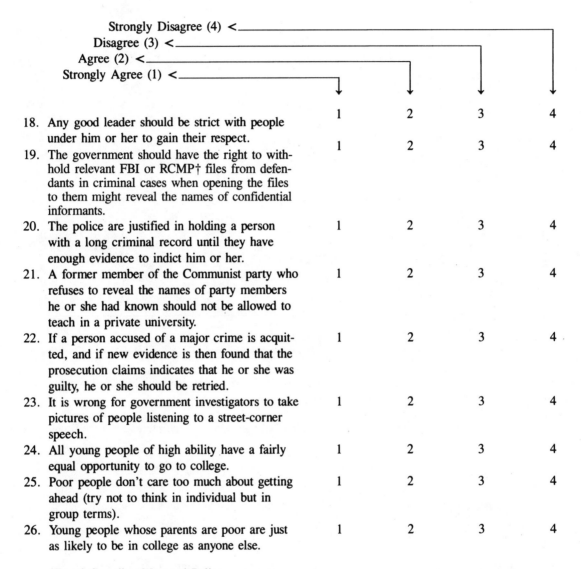

Strongly Disagree (4) <——————————————————————

Disagree (3) <——————————————————

Agree (2) <————————————

Strongly Agree (1) <——————

		1	2	3	4
18.	Any good leader should be strict with people under him or her to gain their respect.	1	2	3	4
19.	The government should have the right to withhold relevant FBI or RCMP† files from defendants in criminal cases when opening the files to them might reveal the names of confidential informants.	1	2	3	4
20.	The police are justified in holding a person with a long criminal record until they have enough evidence to indict him or her.	1	2	3	4
21.	A former member of the Communist party who refuses to reveal the names of party members he or she had known should not be allowed to teach in a private university.	1	2	3	4
22.	If a person accused of a major crime is acquitted, and if new evidence is then found that the prosecution claims indicates that he or she was guilty, he or she should be retried.	1	2	3	4
23.	It is wrong for government investigators to take pictures of people listening to a street-corner speech.	1	2	3	4
24.	All young people of high ability have a fairly equal opportunity to go to college.	1	2	3	4
25.	Poor people don't care too much about getting ahead (try not to think in individual but in group terms).	1	2	3	4
26.	Young people whose parents are poor are just as likely to be in college as anyone else.	1	2	3	4

†Royal Canadian Mounted Police

SECTION 4: GENDER ATTITUDES

Answer questions 27–33 by circling the number in the "Me" column that best represents your attitude toward the statements. In the columns labeled "Father" and "Mother," make your best guess as to your parents' attitudes toward these statements.

27. If there are two candidates for a job, one a man and the other a woman, and the woman is slightly better qualified, the job should nevertheless go to the man because he is likely to have a family.

Me	Father	Mother	
1	1	1	Strongly Agree
2	2	2	Agree
3	3	3	Disagree
4	4	4	Strongly Disagree

28. The talk we hear nowadays about women being an oppressed group in American society is really ridiculous.

Me	Father	Mother	
1	1	1	Strongly Agree
2	2	2	Agree
3	3	3	Disagree
4	4	4	Strongly Disagree

29. I would support the candidacy of a woman for president of the United States.

Me	Father	Mother	
1	1	1	Strongly Agree
2	2	2	Agree
3	3	3	Disagree
4	4	4	Strongly Disagree

30. If a male and female student are equally qualified for a scholarship, it should be awarded to the male student on the grounds that he has greater career potential.

Me	Father	Mother	
1	1	1	Strongly Agree
2	2	2	Agree
3	3	3	Disagree
4	4	4	Strongly Disagree

31. Women who insist on competing in the male world of work and politics tend to lose their femininity.

Me	Father	Mother	
1	1	1	Strongly Agree
2	2	2	Agree
3	3	3	Disagree
4	4	4	Strongly Disagree

32. Prison is too good for sex criminals. They should be publically whipped or worse.

Me	Father	Mother	
1	1	1	Strongly Agree
2	2	2	Agree
3	3	3	Disagree
4	4	4	Strongly Disagree

33. The most important thing to teach children is absolute obedience to their parents.

Me	Father	Mother	
1	1	1	Strongly Agree
2	2	2	Agree
3	3	3	Disagree
4	4	4	Strongly Disagree

34. Circle the number opposite each of the following 26 items that best represents your feelings toward the OPPOSITE-SEX peer whom you are dating or romantically involved. If you are not presently romantically involved, imagine an opposite-sex partner with whom you would desire to be romantically involved.

		Agree								Disagree
A.	If _____ were feeling bad, my first duty would be to cheer him (her) up.	9	8	7	6	5	4	3	2	1
B.	I feel that I can confide in _____ about virtually everything.	9	8	7	6	5	4	3	2	1
C.	I find it easy to ignore_____'s faults.	9	8	7	6	5	4	3	2	1
D.	I would do almost anything for _____.	9	8	7	6	5	4	3	2	1
E.	I feel very possessive toward _____.	9	8	7	6	5	4	3	2	1
F.	If I could never be with _____, I would feel miserable.	9	8	7	6	5	4	3	2	1
G.	If I were lonely, my first thought would be to seek _____ out.	9	8	7	6	5	4	3	2	1
H.	One of my primary concerns is _____'s welfare.	9	8	7	6	5	4	3	2	1
I.	I feel responsible for _____'s well-being.	9	8	7	6	5	4	3	2	1
J.	I would forgive _____ for practically anything.	9	8	7	6	5	4	3	2	1
K.	When I am with _____, I spend a good deal of time just looking at him (her).	9	8	7	6	5	4	3	2	1
L.	I would greatly enjoy being confided in by _____.	9	8	7	6	5	4	3	2	1
M.	It would be hard for me to get along without _____.	9	8	7	6	5	4	3	2	1
N.	When I am with _____, we are almost always in the same mood.	9	8	7	6	5	4	3	2	1
O.	I think that _____ is unusually well-adjusted.	9	8	7	6	5	4	3	2	1
P.	I would highly recommend _____ for a responsible job.	9	8	7	6	5	4	3	2	1
Q.	In my opinion, _____ is an exceptionally mature person.	9	8	7	6	5	4	3	2	1
R.	I have great confidence in _____'s good judgment.	9	8	7	6	5	4	3	2	1
S.	Most people would react very favorably to _____ after a brief acquaintance.	9	8	7	6	5	4	3	2	1
T.	I think that _____ and I are quite similar.	9	8	7	6	5	4	3	2	1
U.	I would vote for _____ in a class or group election.	9	8	7	6	5	4	3	2	1
V.	I think that _____ is one of those people who quickly wins respect.	9	8	7	6	5	4	3	2	1
W.	I feel that _____ is an extremely intelligent person.	9	8	7	6	5	4	3	2	1
X.	_____ is one of the most likable people I know.	9	8	7	6	5	4	3	2	1
Y.	_____ is the sort of person whom I would like to be.	9	8	7	6	5	4	3	2	1
Z.	It seems to me that it is very easy for _____ to gain recognition.	9	8	7	6	5	4	3	2	1

After completing these ratings for your opposite-sex peer, use the same scales to rate your best SAME-SEX friend. Put an "X" through the appropriate response that best expresses your feelings toward your best same-sex friend.

SECTION 5: OCCUPATIONAL PRESTIGE EXERCISE

35. For each occupation mentioned, please circle the rating that gives your own personal opinion of the general standing or prestige that such an occupation has.

	Occupational Category	Excellent	Good	Average	Below Average	Poor	Don't Know
A.	Banker	100	80	60	40	20	DK
B.	Barber	100	80	60	40	20	DK
C.	Bookkeeper	100	80	60	40	20	DK
D.	Carpenter	100	80	60	40	20	DK
E.	Clerk in store	100	80	60	40	20	DK
F.	Coal miner	100	80	60	40	20	DK
G.	College professor	100	80	60	40	20	DK
H.	Electrician	100	80	60	40	20	DK
I.	Farmer	100	80	60	40	20	DK
J.	Janitor	100	80	60	40	20	DK
K.	Lawyer	100	80	60	40	20	DK
L.	Machine operator	100	80	60	40	20	DK
M.	Manager of small store	100	80	60	40	20	DK
N.	Minister	100	80	60	40	20	DK
O.	Physician	100	80	60	40	20	DK
P.	Police officer	100	80	60	40	20	DK
Q.	Public school teacher	100	80	60	40	20	DK
R.	Railroad conductor	100	80	60	40	20	DK
S.	Restaurant waiter	100	80	60	40	20	DK

SECTION 6: RATING CRIME SERIOUSNESS

36. *Criminal law* covers a very large number of different kinds of crime. Some are considered to be very serious, and others not so serious. We are interested in your opinions about how serious you think different crimes are. With a "1" meaning not serious at all and a "9" meaning extremely serious, please rate how serious you believe each of the following crimes to be by circling your rating in the scales below.

Not Serious At All   **Extremely Serious**

A. Impulsive killing of a police officer

1   2   3   4   5   6   7   8   9

B. Assault with a gun on a police officer

1   2   3   4   5   6   7   8   9

Not Serious At All   **Extremely Serious**

C. Beating up a police officer

1	2	3	4	5	6	7	8	9

D. Assault with a gun on a spouse

1	2	3	4	5	6	7	8	9

E. Beating up a spouse

1	2	3	4	5	6	7	8	9

F. Armed street holdup stealing $25 cash

1	2	3	4	5	6	7	8	9

G. Armed street holdup stealing $200 cash

1	2	3	4	5	6	7	8	9

H. Passing worthless checks for more than $500

1	2	3	4	5	6	7	8	9

I. Passing worthless checks for less than $100

1	2	3	4	5	6	7	8	9

J. Theft of a car for the purpose of resale

1	2	3	4	5	6	7	8	9

K. Impulsive killing of a stranger

1	2	3	4	5	6	7	8	9

L. Beating up a stranger

1	2	3	4	5	6	7	8	9

M. Assault with a gun on a stranger

1	2	3	4	5	6	7	8	9

N. Selling pornographic magazines

1	2	3	4	5	6	7	8	9

O. Soliciting for prostitution

1	2	3	4	5	6	7	8	9

P. Employee embezzling company funds

1	2	3	4	5	6	7	8	9

Q. Willfully neglecting to file income tax returns

1	2	3	4	5	6	7	8	9

R. Male homosexual acts with consenting adults

1	2	3	4	5	6	7	8	9

S. Disturbing the peace

1	2	3	4	5	6	7	8	9

T. Being drunk in public places

1	2	3	4	5	6	7	8	9

TABLES A AND B

Table A

CRITICAL VALUES OF RHO

N	Significance Level (one-sided test)	
	.05	.01
4	1.000	
5	.900	1.000
6	.829	.943
7	.714	.893
8	.643	.833
9	.600	.783
10	.564	.746
12	.504	.701
14	.456	.645
16	.425	.601
18	.399	.564
20	.377	.534
30	.306	.432

Note: From *Elementary Statistics* (p. 342, Table X) by P. Hoel, 1976. New York: John Wiley & Sons. Used by permission of the author.

Table B

ABBREVIATIONS

Symbol	Interpretation
=	: a = b means "a is equal to b"
=	: a = b means "a is not equal to b"
≥	: a ≥ b means "a is equal to or greater than b"
≤	: a ≤ b means "a is less than or equal to b"
>	: a > b means "a is greater than b"
<	: a < b means "a is less than b"
Mdn	: means "Median"
N	: means "number or number of cases"
P	: means "probability"
r_s	: means Spearman rank order correlation (Rho)
X	: means "independent variable"
$\bar{X}$	: means "arithmetic mean"
Y	: means "dependent variable"

HM
51
.C68
1993

GLOSSARY

Association   A relationship between two or more variables in which one variable depends upon, follows from, or is connected with another variable.

Cohesiveness   The attractiveness or desirability of a group to individuals. The attraction of cohesive groups gives them more influence and a stronger hold over members.

Concept   A word or set of words expressing an abstract idea about phenomena. In science, concepts are measured with indicators. Indicators often used in research are constants and variables (for example, independent and dependent).

Constant   An unchanging quantity or attribute. For example, in studying educational achievement of blacks only, race is a constant. Constants cannot explain change or variation.

Correlation   The degree of correspondence that exists between the values of two or more variables. When changes in the values of two variables correspond directly, the correlation is *positive*. When change in one variable results in a change in the opposite direction for the second variable, the correlation is *negative*.

Dependent Variable   The presumed effect. It is also called the outcome, effect, or criterion variable. The values of this variable depend on or are influenced by another variable (the independent variable).

Empirical   Gained through the senses, rather than by intuition, authority, or supernatural sources.

Hypothesis   An educated guess, often deduced from theory, that is about to be empirically tested.

Independent Variable   The presumed cause. Changes in the values of this variable are believed to influence the dependent variable.

Indicator   An observable phenomenon taken to indicate the presence, or degree of presence, of a concept. An ideal indicator measures both presence and degree of presence of the concept.

Psychological Fact   Psychological phenomenon that can only be explained by the nature of the individual. It cannot be reduced to or understood by simpler biological phenomena. The working of the mind, for example, is not reducible to the biology of the brain.

Reliability   The consistency or stability of an indicator to get the same results over time. A weight scale, for example, would be considered unreliable if you weighed yourself twice, a few moments apart, and found a five-pound weight difference.

Rho   A statistical measure of association between two sets of ranked variables. It is sometimes called the Spearman rank order correlation and symbolized by r_s.

Science   A logical, systematic method by which empirical knowledge can be obtained and accumulated.

Social Fact   Social phenomenon that can only be explained by the logic of the social order. It cannot be reduced to or understood by simpler psychological phenomena. The homicide rate is not reducible to individual aggression.

Society   A group of interdependent individuals sharing the same territory and culture.

Standardize   To make variables comparable from a common base or scale (for example, percentages, rates, and ratios).

Table   An orderly arrangement of data into rows and columns to simplify description and comparison of data.

Theory   A logically interrelated set of statements about reality. Scientific theory constructs explanations of observable data based upon testable hypotheses.

Validity   The degree to which the indicator measures what it claims to measure. Does the I.Q. test measure intelligence or does it also measure racial, ethnic, and social class background? If the latter is true, the I.Q. test would be an invalid indicator of intelligence.

Value   A measure of the quantity (for example, 0–100) or quality (for example, attends church, does not attend church) of a concept or indicator (for example, religiosity).

Variable   Any concept or indicator that can vary in quality or quantity (that is, has more than one value).